SELFHOOD, AUTISM AND THOUGHT INSERTION

Edited by
Mihretu P. Guta
and Sophie Gibb

Imprint-academic.com

Published in the UK by
Imprint Academic, PO Box 200, Exeter EX5 5YX, UK

Distributed in the USA by
Ingram Book Company,
One Ingram Blvd., La Vergne, TN 37086, USA

ISBN 9781788360562

A CIP catalogue record for this book is available from the
British Library and US Library of Congress

Contents

ABOUT AUTHORS

Lynne Rudder Baker was a Distinguished Professor in Philosophy (Emeritus), and was the author of five books: *Saving Belief: A Critique of Physicalism* (Princeton UP 1987), *Explaining Attitudes: A Practical Approach to the Mind* (CUP 1995), *Persons and Bodies: A Constitution View* (CUP 2000), *The Metaphysics of Everyday Life: An Essay in Practical Realism* (CUP 2007), and *Naturalism and the First-Person Perspective* (OUP 2013). Her research focused on metaphysics, philosophy of mind, and philosophical theology. She also wrote scores of articles in philosophy journals. In 2001, Anthonie Meijers edited a volume of critical essays on her work, *Explaining Beliefs: Lynne Rudder Baker and her Critics* (CSLI Publications).

José Luis Bermúdez is Professor of Philosophy at Texas A&M University, where he previously served as Dean of Liberal Arts and Associate Provost for Strategic Planning. His books include *The Paradox of Self-Consciousness*, *Thinking without Words*, and *Decision Theory and Rationality*. The second edition of his textbook *Cognitive Science: An Introduction to the Science of the Mind* was published by Cambridge University Press in 2014. He recently published a book on understanding the first-person pronoun 'I'.

Angela J. Guta has a PhD from Newcastle University, UK. Her thesis was titled 'A Comparison of the Effectiveness of Video Modelling and Point-of-View Video Modelling on the Social Skills of Primary School Children with Autism'. She is an Assistant Professor at Azusa Pacific University, CA. She has an extensive background as a special educator working with individuals from birth through adulthood.

Mihretu P. Guta completed his PhD in Philosophy at Durham University, where he subsequently worked as a Postdoctoral Research Fellow within the Durham Emergence Project (funded by the John Templeton Foundation). His main research focuses on metaphysics, philosophy of mind, and the philosophy of neuroscience, with special emphasis on the emergence of consciousness and its relation to the brain. His relevant publications include: 'Frank Jackson's Location Problem and Argument from the Self', *Philosophia Christi* (2011). He is currently teaching philosophy at Biola University, Azusa Pacific University, and Addis Ababa University. He is also working on a manuscript entitled *The Metaphysics of Substance and Personhood: A Non-Theory Laden Approach*.

Sophie Gibb is Professor of Philosophy in the Department of Philosophy, Durham University. Her research is in metaphysics and the philosophy of mind, with particular interests in the mental causation debate, the categories of being, and causation, laws, and powers. Recent papers are on the ontology of the mental causation debate, the subset account of property realization, and tropes and laws. She was the leader of the philosophy of mind work group within the Durham Emergence Project, which is an interdisciplinary research initiative involving collaboration between philosophers and physicists, made possible through the support of the John Templeton Foundation.

Andy Hamilton teaches philosophy at Durham University, specializing in aesthetics, philosophy of mind, political philosophy, and history of nineteenth- and twentieth-century philosophy, especially Wittgenstein. His monographs are *Aesthetics and Music* (Continuum 2007), *The Self in Question: Memory, the Body and Self-Consciousness* (Palgrave 2013), and *Routledge Philosophy Guidebook to Wittgenstein and On Certainty* (2014). He also teaches aesthetics and history of jazz at Durham, and published *Lee Konitz: Conversations on the Improviser's Art* (University of Michigan Press 2007).

Wolfram Hinzen is a philosopher-linguist interested in the role that language plays in the organization of human thought. He currently investigates this question through studies of language change accompanying cognitive change in three clinical populations: children with autism spectrum disorders, people with schizophrenia, and people with Huntington's disease. He is currently leading a large AHRC-funded project on 'Language and Mental Health' based in Durham, Newcastle, and London. The theoretical foundations of this research are laid out most recently in Hinzen and Sheehan, *The Philosophy of Universal Grammar* (OUP 2013).

Thomas Metzinger is currently Professor of Theoretical Philosophy at the Johannes Gutenberg-Universität Mainz and an Adjunct Fellow at the Frankfurt Institute for Advanced Study (FIAS). He is also Director of the Neuroethics Research Unit in Mainz and Director of the MIND Group at the FIAS. Metzinger is past president of the German Cognitive Science Society (2005–07) and of the Association for the Scientific Study of Consciousness (2009–11). His research interests lie in philosophy of mind and cognitive science, as well as the intersection between ethics, philosophy of mind, and anthropology. He has edited two collections on consciousness (*Conscious Experience*, mentis and Imprint Academic 1995; *Neural Correlates of Consciousness*, MIT Press 2000), and published one major scientific monograph developing an interdisciplinary theory about consciousness, the phenomenal self, and the first-person perspective (*Being No One: The Self-Model Theory of Subjectivity*, MIT Press 2003). In 2009, he published *The Ego Tunnel: The Science of the Mind and the Myth of the Self* (Basic Books).

Harold Noonan was educated at the University of Cambridge, and taught at the University of Birmingham between 1979 and 2004, before which he was a Research Fellow at Trinity Hall College, Cambridge. He is author of six books including *Kripke and Naming and Necessity* and *Personal Identity*, and many articles in philosophical journals on topics in the philosophy of mind, metaphysics, and philosophy of language.

Eric Olson is Professor of Philosophy at the University of Sheffield. He was previously Senior Lecturer at the University of Cambridge. He is the author of *The Human Animal* (OUP 1997), which argues for animalism, and *What Are We?* (OUP 2007), which compares it with the alternatives, as well as many articles on the topic.

Olley Pearson is currently a Lecturer in Philosophy at the University of Lincoln, UK. He worked for Durham University, where he also completed his doctoral studies under the supervision of E.J. Lowe. Prior to this he studied in Wales, Canada, and Scotland. His primary research interest is metaphysics. He is also interested in its intersection with normativity.

Matthew Ratcliffe is Professor of Philosophy at the University of York. He was Professor for Theoretical Philosophy at the University of Vienna, Austria. Most of his recent work addresses issues in phenomenology, philosophy of psychology, and philosophy of psychiatry. He is author of *Rethinking Commonsense Psychology: A Critique of Folk Psychology, Theory of Mind and Simulation* (Palgrave 2007), *Feelings of Being: Phenomenology, Psychiatry and the Sense of Reality* (OUP 2008), and *Experiences of Depression: A Study in Phenomenology* (OUP 2015).

Kristen Schroeder is a PhD candidate in Cognitive Science and Language at the University of Barcelona and member of the Grammar and Cognition Lab. Her research focuses on how language varies across cognitively diverse populations and to what extent this linguistic variance may dialogue with specific symptomatology. Specifically, she is developing a fine-grained language profile of young children on the autism spectrum in the greater Barcelona area.

Richard Swinburne is Emeritus Professor of the Philosophy of Religion at Oxford University. He is best known as the author of several books on the justification of theism (especially *The Existence of God*) and of Christian doctrine, as well as books on mind and body and on personal identity. He has also written books on space and time, probability, and epistemology. His latest book is *Mind, Brain, and Free Will* (2013).

Sam Wilkinson is a Postdoctoral Research Fellow in Philosophy at Durham University. He works on the Wellcome Trust-funded project 'Hearing the Voice', which examines the phenomenon of auditory verbal hallucinations (namely, hearing voices in the absence of anyone speaking) in a wide variety of clinical and non-clinical contexts. Before that, he did his PhD at the University of Edinburgh on delusions and the nature of belief.

Mihretu P. Guta

Editorial Introduction

1. The Questions and the Background

The essays in this volume focus on the notion of the first-person pronoun 'I', the notion of the self or person,[1] and the notion of the first-person perspective. Let us call these the *three notions*. Ever since Descartes set the initial tone in his *Meditations*, modern philosophical controversies concerning the *three notions* have continued unabated. Part of the reason for ongoing debates has to do with the sorts of questions that the *three notions* give rise to.

(i) The word 'I' raises two distinct but related questions. The first is the linguistic question of whether the first-person pronoun 'I' purports to refer to something. The second is a metaphysical question: whether 'I' succeeds in referring to something; (ii) the central question concerning the notion of the self or person is whether the self or person is distinct from the physical body or any part of it such as the brain and, if it is, what sort of a thing it is supposed to be; and (iii) when it comes to the notion of the first-person perspective, the question is whether or not it reliably informs us about the true state of our subjective experience(s) and, if it is not, whether it should rather be reduced to a third-person perspective, which is said to be a scientifically respected method. As Chalmers (2010) points out, the data for first-person subjective experience(s) come from visual experiences (e.g. colour and depth), or other perceptual experiences (e.g. auditory and tactile), bodily experiences (e.g. pain), mental imagery (e.g. recalled visual

Correspondence:
Email: mihretup@aol.com

---

[1] For present purposes, following Locke, I will use the terms 'self' and 'person' interchangeably to refer to 'a thinking intelligent Being, that has reason and reflection, and can consider itself as itself, the same thinking thing in different times and places...' (Locke, 1975, *Essay* II, XXVII, 9, p. 335).

images), emotional experiences (e.g. anger), and occurent thought (e.g. reflecting). By contrast, the data for the third-person perspective come from the behaviour and the brain processes of conscious systems (*ibid.*, p. 38).

Keeping these questions in mind, the next thing we need to do is to look for ways which will allow us to develop adequate answers to (i)–(iii). But in order to do this effectively, at least initially, we should approach this issue against the backdrop of Descartes' view on the *three notions* and the answers he proposed to (i)–(iii).

Descartes' approach to (i)–(iii) was entirely *non-empirical* (i.e. *a priori*). In the *First Meditation* (e.g. 1996), Descartes' desire to establish a strong epistemic foundation for knowledge led him to deploy his famous methodic doubt. Utilizing this method, Descartes tried to show how the reality of all things, particularly material things, at least in principle, could be called into doubt. On the other hand, in the *Second Meditation* Descartes argues that the reality of one's own existence (which is revealed by one's own first-person awareness of it) cannot be doubted. This is because, at least on Descartes' view, one cannot rule out one's own existence without at the same time inescapably presupposing it. In a nutshell, for Descartes, doubt without a doubter cannot exist. Hence, it (i.e. epistemic doubt) cannot shake the reality of one's existence. Moreover, for Descartes, *a priori* introspective reflection, which is rooted in the first-person perspective, is the most effective way by which one secures self-knowledge. These considerations eventually led Descartes to raise an important ontological question which he phrases as: 'But what then am I?' (Descartes, 1996, p. 19).

Here Descartes' question directly echoes one of the questions that underlies the *three notions*. This is the question that is stated in (i) above. As we recall, the question in (i) comes in two forms, one is whether a singular term 'I' purports to refer to something which is a linguistic question. The other question deals with whether 'I' actually succeeds in referring to anything. This is a metaphysical question. Descartes dealt with each aspect of these questions by presupposing that 'I' purports to refer, and then arguing that it refers to an immaterial substance. Descartes' detailed discussion for the metaphysical question comes in the *Sixth Meditation*, where he portrays an *immaterial substance* as a bearer of all psychological properties such as beliefs, desires, etc., whereas a *material substance* is a bearer of all physical properties such as extension, size, etc. These are all interesting claims in their own right. But where does all this leave us?

One way we can answer this question, in a way that provides a good context for the discussions to follow in the main essays of the present volume, would be to look at some of the main reactions Descartes' thoughts have elicited. Due to space limitations, I will raise only three points.

2. Reactions

2.1. Immateriality of the Self/Person

For many philosophers, the sticking point in Descartes' view on the *three notions* has to do with his characterization of the self or person as an *immaterial substance*. As it is well-known, Locke, Hume, and Kant in their own way denied that selves or people were immaterial substances. For example, Locke thought that by endorsing a Cartesian self or person we run into an intractable epistemic problem of establishing whether or not it (i.e. the same self or person) continues to occupy any given material body at all times. In this case, Locke illustrates his own suspicion via his famous *cobbler* and *prince* thought experiment, which is intended to highlight the possibility of 'soul swap' (see, for example, Locke, 1975, *Essay*, Book II, Ch. XXVII). For his part, having failed to find a Cartesian self via introspection, Hume firmly concluded that there is no such thing (see, for example, Hume, 1978, *Treatise*, Part IV). Partly motivated by Hume, in his 'First Paralogism' Kant also argued that we could have no knowledge of an immaterial substance (see Kant, 1929, *Critique of Pure Reason*, A349–A351).

Largely following the lead of Locke, Hume, and Kant, most contemporary philosophers (not to mention psychologists and cognitive neuroscientists) also object to the immateriality (perhaps not necessarily *substantiality*) of the self or person, stating that since an immaterial thing is unobservable, its existence cannot be established (see, for example, Quinton in Perry, 1975, pp. 54–5; Dennett, 1991; Kolak and Martin, 1991, p. 339). Moreover, the separation Descartes introduced between the immaterial self or person and the material body on the one hand, and the corresponding distinctions he introduced between mental states and physical/brain states on the other was directly responsible in paving the way for a number of issues still debated in philosophy of mind. Here as a good case in point we can mention well-known contemporary debates on mental causation, the problem of overdetermination, epiphenomenalism, the supervenience of the mental on the physical, reductive physicalism, non-reductive physicalism, property dualism, and various formulations of a non-Cartesian substance dualism (see for details Gibb, Lowe and Ingthorsson, 2013; Kim, 2006; 2005; Lowe, 2008; 2000; Hasker, 1999). The question remains: what would follow from such reactions against Descartes' characterization of the self or person? My own response (although I cannot defend it here) would be to say that such objections (i.e. those of Locke, Hume, Kant, as well as their modern formulations) by themselves neither conclusively established the non-existence of a non-physical substantial self or person nor did they prevent anyone from holding various views of the self or person such as Hasker's 'emergent self view' (1999). Moreover, some of the essays in this volume would also illustrate this very point in an excellent way.

2.2. The Referentiality of the 'I'

Largely reacting to Descartes' characterization of the self or person, Anscombe in her classic paper 'First Person' argues, '"I" is neither a name nor another kind of expression whose logical role is to make a reference, *at all*' (in Cassam, 1994, p. 154). Similarly, Kenny remarks, 'the grammatical error which is the essence of the theory of the self is in a manner obvious when it is pointed out... It will not do, for instance, to say simply that "I" is the word each of us uses to refer to himself, a pronoun... synonymous with the name of the utterer of the sentence. I is not a referring expression at all, since it is possible to describe one's own action in the third person' (Kenny, 1989, p. 87). If both Anscombe and Kenny are right here, then the question arises: what is the role of 'I' whenever it appears in grammatical sentences such as 'I am feeling dizzy'? In this case, one just can't convincingly assert that, although 'I' is not a referential term, its presence somehow is still important to make sense of a particular grammatical sentence(s) in which it happens to appear. Again such a response misses the point by ignoring/violating a simple semantic rule of *token-reflexivity*, according to which 'any token of "I" refers to whoever produced it' (Campbell, 1994, p. 120). Similarly, Lowe remarks, 'it is a curious feature of the word "I" that it seems to be *guaranteed* to refer to a quite specific person on any occasion of its use, in such a way that the person using it cannot mistake which person it refers to, namely, him or herself. No such feature attaches to other ways of referring to ourselves' (Lowe, 2000, pp. 226–7; also see Olson, 2007, pp. 11f.).

Of course, this does not mean that we do not have aspects of the concept of 'I' that do not puzzle us. For example, in his 'On the Phenomeno-Logic of the I', Castañeda remarks, 'many mysteries surround the self, but many of them arise from the fact that a self refers to itself in the first-person way' (in Cassam, 1994, p. 160; see also Evans, 1982, p. 205). The bottom line here is that the referentiality of the term 'I' should be kept distinct from the difficulty it poses in understanding what exactly it stands for. Two essays in the present volume will elaborate on this issue in great depth.

2.3. Descartes' Non-Empirical Approach

As pointed out earlier, Descartes strongly believed that a purely *a priori* method can establish an unshakeable foundation not only for knowledge taken in general, but also for self-knowledge in particular. While *a priori* first-personal introspective reflection gives us access to our own mental life, it may not be sufficient all by itself.

For example, as some of the essays in this volume will show, there are cases where self-knowledge or even self-concept (i.e. a capacity to reflectively think about oneself) seems to break down. For example, what conclusion should be drawn when individuals with autism demonstrate what is known as *pronoun reversals*, that is, when a child utters 'you' instead of 'I' or 'me' when intending to refer to himself or herself? Will a child's inability to use 'I' to refer to himself or herself in any way jeopardize the capacity he or she has for a self-concept? Similarly, what conclusion should be drawn concerning the problem of 'thought insertion', say in schizophrenia, where someone ends up experiencing their own thoughts as someone else's? Can we then say that, in such situation(s), one would still continue to maintain a clear sense of self-knowledge as understood from one's own first-person perspective? There are also cases of 'mind-wandering' which is contrasted with 'mental autonomy'. Mental autonomy refers to a capacity to manage one's own mental life. However, it has been said that we do not in fact have such a capacity for mental autonomy to the extent we naturally believe that we have. This is because, according to the view (proposed by one of the contributors to this volume), for roughly two thirds of their lives, humans are not mentally autonomous subjects. If this view is correct, then we wonder whether we would be forced to revise our estimation of what we can know from the first-person perspective. If so, in what way? We can add to the list modern day neuroimaging techniques in neuroscience via which it is now possible to peer into people's brains while people are still alive. Does such progress in brain science render our reliance on the first-person perspective less relevant, thereby elevating the prominence of the third-person perspective?

Once we seriously begin to ponder on these questions, the limitations of Descartes' non-empirical method become increasingly evident. This is because these are not the sorts of questions that we can hope to tackle via sustained privately exercised *a priori* reflection by introspection. Moreover, it could also be said that one cannot know *a priori* what sort of thing one is (or what your 'I' refers to). So these questions, *inter alia*, require direct engagement with people who suffer from some of the situations described above on the one hand, and the experts who do research in these areas on the other.

So where does all this leave us? The answer to this question must not be too difficult. If we really want to make some significant inroads into our understanding of the *three notions*, the most fruitful course of action we can take has to do with bringing non-empirical and empirical methods together. In short, we need to think about these issues within an *interdisciplinary* setting. And that is precisely what the present volume attempts to do by bringing together experts from academic disciplines as diverse as metaphysics, philosophy of mind, linguistics, phenomenology, education, and cognitive neuroscience.

Given that this volume is interdisciplinary in its approach, readers should expect different ways by which the authors develop their arguments in dealing with the *three notions*. As it should be expected, the authors may not share similar convictions with respect to what they say regarding the *three notions*. However, points of agreement among the authors outweigh points of disagreement. Figuring out this common ground at times may appear to be difficult, but with a little bit of extra effort readers should not find it too demanding. With this in mind, in §3 I will briefly explain the structure of the essays.

3. The Essays

3.1. Part One

This section consists of seven essays which collectively deal with selfhood and the first person.

The first essay begins with José Luis Bermúdez's 'Selves, Bodies, and Self-Reference: Reflections on Jonathan Lowe's Non-Cartesian Dualism'. In this essay, Bermúdez examines Lowe's Non-Cartesian

Substance Dualism (NCSD), according to which the self or person is distinct from the physical body or any part of it such as the brain. Bermúdez evaluates Lowe's arguments for NCSD, namely mental causation and personal agency, the unity argument, individuation of psychological states, as well as the theory of direct demonstrative reference, all of which Lowe uses to defend his theory of NCSD on the one hand, and to reject reductionism about the self (e.g. the bundle theory of the self) on the other. Bermúdez concludes his essay by claiming that neither Lowe's positive argument for NCSD nor his arguments against reductionism about the self are persuasive.

Richard Swinburne, in his paper 'The Inevitable Implausibility of Physical Determinism', argues against physical determinism, the doctrine he states as every event has a physical event as its necessary and sufficient cause and no non-physical or mental event as either a necessary or sufficient cause. But Swinburne argues that there is robust room for causal efficacy of mental events (e.g. one's intention) which can be accessed only from one's first-person perspective. Swinburne claims that there is no justification for epiphenomenalism for which the recent neuroscientific work such as Libet-type experiments offer no help. Swinburne concludes his essay by claiming that physical determinism is false, since the physical domain is not causally closed. His conclusion is very much compatible with Lowe's view of mental causation, which Bermúdez criticizes.

Looking at reductive account of the self, Andy Hamilton, in his paper 'The Metaphysics and Anti-Metaphysics of the Self', begins his discussion with the modern conception of self-consciousness, which he attributes to Kant (as its originator), and connects this notion to controversies surrounding the ontology of the self. Hamilton develops his own position of self-consciousness by appealing to what he calls the *Analytic Principle*, which construes self-consciousness via the use of the first-person referring device, 'I'. Hamilton further develops this principle by merging the notion of self-consciousness with the notion of self-reference via what he calls *conceptual holism*. Hamilton concludes his essay by emphasizing, *inter alia*, the centrality of 'I' for self-consciousness.

Eric T. Olson, in his paper 'What Does it Mean to Say That We Are Animals?', focuses on developing a clear account of what the doctrine of animalism comes down to. He begins his discussion by contrasting animalism with Lockeanism. He then moves on to discussing how animalism should be stated. In light of this, Olson points out the different formulations of animalism, thereby showing their inadequacy as well as the problems associated with them. Olson also discusses the central claims of weak animalism, strong animalism, and new animalism. According to Olson, weak animalism is the bare claim that we are animals (in the ordinary sense of 'are'). Strong animalism is the conjunction of weak animalism with further claims such as animals are animals fundamentally, animals do not persist by virtue of psychological continuity, animals persist by virtue of some sort of brute-physical continuity, etc. New animalism embraces the claim that we are animals, but takes our persistence to consist in psychological continuity. Olson concludes his essay by pointing out that animalism comes in different forms, for which weak animalism serves as their unifying feature.

Harold Noonan, in his paper 'Plenitude, Pluralism, and Neo-Lockean Persons', discusses, among other things, the debates between neo-Lockeans and proponents of strong animalism. Noonan understands strong animalism as the view that denies the relevance of psychology for the persistence of animals, the view he attributes to Olson. At the centre of Noonan's discussion lies the solution he proposes to accommodate the well-known 'too many thinkers objection', often raised against defenders of the neo-Lockean psychological continuity theory of personal identity. Noonan claims that by accepting that biologically individuated animals think, the neo-Lockean can effectively deflect the too many thinkers objection. In light of this, Noonan concludes his essay by urging other neo-Lockeans also to embrace a multiplicity of thinkers.

Olley Pearson, in his paper 'Rationality and the First Person', discusses how a theory of rationality provides an argument for the existence of a self. The sort of a self that Pearson has in mind is the one that can be captured only in first-personal beliefs, that is, beliefs best expressed with utterances in the first person. For Pearson, a self is distinct from the physical body, which can be captured in third-person beliefs, that is, beliefs best expressed with utterances in the third person. After discussing first-personal beliefs in relation to certain actions, Pearson discusses two accounts of rationality, namely one that is said to consist in fitting complex normative requirements, and one which is reasons-based. Pearson concludes his paper by pointing out why a reasons-based account of rationality is preferable.

Wolfram Hinzen and Kristen Schroeder, in their paper 'Is "the First Person" a Linguistic Concept Essentially?', seek to reverse the marginalization of linguistics in philosophical discussions of the 'self', 'the first-person perspective', and 'subjectivity'. Hinzen and

Schroeder forcefully argue that non-theoretical notions such as the 'self' and 'the first person' are intimately linked to the grammatical forms used to engage in acts of self-reference. The central claim Hinzen and Schroeder defend is that the first person is inherently linguistic and cannot be defined in non-grammatical terms. They also highlight problems related to pronominal systems in the case of conditions such as autism spectrum disorder. They conclude their paper by claiming that grammar and selfhood are intimately related, which they also say shows why a renewed attention should be given to language.

3.2. Part Two

Building upon the discussion undertaken in the preceding seven essays, the five essays in this section collectively focus on the first-person perspective.

In this case, Lynne Rudder Baker, in her paper 'Autism and "I"', discusses her view of the first-person perspective and its importance for understanding personhood by applying it to a well-known person with autism, Temple Grandin. Central to Baker's discussion is Grandin's claim that she thinks only in pictures. But Baker, without denying Grandin's personal experiences, however insists that the fact that Grandin has a mental life requires that language plays a central role in how she communicates her experiences as well as in the things she writes, for example. Baker concludes her essay by claiming that Grandin does not lack language or a robust first-person perspective.

Angela J. Guta, in her paper 'First-Person and Third-Person Perspectives and Autism', proposes a new way to help children with autism who suffer from social impairment such as a lack of seeking enjoyment and interest in others. Guta examines whether or not video modelling filmed from the first-person perspective or the third-person perspective is more effective in terms of increasing the verbal and action imitation skills of children with autism. Guta claims that video filmed from the first-person perspective is more effective in increasing the imitation skills of children with autism. She concludes her essay with some recommendations for further research in the area of video modelling filmed from the first-person perspective.

Mihretu P. Guta, in his paper 'Consciousness, First-Person Perspective, and Neuroimaging', introduces a capacity-based account of the first-person perspective, thereby clarifying a number of notions such as intersubjectivity, scientific objectivity and its relation to subjectivity, and the asymmetry that holds between the first-person perspective and the third-person perspective. Guta argues that any attempt to reduce the first-person perspective to that of the third-person perspective fails. Guta also makes a case for the integration between subjectivity and scientific objectivity. He concludes his paper by briefly discussing an objection from neuroscience.

Unlike Baker's and Guta's papers, each of which strongly argue for the centrality of the first-person perspective, the remaining two papers deal with some phenomena that seem to disturb first-person experiences in general and the notion of self in particular.

In this case, Matthew Ratcliffe and Sam Wilkinson, in their paper 'Thought Insertion Clarified', explain the phenomenon of 'thought insertion' which involves one experiencing one's own thought as someone else's. Ratcliffe and Wilkinson point out that some philosophers try to make sense of thought insertion in terms of ownership and agency. However, Ratcliffe and Wilkinson find such an approach unsatisfactory. In light of this, they argue that thought insertion should be understood in terms of experiencing thought *content* as alien, as opposed to episodes of thinking. They conclude their essay by pointing out how the experience of thought insertion results in disturbances of the notion of the self as well as first-person experience.

Finally, Thomas Metzinger, in his paper 'M-Autonomy', makes a case for two main claims. First, Metzinger claims that for roughly two thirds of their conscious lives human beings lack mental autonomy; and second, he claims that conscious thought is a subpersonal process. The idea here relates to spontaneous, task-unrelated thought (e.g. daydreams). Metzinger claims that each of these claims can be backed up by empirical evidence and he presents some of these in his essay. In light of this, he also argues how the notion of the first-person perspective and personhood should be understood. He concludes his paper by claiming that most of the time it is the brain that thinks, not us.

Acknowledgments

The essays contributed to this Special Issue are an important output of the international interdisciplinary conference that took place on 15–17 May 2014 at Durham University, UK. The title of the conference was Perspectives on the First Person Pronoun 'I': Looking at Metaphysics, Linguistics and Neuroscience. This conference was generously funded by the Mind Association; the John Templeton Foundation; Durham Institute for Advanced Study; Durham Philosophy Department;

Durham Faculty of Arts and Humanities Postgraduate Training Grants; Newcastle University School of Education, Communication and Language Sciences; the Analysis Trust; and Durham Ustinov College. We would like to thank the speakers at the conference: Sophie Gibb (Durham University); Harold Noonan (University of Nottingham); Raymond Tallis (Manchester University); Richard Swinburne (University of Oxford); Eric Olson (University of Sheffield); Lynne Rudder Baker (University of Massachusetts); Wolfram Hinzen and Kristen Schroeder (University of Barcelona); Matthew Ratcliffe (University of Vienna); Anders Holmberg (Newcastle University); Angela Guta (Newcastle University); and Mihretu Guta (Durham University). Postgraduate Speakers: Amelia Mihaela Dascalu (Université Sorbonne Nouvelle, Paris); Eleonora Mingarelli (Higher Institute of Philosophy, KU Leuven, Belgium); Brandon L. Rickabaugh (Azusa Pacific University/Biola University, USA); and Alexander Moran (Oxford University). Invited contributors: José Luis Bermúdez (Texas A&M University); Thomas Metzinger (Johannes Gutenberg-Universität Mainz); Olley Pearson (Durham University); and Andy Hamilton (Durham University).

The conference was originally organized by E.J. Lowe (in memoriam), Mihretu P. Guta, and Angela J. Guta. We dedicate this Special Issue to the loving memory of Professor E.J. Lowe.[2]

References

Campbell, J. (1994) *Past, Space and Self*, Cambridge, MA: MIT Press.

Cassam, Q. (1994) *Self-Knowledge*, Oxford: Oxford University Press.

Chalmers, D.J. (2010) *The Character of Consciousness*, Oxford: Oxford University Press.

Dennett, D.C. (1991) *Consciousness Explained*, Boston, MA: Little, Brown and Company.

Descartes, R. (1996) *Meditations on First Philosophy*, Cottingham J. (ed.), Cambridge: Cambridge University Press.

Evans, G. (1982) *The Varieties of Reference*, Oxford: Oxford University Press.

Gibb, S., Lowe, E.J. & Ingthorsson, R.D. (2013) *Mental Causation and Ontology*, Oxford: Oxford University Press.

Hasker, W. (1999) *The Emergent Self*, Ithaca, NY: Cornell University Press.

Hume, D. (1978) *David Hume: A Treatise of Human Nature*, Selby-Bigge, L.A. (ed.), Oxford: Clarendon Press.

---

[2] Many thanks to Eric T. Olson for excellent comments on the original draft of this introduction. My thanks also go to a referee for helpful comments. I am also grateful for the Durham Emergence Project (funded by the John Templeton Foundation), where I was a Postdoctoral Research Fellow at the time of editing this volume.

Kant, I. (1929) *Critique of Pure Reason*, Smith, N.K. (trans.), London: Macmillan Press.

Kenny, A. (1989) *The Metaphysics of Mind*, Oxford: Clarendon Press.

Kim, J. (2005) *Physicalism, or Something Near Enough*, Princeton, NJ: Princeton University Press.

Kim, J. (2006) *Philosophy of Mind (2nd edition)*, Cambridge, MA: Westview Press.

Kolak, D. & Martin, R. (1991) *Self and Identity: Contemporary Philosophical Issues*, New York: Macmillan Publishing Company.

Locke, J. (1975) *An Essay Concerning Human Understanding*, Nidditch, P.H. (ed.), Oxford: Clarendon Press.

Lowe, E.J. (2000) *An Introduction to the Philosophy of Mind*, Cambridge: Cambridge University Press.

Lowe, E.J. (2008) *Personal Agency: The Metaphysics of Mind and Action*, Oxford: Oxford University Press.

Olson, E.T. (2007) *What Are We? A Study of Personal Ontology*, New York: Oxford University Press.

Perry, J. (ed.) (1975) *Personal Identity*, Berkeley, CA: University of California Press.

José Luis Bermúdez

Selves, Bodies, and Self-Reference

Reflections on Jonathan Lowe's Non-Cartesian Dualism

Abstract: *This paper critically evaluates Jonathan Lowe's arguments for his non-Cartesian substance dualism (henceforth: NCSD). Sections 1 and 2 set out the principal claims of NCSD. The unity argument proposed in Lowe (2008) is discussed in Section 3. Throughout his career Lowe offered spirited attacks on reductionism about the self. Section 4 evaluates the anti-reductionist argument that Lowe offers in* Subjects of Experience, *an argument based on the individuation of mental events. Lowe (1993) offers an inventive proposal that the semantic distinction between direct and indirect reference delineates the metaphysical boundary between self and world, and uses this as a further argument against reductionism about the self. This proposal is discussed in Sections 5 and 6.*

With the untimely death of Jonathan Lowe in January 2014, analytic philosophy lost one of its most productive and innovative thinkers. Lowe was a very wide-ranging philosopher who made significant contributions to philosophical logic, metaphysics, and the philosophy of mind. He was never one to follow the shifting tides of philosophical fashion. In fact, many of us will remember him fondly for his spirited defence of a number of positions that many (most?) philosophers would deem to be self-evidently false. A fierce opponent of physicalism in both its reductionist and non-reductionist forms, Lowe vigorously propounded his own version of substantival dualism, combined

Correspondence:
Email: jbermudez@tamu.edu

Journal of Consciousness Studies, **22**, No. 11–12, 2015, pp. 20–42

with a robust psychophysical interactionism. As if this were not enough, he offered ingenious defences of the sense datum theory of perception, the volitional theory of action, and the ideational view of language. Proponents of these currently unfashionable positions have a tendency to argue for them indirectly by attacking the competing positions. One of the many merits of Lowe's philosophical style and temperament is that he offered a series of clearly articulated and carefully developed arguments in support of almost all his major theoretical claims, in addition to trenchant criticisms of competing views.

1. Lowe's Non-Cartesian Substance Dualism

According to NCSD selves are enduring and irreducible substances that are non-identical with their bodies. But Lowe's version of this claim is not Descartes'. He emphasizes that selves are subjects of experience, rather than immaterial entities. What distinguishes selves from their bodies is not a radical ontological distinction between material and immaterial substances, but rather more prosaic considerations of persistence and causation. Selves have different persistence conditions from bodies and different causal powers.

As he explicitly states (Lowe, 1996, p. 35), NCSD is intended to do justice jointly and severally to the Cartesian view that persons are a distinctive type of entity, to the Lockean view that this type of entity is essentially a psychological type, and to the Aristotelian view that persons are not essentially immaterial. For Lowe, selves are psychological substances (that is, they require suitably unified successions of psychological states) — that is a point of agreement with Locke. And (a point of agreement with Descartes) selves are simple — that is, they are substances that have no substantial parts — and in particular no physical substantial parts. But Lowe denies (with Aristotle) that selves can be separated from their bodies. In fact, he allows that subjects of experience can be the bearers not just of mental properties but also of those physical properties that they have in virtue of possessing a body that possesses those properties (Lowe, 2008, p. 95).[1]

The first difficulty for the sympathetic reader is clarifying the precise metaphysical doctrine being defended. There is, for example, an

---

[1] Following Lowe (see 1996, p. 1), I am using 'self', 'person', and 'subject of experience' interchangeably.

equivocation in Lowe's presentation of Aristotle's insight that persons
are not essentially immaterial. Is this supposed to entail that persons
are essentially embodied? We are told that persons cannot be
separated from their bodies 'except perhaps conceptually or purely in
imagination' (Lowe, 1996, p. 35), and this seems to be reinforced by
the stress on the self perceiving and acting through a particular body.
But what is the content and force of the claim that self and body are
distinct? Like Duns Scotus, Lowe believes that two things can fail to
be really distinct and yet be more than conceptually distinct.[2] Two
points secure for Lowe what Scotus would call a 'formal' distinction.
First, even though it seems to be necessary that any given self have
some body, the connection between any given self and its body is
purely contingent — as he puts it, 'this body is only *contingently
mine*' (*ibid.*, p. 7, emphasis in original). Second, the self and its body
have different persistence conditions (*ibid.*, p. 34).

One might reasonably wonder how either of these two claims could
be motivated without begging the question. The first point could
neutrally be put as the intuitively plausible claim that I could have had
physical characteristics other than the ones that I do have. But this
intuition can be cashed out in two ways — as saying either that my
body could have been different or that I could have had a different
body. Only the second version suggests a contingent connection
between self and body, but there is nothing in our initial neutral
intuition to suggest the second version. In order to motivate the idea
that I could have had a different body, Lowe needs to appeal to
thought experiments in which, for example, as Locke suggests, a
Prince and a Cobbler swap bodies. These thought experiments would
be accepted by many reductionists about the self, but quite plainly
would fail to convince anyone who thinks that selves are human
animals.

Nor is it clear that Lowe's own theory allows him to assert that the
self and the body have different persistence conditions, since his
doctrine of the simplicity of the substantival self entails that 'we lack
any proper grasp of what would constitute the ceasing-to-be of a self'
(*ibid.*, p. 43). We do not, Lowe thinks, have criteria of identity for
simple substances, because simple substances lack substantial parts
and all criteria of identity rest upon the holding of certain relationships
among a substance's substantial parts. Of course, Lowe does not think

---

[2]   For discussion of Scotus's views in this area see Adams (1982).

that selves are immortal. So there must be circumstances in which they cease to be. We just don't know what those circumstances are. But then, by the same token, we cannot responsibly say that the circumstances in which selves cease to be are different from the circumstances in which their respective bodies cease to be. We have to be agnostic.

Lowe's argument would be better put, I think, as the inference that the self cannot be identical with the body from the principle of the non-identity of discernibles and the lemma that the body but not the self has determinate persistence conditions. This, however, places the full weight of the argument onto the claim that the self is a simple substance, which in turn is derived from the thought that the self cannot have substantial parts since such parts could only be the parts of the body, which would have the result that the body and the self would share all their parts (and hence, on standard mereological assumptions, be the same thing). Of course, one man's *modus tollens* is another man's *modus ponens* and some philosophers will simply conclude from all this that the body and the self are necessarily identical.

In any event, the reasoning here does seem to be moving in a rather tight circle. If the self is a simple substance, then we should certainly grant Lowe that the self is distinct from its body, since bodies do have substantial parts. But why think that the self is a simple substance? Because otherwise it would end up being identical to the body, since its substantial parts would be bodily parts. Wait — that's the very conclusion we are trying to establish!

In Section 3 we will turn to Lowe's 'master argument' for NCSD — the unity argument — which offers a different way of motivating the non-identity of self and body. Before doing so we turn in Section 2 to the second aspect of NCSD, *viz.* the idea that selves have distinctive causal powers.

2. Lowe on Mental Causation and Personal Agency

In Chapter 3 of *Subjects of Experience* Lowe considers and eventually rejects three interactionist proposals to reconcile the notion of independent mental causal powers with the conservation laws of physics. His main objection is that they all display a misplaced allegiance to the Cartesian principle that the mind can only exert causal influence on the body by setting matter in motion. Lowe thinks that the Cartesian principle is incompatible with the structure of the causal chains involved in deliberative action. He models these causal

chains as fractally structured trees converging on a bodily movement.
There is no single linear causal chain. Instead, going backwards from
every event there are many different chains, splitting and separating
off from each other like branches on a tree. Unlike real trees, though,
these causal trees have no identifiable tips (at which the mind might
set the whole causal process in motion) because the causal ancestry of
any bodily movement merges into the prior causal history of the
whole brain (Lowe, 1996, p. 65, n. 15). Instead, Lowe suggests, we
need to replace the dominant conception of mental causation with a
model of mental events as indirect rather than direct causes of bodily
movements. Mental events do not directly cause all (or any) of the
physical events in the fractal tree convergent upon a bodily movement. Rather, the causal efficacy of a given mental event lies in the
fact that such a convergent fractal tree exists at all (*ibid.*, p. 67). We
need to appeal to mental events because the existence of such a convergence seems inexplicable in purely physical terms.

Here is Lowe's example in *Personal Agency*. Suppose that someone
deliberately raises their arm in order to ask a question in a lecture.
Tracing the purely bodily causes of the arm movement back in time
would yield a highly complex branching structure in the brain and
nervous system, but introspectively things seem very different.

> Many of the neural events concerned will be widely distributed across
> fairly large areas of the motor cortex and have no single focus any-
> where, with the causal chains to which they belong possessing no
> distinct *beginnings*. And yet, intuitively, the agent's mental act of
> decision or choice to move the arm would seem, from an introspective
> point of view, to be a singular and unitary occurrence which somehow
> initiated his or her action of raising the arm. (Lowe, 2008, p. 102)

Here is how Lowe proposes to reconcile the tension.

> First of all, the act of choice is attributed to the *person* whereas the
> neural events are attributed to parts of the person's *body*: and a person
> and his body are, according to this conception of ourselves, *distinct*
> things, even if they are not *separable* things. Moreover, the act of
> choice *causally explains* the bodily movement — the upward movement
> of the arm — in a different way from the way in which the neural
> events explain it. The neural events explain why the arm moved *in the
> particular way* that it did — at such-and-such a speed and in such-and-
> such a direction at a certain precise time. By contrast, the act of choice
> explains why a movement of that general kind — in this case, a rising
> of the agent's arm — occurred around the time it did. It did so because
> shortly beforehand the agent decided to raise that arm. (*ibid.*, p. 102)

These two causal explanations differ counterfactually. Had the decision not taken place there would not have been an arm movement of that kind at all. And yet, Lowe claims, there is no set of neural events in the bodily antecedents of the arm-raising of which it is true to say that had those events not occurred there would not have been an arm movement of that kind at all. From which he concludes, first, that the decision cannot be identified with any set of neural events, and, second, that the decision is an instance of a fundamentally different type of causation from that operative at the neural level.

Lowe has done philosophers a service by reminding us how impoverished and implausible the causal models which inform contemporary discussion of mental causation are. He may well be right that once we take causal chains to be fractal trees rather than linear successions of billiard-ball-like interactions it becomes completely inappropriate to look for a single initiating cause of a bodily movement that can then be either caused by or identified with a mental event. As he readily admits, however, we really need a positive account of how mental events can have the indirect causal powers that Lowe claims they have. Unfortunately any such account runs into a significant dilemma.

The dilemma comes when we ask whether there is any causal contact that would allow the mental act of choosing to intervene in the branching neural tree. Suppose, first, that there is such an intervention. If there is then there must be an earliest such causal contact, and then Lowe needs to explain why this does not qualify as exactly the type of initiating cause that he is trying to move away from. If the act of choice plays a causal role within the branching neural tree then Lowe seems to lose the distinction between, on the one hand, the neural events that (causally) explain the precise contours of the arm movement and, on the other, the mental event that (causally) explains why there is an arm movement of that type (a signalling).

We can appreciate the problem by looking at the subtle model of mental causation that he offers in Section 3.4 of *Personal Agency*. It is easier to see what is going on in Lowe's own diagram, reproduced as Figure 1.

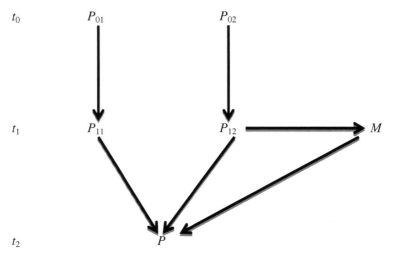

Figure 1. Lowe's model of mental causation (from 2008, p. 71). Note that mental event M is simultaneous with physical events P_{11} and P_{12}.

Lowe's suggestion is that at time t_1 there are two physical events P_{11} and P_{12}, each of which has a purely physical causal history. Those two events are causally sufficient for event P. But P_{11} and P_{12} are only causally sufficient for P because P_{12} simultaneously causes mental event M, which 'helps' bring about P.

Setting aside scruples about simultaneous causation, the real problem comes when we ask just how M helps bring about P. What the diagram shows is a contributing cause. In that regard M is no different from P_{11}. This may (or may not) make sense. But it is certainly not an example of the type of causation that Lowe claims to be offering. Recall that Lowe is proposing a model on which mental causes are indirect rather than direct. M is not supposed to intervene directly in the convergent causal tree. Rather it explains why there is a convergent causal tree at all — or, as he puts it in *Personal Agency* (2008, p. 36), why P is not a coincidence. But M cannot be doing any such job in the model depicted in Figure 1, since M is actually the causal product of one of P's immediate physical causes.

This drives Lowe to the other horn of the dilemma, on which the mental act of choosing does not causally intervene in the branching tree of neural events. But now he needs to answer an even more difficult question: how can the mental act have any causal influence on the arm movement at all? *Ex hypothesi* the branching tree of neural events is causally sufficient for the particular bodily movement that occurs (or at least, in a probabilistic universe, sufficiently fixes the chances of that movement). And yet Lowe is committed to it being the case that had the mental act not occurred, not only would <u>that</u> bodily movement not have occurred, but nor would there have been any bodily movement of that type at all. In virtue of what could this counterfactual dependence hold, if the mental act is causally insulated from the physical antecedents of the bodily movement? It certainly looks as though we have the mere statement of a counterfactual dependence without any account of what could possibly make it true.

In *Personal Agency*, Lowe does give a theological example to illustrate how his proposed account is at least possible on the assumptions that I am terming the second horn of the dilemma. Imagine a world in which it is true that physical events only have other physical events in their causal history and in which every physical event has a sufficient physical cause. Such a world would, he thinks, have no beginning in time. He continues:

> And yet we could still ask of this world why *it* should exist or be actual rather than any other. One intelligible answer would be that this world was actual because God had chosen it to be actual. God's choice, then, would have caused it to be the case that a world containing certain physical facts was actual — and this would be mental causation of physical causal facts. (*ibid.*, p. 55)

This is a desperate move. Leaving aside the question of whether the theological scenario really is intelligible, taking this example literally would seem to require that ordinary mental causation operate outside space and time. If ever there was a cure that killed the patient this is it!

3. The Unity Argument

In Section 5.2 of *Personal Agency* Lowe offers what he terms the unity argument for NCSD. The argument is intended to show that the self cannot be identical to the body or to any part of the body (such as the brain or central nervous system, for example). Here is the argument:

(1) I am the subject of all and only my own mental states.
(2) Neither my body as a whole nor any part of it could be the subject of all and only my own mental states.
(3) I am not identical with my body or any part of it.

Clearly the weight of the argument is being carried by premise (2).

In support of (2) Lowe observes that my body as a whole does need to exist in order for me to have all, or at any rate almost all, of the mental states I currently have. So, for example, if I were to lose the tip of the little finger on my left hand, that would have no implications for any of my mental states of any of my mental states (except for any non-phantom sensations that I might feel at the tip of my little finger). Lowe then applies the following principle.

> No entity can qualify as the *subject* of certain mental states if those mental states could exist in the absence of that object. (Lowe, 2008, p. 96)

Since he believes that the fingertip example shows that the overwhelming majority of my mental states could exist in the absence of my body, he concludes that my body cannot be the subject of those mental states. Since exactly the same argument could be applied to any part of my body (imagine, for example, my brain lacking a few brain cells), Lowe concludes that no part of the body could be the subject of all and only my own mental states.

The obvious objection to this line of argument is to deny that my body would cease to exist if I were to lose the tip of the little finger on my left hand. It seems much more plausible to say that my body would persist through such a change. After an involuntary digital amputation, for example, I would end up with the same body, slightly changed, rather than with a different body that almost completely overlaps with the old one. To hold the opposite, as Lowe does, would seem to entail that one's body disappears when a hair drops out or a toenail falls off.

Lowe acknowledges this objection and revises his defence of (2) to accommodate it. Let 'T' denote the set of occurrent thoughts that do not depend upon my body having the tip of the little finger of my left hand as a part, let 'O' denote my body minus the tip of the little finger of my left hand, and let 'B' denote my body as a whole. Now, Lowe asks, what reason could there be for identifying O rather than B as the subject of the thoughts in T? He finds none, claiming that the material difference between O and B is irrelevant to either of them being the subject of the thoughts in T. But then, he continues, it must either be the case that B and O are both the subjects of the thoughts in T or that neither of them is. Since thoughts cannot have two distinct subjects, and B and O are distinct objects, the first option is ruled out.

It would be dialectically unsatisfying simply to respond to this line of argument that only B is a genuine object. That would be to beg the question against Lowe, who has written at great length on the meta-physics of identity and constitution. However, even if we put aside the question of whether O is a genuine object (as we probably should, since 'object' is not a term that has clear criteria of identity), it is not clear that on his own metaphysical principles Lowe is entitled to assume that O and B are equally eligible to be subjects of the thoughts in T. Lowe is firmly committed to the metaphysical significance of the category of substance. Although he does not, to my knowledge, directly consider the issue, I think that he is committed to holding that only substances can be the subjects of thoughts and experiences. This is the crucial difference between B and O. Only B is even a candidate to be a substance, because B is an appropriately organized and structured physical organism that falls under a sortal term with clear criteria of identity (the sortal 'human body').

It is certainly true that in a possible world W in which I had had the tip of the little finger on my left hand amputated, I would still count as a substance, because in that possible world my body would be appro-priately organized and structured. Being a human body does not require possessing all one's fingertips. But it doesn't follow that in this world, where I do have all my fingertips, O, as a proper part of me, is a substance. In fact, it fails to qualify even by Lowe's own defi-nition of substance, which is x is a substance if and only if it is not dependent for its existence upon anything else (Lowe, 1998, p. 138). O would not be dependent upon anything else in the counterfactual scenario, but in this world O is dependent for its existence upon the human body B of which it is a proper part.

For these reasons Lowe is not entitled to his crucial claim that it must either be the case that B and O are both the subjects of the thoughts in T or that neither of them is. And so the revised argument for (2) fails. The unity argument is ingenious but ultimately unsuccessful.

4. Individuating Psychological Modes: Lowe's Objection to Reductionism about the Self

Throughout his career Lowe complemented his positive arguments for NCSD with probing criticisms of what he took to be the principal alternatives. Since it is integral to his view of selves as simple sub-stances that they be the subjects of psychological events, process, and states, a natural target for him was reductionism about the self. His

objections to reductionism clarify and sharpen his conception of what
it is for a self to be a subject of experience.

The reductionist position was put most pithily by Hume in *A
Treatise on Human Nature* when he described the self as 'nothing but
a bundle or collection of different perceptions, which succeed each
other with an inconceivable rapidity, and are in a perpetual flux and
movement' (Hume, 1739–40/1978, p. 252). Hume continues:

> The mind is a kind of theatre, where several perceptions successively
> make their appearance; pass, re-pass, glide away, and mingle in an infi-
> nite variety of postures and situations. There is properly no *simplicity* in
> it at one time, nor *identity* in different; whatever natural propensity we
> may have to imagine that simplicity and identity. (*ibid.*, p. 253)

The most celebrated modern exponent of reductionism (also known,
for obvious reasons, as the bundle theory) is Derek Parfit (Parfit,
1984).[3]

Lowe uses the expression 'psychological modes' to cover mental
events, process, and state. I will follow him in this convenient short-
hand. Lowe's basic objection to reductionism about the self is that
psychological modes are necessarily 'owned'. They cannot, he thinks,
be identified and individuated in the way that the reductionist maintains. The reductionist needs psychological modes to be individuated
impersonally — namely, without reference to the subject of which
they are modes. But Lowe, like many others, thinks that this is
impossible.

> Such individual mental states are necessarily states *of persons*: They are
> necessarily 'owned' — necessarily have a *subject*. The necessity in
> question arises from the metaphysical-cum-logical truth that such
> individual mental states cannot even in principle be individuated and
> identified without reference to the subject of which they are states.
> (Lowe, 1996, p. 25)

Of course, no reductionist is going to accept that there really is such a
metaphysical-cum-logical truth. So Lowe's position ultimately rests
upon his objections to impersonal criteria for individuating psychological modes.

---

[3]   I don't actually believe that Parfit offers the only way, or even the best way, to formulate reductionism about the self. But it is the version that Lowe considers, and in the
remainder of the paper 'bundle theorist' should be understood to refer to 'Parfit-style
bundle theorist'.

Perhaps the best-known proposal for individuating psychological modes comes from Donald Davidson, as an application of his general criterion for individuating all events. Davidson held that we can individuate mental events causally. Two events are identical iff they have the same causes and effects (Davidson, 1969). Plainly this causal conception of individuation can be applied within an impersonal conception of the world. So Lowe discusses Davidson's position at some length.

Before we look at the details of Lowe's discussion of Davidson we should recognize that Davidson himself abandoned this theory of events (Davidson, 1985). It is still worth considering, however, for two reasons. The first is that a recognizable descendant of the theory still lives on in the philosophy of mind in functionalist theories of mind, which typically identify mental states/events, including experiences, in terms of their typical causes and effects. The second, and for our purposes more important, is that Lowe's objection to Davidson is really a more general objection to a certain model of individuation (impredicative individuation) and it is highly plausible that any reductionist account of how to individuate mental events will be impredicative.

Lowe's principal objection is that the causal criterion of event identity is, if not strictly speaking circular, then at least impossible to apply — a charge that, as he freely admits, has been levelled many times at Davidson (for a pithy example see Quine, 1985). Since the relata of the causal relation are themselves events, in order to apply the criterion to individuate an event we would have already had to have individuated the events that are its causes and effects. Davidson's definition of event identity is an example of impredicativity, whereby something is defined with reference to a totality of which it is an element. Philosophers are divided on whether impredicative definitions are acceptable as definitions, or whether they are viciously circular (this is a particularly lively topic in the philosophy of mathematics). But Lowe agrees with Quine that impredicative individuation is a non-starter.[4]

---

4   Actually Lowe is not entirely on the same page as Quine with respect to impredicative individuation. He discusses Quine's views in Lowe (1989). What Quine should have said, according to Lowe, is that impredicative individuation is impermissible in the absence of a supporting theory that will allow an impredicative principle to be applied (in the way that the impredicative axiom of extensionality in Zermelo-Frankel set theory

This proscription on impredicative individuation needs closer examination, however. The topic of individuation is one that Lowe has explored at length throughout his career and his own discussion is an excellent starting point. We can start with some general points about individuation that would be accepted by most philosophers and certainly by Lowe. First, individuation is relative to a given category or sortal. We need to know the kind of thing that we are dealing with before we can specify how that thing is individuated. Second, there is a close connection between individuation and criteria of identity. To individuate an object is to give criteria that determine whether an object is the same at different times and that will settle the question of whether at a given time we have two objects of a given kind or just one.

In *More Kinds of Being* Lowe gives the following as the general form for criteria of identity.

> (1) If x and y are φs, then x is identical to y if and only if x and y satisfy $C(\varphi)$ (Lowe, 2009, p. 16).

This general schema can be read both at a time and over time, and it is sortal-relative — that is to say, it gives a criterion for identity for x and y relative to some sort or category φ under which they both fall.

The general form (1) allows us to clarify what would count as impredicative individuation. We have impredicativity when the condition $C(\varphi)$ makes reference to a set or totality in which x and y both feature. Davidson's criterion for event identity certainly counts as impredicative in this sense. The condition he proposes where φ is the category of events is that $x = y$ iff x and y have the same causes and effects. The most natural way of formulating that condition would be

> (2) $x = y$ iff $\forall z$ [(z causes $x \Leftrightarrow z$ causes y) & (x causes $z \Leftrightarrow y$ causes z)].

In (2) we assume that the universal quantifier $\forall$ ranges over all events. Since x and y are events, they fall within the range of $\forall$ and so (2) is impredicative.

Why is this supposed to be a problem? Here is Lowe.

> Briefly, the trouble with Davidson's criterion is that if (as Davidson himself proposes) the causes and effects of events are themselves events

---

is supported by the remaining axioms). These differences are not relevant to the current discussion, however.

then the question of whether events $e1$ and $e2$ have the *same* causes and effects (and hence turn out to be the same event according to the criterion) is itself a question concerning the identity of events, so that in the absence of an independent criterion of event identity Davidson's criterion leaves every question of event identity unsettled. (Lowe, 1996, pp. 27–8)

I find this reasoning unconvincing. Consider the following reformulation in which talk of questions is replaced by talk of facts.

> Briefly, the trouble with Davidson's criterion is that if (as Davidson himself proposes) the causes and effects of events are themselves events then the *fact* of whether events $e1$ and $e2$ have the *same* causes and effects (and hence turn out to be the same event according to the criterion) is itself a *fact* concerning the identity of events, so that in the absence of an independent criterion of event identity Davidson's criterion leaves every *fact* about event identity unsettled.

This, I submit, would not be compelling. There is nothing mysterious about the idea that a fact about the identity of an object of a given type depends upon facts about the identity of other objects of the same type. Consider for example the well-known theory of origin essentialism proposed by Saul Kripke. According to Kripke, a human being's origins are essential to that human being (Kripke, 1980). One way of formulating this would be to say that it is essential to any human being that they should have developed from the actual zygote that they did develop from. Since a zygote is the immediate product of a sperm cell originating (essentially) in a man fertilizing an egg cell originating (essentially) in a woman, it follows that it is essential to any human being that they have the parents that they actually have. This has obvious implications for how we think about identity. It means that x is the same human being as y iff x and y have the same parents. But parents are human beings, and so we have a fact about the identity of a human being dependent upon facts about the identity of human beings. Such dependence would be unacceptable by the reformulated argument. But there's absolutely nothing wrong with it. Whatever problems there might be with Kripke's origin essentialism this is not one of them.

The lesson to draw from this, I think, is that we need to distinguish two different senses of the term 'individuation'. On the one hand, individuation can be taken metaphysically. From a metaphysical point of view individuating an object is a matter of specifying what makes that object the object that it is — giving the criteria that determine that object's identity at a time and over time. On the other we can think about individuation as an epistemic undertaking, as a process by which we actually go about establishing whether there really is one object when there appear to be two, or whether an object really has persisted over time. The contrast is between what makes it the case that $x = y$ or $x \neq y$ and how we go about determining whether $x = y$ or $x \neq y$.

The objection to impredicative individuation that we are discussing depends upon framing individuation epistemically. His objection is really that it would be in practice impossible to apply Davidson's criterion for event identity — in order to apply it to settle a question about the identity of two events we would already have to have settled questions about the identity of the events that are the causes and effects of the given event(s). But the objection misses its target. The issue we started with was a metaphysical issue, not an epistemic one. The reductionist is trying to give the identity conditions of mental events without reference to selves or persons. That requires explaining what makes mental events the same or different, not how we go about establishing whether they are the same or different. And, as the example of Kripke's origin essentialism shows, from a metaphysical perspective impredicative individuation can be perfectly acceptable.

Lowe might object that metaphysical and epistemic individuation cannot be so easily separated. He could argue, for example, that a metaphysical identity criterion must be something that we are in principle able to apply, and so to the extent that impredicativity is an epistemic problem it is equally a metaphysical one.

However, there are different contexts in which we might be thinking about individuation. In some situations we have independent modes of access to the object under consideration. The origin essentialism case is like this. We have many different ways of identifying human beings, and we can use them to apply the essentialist criterion of identity. We do not need to investigate the parents of x and y's parents in order to determine whether or not x and y have the same parents. The same holds, I submit, for mental events. We have sufficient grip on what mental events are in order to be able to work out for any mental events w and z whether or not they have the same causes and effects without getting into an endless regress of identifying and comparing the causes and effects of the causes and effects, and so on, of w and z. In situations such as these we do not need to apply criteria of identity all the way down, because we can reply on a more intuitive grasp of, say, mental events. From an epistemic point of view, we use a formal principle of individuation such as Davidson's in order to help resolve problem cases of mental event identity. We do this, though, in the context of being able to resolve ordinary, non-problem cases, and that ability allows us to apply impredicative criteria of identity.

There are situations, though, where we do not have an independent mode of access to the objects under consideration. This may well be the case in mathematics. If a class of mathematical objects is introduced impredicatively and we have no independent grasp of how to individuate objects in that class, then there seems to be room for doubts about how we might (epistemically) individuate objects in that class. The issue is very much alive in the philosophy of mathematics (see Shapiro, 2000, for discussion and further references). But we are obviously in a very different epistemic position with respect to mental events than we are with respect to mathematical objects.

It is true, as a referee observed, that in other publications (e.g. Lowe, 2002, pp. 226–8, and 2010) Lowe offers a different type of objection to Davidson's causal criterion for event identity. He describes a simple possible world with a handful of events where the causal relations are in effect symmetrical, so that (he argues) the causal criterion fails uniquely to individuate the events in that world. This is certainly a metaphysical argument, not an epistemic one. But, as emphasized earlier, the important point is not really whether Davidson's theory of identity can ultimately be maintained. I have been focusing on the legitimacy of impredicative individuation, because it is highly plausible that any reductionist proposal for individuating mental events will have to be impredicative. And what I have tried to show is not that Davidson's theory should be maintained, but rather that Lowe's objection to impredicative individuation (illustrated by Davidson, but not exclusive to Davidson) rests upon an illegitimate appeal to epistemic criteria.

Let me take stock. His attack on reductionism about the self is an important plank in Lowe's case for NCSD. In this section we have been reviewing the objection to reductionism that he levels in *Subjects of Experience* (1996). Lowe argues that reductionism is false because there is no possibility of individuating mental events without reference to selves as their owners. He considers a causal criterion derived from Davidson's well-known discussion of event identity and objects, in essence, that such a criterion would be illegitimately impredicative. Against this I have argued that impredicative individuation is perfectly acceptable for mental events. This falls short, of course, either of a definitive formulation of reductionism or of a convincing argument in favour of reductionism. Nonetheless, reductionism about the self remains in play and we still lack compelling support for NCSD. In the final two sections I turn to another of Lowe's anti-reductionist arguments.

5. Self-Reference and the Boundaries of the Self

In his paper 'Self, Reference, and Self-Reference' (Lowe, 1993), a precursor of the final chapter of *Subjects of Experience*, Lowe offers an account of selfhood that ties it to the self's *de re* knowledge of its own thoughts and experiences. It is, he argues, constitutive of the concept of selfhood that a self be able to make direct demonstrative reference to his or her own occurrent thoughts and experiences, as well as to those parts of the body that can be moved at will. In fact, those parts of the body that can be moved at will are the only physical objects to which Lowe thinks it possible to make direct demonstrative reference, so that the semantic limits of direct demonstrative reference (DDR) track the metaphysical boundary between self and world. He then goes on to develop a further argument against reductionism about the self. This section discusses his conception of direct demonstrative reference. The final section evaluates the anti-reductionist argument.

Standard accounts of reference make a contrast between DDR and indirect reference according to whether the object referred to is sensibly present. We can make DDR both to our own thoughts and experiences and to appropriately situated objects in the external world. According to Lowe, however, reference to non-bodily physical objects is indirect, where this means that a particular demonstrative reference is fixed (implicitly or explicitly) by one or more independent acts of reference involving definite descriptions. Only when we refer to what we are presently thinking or experiencing, or to those parts of our body that we can move 'at will', can we refer demonstratively without relying upon such independent acts of reference.

The standard view permits DDR to non-bodily physical objects such as chairs, provided they can be sensibly discriminated. But, Lowe asks (1993, pp. 28–30), how do I know to which chair I am referring? Only, he replies, through some definite description, such as 'the chair on which I am now fixing my gaze' or 'the chair which I can see on my extreme left out of the corner of my eye'. Such definite descriptions involve an implicit reference to myself, and that is enough to make the reference to a chair indirect. In contrast, no such definite descriptions are required when referring to my present conscious thoughts and experiences.

In the case of a chair Lowe thinks that a definite description is required to provide completely unambiguous reference-fixing. The contrast he draws rests on the claim that reference to one's mental states is always unproblematic and unambiguous. The need for disambiguation in reference to chairs arises because of the possibility of confusion, because there may be more than one chair in front of one (*ibid.*, pp. 28–9). But a similar possibility of confusion exists in reference to one's mental states. Perhaps my toothache is playing up just as my sprained ankle twinges, or perhaps I've just incurred multiple fractures. In these and many other cases one has a plethora of distinct pains, not one composite pain. And, for Lowe's purposes, there is surely no relevant difference between such a situation and one in which one is confronted by a plethora of chairs. Disambiguation is clearly required for reference-fixing in both cases.

How might such disambiguation be provided for multiple pains? Well, I might be referring to the pain to which I am attending. But here we seem drawn to a definite description, 'the pain I am attending to', and with it an indirect reference to myself. Alternatively, I might be referring to a pain in a particular location, 'the pain that I can feel in my arm'. This too brings with it an independent demonstrative reference to myself, as well as to my arm. Or perhaps reference could be fixed through qualitative feel ('the most excruciating pain', for example). But this would be equally unsuccessful, because an independent demonstrative reference is needed to fix the range of the quantifier. I am not referring to the most excruciating pain in the world or in the room, after all, but just to the most excruciating pain that I am feeling now. To appreciate this, consider how I might disambiguate the statement 'that pain is excruciating', uttered when I am lying in a hospital bed looking at the fellow victims of a multiple car crash.

Of course, these examples yield what might seem a trivial sense in which reference to my pains counts as indirect. But it is in precisely this sense that reference to perceptually presented objects is indirect, acording to Lowe. If he thinks that I might need to make clear which chair I am referring to by means of a definite description like 'the chair on my right' or 'the chair in front of me', then he must accept that I might need to make clear which pain I am referring to by means of a definite description like 'the sharp pain I am feeling now' or 'the pain in my right hand'. And if he thinks that the former count as indirect reference, then so too must the latter.

Lowe cannot object that a theory of reference should not be based on extrapolation from these unusual cases of multiplicity and potentially ambiguous demonstrative reference, for he explicitly holds the opposite: 'Cases of actual observable multiplicity only serve to make the indirect nature of all such demonstrative reference more evident' (*ibid.*, p. 30). In the case of perceptually based demonstrative reference to chairs Lowe thinks it legitimate to conclude that such reference must always be indirect from occasional cases of multiplicity. Hence he cannot avoid doing so in the case of reference to one's own thoughts and experiences.

Lowe does on one occasion wonder whether the possibility of multiplicity might not also exist in the case of conscious mental states, but dismisses it on the grounds that one cannot have qualitatively identical but distinct thoughts and experiences (*ibid.*, p. 30 — see also Lowe, 2008, pp. 26–31). I am not convinced by this. Nobody would deny that I can, at two different times, have two qualitatively identical pains, one in my right foot and one in my left foot. So why should it be impossible for me to have those two qualitatively identical pains at the same time? There seems no *a priori* reason for demanding that they suddenly merge into one pain, or acquire a qualitative difference. The view that all pains must be qualitatively different is surely wildly implausible. So why should the view that all the pains one is experiencing at any given moment must be qualitatively different be any less implausible? But in any case, as I have shown, problems of multiplicity arise even when qualitative identity is not assumed, because we saw that an implicit self-reference can be required even when a pain is being identified qualitatively (as 'the excruciating pain that I am feeling now').

Lowe's paper suggests how he might respond. Considering the possibility that one might identify a pain via the definite description 'the toothache that I am now feeling', he asks '...can it seriously be suggested that demonstrative reference by me to my own current toothache necessarily relies, even if only implicitly, upon an independent act of reference to myself? That would seem to suggest that without implicitly specifying to myself that it is my toothache to which I intend to refer as "this pain", I might mistakenly be referring to someone else's...' (Lowe, 1993, p. 21). He finds this completely absurd (because he holds it a logical truth that one can only feel one's own pain). But even granting that there is no ambiguity about who the pain belongs to, there remains an ambiguity about which one it is of the pains that (unquestionably) belong to me. This ambiguity about which pain it is precisely matches the ambiguity Lowe thinks there is when I have several chairs in front of me. So, if an implicit self-reference is required in the latter case, it must also be required in the former.

He also suggests that no reference to oneself is involved in demonstrative reference to one's body (so that one could, despite my suggestion earlier, directly refer to the pain in one's arm, and hence individuate pains by their bodily location): '...it seems absurd to suppose that I need to specify that a hand is mine in order to make it an object of my volitions — for the idea that I might move another's hand at will (that is, as a basic action) is just incoherent' (*ibid.*, p. 32). But ruling out the possibility that it actually belongs to somebody else is not the only reason one might have for appealing to such descriptions to fix the reference of 'this hand'. For example, one might think that in some situations the reference of 'this hand' (e.g. an answer to the question 'which hand?') can only be fixed by a definite description such as 'not the hand I write with'. I might be confused about which hand I am going to pick up the potentially scalding object with until I think of it under the description 'not the hand I write with'. Here, as in the case of multiple pains, the ambiguity is between my two hands, rather than between my hand and somebody else's hand.

Lowe's distinction between direct self-reference and indirect reference to non-bodily physical objects cannot be maintained on the grounds that he presents for it. His construal of direct reference has the consequence that not even reference to our own thoughts and experiences count as instances of DDR. So, assuming that a distinction between indirect reference and DDR is a necessary feature of a satisfactory theory of reference, the standard theory is still the only serious candidate.

6. Direct Self-Reference and Reductionism

Lowe uses his theory of demonstrative reference against the reductionist view of the self, objecting that reductionism about the self makes first-person self-reference into a form of indirect reference. Section 5 shows that, if this is a genuine criticism of reductionism, it is an equally valid criticism of Lowe's own theory of DDR. But his anti-reductionist argument can be freed from his theory of DDR, and is independently interesting.

The argument runs as follows (Lowe, 1993, pp. 25–7). It is a defining feature of selfhood that the self knows necessarily that it is the unique subject of its present conscious thoughts and experiences. This knowledge, expressible in propositions such as '*This* pain is *my* pain', is genuine and informative. But on the bundle theory such genuine and informative self-knowledge would not be available, because the bundle theorist can only refer to the self indirectly, through the thoughts and experiences to which it reduces. If the self can only refer to itself indirectly, by means of independent reference to these experiences and thoughts, then '*This* pain is *my* pain' will come out as trivially true, because it is trivial that *this* pain is one of *these* pains.

An initial response might be that the bundle theorist *can* provide an account of indirect self-reference which will make propositions such as '*This* pain is *my* pain' into informative self-knowledge, by construing '*This* pain is my pain' as '*This* pain is co-conscious with other thoughts and experiences to which DDR could now be made'. This is not trivial in the way that '*This* pain is one of *these* pains' is trivial, because *this* pain is not included in the set of other thoughts and experiences with which it is co-conscious. And nor should it be thought that 'other thoughts and experiences...' is effectively equivalent to '*these* other thoughts and experiences...', so that the original difficulty reappears. It is trivially true that a pain is co-conscious with itself, because co-consciousness is a reflexive relation, but this is not what is doing the work here. The point of the bundle theorist's proposal is precisely that *this* pain is co-conscious with a range of mental states that are distinct from itself and to which DDR *could* now be made.

But this is not quite right yet, since at any given moment any thought or experience is such that DDR could now be made to it. We clearly do not want the result that all thoughts and experiences are co-conscious with each other. Nor, on the other hand, can the bundle theorist get round the problem by reformulating 'This pain is my pain' as 'This pain is co-conscious with other thoughts and experiences to which *I* could now make DDR'. That would be to concede the point to the anti-reductionist, by making an appeal to the self ineliminable.

But Lowe's bundle theorist does have a way out. There is more to thoughts and experiences being co-conscious than the possibility of making DDR to them. For example, the co-consciousness of mental states is manifest in various dispositions to draw conclusions — if a desire for x is co-conscious with a memory that x is to be found at p, then there will be a disposition to infer that *p* is a desirable place to go to. By the same token, and more generally, the co-consciousness of mental states brings with it the *a priori* ability to conjoin them in a more inclusive mental state. Take the judgment 'I am in pain', or, as a reductionist might say, 'there is pain here' — I won't spell out the impersonal rewording in the following. Suppose it is co-conscious with the judgment 'I am tired', then without recourse to experience the conjunctive thought 'I am in pain and I am tired' can be formulated. This is obviously not the case if you think 'I am in pain' and I think 'I am tired' (taking this as a paradigm case of two thoughts that are not co-conscious). The bundle theorist can take this capacity to form *a priori* conjunctive thoughts as constitutive of co-consciousness, so that two thoughts are co-conscious iff thinking of them makes it possible to form *a priori* a thought conjoining them.

Understanding co-consciousness in this way enables the bundle theorist to construe 'This pain is my pain' as informative self-knowledge. He can reformulate it as 'This pain is a member of a set of thoughts and experiences which supports *a priori* conjunctive thoughts'. Because this is neither trivial nor uninformative, Lowe's argument from self-reference against reductionist accounts of the self cannot be sustained.

***

Lowe's non-Cartesian substance dualism is a provocative and ingeniously defended theory. I remain unconvinced both by his positive arguments for NCSD and by his criticisms of reductionism. However, he has done us all a service by presenting his theory so clearly and by forcing defenders of opposing views to clarify their own thoughts and arguments.

Acknowledgments

The special issue in which this paper is published had its origins in a conference in honour of E.J. Lowe at Durham that sadly turned into a memorial conference. I was unable to attend the conference due to prior commitments and I am very grateful to Mihretu Guta and Sophie Gibb for allowing me to contribute a paper to the special issue. The paper was much improved by the acute comments of two referees.

References

Adams, M.M. (1982) Universals in the early fourteenth century, in Kretzmann, N., Kenny, A. & Pinbirg, J. (eds.) *The Cambridge History of Later Medieval Philosophy*, Cambridge: Cambridge University Press.

Davidson, D. (1969) The individuation of events, in Rescher, N. (ed.) *Essays in Honor of Carl G. Hempel*, pp. 216–34, Dordrecht: Reidel.

Davidson, D. (1985) Reply to Quine on events, in LePore, E. & McLaughlin, B.P. (eds.) *Actions and Events: Perspectives on the Philosophy of Donald Davidson*, pp. 120–3, Oxford: Basil Balckwell.

Hume, D. (1739–40/1978) *A Treatise of Human Nature*, Oxford: Oxford University Press.

Kripke, S. (1980) *Naming and Necessity*, Cambridge, MA: Harvard University Press.

Lowe, E.J. (1989) Impredicative identity criteria and Davidson's criterion of event identity, *Analysis*, **49** (4), pp. 178–181.

Lowe, E.J. (1993) Self, reference, and self-reference, *Philosophy*, **68**, pp. 15–33.

Lowe, E.J. (1996) *Subjects of Experience*, Cambridge: Cambridge University Press.

Lowe, E.J. (1998) *The Possibility of Metaphysics: Substance, Identity, Time*, Oxford: Oxford University Press.

Lowe, E.J. (2002) *A Survey of Metaphysics*, Oxford: Oxford University Press.

Lowe, E.J. (2008) *Personal Agency: The Metaphysics of Mind and Action*, Oxford: Oxford University Press.

Lowe, E.J. (2009) *More Kinds of Being: A Further Study of Individuation, Identity, and the Logic of Sortal Terms*, Oxford: Wiley-Blackwell.

Lowe, E.J. (2010) On the individuation of powers, in Mormodoro, A. (ed.) *The Metaphysics of Powers: Their Grounding and their Manifestations*, London: Routledge.

Parfit, D. (1984) *Reasons and Persons*, Oxford: Oxford University Press.

Quine, W.V.O. (1985) Events and reification, in Lepore, E. & McLaughlin, B. (eds.) *Acitons and Events: Perspectives on the Philosophy of Davidson*, Oxford: Blackwell.

Shapiro, S. (2000) *Thinking about Mathematics: The Philosophy of Mathematics*, Oxford: Oxford University Press.

Richard Swinburne

The Inevitable Implausibility
of Physical Determinism

Abstract: *I shall understand physical determinism as the doctrine that every physical event has a physical event as its necessary and suffici-ent cause (and no non-physical event as either a necessary or a sufficient cause). This paper seeks to show that no one would be justified in holding this doctrine unless it could be shown to make successful predictions; and that such predictions could only be obtained if we assume the doctrine to be false.*

1. Ontology

Before proceeding further I need to define a 'physical' event. Philosophers who attempt a definition of the 'physical' usually define it in terms of the subject matter of a future true and complete physics and what supervenes thereon.[1] On such a definition a 'physical' event would be an event canonically describable in terms of the categories of that physics or an event supervening on events of that kind. But since we do not have an adequate idea of what a future physics would be like, that definition is not very useful. However, whatever other characteristics a future physics might have, there is one characteristic which any event lying within the scope of a future physics will surely have, the characteristic of being a public event, necessarily equally accessible to any investigator who is properly located, equipped with the right instruments, and possessing the categories and expertise

Correspondence:
Email: richard.swinburne@oriel.ox.ac.uk

---

[1]   See the various slightly different definitions of the 'physical' analysed in Montero (2009).

Journal of Consciousness Studies, **22**, No. 11–12, 2015, pp. 43–59

needed to recognize it. I shall therefore define a 'physical' event as one to which no one necessarily has 'privileged' access (in the above sense). A brain event, for example, is a physical event; anyone suitably located, etc. can find out about my brain events as well as can anyone else. As I need also for this discussion the concept of a 'mental' event, I shall define it as an event to which necessarily there is privileged access; and I shall assume hereafter that the event consists in some individual having some property and that that individual is the only one who has privileged access to that event. And it does rather look as if most events normally considered to be mental events in virtue of being phenomenal and/or intentional events[2] are in my sense mental events. ('Phenomenal' events are conscious events, such as sensations and the ways things seem to be; 'intentional' events are attitudes, such as beliefs and thoughts, towards some state of affairs. 'Intentional' events are not as such the same as 'intentions', which are a particular class of 'intentional' events.) Whatever ways others have of finding out whether I am in pain, or have a thought that today is Thursday, I can also use; like others, I can study my behaviour (by watching a film of it) or inspect my brain (via some instrument). But I have an additional way of finding out whether I am in pain or have a thought that today is Thursday, by actually experiencing the pain or thought; and necessarily no one else has that way. So these events are mental events. In my sense of 'mental event', necessarily mental events are not identical to and do not supervene on physical events. The only remaining philosophical issue is which kinds of events are mental events, and I shall make below some debated but (to my mind) fairly obvious assumptions about what these are.

I define a pure mental event as one which does not entail the occurrence of a physical event. Perceptions such as my seeing a tree are mental events since I can know better than can anyone else whether or not I am seeing a tree, but they are not pure mental events since seeing a tree entails that there is a tree present — and that is a physical event. But sensations such as pains, and beliefs such as the belief that I am seeing a tree, are pure mental events, since it is not entailed by the occurrence of those sensations or beliefs that anything public is happening.

Conscious events are a sub-class of pure mental events. They include both those pure mental events which occur only while the

---

[2]   See the analysis of these terms in Graham, Horgan and Tienson (2009).

subject is conscious of them, and also pure mental events of which the
subject is conscious but which may occur while the subject is not conscious of them. The first group includes not merely sensations such as
pains, but also, as I have assumed above, occurrent thoughts. If I am
not in any way aware that the thought 'today is Friday' is now
crossing my mind, it isn't crossing my mind. It also, I suggest,
includes — as I shall use the word — intentions (intentions in what I
am doing, not intentions for the future), what I am trying to achieve by
my bodily movements. If my body performs some movement of a
kind which I normally make intentionally, but which on this occasion
was simply an unintended reflex, then (in my sense) there was no
intention in what I was doing. If an intention causes my bodily movements it clearly does so by causing the brain events which cause those
movements. Among the pure mental events of which I can become
conscious but which may continue to occur while I am not conscious
of them are beliefs and desires. As I shall use these words, if I behave
in the way I would behave if I had some belief or desire, but am
entirely ignorant of having that belief or desire (even when helped by
some psychiatrist to probe my 'unconscious'), I am not to be counted
as having that belief or desire.

Physical determinism, as I am defining it, is the doctrine that every
event has a physical event as its necessary and sufficient cause (and no
non-physical event (and so no mental event), as either a necessary or
sufficient cause). Epiphenomenalism is the doctrine that physical
events (in effect brain events) often cause conscious events, but conscious events never cause physical events. It is fairly obviously
implausible to deny the first clause of this definition, and so I shall in
future understand by 'epiphenomenalism' merely the contested
doctrine of the second clause, that conscious events never cause
physical events. If epiphenomenalism (on this narrower understanding) is implausible, so too is physical determinism. It would
follow from epiphenomenalism that such common-sense views as that
my intention to come to the Humanities Building caused my leg
movements which brought me to that building are false. It follows
that, in the way these terms are analysed above, no conscious event is
identical to or supervenes on a physical event. Hence these theories
(physical determinism and epiphenomenalism) are theories about
which kinds of thing cause which other kinds of thing, and so they are
scientific theories. In this paper, I argue the epistemological thesis that
no one could ever be justified in believing epiphenomenalism and so
in believing physical determinism, and that claims that recent

neuroscientific work provides that justification are not merely false, but couldn't possibly be true — and that is because of what constitutes a justified belief in a scientific theory. For a justified belief in epiphenomenalism requires a justified belief in a particular scientific theory; and to have a justified belief in a scientific theory requires a justified belief that it makes successful predictions, and that means both a justified belief that it predicts certain events and a justified belief that those events occurred. This will hold on any mildly plausible internalist or externalist account of justification. The internalist will regard successful prediction as an *a priori* requirement for justification, while the externalist will hold that the scientific method requiring successful prediction is a reliable truth-conducive method (or satisfies some other externalist requirement) and that that is what makes a belief acquired by that method justified. In this paper I will be arguing that (at least one of) those justified beliefs couldn't be had if physical determinism were true. Hence physical determinism is in a crucial sense self-defeating; if it were true, we could not be justified in believing it.

2. Epistemology

So how can anyone have a justified belief that some scientific theory predicts certain events? Scientists in the relevant field will have calculated that it makes these predictions. And if a scientist can hold all the calculations in her mind at one time, it will be for her a deliverance of reason, evident *a priori*, that the theory does make these predictions. Alas, for any scientific theory of any complexity most experts at the centre of the field will be unable to hold in their minds at one time all the relevant calculations; even as the scientist reads through the text of her calculations, she depends on her memory towards the end of the calculations for her belief that the initial calculations were correct. Later in life all that she may remember is that it did seem to her earlier that the theory made those predictions. She may have a diary in which she recorded this, which will be — as it were — her testimony about this to herself and others. Non-scientists and scientists less central in the field will depend on the testimony of those whom they regard as experts, that they have made those calculations. So what makes someone's belief that the theory predicts certain events justified is (if it can be had) experience (of oneself currently 'seeing' that the calculations are correct), memory (of having made the calculations in the past), or testimony (from oneself or others that they have made the calculations); or rather, since all of these sources may be mislead, it is apparent experience, memory, or testimony which provide our justified belief that the theory makes true predictions — justified in the absence of counter-evidence, that is, in the absence of defeaters.

And how can anyone have a justified belief that the events predicted in fact occurred? They will normally depend on the evidence of the same three sources. Certain observers will (apparently) in a wide sense experience these events — that is, if they are physical events they will perceive them, or if they are conscious events they will experience them (in a narrow sense). Later, the observers may (apparently) remember having experienced the events; and others will depend on the (apparent) testimony of observers about these (or the observers may depend on their own apparent written testimony). Alternatively, a believer may have a justified belief that the events predicted occurred because it is a consequence (deductive or probabilistic) of some other justifiably believed theory that they did. But in that case a justified belief in that other theory would itself depend on the evidence of the same three sources.

It is a fundamental epistemic principle that what we seem to (that is, apparently) experience is probably so — barring counter-evidence; this includes what we seem to observe in the public world, what we seem to experience as conscious events, and the logical consequences we seem to 'see'. This principle has had a number of different names, among them 'the principle of credulity'.[3] If this were not a fundamental epistemic principle, total scepticism would follow. It is a second epistemic principle (which follows from the former, though I shall find it useful to treat it separately) that what we seem to (that is, apparently) remember having experienced, we probably did experience — barring counter-evidence. I shall call this the Principle of Memory. And it is a further fundamental epistemic principle that what people seem to be (that is, apparently are) telling us that they experienced, they probably did experience — again barring counter-evidence; and I shall call this the Principle of Testimony. Beliefs

---

[3] Other names are 'Phenomenal Conservatism', 'Epistemic Conservatism', and 'Dogmatism'. See the discussion of these principles in Tucker (2013). Different philosophers have sought to put qualifications on this principle — for example by restricting its application to propositions of certain kinds, such as propositions about what we seem to perceive with our senses. For my arguments against any such restrictions see Swinburne (2013, pp. 42–4). For arguments supporting the Principle of Memory, and the Principle of Testimony, see *op. cit.* (pp. 55–7).

acquired by apparent experience, memory, and testimony are probably true — in the absence of counter-evidence. Science relies on the applicability of these principles to determine what constitutes evidence. A scientist takes his (apparent) observations, experiences, and calculations as probably correct, at least when he has looked carefully and checked. Almost all scientific knowledge relies on (apparent) memory (e.g. of the results of experiments or calculations only written up the following day). And, for all science, we all rely most of the time on the (apparent) testimony (written and spoken) of observers to have had certain experiences (normally in the form of observations) and of theoreticians to have done certain calculations. And the wider public relies entirely on the (apparent) testimony of scientists with respect both to their calculations and to their experiences.

Beliefs acquired by apparent experience, memory, and testimony are however open to counter-evidence or defeaters. There are two kinds of defeaters — undermining defeaters and overriding defeaters. If we have inferred (consciously or subconsciously) the occurrence of some event y from present evidence x, then an undermining defeater is evidence (making it probable) that x did not occur or is not good evidence for y, whereas an overriding defeater is new evidence that y did not happen. If, for example, I apparently experience hearing my telephone ring, and then someone points out to me that the noise (from which I subconsciously inferred that my telephone is ringing) is coming from the television set where someone is depicted as hearing a telephone ring, that constitutes an undermining defeater for my apparent experience. It doesn't show that my telephone was not ringing, but it does show that the noise was not evidence that it was, because the noise had a different cause. Again, if I have come to believe that y happened because some person apparently testified that he saw y, evidence that that person was somewhere else at the relevant time and so could not have seen y undermines his evidence, and I no longer have reason to believe that y happened. By contrast the apparent testimony of two independent witnesses that they were at the place of the alleged occurrence of y, and that they saw that y did not happen, overrides the evidence of the original witness. But the evidence constituting the defeater must itself be provided by apparent experience, memory, or testimony. This evidence need not be direct evidence of, for example, the non-occurrence of the event or of the evidence for it — for example in the form of apparent testimony that the testifier was not present at the site of the alleged event — it may be indirect evidence, in the sense that it may be evidence supporting a theory which has the consequence that the event or the evidence for it apparently experienced, remembered, or testified to couldn't have happened — for example, evidence supporting a theory that the testifier was blind and so couldn't have seen what he testified to having seen.

Further, I claim, in having beliefs resulting from experience of physical events such as the apparent observation of a desk, we assume that the event (of the presence of the desk) experienced caused the belief (with its accompanying sensations), 'caused', that is, in being a necessary part of the total cause. In perception we seem in contact with the event apparently observed. That event seems to force itself upon us; the presence of the desk seems to force itself upon me, and so I have no option but to believe that it is there. That, we assume, is because there is a causal chain from the desk to the belief — only causes exert 'force'. Hence the generally accepted causal theory of perception. (Maybe not any perceptual belief caused by the object apparently observed constitutes an observation of it. Maybe the causal route must not be 'deviant'. But that does not affect my point that a causal route is necessary for perception.) It is natural to suppose that the same goes for our beliefs about our currently conscious events; that in believing that we are having certain sensations we assume that the belief is forced upon us by those events, and in believing that our calculations are correct we assume that that belief is forced upon us by the calculations — the marks on the paper or in our mind symbolizing the calculations cause us to have the belief that the calculations are correct. But, as some writers (for example, Chalmers, 1996, pp. 172–209) have denied that our beliefs about currently experienced conscious events are caused by those events, and claim instead that in this special case we have direct access of a non-causal kind to our conscious events, I shall not assume that a causal route is required for access to our presently conscious events.

So with respect to beliefs resulting from experience (with the above mentioned exception) evidence that such a belief was not caused by a causal chain (of necessary parts of total causes) from the event believed constitutes an undermining defeater for it — as in my example of the telephone ring. A similar assumption of the existence of causal chains, although longer ones than for experience and ones involving different kinds of event, undergirds our beliefs in the deliverances of apparent memory and testimony. I trust my apparent memory of an event because I assume that that apparent memory was

caused by a past apparent experience of the event recalled, and that
the experience was caused by the event itself. Thus in trusting my
apparent memory that I was in London on Monday I assume that it
was caused by my apparent experience on Monday of being in
London, itself caused by my being in London. Hence the generally
accepted causal theory of memory. (The apparent memory must of
course correspond to the previous experience, and maybe the causal
route must not be 'deviant'. My point is merely that a causal route is
necessary for memory.) Any evidence that the (apparent) memory was
planted in me by a hypnotist or a brain surgeon constitutes an undermining defeater for that apparent memory belief.

Similarly, in believing someone's apparent testimony to be experiencing or have experienced some event I assume that they say what
they do because they are apparently experiencing or apparently
remember having experienced that event and have the intention of
telling me the truth about it; that is, their apparent experience or
memory and their intention causes them to say what they do, 'causes'
in the sense of being a necessary part of the total cause. In the case of
a past event I believe that their apparent memory was caused by an
apparent past experience of the event, the latter being caused by the
event itself. So, if I get evidence that the words coming out of some
person's mouth were not caused by any intention of his (e.g. that the
words were caused by a neurophysiologist stimulating that person's
neurons to cause his mouth to make the sounds, or simply as in fluent
aphasia where a neural malfunction causes a stream of words to come
out of a subject's mouth), that evidence constitutes an undermining
defeater to belief in the truth of what that person seemed to be saying.
(The intention does of course have to be of a particular kind, an
intention to tell the truth; and evidence that the person was intending
to deceive me would also undermine his testimony. But my point is
simply that evidence that there is no causation at all by the apparent
testifier's intention undermines his apparent testimony.) In all of these
cases the counter-evidence (in the form of an undermining defeater)
must itself come (directly or indirectly) from apparent experience,
memory, or testimony.[4]

---

[4] Audi (1998) defends the causal nature of perception, memory, consciousness, and (in
effect) testimony. Thus (his p. 28) 'perception is a kind of causal relation', (p. 56)
'causal connections to the past are essential to genuine remembering', (p. 81) 'the process by which introspection leads to introspective beliefs... is... causal', and (p. 137)
'with testimonially grounded knowledge... there must be a certain kind of unbroken

In summary, then, I am making the epistemic assumption (EA) that:

(1) A justified belief in a scientific theory (which is not itself a consequence of any higher-level theory in which the believer has a justified belief) requires a justified belief that the theory makes true predictions.

(2) A justified belief that a theory makes true predictions is (unless this is a consequence of some other theory in which the believer has a justified belief) provided by and only by the evidence of apparent experience, memory, and testimony that the theory predicts certain events and that these events occurred.

(3) Such justification is undermined by evidence that any apparent experience was not caused by the event apparently experienced, any apparent memory was not caused by an apparent experience of the event apparently remembered, and any apparent testimony was not caused by the testifier's intention to report his apparent experience or memory.

I hope that the few examples by which I have illustrated its application show the centrality of EA in our noetic framework. The fundamental criterion (FC) behind EA is that justified belief that some event occurred requires the assumption that that event is (privilegedly) accessible to or causes effects (privilegedly) accessible to the believer (unless it is justifiably believed to be the consequence of some theory which predicts events justifiably believed to occur on grounds independent of that theory). Then justified belief that a theory makes true predictions requires (unless justified by a higher-level theory) the assumption that both a scientist's awareness of the calculations that the theory predicts certain events and the events predicted are accessible or cause effects accessible to the believer. FC, I suggest, is a criterion central to our judgments about the credibility of a scientific theory.

3. Epiphenomenalism

Now there could be two kinds of scientific evidence for epiphenomenalism. The first kind, which I shall call α-type evidence, is evidence about when (relative to brain events) various conscious events occur. For epiphenomenalism claims that the occurrence of any conscious

chain from the belief constituting that knowledge to a source of the knowledge in some other mode'.

event makes no difference to the pattern of later brain events. So it predicts that whether or not some type of conscious event occurs during the first part of some sequence of brain events will make no difference to whether or not the sequence is completed (and so cause public behaviour). It would seem that if this prediction were tested for a large random sample of different types of sequences of brain events and different types of conscious events (especially intentions), and found to be correct, this would be strong evidence for epiphenomenalism. To test such predictions, a scientist would have to learn about the times of occurrence of various conscious events. The paradigm way to learn about this is from apparent experience, memory, and testimony about when the conscious events occurred. Although a scientist could learn about times of occurrence of conscious events of some narrow kind from some wider theory, that theory would be a theory about when conscious events of some wider kind occurred and could itself be justifiably believed only on evidence of the same kind.

Yet, if apparent testimony is to constitute evidence that conscious events occurred, the scientist must — by EA — assume that the testifying subjects are caused to say what they do by a belief that the conscious events occurred and an intention to tell the truth about their belief — a causal route which must go through a brain event. But, if epiphenomenalism were true, no conscious events will cause any brain event to cause the subjects to say what they do. Yet no theory could be justifiably believed on the basis of evidence about the occurrence of events about the occurrence of which we could have evidence only if we assume that theory to be false. Hence epiphenomenalism couldn't be justifiably believed on the basis of apparent testimony. A scientist might remember his own conscious events. (By EA) someone is justified in trusting his apparent memories on the assumption that they are caused by his past experiences. But we know that true memories are caused directly by brain events, and so, in order to be justified in believing that his memories are caused more ultimately by his past experiences, he must believe that those experiences cause brain events, and so he must assume that epiphenomenalism as a whole is false. Hence apparent memories of past experiences cannot provide a justified belief that epiphenomenalism makes true predictions, any more than can the apparent testimony of others. I have conceded that a scientist might have a justified belief about which conscious event he was currently experiencing, without assuming that the conscious events caused that belief. But the evidence of one private event currently experienced by a scientist would hardly constitute enough evidence of successful predictions to make it (together with any amount of evidence about brain events) at all probable that epiphenomenalism is true. I conclude that no one could have a justified belief in epiphenomenalism on the basis of α-type evidence for it.

I now apply this result to the research programme initiated by Benjamin Libet which seeks to provide evidence of α-type showing (i.e. providing a justified belief) that a sample of brain events of one kind which cause intentional actions (i.e. actions which the agent believed that he had the intention to perform) are not caused by intentions. In the original and most influential Libet experiments (Libet, 2004, pp. 123–137) participants were instructed to move their hand at a moment of their choice within a period (e.g. 20 seconds). They watch a very fast clock, and report subsequently the moment at which they first had the 'intention'[5] to move the hand. They reported the 'intention' to move the hand as occurring (on average) 200 msecs before the onset of muscle activity initiating a hand movement. However, electrodes placed on their scalp recorded (on each occasion of hand moving) a build up of 'readiness potential' (RP), which was evidence of a particular kind of brain event (which I'll call B_1) occurring an average 550 msecs before the muscle activity. Experiments of other kinds, Libet claimed, showed that subjects report the time of sensations as occurring 50 msecs before the time of brain events which caused them. That led Libet to hold that subjects misjudge the time of all conscious events by 50 msecs, and so he concluded that the 'intention' first appeared 150 msecs before the muscle activation.[6]

So, if the subjects' reports are at all accurate there is a succession of events: a brain event (B_1), then a conscious event (the intention, which

---

[5]   One problem with Libet-type experiments is that Libet and other experimenters describe the conscious event which the subjects report, and which I have described as the onset of an 'intention', sometimes instead as the onset of a 'wish', or of an 'urge' or a 'wanting', or as a 'decision'. These are events of very different kinds — 'wishes', 'urgings', and 'wantings' are experienced as involuntary occurrences which happen to us, and to which we may or may not yield, whereas 'intentions' and 'decisions' which initiate intentions are experienced as voluntary chosen occurrences. On this see Mele (2006, pp. 32–4).

[6]   For Libet's description of his own work, see Libet (2004). For accounts and interpretations of the development of this work on the neural basis of intentional actions over the last twenty years, using new methods of discovering what is happening in the brain at different times, see the surveys by Hallett (2007), Haggard (2008); and philosophical commentary in Banks and Pockett (2007) and Mele (2009).

I'll call M_2), and then some brain event (which I'll call B_3) which directly causes the muscle activity and so the movement. Many neurophysiologists proceed from that to reach the extraordinary conclusion that the intention does not cause the movement. Thus Roediger, Goode and Zaromb (2008) conclude that Libet's data 'contradict the naïve view of free will — that conscious intention causes action. Clearly conscious intention cannot cause an action if a neural event that precedes and correlates with the action comes before the conscious intention'.[7] But that is a totally unjustified conclusion, since it is equally compatible with all the data and the most natural explanation of them to suppose that B_1 causes (in the sense of being a necessary causal condition for) the 'conscious intention' (M_2), and that the intention causes the brain event (B_3) which directly causes the movement. Causation is transitive. If I flip the light switch and thereby cause the light bulb to light up, that doesn't rule out the possibility that my flipping the switch caused an electric current to pass to the bulb and that the current caused the bulb to light up. Despite this obvious point many neurophysiologists prefer one of two rival explanations of the data over the natural explanation, of which the favoured one is that an earlier brain event (B_1) causes both the intention (M_2) and (in 'parallel') a sequence of brain events leading to B_3 which causes the hand movement without the intention causing any brain event.

Even if it were shown that B_1 causes a sequence of brain events which are necessary for the bodily movement, when that constitutes an intentional action (in virtue of the agent believing that he had the intention to make that movement), that wouldn't show that the intention was not also a necessary part of the cause. To show that you would need to show that B_1 causes the very same sequence of brain events with or without subjects having the requisite intention (to produce that bodily movement) and so with or without the bodily movement constituting an intentional action. As far as I know, no one has attempted to show this. If this were shown, we would have evidence against the natural interpretation of the Libet experiments, that a brain event causes the intention which causes the brain event which causes the bodily movement.

---

[7]   See Roediger, Goode and Zaromb (2008, p. 208). For a collection of similar quotations from neuroscientists, see Mele (2009, pp. 70–2).

Experimenters seeking to establish a scientific theory, such as those performing Libet-type experiments, assume that they have access to the conscious lives of many different subjects (and so evidence of α-type about them), in order to test the predictions discussed in the last paragraph, that the same sequence of brain events would occur in the absence of the intention, without which the experimental results do not show that the intention does not cause the movement. The only way for experimenters to acquire this information about the conscious events of subjects is from what those subjects tell them (or by a higher-level theory itself justified by what subjects say). So experimenters assume that subjects' beliefs about their conscious events (including their memory beliefs) are correlated with their testimony (in the sense that the testimony is a true report of their beliefs). The normal reason for assuming this is provided by EA — subjects' intentions to tell the truth about their beliefs plus their beliefs cause the testimony. If we assume that the correlation holds for this reason, then we would already be assuming the falsity of epiphenomenalism in one respect in order to test the crucial prediction necessary to provide justification of either of the interpretations of the Libet experiments which claim that intentions do not cause the hand movements. We can only justifiably believe that intentions do not cause the hand movements if we justifiably believe that they do cause the apparent testimony about them.

However, we might have good grounds to believe that, in the particular circumstances of Libet-type experiments, apparent testimony is not caused by the intention to produce it, while nevertheless being in general reliable (i.e. correctly reporting the testifiers' beliefs). But these grounds could only be provided by a wider scientific theory about when apparent testimony to a belief about a testifier's conscious life was or was not correlated with the occurrence of that belief, and about when someone's apparent memory of their past conscious life was true. A justified belief in that scientific theory would require a justified belief that the theory made true predictions. The predictions would need to be predictions of when on other occasions subjects' apparent testimony was correlated with their beliefs and their own apparent memories were true. But in order to have a justified belief that these predicted correlations occurred we must rely ultimately on apparent testimony and memory and so — by EA — assume that subjects' apparent testimony was caused by intentions to report true beliefs, and apparent memory was caused (via brain-events) by the conscious events apparently remembered.

I conclude that the Libet-type experiments have not so far shown that in their experimental circumstances intentions do not cause bodily movements; and — even if the crucial predictions necessary to show this proved correct — that would only show that epiphenomenalism held in these circumstances on the assumption that in general it was false. And, more generally, no α-type evidence could have any tendency whatever to show that epiphenomenalism is true, and thereby begin to show that physical determinism is true.

It might, however, seem that someone could have a justified belief in physical determinism, not because of α-type evidence for epiphenomenalism, but because of a justified belief in some physical theory, that every physical event has another physical event as its immediate necessary and sufficient causal condition. In that case of course no brain event could have a conscious event as its necessary causal condition; overdetermination would be excluded. It might be thought that we could establish that deterministic physical theory on evidence solely about which physical events occur when, which I will call β-type evidence. If we found that for any random sample of physical events (including brain events) that each of them is related to some other physical event as its immediate necessary and sufficient cause in a way calculable from such a theory, that would seem to be powerful evidence in favour of that theory and so in favour of physical determinism.

Someone could justifiably believe certain physical events to be occurring on the evidence of apparent experience (a current observation). But to get enough evidence to acquire a justified belief that the deterministic physical theory is true, a scientist would require evidence provided by apparent memory of past observations and apparent testimony by others to having observed various physical events in the past. But a justified belief in the deliverances of apparent memory of past experiences and apparent testimony to them is — by EA — undermined by evidence that they are not caused by experiences of those events. So — given EA — there could not be a justified belief in a physical theory which entailed epiphenomenalism.

However, a modified understanding of memory and testimony is possible, which keeps apparent memory and testimony as sources of justified belief, and is still compatible with the fundamental criterion (FC) (lying behind EA) that (barring justification by a justified theory) justified belief in the occurrence of an event is dependent on the assumption that that event is accessible to or causes an effect accessible to the believer. One could understand memory simply as memory of the occurrence of events, and not only of events which are experiences of the occurrence of events. A subject could be said to 'remember' past physical events in virtue of those events causing traces in his brain, which at a later time cause the apparent memory of those events without any mental-to-physical causation being involved. People sometimes become aware later of details of some event which they observed and of which they were not at the time aware; and it does not seem too unnatural a use of the word 'remember' to say that they 'remembered' those details. And we could come to understand testimony to amount merely to the public utterance of sentences reporting that an event occurred caused by a chain of events in the utterer, itself caused by the event reported, a chain which need not include any conscious events. The 'testimony' would not be testimony that the testifier had observed the events, but merely testimony that the events had occurred. This certainly seems to involve giving a stretched meaning to 'testimony', but relying on apparent testimony of this kind to the occurrence of physical events would still be compatible with the fundamental criterion (FC). Given these modified senses of memory and testimony, someone could have an apparent memory of or receive apparent testimony to the occurrence of physical events without making any assumption about anyone's conscious events causing physical events. Thus someone's eyes could receive light rays from physical events and — because those physical events caused brain events in that person — subsequently report them, without that causal chain proceeding through any conscious events. Given this modified understanding of apparent testimony and memory, anyone could have justified beliefs in the occurrence of any set of physical events (including brain events) which occurred without presupposing causation of the physical by the mental; and so come to believe in the occurrence of the physical events (the β-type evidence) predicted by a deterministic physical theory.

There is, however, a further problem in supposing that we could have a justified belief that some deterministic physical theory gave true predictions about relations between physical events. This is that we would also need, not merely a justified belief that certain relations between physical events occurred, but also a justified belief that these relations were predicted by that deterministic theory. But anyone who had not calculated for himself what that theory predicted about the relations between physical events must depend on the evidence provided by the apparent testimony of scientists to have calculated this and 'to have seen' (that is, had a conscious belief) that that was what the theory predicted, that is evidence of the conscious events of scientists. But if the deterministic physical theory were true, the scientist would not have been caused to give that testimony by any conscious event — neither by his intention to tell the truth nor even merely by his conscious belief about what the theory predicted. Hence no one could justifiably believe what the scientist reported about his calculations, and so believe that the theory made the predictions which he claimed that it did (as well as believing that the predicted events occurred), since believing what the scientist reported would undermine the credibility of his apparent testimony to it. Scientists normally check each other's calculations, but for the same reason — if the deterministic physical theory were true — no scientist could rely on the testimony of another scientist to have made the same calculation as he had. Neither — for the same reason — could any scientist rely on his own testimony to himself recorded in a diary that he had previously calculated the consequences of the deterministic theory. Nor could a scientist rely on his own memory of having calculated these consequences. For, since this would involve the causation by his past experiences (of his calculation) of the brain event which caused his memory, he would not be justified in relying on his own apparent memory about his calculations. Only if a scientist could hold in his mind at one time all his calculations from which it apparently followed that the deterministic theory predicted certain events could he have a justified belief that that theory made successful predictions, and so a justified belief in epiphenomenalism. For most scientific theories and most scientists, this is most unlikely.

I conclude that, given the fundamental criterion (FC) which guides the acceptability of scientific theories, (with the above very small exception) no one could have a justified belief that any deterministic physical theory made certain predictions, and so no one could have a justified belief in physical determinism. Hence, given the principle of credulity, we should believe that things are as they seem to be, that often our intentions do cause our bodily movements, which clearly they do by causing brain events; and so we should believe that physical determinism is false, because the physical domain is not causally closed.

Acknowledgments

I am grateful to the guest editor for agreeing to publish this paper, despite its considerable similarity to Swinburne (2011). The arguments of this paper are developed more fully in Swinburne (2013).

References

Audi, R. (1998) *Epistemology*, London: Routledge.

Banks, W.P. & Pockett, S. (2007) Benjamin Libet's work on the neuroscience of free will, in Velmans, M. & Schneider, S. (eds.) *The Blackwell Companion to Consciousness*, Oxford: Blackwell Publishing.

Chalmers, D. (1996) *The Conscious Mind*, Oxford: Oxford University Press.

Graham, G., Horgan, T. & Tienson, J. (2009) Phenomenology, intentionality, and the unity of mind, in McLaughlin, B., *et al.* (eds.) *The Oxford Handbook of Philosophy of Mind*, Oxford: Oxford University Press.

Haggard, P. (2008) Human volition: Towards a neuroscience of will, *Nature Reviews Neuroscience*, **9**, pp. 934–946.

Hallett, M. (2007) Volitional control of movement: The physiology of free will, *Clinical Neurophysiology*, **118**, pp. 934–946.

Libet, B. (2004) *Mind Time*, Cambridge, MA: Harvard University Press.

Mele, A.R. (2006) *Free Will and Luck*, Oxford: Oxford University Press.

Mele, A.R. (2009) *Effective Intentions*, Oxford: Oxford University Press.

Montero, B. (2009) What is the physical?, in McLaughlin, B., *et al.* (eds.) *The Oxford Handbook of Philosophy of Mind*, Oxford: Oxford University Press.

Roediger, H.L., Goode, M.K. & Zaromb, F.M. (2008) Free will and the control of action, in Baer, J., Kaufman, J.C. & Baumeister, R.F. (eds.) *Are We Free?*, Oxford: Oxford University Press.

Swinburne, R. (2011) Could anyone justifiably believe epiphenomenalism?, *Journal of Consciousness Studies*, **18** (3–4), pp. 196–208.

Swinburne, R. (2013) *Mind, Brain, and Free Will*, Oxford: Oxford University Press.

Tucker, C. (ed.) (2013) *Seemings and Justification*, Oxford: Oxford University Press.

Andy Hamilton

The Metaphysics and Anti-Metaphysics of the Self

Abstract: *The modern conception of self-consciousness holds that, in self-conscious thought, I think of myself as both subject and object; and that the subject is essentially embodied. This understanding begins with Kant. An anti-metaphysical treatment regards 'What is a self?' as expressing a pseudo-problem; it regards the claim of an immaterial self as nonsensical, and diagnoses its postulation. A moderate anti-metaphysical position analyses self-consciousness by appeal to the Analytic Principle: that self-consciousness is a phenom-enon expressed — or interpreted — by use of a device with the pro-perties of the first person. This article proposes a strong interpreta-tion of the Principle, involving the <u>conceptual holism of self-consciousness and self-reference</u>. But how essential is the use of 'I' to self-consciousness? In the name-user scenario, each speaker uses their own name self-consciously to self-refer. However, in this scenario, against appearances, 'I' is not in fact eliminated without loss of the language's expressive power, and so the Analytic Principle is preserved.*

1. The Modern Conception of Self-Consciousness

The modern conception of self-consciousness in Western philosophy — the dominant and guiding conception — has two main components:

(1) *Reflexivity*: in self-conscious thought, I think of myself as both subject and object ('reflexive' means 'bends back on itself', i.e. when I say 'I am in pain', I speak or think, and refer, to myself).

Correspondence:
Email: a.j.hamilton@durham.ac.uk

Journal of Consciousness Studies, **22**, No. 11–12, 2015, pp. 60–83

(2) *Embodiment*: the subject is essentially embodied.

This conception tends towards an anti-metaphysical one, in the sense that feature (1) implies the rejection of any introspectible or immaterial entity distinct from thinker or speaker; and feature (2) suggests that the only entity in question here is the person. But in order to be anti-metaphysical it must regard the claim of an immaterial self as nonsensical, and therapeutically diagnose the temptation to postulate one.

It might be argued that the modern conception cannot be 'anti-metaphysical' since it offers a metaphysical account of the self, identifying it with a person or with a human animal. But for the anti-metaphysician, selves are not entities, identical with persons; the term 'self' is misleading and should be abandoned. Certainly one must distinguish abstemious metaphysics from anti-metaphysics. But one can be anti-metaphysical about the self, and at the same time a metaphysician, I believe — even, perhaps, a revisionary one. Abstemious metaphysicians regard 'There are selves' — or 'There are numbers' — as in good order as they stand — that is, as making sense, but false. In contrast, anti-metaphysicians regard such statements as nonsensical. Realist metaphysicians might be anti-metaphysical on questions like the existence of selves or universals, if they diagnose why other realist metaphysicians wish to postulate such entities.

The modern understanding of self-consciousness began with the 'Transcendental Deduction' in Kant's *Critique of Pure Reason* (1781/ 1929). According to most writers, Kant recognized (2) — the embodiment condition — insufficiently, and philosophers up to Schopenhauer tended to follow Descartes in rejecting or neglecting it; though Descartes' position is subtler than is often thought.[1] Hume neglected both features. He did not seem to realize that, in asking 'Is there a persisting self?', I think of myself as both subject and object, and so — in that sense — the existence of a self is presupposed.[2] Descartes

---

[1] Descartes' position is examined in Hamilton (2013, Chapter 5). This article brings together ideas on self-consciousness from that volume, and on anti-metaphysics from Hamilton (2014).

[2] Kemp Smith argues that 'the denial in Book 1 of the *Treatise* [of] an impression of the "self" is incompatible with passages in Book 2 describing the indirect passions, in which Hume admits that there is an idea of the self which is the effect of pride and humility' (Kemp Smith, 1948, pp. 555–8). Note, however, Kemp Smith's conflation here of 'impression' and 'idea'; Hume does not deny in Book 1 that we have an *idea* of the self. Some have argued that the 'Appendix' to Book 1, where Hume confesses

provided the beginnings of such an understanding — as he points out, the *cogito* is a principle that *anyone at all* can apply to himself or herself — but recognizes (1), the reflexivity condition, insufficiently. The *cogito* anticipates the modern conception, but does not really grasp it. The modern conception recognizes what Hume failed to, and what Descartes did only dimly — that the self is not merely an object, but a subject also.

Though he neglects the second, embodiment feature of the modern conception, Kant provides the beginnings of an understanding that, in self-conscious thought, I think of myself *as subject* as object. Reflexivity is found in the most mundane self-conscious thought — when I think, self-consciously, 'I've got a backache', I think of myself as subject and object, simultaneously. This notion of reflexivity is largely absent from Descartes' understanding of 'I', and completely so from Hume's. Descartes' failure to distinguish these two kinds of consciousness of oneself as subject of thought, from consciousness of oneself as an object, led him to regard the 'I think' as an immaterial or thinking substance, he believed. However, Kant was insufficiently aware that I do think of myself as embodied. As Cassam argues, 'Self-consciousness... is intimately bound up with awareness of the subject "as an object" — not as an "immaterial" substance but as a physical object in a world of physical objects' (Cassam, 1997, p. 25; p. 198). My criticism of Cassam is that we *conceive* of, but do not *experience*, ourselves as bodily (Hamilton, 2013, Chapter 5; see also Longuenesse, 2015).

Examining Kant's treatment of self-consciousness shows how the modern conception is anti-metaphysical. Kant's grasp of reflexivity is expressed in what one may term the *apperception or self-conscious-ness condition* of the Transcendental Deduction of *Critique of Pure Reason*, which says that a unified subject is a presupposition of experience. Kant argues in the Paralogisms that the 'necessary unity of the subject' cannot be derived from experience, but is a necessary condition of it: 'This proposition ["I think"] is... but the form of apperception, which belongs to and precedes every experience; and as such it must always be taken only in relation to some possible knowl-edge, as a *merely subjective condition* of that knowledge' (Kant,

---

himself in a state of agonized perplexity concerning personal identity, plays a rhetorical role. A better answer is that he moves from a metaphysical to a social self, and the dissolution of the problem.

1781/1929, A354). Kant took the phrase 'I think' from Descartes, while rejecting the latter's metaphysical implication of substantiality.

The apperception or self-consciousness condition may seem tautological; 'necessary condition of experience' seems elliptical for 'necessary condition of experience had by a unified subject', and Kant appears to be arguing, otiosely, that experience requires a unified subject. The argument is not otiose, however, given the treatments by Hume, and later reductionists — as with other fundamental issues in the Critical philosophy, one can usefully understand Kant as responding to Hume. For Kant, a unified subject is one that judges that it is unified. His *self-ascription requirement* says that a self-conscious subject must be capable of self-ascribing representations; it must be possible for the 'I think' to accompany all my representations (*ibid.*, B131).[3] The requirement involves *reflexivity*, the ability to conceive of oneself *as subject as object* — the core of the modern conception of self-consciousness.

Kant offers a modern account of self-consciousness, but is it anti-metaphysical? The consensus is that it is. For Zöller, interpreters '[agree] in their understanding of Kant's thinking self as a form or structure that eludes any attempt at reification' (Zöller, 1993, p. 460).[4] Rödl holds that self-knowledge arises from spontaneity rather than sensory reception; its object and source are the subject's own activity (Rödl, 2007, p. vii). This line of interpretation is correct in that Kant rejects the transcendental self as an entity, while the Paralogisms offer a diagnosis of the reifying tendency. But it does not belong to the mainstream anti-metaphysical modern conception, which instead of treating 'the self' as an activity or structure refers to persons with self-consciousness.

For some writers, Kant does have a metaphysics of the self.[5] At issue is a long-standing debate. Kant rejected as unacceptably dogmatic the attempt to demonstrate the reality of God, freedom, and immortality through pure reason, but allowed that the description 'metaphysics... can [also] be given to all pure philosophy including this critique' (Kant, 1781/1929, A841/B869). Thus, for many writers,

---

3 The label is Cassam's (1997, pp. 118–9).

4 Melnick (2009) argues that in Kant's theoretical philosophy the self is understood as an activity, not an entity. See also Kitcher (1984, p. 113).

5 Marshall (2010) argues that Kant offers a metaphysical account, with selves individuated by experiences.

Kant supplants transcendent or dogmatic metaphysics with a 'meta-physics of experence'. On this view, his metaphysics of the self involves grasping its status as a necessary condition of experience. A judicious view sees Kant as both metaphysician and anti-metaphysician, and Wittgenstein and the Vienna Circle as thorough-going anti-metaphysicians.

Twentieth-century analytic philosophers have expressed the reflex-ivity of self-consciousness in linguistic terms, treating it as a phenom-enon expressed by use of a device with the properties of the first person, notably indexicality. Hence what I call *the Analytic Principle*, which says that self-consciousness is a set of capacities manifested through use of a device like 'I', or through behaviour interpretable only by using such a device. That is, it is manifested in a capacity to self-refer self-consciously.[6] The principle is Analytic in the sense of being widely accepted in the Analytic Tradition, not in being true purely in virtue of meaning.

The modern conception is dominant but not universal. In endorsing it, analytic philosophy tends to reject a metaphysics of the self; it tends to accept, consciously or more usually unconsciously, the Wittgensteinian view that 'the self' — the alleged irreducible entity — is a grammatical phenomenon. Analytic philosophers agree that the referent of 'I' is a person, or alternatively, a human animal.[7] E.J. Lowe did argue that dogs and dolphins are, or have, selves, in that they have rudimentary mental powers; but usually he uses 'self' and 'person' interchangeably, a more mainstream analytic view, also found in Strawson's *Individuals* (Lowe, 2008; Strawson, 1959). A development of the view is to regard dolphins, elephants, and other creatures that pass the mirror and similar tests — that can recognize themselves in a mirror — as primitively self-conscious.[8]

2. Anti-Metaphysics and the Self

To reiterate, the anti-metaphysical temper questions whether a philo-sophical claim is in good order as it stands; anti-metaphysics rests on a reluctance to give definite meaning to philosophical utterances in a

---

[6] Anscombe (e.g. 1981) regards self-consciousness as a set of capacities manifested through use of a device like 'I', but denies that this involves a self-referential capacity. Other writers might refer to a mode of presentation rather than a capacity.

[7] The maverick 'no-reference' view of 'I', discussed below.

[8] A view developed in Hamilton (2013, Chapter 7).

certain domain of discourse. 'What is a self?' is regarded by some philosophers as in good order, but by others as expressing a pseudo-problem. Thoroughgoing, general anti-metaphysics rejects what it regards as the fruitless search for transcendent explanations of human concepts and practices; it aspires, in contrast, to something like Wittgenstein's 'logical clarification of thoughts' (Wittgenstein, 1961, 4.112). Wittgenstein's therapeutic method regards philosophical disputes as pseudo-problems resting on grammatical illusion. Language misleads us into thinking of the mind as a receptacle for mental entities, of understanding as an internal mental state — and, most pertinent for present purposes, that 'I' refers to an immaterial self.

The philosopher's proper concern, on this view, is with what is conceivable, given how our concepts fit together. For Wittgenstein, metaphysics is associated with scientism, and excites in him a particular animus. However, not all contemporary metaphysics is scientistic; it can allow that discovery of what contingently exists or does not exist is the preserve of science. It seeks to delimit what could and could not possibly exist — to discover the nature of *possible* reality through pure reason.

Here I simply distinguish pervasive anti-metaphysics from a restricted anti-metaphysics concerning the self or other domain of discourse such as mathematics. Whether this view amounts to anti-metaphysics, or merely abstemious metaphysics that excludes the self from its ontology, depends on whether it is associated with a general programme of anti-metaphysics, or whether there is, at least, a diagnosis of the tendency to reification. (So the contrast between anti-metaphysics and abstemious metaphysics is not clear-cut.) Abstemious metaphysicians regard 'There are selves' — or 'There are numbers' — as in good order but false; anti-metaphysicians regard such statements as nonsensical. Radical and more conservative versions of the latter view arise from more and less radical anti-metaphysical contexts. A more conservative rejection of selves as entities rejects their metaphysics in favour either of that of persons, or of human animals — supplemented by an epistemology of self-consciousness which sees it consisting in, or least involving, use of the first person. On this view, questions about that dubious entity 'the self' are explored through the semantics or grammar of 'I', analysed in terms of a first/third-person asymmetry or first-person inflection.[9]

Wittgenstein's radically anti-metaphysical stance led him to suggest a radical anti-metaphysics of the self — the 'no-reference' view of 'I'. This was developed further by Anscombe (1981), who held that the only possible referent for 'I' is a Cartesian immaterial subject — nothing else will give rise to the distinctive features of 'I', *viz.* guaranteed reference, and immunity to error through misidentification.[10] The contemporary analytic consensus holds, in contrast, that 'I' is a genuinely referring expression. Strawson, Evans, and McDowell tried to characterize a Fregean mode of presentation that accommodates the features Anscombe cites; Kaplan favoured a direct reference view. The Fregean project is moderately anti-metaphysical, and diagnoses the 'no-reference' view as an overreaction to the phenomena in question. I would argue that Wittgenstein's target is not the claim that 'I' refers, but the more important claim that first-person judgments always effect a genuine identification (Hamilton, 2013, Chapter 6).

To reiterate, rejection of the self may be abstemious metaphysics, not anti-metaphysics; Olson's rejection of the 'problem of the self' is the former, and he offers no diagnosis of the tendency to postulate selves. He writes that 'there must at least be some problematic idea or concept of a self, if there is to be a problem of the self... no concept could be so problematic that no one could agree about anything to do with it' (Olson, 1998). For Olson, discussion of the self concerns issues like personal identity, the semantic properties of first-person pronouns, the unity of one's mental contents, and the varieties of first-person knowledge. His account offers no diagnosis of the pseudo-problem — no recognition that the question is not in good order as it stands, but requires therapeutic investigation to uncover the real questions underlying it. Without this diagnosis, the position is not anti-metaphysics, but naturalist metaphysics — a fact that may be obscured by the naturalistic tenor of contemporary metaphysics. Naturalists may not see themselves as metaphysicians, perhaps, because contemporary metaphysics is predominantly naturalistic. Hume's rejection of the self should not be assimilated to that of contemporary naturalism, however. Scientific, i.e. scientistic, naturalism

---

[9] 'First/third-person asymmetry' is preferable to 'first-person perspective', which suggests that thought is more basic than language — see final section.
[10] Wittgenstein's view is illustrated in his oriental despot thought experiment, below.

is metaphysical. Hume's naturalism predates scientism; when he advocates a Newtonian 'science of the mind', he does not take 'science' in its post-Whewell sense.[11] To regard him as advocating a naturalistic metaphysics is anachronistic, therefore.

It might be responded that many philosophers reject the self — the bearer of self-consciousness, and so on — as an entity distinct from persons or from human animals, but would regard the claim that there are selves as making sense. Cartesian dualists regard the self as a substance of a certain sort — not a common view, but, so the objector claims, one regarded as a wrong answer to a question that makes sense. Furthermore, someone who regards experiences as identical with brain states offers a metaphysical conception of experiences, often accompanied by a diagnosis of why their opponents postulate them as something other than brain states — one that usually regards the statements to be diagnosed as false, not nonsensical.

I concede that thse issues are disputed. But the idea that 'There is a self' is simply false — that there just happen not to be selves — is surely perplexing. On a modern understanding of self-consciousness, it is more than a simple error to regard the self, as Cartesians or materialists do, as just a kind of object. Rather, it is to fail to take seriously the grammar of self-consciousness expressed in the modern conception. Against Olson, one must press the question: if the self is an illusion, why is it such a persisting one? The fact needs explanation; it is too big to be a mistake.[12] The anti-metaphysical claim is that 'selves' are not a coherent entity. To postulate them is to confuse an epistemological for an ontological question — as Kant saw in the Paralogisms. The objection is to reifying self-consciousness as such — not just to an immaterial self, but to any reified self, material or immaterial. '"I" refers to a living human being' is one proper answer to the question 'What is a self?'. Self-consciousness is not a matter simply of reference to a certain kind of object; it is, rather, a certain *kind* of self-reference by and to a person. If someone says, 'I consider myself a self', one should point out that what they really mean is 'I am a self-conscious being — a self-conscious human'. It is true that one also seeks explanations for illusions which are false beliefs — ones which are not simply mistaken beliefs. Dog-heads — dog-headed

---

[11] In 1833, responding to Coleridge's challenge, Whewell coined the word 'scientist', to replace 'natural philosopher' or 'man of science'.

[12] The epistemology of 'mistake' is discussed in Hamilton (2014, Chapter 10.3).

races, or cynocephali — contingently do not exist; they could, perhaps, have evolved. Belief that they exist was not just a false belief — they were a pervasive illusion of ancient and medieval societies. So there is a further level of implausibility to belief in selves.

This debate must be pursued elsewhere. What I would insist is that there is a continuum of views, and that metaphysicians perhaps can have an anti-metaphysics of the self. An example is found in Cassam's defence of materialism about self-consciousness — the view that I experience myself, as subject, as embodied. This view seems to face an *ownership challenge*: 'What makes a given body my body?'[13] Cassam cannot give the same response as he did concerning body-parts — that X's body belongs to X in virtue of being materially united with X. However, he maintains that the ownership challenge is illegitimate, since there is no body-independent 'I' whose ownership of a particular body can be in question: 'the "me" can only properly be conceived of as a *bodily* me' (Cassam, 1997, p. 67). This response involves a salutary recognition that — as Wittgenstein insisted — some philosophical claims or questions are not in good order as they stand, and require therapeutic elucidation. Certainly the claim that there is a 'soul', to which one's body belongs, is imponderable; Cassam is right that the 'me' must be conceived of as bodily.

Pursuing the debate shows an anti-metaphysical approach in operation. Thus one can respond to Cassam that 'bodily' does not mean simply 'materially unified'. Although the ownership challenge is not a demand for a criterion — 'Which is my body?' never requires an answer — it does have a sense, *viz.* one inviting the same response as the challenge concerning body-parts: 'My body is the one concerning which I have knowledge that exhibits immunity to error through mis-identification, and can move basically' (glossed in Hamilton, 2013, Chapter 3.4). Cassam's rejection of the initial question 'What makes a given body my body?' may be turned back on itself, therefore. The materialist reply assumed that the question made no sense because there was nothing to be decided. But neither — normally — does it need to be decided whether a given body-part is mine; yet materialists still offer criteria for ownership of body-parts. Exceptions might be

---

13 His version of materialism about self-consciousness takes the form of what I term the self-presentation thesis: 'we can and must be presented to ourselves, *qua* subjects... as physical objects among physical objects' (Cassam, 1997, p. 6) — criticized in Hamilton (2013, Chapter 5.3).

intertwined fingers, or a photograph of arms — one of them mine — with everything else blanked out. But comparable photographs of torsos and arms would elicit the question 'Which one is me?' rather than 'Which one is my body?'. Materialists about self-consciousness assume that ascriptions are made to a body, when in fact they are made to a person.

This debate shows how an anti-metaphysical approach might be developed. Both Cassam and his anti-materialist critic recognize that some philosophical claims are not in good order as they stand. Cassam's readiness to do so perhaps reflects his standpoint as a Strawsonian or descriptive metaphysician. This kind of approach offers a diagnosis of why philosophers have thought that there is an entity, the self — a diagnosis such as Kant provides in the Paralogisms, where, as Strawson (1966) argued, he holds that the unity of experience has been mistaken for experience of a unity.

A *moderate anti-metaphysics of the self* holds that there is a real question that the pseudo-problem 'What is the self?' tries but fails to express — *viz.* 'What is the nature of self-consciousness?'. On this view, Olson is correct in holding that discussion of the self really concerns issues like personal identity, the semantic properties of first-person pronouns, the unity of one's mental contents, and the varieties of first-person knowledge. Where Olson is wrong, it continues, is in denying that these issues form a distinctive set of problems concerning self-consciousness. The phenomena grouped under its heading are not a disparate collection. One connection, I would argue, is that the truth in the memory criterion of personal identity is that memory-judgments are immune to error through misidentification — a key feature of self-consciousness.[14]

A *more radical anti-metaphysical stance* — it has roots in Wittgenstein's thought, but is distinct from the radically anti-metaphysical 'no-reference' view of 'I' — rejects the preceding view. It holds instead that there is no real question underlying the pseudo-problem 'What is the self' — that 'What is self-consciousness?' is itself a pseudo-problem. In order to address this view, one must say something about the almost universal assumption that self-consciousness is a well-defined and unified concept. One can allow that it is — which is what I am inclined to do — while denying the further assumption, of Evans (1982) and others, that it has an essence; we see

---

[14]   As argued in Hamilton (2013, Chapter 3.4).

later how, when this essence is taken as non-behavioural, it is illustrated by the name-user scenario. 'Self-consciousness', as used in
contemporary analytic philosophy of mind, is not entirely a philosophical term of art or theoretical concept (Hamilton, 2013). Analytic
philosophy, in its less scientist forms, grounds philosophical specu-
lation in pre-philosophical thought, encouraging us to explore the
everyday meanings of its concepts (as Soames, 2003, suggests).
According to the *OED*, self-consciousness in its philosophical sense is
'consciousness of one's own identity, one's acts, thoughts, etc.'. Self-
awareness is insight that involves understanding how one's actions
appear to others. Hence Strawson's plausible requirement, that to be
self-conscious involves viewing oneself as a person among persons
(Strawson, 1959).[15] His account of persons is 'descriptive metaphysics' that supplements a conceptual analysis of self-consciousness.

Setting aside the worry about whether self-consciousness is well-
defined, therefore, we can say that understanding self-consciousness
involves grasping 'I''s role as a device of self-reference, but also
understanding the grounds of self-knowledge. Thus Evans comments
that although self-consciousness essentially involves self-reference,
'our self-conscious thoughts about ourselves also rest upon various
ways we have of gaining knowledge of ourselves as physical things'
(Evans, 1982, p. 213). We now see a further way in which the
questions that Olson presents as disparate in fact form a connected set.
Self-consciousness may be characterized in terms both of first-person
judgments involving self-identification, and of those that do not —
those which are immune to error through misidentification.[16] An
understanding of the epistemology of self-consciousness focuses on
the important sub-class of 'I'-thoughts that exhibit this immunity,
including personal memory-judgments.

This view need not imply an essence of self-consciousness — at
least, not a non-behavioural essence. Rather, in its philosophical
sense, self-consciousness implies a network of interrelated capacities,
involving intelligence, rationality, and intentional agency. How
extensive these capacities must be, in order for a creature to be self-
conscious, is a matter of debate in particular cases; self-conscious
behaviour exists on a continuum, and attributions of self-consciousness may not be unqualified. There are degrees of primitive self-

[15] The claim is considered in Hamilton (2013, Chapter 7).
[16] As Hamilton (2013, Chapters 2–3) argues.

consciousness across species.[17] However, it does not admit of degrees within species — one would not say that one person had more self-consciousness than another, except perhaps in the everyday sense of being more prone to embarrassment.

Other terms of art in philosophy of mind that are based on ordinary usage include 'perception' and 'intention'. The philosophical significance of denying, for instance, that proprioception is a mode of perception depends in part on the role of ordinary usage in deciding whether a faculty counts as perceptual. 'Aesthetic' is another semi-technical term which has come to denote a philosophical sub-discipline. Although 'aesthetic' is a term of art in more than one sense, it describes an ordinary and unmysterious attitude of intensified or enriched experience which Kant rightly described as disinterested, by which he meant devoid of practical interest. 'Self-consciousness', like the preceding, is a term of art with some basis in ordinary language. We now pursue further what its modern conception involves.

3. Moderate Anti-Metaphysics: Self-Consciousness and Conceptual Holism

To reiterate, the modern conception of self-consciousness, in its contemporary form, endorses the *Analytic Principle*: that self-consciousness is a phenomenon expressed — or interpreted — by use of a device with the properties of the first person. That is, we have no grasp of the notion of self-consciousness independently of our understanding of self-reference. Anscombe, for instance, writes that 'when we speak of self-consciousness we... mean something manifested by the use of "I"' (Anscombe, 1981, p. 25), while Evans comments that:

> The essence of self-consciousness is self-reference, that is to say, thinking, by a subject of judgments, about himself, and hence, necessarily, about a subject of judgments. (Evans, 1982, p. 213)

Bermúdez holds that the ability to have 'I'-thoughts is distinctive of self-consciousness (Bermúdez, 1998, p. 295). Rödl writes that 'self-consciousness... manifests itself in... thinking thoughts whose linguistic expression requires the use of the first person pronoun "I". [It is] a manner of thinking of an object, or a form of reference... a form [of] knowledge of oneself as oneself' (Rödl, 2007, p. vii).

---

[17] As Hamilton (2013, Chapter 7) discusses in connection with chimps.

Clearly it is not use of the English word 'I' that is essential, according to the Analytic Principle — there are many self-conscious non-English speakers — but grasp of the first person as a grammatical category, expressed as pronoun or verbal inflection. The Analytic Principle involves:

(1) the *conceptual claim* that self-consciousness must be understood as a phenomenon expressed — or interpreted — by use of a device with the properties of the first person.
(2) the *methodological claim* that understanding of the first person is the route to understanding self-consciousness.

Self-consciousness is an elusive phenomenon, which the Analytic Principle anchors in concrete linguistic practice. I have defended a strong interpretation of the Principle, involving what I describe as the *conceptual holism of self-consciousness and self-reference* — an account sometimes described as 'no-priority' (Hamilton, 2013, Chapter 3). Elucidation of conceptual holisms is essential to understanding fundamental philosophical concepts such as self-consciousness. A conceptual holism involves an equivalence or interdependence between the concepts concerned; neither is more basic than the other. Thus, a definition or understanding of concept X makes essential reference to that of concept Y, and vice versa. There is a relation of mutual presupposition; one can neither acquire, nor manifest understanding of, one concept without the other. In contrast are those connected concepts that do not form a relation of mutual presupposition. A photograph is a kind of picture, and 'photograph' cannot be understood without an understanding of 'picture'; but 'picture' is a more basic concept, and can be understood without understanding 'photograph'.

The claim about acquisition is not empirical or psychological. An empirical holism between concepts could be a merely contingent association of ideas, such as that between morality and religion. Only a divine command ethics that regards God and goodness as inter-defined — so that it was inconceivable for God to command other than the good — would regard 'good' and 'commanded by God' as a *conceptual* holism. To claim a conceptual holism is to say that, given the nature of the concepts in question, to acquire one concept is necessarily to acquire the other.

To claim a holism between two concepts is not to assert their identity. Conceptual holisms occupy a middle ground between analytically inter-defined concepts and cases where one concept has epistemic priority. A philosophically uninteresting holism such as that between 'monarch' and 'subject' rests on the dictionary definition that a monarch is a ruler of subjects, and subjects are those ruled by a monarch. Genuinely conceptual holisms include: memory and personal identity; proprioception and bodily individuation — whose recognition enables one to transcend the traditional opposition between psychological and bodily criteria for personal identity; my body and objectivity concepts; belief and assertion; concept and object; intention and action; natural law and causation; the right and the good; art and the aesthetic.[18]

The claim of conceptual holism contrasts with that of an *ability holism*. The former says that understanding of self-consciousness and self-reference is interdependent, the latter that the abilities underlying self-consciousness and self-reference are interdependent. Ability holism consists in a two-part claim: that to be self-conscious one must be able to self-refer; and that to be able to self-refer one must be self-conscious — that is, only selves can self-refer. (In a sense, a conceptual holism involves an ability holism, since understanding of concepts is manifested in one's ability to use them.)

Analytic philosophers have been sceptical about circles of concepts, a concern perhaps originating with Quine's critique of the analytic-synthetic distinction (Quine, 1953, 'Two Dogmas of Empiricism'); Bermúdez (1998, p. 16), for instance, worries about how language-learners penetrate the circle of 'I'-use and 'I'-thoughts. But if the basic concepts involved in a holism are introduced to language-users by example, not verbal definition, and are thus shown to be anchored in our practices and activities, such concerns are allayed. Far from exhibiting a vicious circularity, conceptual holisms are an essential feature of language; recognition of them shows how philosophical understanding must be both analytic *and* synthetic.

It may be that, in rejecting the idea of explicit introductory explanation, conceptual holism provides a distinctive anti-metaphysical interpretation of the Analytic Principle that self-consciousness is expressed by use of a self-referring device with the properties of the first person. That question will have to be addressed on a later occasion. In any case, an holistic account argues that self-consciousness and use of 'I' are inter-defined; neither can be understood independently of the other.

---

18   These holisms are defended in Hamilton (2000) and (2013).

4. Self-Conscious Self-Reference and Indexicality

An anti-metaphysical approach rejects both the self as object, and an essence of self-consciousness. It therefore attends carefully to self-reference and reflexivity, and what I termed the Analytic Principle. In particular it addresses the question: 'How essential is the use of "I" to self-consciousness?' A brief tradition of using thought experiments in pursuing this question originates with Wittgenstein's oriental despot. In *Philosophical Remarks* (14 December 1929 and 11 October 1929; see for example, Wittgenstein, 1975) he argues for a 'no-reference' view of 'I'. He comments that 'I am experiencing a red patch' might be paraphrased to eliminate the implicit reference to a Cartesian ego: '[Wittgenstein's] idea is to externalize the privileged position of subjectivity by designating one particular person as a universal point of reference' (Hrachovec, 2000). If 'I' is LW, 'I have toothache' becomes 'There is toothache' and 'A has toothache' becomes 'A behaves as LW does when there is toothache' (Wittgenstein, 1975, paragraph 58). Any subject can take centre stage in this language. Wittgenstein asks us to imagine an oriental despotism, with the subject taking the place of the despot in providing the origin of the system of communication. Note the behaviourist assumption of Wittgenstein's middle period.

The thought experiment is under-described; and Wittgenstein is not expansive on what it is to dispense with 'I', or to deny that 'I' refers. Anscombe's 'A'-users in her 1981 develops the eliminative scenario — 'A' is meant to be a self-referring term that is not expressive of self-consciousness. Her example is also under-described, and seems incoherent. Since the 'A'-users have to check by observation whether it is a part of their body rather than someone else's which has moved, they must lack proprioception; but then they cannot be said to act at all, and so cannot be said to self-refer.[19]

We can pursue the line of eliminative thought experiment by imagining a linguistic community whose members self-consciously self-refer using their own name, lacking any uniform device of self-reference. Wittgenstein's 'There is pain' is unambiguous; a name such as 'de Gaulle' is not — or at least, not transparently so, i.e. not everyone can recognize its lack of ambiguity. The *name-user scenario* is intended as a critique of the Analytic Principle, and rests on the fact

---

[19]   Argued in Hamilton (2013, Chapter 4); but see Wiseman (2010).

that one can self-refer self-consciously by means of devices other than
'I'. Thus, the present writer uses the self-referring definite description
'the present writer' in order to avoid the intrusive 'I'; and historical
personages have self-consciously self-referred using their own name:
Julius Caesar, Henry James, and Charles de Gaulle. The General
would reportedly remark that, when faced with a particularly knotty
problem, he would ask himself 'What would *de Gaulle* do in this
situation?'. He is being ironic, asking himself, 'What would the
character that people regard as "de Gaulle" do?' (like Churchill, De
Gaulle was a megalomaniac with an acute sense of irony — an
unusual combination).

In a *community of name-users*, a linguistic convention echoes the
great general's habit: each speaker uses their own name self-
consciously to self-refer. Each name-user adopts an *alternative self-
reference rule* for a term used knowingly and intentionally to self-
refer: 'Their own name is the word which each one uses to refer to
him- or herself.' There is a uniform rule, but no uniform term, across
persons. A conservative variant abolishes only 'I' and its cognates; the
most radical variant replaces all personal pronouns and inflections by
a uniform 'third person'. The speaker's name does not count as an
indexical term, since its reference does not vary with the context of
utterance, namely, who uses it. 'De Gaulle' always refers to de Gaulle,
but only de Gaulle himself can use it to self-refer self-consciously. So
there would be self-conscious self-reference without indexicality —
or, at least, without use of an indexical term.

Our question is whether the name-user community has lost anything
essential to the means of linguistic expression. What features does 'I'
have that name-use lacks? The first person is a self-referring term or
verbal inflection which, unlike the speaker's own name, is *typographically identical* — the same word — for all speakers.[20] 'I' is
used comprehendingly only if it is understood as such a device; it is
privileged as a device of self-reference in effecting self-reference
unambiguously and transparently. Definite descriptions and proper
names, in contrast, may be used self-consciously to self-refer, but are
not devices of self-reference exclusively. Oedipus grasps the use of
the definite description 'the person who brought trouble to Thebes'
without realizing that he satisfies it. Later, after discovering that he

---

[20] The problematic elucidation of words and sentences as 'typographically identical' is
discussed in Hamilton (2014, Chapter 6.6).

does — that he himself brought trouble to Thebes — he could use the definite description in order to self-refer self-consciously. A description can function as a self-referring term, but not as a *general device* like 'I', which effects self-reference unambiguously and transparently — that is, as an indexical term. Indexicality, in the case of the first person, may therefore just amount to unambiguous self-reference.

In a sense, name-use is more primitive than 'I'-use. It echoes children's less than fully self-conscious use of their own name before they acquire a grasp of 'I' — a grasp that is interestingly late in linguistic development. When Jacob says 'Jacob wants a biscuit', and becomes upset when not given one, we naturally interpret him to mean 'I want a biscuit' — as self-consciously self-referring. Although he does not yet grasp the first person, we infer that, given his normal linguistic development thus far, he is about to do so. Comprehending use of 'I' goes with a pattern of behaviour inviting ascriptions of intention and self-consciousness. If there is behaviour without the use, one may ascribe the ability self-consciously to self-refer; conversely, given the use without the behaviour, one may decline to do so. Indeed, 'Jacob wants a biscuit' may not really require *interpretation* any more than 'I want a biscuit' does; what Jacob is saying is transparent. We assume that he knows that he is Jacob, that is, that he knows his own name — if that really is an assumption, since children usually do.[21]

Self-referring uses of descriptions and proper names are peripheral to linguistic practice. De Gaulle mostly used 'de Gaulle' for rhetorical effect, and continued to use 'I'. Our question is whether the name-user community has lost anything essential to the means of linguistic expression. Is lack of a uniform device of self-reference, one that exhibits unambiguous reference, merely an inconvenience — or does it signal a more radical loss? The distinction is not clear, and the question hard to answer. Certainly there are major inconveniences, as follows:

(1) *Not knowing the speaker's name.* With 'I', the audience can identify the referent immediately — there is no doubt that the speaker is self-referring. Ventriloquism provides only a minor qualification of the immediate, unambiguous self-reference of 'I', which rests on the very general fact of nature — as Wittgenstein would put it — that we

---

21 Primitive name-use is illustrated by behaviour of autistic subjects — Hinzen and Schroeder (2015).

can tell by movements of the mouth, and the apparent origin of the sound, who is speaking. In a name-user community, however, it would not be clear whether someone were self-referring with their own name or referring to someone else. In a community of modern size, one would have to learn thousands of self-referring names to gain an equivalent of the practical use of 'I'.

We now see that 'I' has two functions: If I say 'AJH would like more beans', others at the meal would not know who wanted beans unless they knew who was AJH, even if they knew who was speaking; with 'I' they just have to know who spoke. For clarity, I would have to say 'AJH — speaking — wants more beans', but then the name-use is gratuitous — unless one cannot see or work out who is speaking, in which case it gives extra information. So either names do not fully replace personal pronouns, or they do so only in association with a device that makes them redundant; in any case, they would no longer be names. When Lara screams '(Want) ice-cream!', she may receive it if the donor realizes who is shouting. '(Wants) ice-cream!' is not an 'I'-thought; it precedes both mastery of names and use of 'I'. When Lara has learned her name, she may shout 'Lara wants ice-cream', and may receive it even if the donor does not realize who shouted; but she may not, if they do not know her name. When she learns to say 'I — Lara — want ice-cream' that is not two words doing the same job, but two complementary devices — closing both loopholes, as it were. (This may be another way to try to elucidate 'the intention to self-refer'.)

Analogously, a secretary records the committee's votes by ticking off a list. When Baldy says, 'I vote against', the secretary, who does not know him, asks 'Who *are* you?' (not, 'Who were you referring to?'). The example shows that in many cases 'I' works properly only if those who hear it know who the speaker is. If Baldy had voted by saying 'Baldy votes against', the secretary might have paused before asking, 'You were referring to yourself?' — is he casting a vote, or describing someone else's voting? Arising from the two functions of 'I' are two inconveniences of name-use: the ambiguity of two people with the same name, and the further uncertainty — given that the listener does not know their name — of whether the person who refers to 'Baldy' is self- or other-referring. Only a close-knit society with no duplication of names, where everyone knew everyone else, would avoid these problems.

(2) *Learning names*. People tend not to forget their names. But doing so may seem slightly less drastic than forgetting the use of 'I',

since it is loss of an item of empirical knowledge, not a species of
linguistic competence — the capacity self-consciously to self-refer.
Indeed, one cannot simply 'forget' how to use 'I', since it is not a
name and one cannot forget it as one can forget a name. This
appearance results from *the seemingly indissoluble connection
between the first person and self-consciousness.* However, a speaker
might simply forget the *word* 'I'. A victim of brain damage might ask,
'What's that word, the one for "This person here [pointing to
himself]"?' or '...the word that people use to refer to themselves?'.
Since 'themselves' is a cognate of 'I', the example may seem unpersuasive. But note that the speaker is simply meant to forget a word,
not lose the associated concept or capacity; they can provide a paraphrase. So both in 'I'- and name-user notations, the speaker might
forget the word without losing the linguistic competence involved in
self-referring. In the name-user community, the need for a new name
in cases of amnesia would be more urgent, but that is all.

   These are inconveniences, for sure. But it might be argued that,
especially in a close-knit society with no duplication of names, where
everyone knew everyone else, members could enjoy self-consciousness without self-reference by a first-personal pronoun. Is this correct?

5. A Conceptual Holism of Thought and Language

The name-user scenario tried to separate grasp of a first-person device
from the intention self-consciously to self-refer; the name-users have
the intention, but no uniform device by which to express it. My
suggestion now is that the scenario fails to show that 'I' is eliminable,
because one must implicitly assume that the name-users are self-
conscious. There is a question whether, although they do not use a
first person, we must nonetheless understand their behaviour in terms
of one — because of the stubborn intertwining of 'I'-use, and the
intention to self-refer. One is asked, 'Imagine this scenario...'. But
who is doing the imagining — an 'I'-user? 'Well, let's imagine a non-
"I"-user thinking about it.' Can we assume that they are self-
conscious, i.e. a person? It seems that in order to *interpret* the utterances of the name-users in the thought experiment, one must use terms
involving 'I' — that is, the scenario is intelligible only because name-
using judgments are interpreted implicitly as 'I'-judgments.

   Metaphysicians will say: 'There is an essence of self-consciousness,
so one *can* say "Imagine a community of self-conscious creatures".'
Anti-metaphysicians will reply: what is it about those creatures'

behaviour that justifies the ascription of self-consciousness? Meta-physicians are stipulating *a prior fact of the matter* about whether the creatures are self-conscious, independent of the behaviour that they manifest — which assumes that self-consciousness has a non-behavioural essence. While Wittgenstein's oriental despot thought experiment is anti-metaphysical, this new version of the name-user scenario would have to assume a metaphysical non-behavioural essence of self-consciousness in order to show the eliminability of 'I'.

The alternative would be to describe a behaviour and then decide whether those exhibiting it were self-conscious. However, the behaviour of the name-users is designed to be of a complexity that invites the attribution of self-consciousness. And indeed, the *self-reference rule for name-users* — which it was stipulated that the name-users followed — assumes grasp of self-consciousness, just like the self-reference rule for 'I'. The name-user rule is: 'Their own name is the word which each one uses to refer to him- or herself.' In order to understand the generality expressed by 'each one', one must have an ability to distinguish between oneself and others, which is expressed, at least incipiently, in an ability self-consciously to self-refer. So it seems to follow trivially that the name-user scenario involves no loss of expressive power.[22]

It is true that a device of self-reference is simply a means of ful-filling an intention to self-refer, which, like any such means, exploits linguistic conventions. But, in the case of 'I', the intention to self-refer seems inbuilt because one does not have to distinguish self-consciously self-referring uses of the term from other uses; there *are* no other comprehending uses. (The use must be comprehending; someone who *says* 'I...' is not guaranteed to understand it.) We attri-bute to the child that uses its own name an intention to self-refer with-out a grasp of 'I', because such grasp seems incipient. Thus it is an illusion that 'I' has been eliminated without loss of expressive power. For self-conscious creatures, Evans' 'method of description' using 'I' or equivalent device is unavoidable, and not one possible conceptual scheme among others.

The name-user scenario apparently dispenses with *indexical self-referring terms* if one defines *indexicality* as 'systematic variation of a term's reference with context'. Is this merely a superficial linguistic characterization of indexicality, resting on a deeper notion of indexical

---

[22] Argued in Hamilton (2013, Chapter 1).

thought? One could argue that the thought experiment smuggles in indexicality, as each proper name can refer only to the person to whom it belongs, even though confusion arises if two people had the same name. All proper names exhibit the rule 'refers only to the person to whom it belongs' — a rule that is the essence of 'I', since it is more important than the word. But could one understand what that meant without having grasped a uniform *term* such as 'I' on which the replacement term was imperfectly modelled? This seems unlikely. And so it seems that the name-user thought experiment does not vindicate Anscombe's view — part of her case against the reference of 'I' — that it is a triviality that 'I' is a word which everyone uses only to speak of him- or herself.

My account of the scenario rejects the primacy of thought that underlies Perry's (e.g. 1979) claim that 'I' is the essential indexical. On the primacy of thought view, self-consciousness involves having indexical thoughts, but does not require any (uniform) indexical term by which they are expressed. Hence the objection that my account offers only a superficial linguistic characterization of indexicality, and that one should appeal instead to a deeper notion of indexical thought.

There is no deeper notion, I believe. The moral of the name-user scenario is *not* that while self-consciousness does not require actual use of 'I' it requires having *'I'-thoughts*. Thought is more basic than language only in the anodyne sense that 'I am hungry' and 'De Gaulle is hungry', both uttered by de Gaulle, express the same thought. That thought may be termed an 'I'-thought; one could say 'De Gaulle has "I"-thoughts but expresses them by using "de Gaulle" instead of "I"'. But the attempt to make thought more basic than language in any deeper sense proves non-explanatory; rather, there is a *conceptual holism of thought and language*. By a 'deeper sense' of the basic nature of thought I mean a *thesis of the primacy of thought*, which says that unexpressed thoughts are more fundamental than their linguistic expression, and that they appear clothed in different linguistic garb.

An extreme version of this thesis is the 'language of thought' hypothesis, that thinking is performed in a mental 'language', a symbolic system physically realized in the brain. (This is really a thought-over-(natural)-language hypothesis.) A less radical form of the thesis says that indexical utterances express perspectival knowledge of oneself and one's environment that is essential for action and self-consciousness. Thus, if I believe that the treasure is buried in Durham, I will not start digging unless I believe that Durham is 'here';

a particular indexical term may be dispensable, it is argued, but indexicality in the sense of beliefs with perspectival content is essential to self-consciousness. This is the sense in which Perry holds that 'I' is an 'essential indexical'. 'Perry is making a mess', framed in the manner of de Gaulle, cannot explain his own behaviour without the additional explanation 'and I believe that I am Perry' (*ibid.*, pp. 4–5). 'Hamilton is making a mess', asserted by myself, explains my adjusting the sack of sugar in my trolley only if it expresses a first-personal conception, and not a conception of someone who happens to be me.

'I' is indeed an essential indexical, but not in the way that Perry suggests. Perspectival or indexical thought cannot be understood independently of indexical terms or language such as 'I', 'here', 'now', and 'this'. Indexicality is a feature of thought *and* language — there is a conceptual holism between them. The claim that indexicality is essential to self-consciousness therefore concerns the nature of self-conscious thought and linguistic expression jointly. They are inseparable, not in that all thoughts are expressed, but in that they form a conceptual holism. Elucidation of perspectival thought involves elucidation of 'I'-thoughts, demonstrative thought, and so on — which involves elucidation of the features of 'I', 'this' and 'that', and so forth. The conceptual holist position rests on two principles:

(1) the capacity to think a certain range of thoughts must be analysed through the capacity for their canonical linguistic expression;
(2) the capacity for linguistic expression must be analysed in terms of the range of thoughts that are canonically expressed.

It must be conceded that a developed case needs to be made for the preceding claims; this would involve a fundamental critique of the notion of 'content', which is obviously a large project for another occasion.

The conceptual holist position advanced here, therefore, denies that thought has primacy over language. The human case, where thoughts are articulated in language, is central to self-consciousness; primitive self-consciousness may be attributed to non-language-using creatures, but it does not follow that, while thought is essential for self-consciousness, linguistic expression is incidental. There are forms of non-linguistic thinking: music is thinking in sound, for instance. But one should not suppose that some basic prior thinking *explains* how these accomplishments involving language, sound, or physical materials are possible. Rather, the accomplishments are some of the *forms that thinking takes* (Hamilton, 2007). While expression — musical, sculptural, or linguistic — is necessary for thought as such, linguistic expression is necessary for *propositional* thought.

We were trying to understand self-consciousness by contrasting self-conscious and non-self-conscious self-reference. But 'I'-use seems to be unanalysable; indexicality must be understood in terms of 'I', 'now', and the demonstratives. Other forms of self-reference are either accidental self-reference by creatures capable of self-conscious self-reference, or else rest on naming conventions themselves parasitic on 'I'-use. Not achieving much success in understanding self-consciousness through direct examination of self-reference, one might try defining self-conscious self-reference as the mode of self-reference by self-conscious creatures. This would be an elucidation, since, as I have argued elsewhere, there are no other genuine self-referrers; only selves self-refer. That is, all self-referrers are self-conscious self-referrers, who occasionally self-refer accidentally or non-self-consciously.[23]

We must conclude that the presupposition that the name-users are self-conscious, and the need to understand name-use in terms of 'I', means that the scenario does not prove the dispensability of 'I'-use. 'I' is a basic concept whose connections with other concepts can be elucidated, but which cannot be fundamentally and introductorily defined. What is required is an account of 'I' that is synthetic as well as analytic, and is anti-metaphysical in so far as it resists the idea of an essence of self-consciousness, not essentially expressed in linguistic behaviour.

Acknowledgments

I am grateful for comments from Mihretu Guta, Matthew Tugby, Rachael Wiseman, and anonymous referees.

References

Anscombe, G.E.M. (1981) The first person, in *Collected Philosophical Papers Vol. II: Metaphysics and the Philosophy of Mind*, Oxford: Blackwell.
Bermúdez, J. (1998) *The Paradox of Self-Consciousness*, Cambridge, MA: Bradford/MIT Press.
Cassam, Q. (1997) *Self and World*, Oxford: Clarendon Press.

---

[23] Implications of this approach are considered in Hamilton (2013, Chapter 7).

Evans, G. (1982) *The Varieties of Reference*, Oxford: Clarendon Press.

Hamilton, A. (2000) The authority of avowals and the concept of belief, *European Journal of Philosophy*, **7** (2), pp. 20–39.

Hamilton, A. (2007) *Aesthetics and Music*, London: Continuum.

Hamilton, A. (2013) *The Self in Question*, Basingstoke: Palgrave.

Hamilton, A. (2014) *Routledge Philosophy Guidebook to Wittgenstein and On Certainty*, London: Routledge.

Hinzen, W. & Schroeder, K. (2015) Is 'first-person' a linguistic concept?, *Journal of Consciousness Studies*, **22** (11–12), this issue.

Hrachovec, H. (2000) *Wittgenstein on Line/on the Line*, [Online], http://wab.uib.no/wab_contrib-hh.page [30 August 2015].

Kant, I. (1781/1929) *Critique of Pure Reason*, Kemp Smith, N. (trans.), London: Macmillan.

Kemp Smith, N. (1948) *The Philosophy of David Hume*, London: Macmillan.

Kitcher, P. (1984) Kant's real self, in Wood, A. (ed.) *Self and Nature in Kant's Philosophy*, Ithaca, NY: Cornell University Press.

Longuenesse, B. (2015) *Self-Consciousness and Consciousness of One's Own Body: Variations on a Kantian Theme*, [Online], http://philosophy.fas.nyu.edu/docs/IO/2575/longuenesse2.pdf [30 August 2015].

Lowe, E.J. (2008) *Personal Agency: The Metaphysics of Mind and Action*, Oxford: Oxford University Press.

Marshall, C. (2010) Kant's metaphysics of the self, *Philosophers' Imprint*, **10** (8), pp. 1–21.

Melnick, A. (2009) *Kant's Theory of the Self*, London: Routledge.

Olson, E. (1998) There is no problem of the self, *Journal of Consciousness Studies*, **5** (5–6), pp. 645–657.

Perry, J. (1979) The problem of the essential indexical, *Nous*, **13**, pp. 3–21; also in Perry, J. (1993) *The Problem of the Essential Indexical and Other Essays*, Oxford: Oxford University Press.

Quine, W. (1953) *From a Logical Point of View*, Harvard, MA: Harvard University Press.

Rödl, S. (2007) *Self-Consciousness*, Harvard, MA: Harvard University Press.

Soames, S. (2003) *Philosophical Analysis in the Twentieth Century*, Vol. 2, Princeton, NJ: Princeton University Press.

Strawson, P. (1959) *Individuals: An Essay in Descriptive Metaphysics*, London: Methuen.

Strawson, P. (1966) *The Bounds of Sense*, London: Methuen.

Wiseman, R. (2010) *Speaking of Oneself: Self-Consciousness and the First-Person Pronoun*, PhD dissertation, York University.

Wittgenstein, L. (1961) *Tractatus Logico-Philosophicus*, London: Routledge.

Wittgenstein, L. (1975) *Philosophical Remarks*, Oxford: Blackwell.

Zöller, G. (1993) Main developments in recent scholarship on the Critique of Pure Reason, *Philosophy and Phenomenological Research*, **53** (2), pp. 445–466.

Eric T. Olson

What Does it Mean to Say That We Are Animals?

Abstract: *The view that we are animals — animalism — is often mis-understood. It is typically stated in unhelpful or misleading ways. Debates over animalism are often unclear about what question it purports to answer, and what the alternative answers are. The paper tries to state clearly what animalism says and does not say. This enables us to distinguish different versions of animalism.*

1. Preliminaries

One of the main questions about the metaphysics of human people is whether we are animals: biological organisms. Snowdon, van Inwagen, and I say yes; Baker, Johnston, Parfit, and Shoemaker say no.[1] Snowdon has called the view that we are animals *animalism*, and the name has stuck. Sometimes 'animalism' means something else — a point I will return to — but I will use it in this sense.

Simple though it is, animalism is often misunderstood. It is typically stated in misleading ways — usually by its enemies, but sometimes by its friends as well. There is confusion about what it does and doesn't say. Debates over animalism are often unclear about what question it purports to answer, and what the alternative answers are. There are various propositions it has been taken to express, and arguments for and against it apply to different ones. My aim in this paper is to clear

Correspondence:
Eric T. Olson, University of Sheffield, UK.   *Email: e.olson@sheffield.ac.uk*

---

[1] Snowdon (2014); van Inwagen (1990); Olson (1997; 2003); Baker (2000); Johnston (2007); Parfit (2012); Shoemaker (1984; 2011). Other animalists include Ayers (1990), Blatti (2014), Carter (1989), and Luper (2014); other anti-animalists include Campbell and McMahan (2010), Hudson (2007), Noonan (1998), and Unger (2000).

Journal of Consciousness Studies, **22**, No. 11–12, 2015, pp. 84–107

up some of these points. This will enable us to distinguish a number of different versions of 'animalism'.

2. Animalism versus Lockeanism

Animalism is frequently contrasted with 'Lockeanism'.[2] Lockeanism is another name for the psychological-continuity view of personal identity over time: that the persistence of a person through time consists in some sort of psychological continuity. That is, a person x existing at one time and something y existing at another time are one and the same just if there is an appropriate chain of causal dependence between the mental states x is in at the one time and the mental states y is in at the other time (Shoemaker, 1984, pp. 89ff.).

Animalists reject Lockeanism on the grounds that animals, even the human animals that they believe us to be, do not persist by virtue of psychological continuity. Lockeans reject animalism for the same reason. Everyone takes animalism and Lockeanism to be incompatible. And as they are perhaps the two most widely held views in the philosophy of personal identity, it's unsurprising that they are often contrasted.

But this contrast can be misleading, because the two views are answers to different questions. Animalism answers the question, *What are we?* Lockeanism answers the question, *What does it take for us* (or for a person generally) *to persist through time?* Call these the *personal-ontology question* and the *persistence question*. The point is easy to miss because both questions are called 'problems of personal identity', and that catch-all term can lead us to think that they come to the same thing. Yet there are at least half a dozen more-or-less unrelated questions called 'problems of personal identity' (Olson, 2015, §1). It is possible to read lengthy discussions of 'personal identity' without having any idea what question they aim to answer.

Animalism does not answer the persistence question. Combined with an account of what it takes for a human animal to persist through time, it will *imply* an answer: that we persist by virtue of some sort of brute-physical continuity, perhaps. But it does not explicitly state any answer, and the implication is disputable, even if not many do dispute it. Nor does Lockeanism answer the personal-ontology question. In

---

2   This is illustrated in the title of Noonan's (1998) paper 'Animalism *versus* Lockeanism: A Current Controversy'.

fact there is no simple or even reasonably uncontroversial way of inferring an account of what we are from Lockeanism: nothing analogous to the easy inference from our being animals to the view that our persistence consists in brute-physical continuity. Most Lockeans say little about what we are, and there is deep disagreement among those who say anything about our non-mental properties of metaphysical interest. (I will return to these points.)

This is important because seeing Lockeanism as the main rival to animalism gives Lockeans an unfair dialectical advantage. The usual way of defending Lockeanism is to see how well it conforms to our 'intuitions' about stories where different accounts of our persistence conditions give different verdicts about who would be who. The most famous of these is the brain transplant. If your brain (or cerebrum) were put into my head, so that the recipient were psychologically continuous only with you but brute-physically continuous in the relevant way only with me, Lockeanism implies that the resulting person would be you 'with a new body',[3] whereas animalism (combined with the assumption that a human animal persists by virtue of some sort of brute-physical continuity, nothing to do with psychology) implies that he would be me with a new brain. In many of these cases it's easy to find the Lockean verdict more attractive,[4] leading people to accept Lockeanism and reject animalism.

But this gives only half the picture. Animalism is attractive not because of what it implies for our persistence through time, but because it looks like an excellent answer to the personal-ontology question. We seem, on the face of it, to be animals. We don't seem to be *non*-animals. So it's not enough for opponents of animalism to point out that it has implausible consequences about what would happen to you in a brain transplant. They need to defend their own view of what we are. Animalism should be contrasted not with Lockeanism, but with other answers to the personal-ontology question: that we are literally brains, for instance (which would explain why you would go with that organ if it were transplanted); or

---

3   The reason for the shudder quotes is that philosophers' talk of people's bodies is irremediably loose and cannot be relied upon; see van Inwagen (1980), Olson (1997, pp. 142–53).

4   It's less attractive in others: for instance, Lockeanism implies that none of us was ever a 5-month-old foetus. But these cases are seldom discussed. Snowdon (2014, p. 234) has argued that our intuitions even in the brain-transplant case are less robust than they at first appear.

that we are non-animals 'constituted by' animals, or temporal parts of animals, or Humean bundles of perceptions, or immaterial substances. These are the true rivals to animalism. Lockeanism can be true only if one of them is true as well. Each of them faces grave metaphysical objections, which anyone opposed to animalism ought to worry about (Olson, 2007). But Lockeans are encouraged to ignore all this by the thought that they are answering only the persistence question. Many Lockeans are completely unaware of these objections, or at any rate feel no need to address them.

So restricting the debate to the persistence question and ignoring the personal-ontology question emphasizes Lockeanism's main strength — its attractive account of who would be who in certain thought experiments — while hiding its main weakness — the difficulty in saying what we are in a way that is compatible with that account.

Someone might think that Lockeanism *does* tell us what we are. Just as animalism says that we are animals, Lockeanism says that we are rational, conscious beings that persist by virtue of psychological continuity. And this does tell us something about what we are, though not much. An account of personal ontology ought to say whether we are material or immaterial. It should say whether we are substances or events or processes, and whether we have parts or are simple. It should say something about where our boundaries lie and what determines them, and of course whether we have any spatial location at all. These questions must have answers. Yet here Lockeanism is completely silent. Nor does it say or even straightforwardly imply anything about whether we are spatial or temporal parts of animals, things constituted by animals, bundles of perceptions, immaterial substances, or what have you. It does not by itself even rule out our being animals. It leaves the question of what we are almost entirely open (*ibid.*, pp. 17f.).

I concede that animalism does not give a complete answer to the personal-ontology question either: its implications about what we are depend in part on the metaphysical nature of animals, which is independent of whether we are animals. But it tells us far more about what we are than Lockeanism does. And there is far more agreement about the metaphysical nature of animals than there is about the metaphysical nature of beings that persist by virtue of psychological continuity.

3. The 'Is' of Constitution

I turn now to the question of how animalism should be stated, or what it means to say that we are animals.

Many people say that the simple statement that we are animals is ambiguous, and can express views opposed to animalism. The idea is that I could 'be' an animal in the sense of being *constituted by* one, where constitution is defined so that nothing can constitute itself. That would make me one thing and the animal sitting here another, which is precisely what animalists oppose. Thus, Shoemaker says, 'a person "is" an animal, not in the sense of being identical to one, but in the sense of sharing its matter with one' (Shoemaker, 1984, p. 113). Whether there is such a thing as the 'is' of constitution presumably depends on whether there is such a thing as constitution itself — that is, whether one thing ever constitutes another thing. But as that is an open question, we don't want to state animalism in a way that pre-judges it.

And if we could 'be' animals in the sense of being constituted by them, we could equally be animals in the sense of having bodies that are animals: if there can be an 'is' of constitution, there can be an 'is' of embodiment. Our being animals in that sense is consistent with our being wholly immaterial — and no biological organism is wholly immaterial. Likewise, the view that each of us is a proper temporal part of an animal — a thing composed of all the stages of an animal except its insentient embryonic and foetal stages, say — is consistent with my being an animal in the sense of sharing stages with one.[5] Almost any account of our metaphysical nature allows that we 'are' animals in some sense or other.

So animalism must say that we are animals in a stricter sense than merely being constituted by or embodied in or sharing stages with them, and an adequate formulation of it needs to specify this stricter sense. In what sense of 'are', then, does animalism say that we are animals?

4. The Identity Formulation

The most common answer is implicit in Shoemaker's statement: animalism says that we are animals in the sense of being *numerically*

---

[5] Lewis said that if I share my stage located at time *t* with something, that makes me 'identical-at-*t*' with it (Lewis, 1976, pp. 26f.).

identical to them. You and a certain animal are one thing and not two. On the constitution view and other rivals to animalism, by contrast, each of us is numerically distinct from the animal that she 'is' loosely speaking. Call this the *identity formulation* of animalism. Some go on to say that when animalists say we are animals, they are using the 'is' of identity. We will see later that this is a mistake.

The identity formulation has an obvious attraction. Animalism really does imply that we are identical to animals, and rival views imply that we're not. So it is no mistake to state animalism by saying that we are identical to animals. It is, however, entirely unhelpful. The identity formulation cannot specify the strict sense of 'is' that animalism needs. The reason is that to be identical to an animal is to be identical to a thing that is an animal. ('An F' is logically and grammatically equivalent to 'a thing that is an F'.) And if the word 'am' in 'I am an animal' could be an instance of the 'is' of constitution, so could the word 'is' in 'I am identical to a thing that is an animal'. So if I could be an animal by being constituted by an animal, then I could be identical to an animal by being identical to something constituted by an animal. Or I could be identical to an animal in the sense of being identical to a thing that 'is' an animal in some other loose sense: a thing embodied in an animal or sharing stages with one, say.

Of course, this is not how the authors of the identity formulation intended it to be understood. When they say that I am (or am not) identical to an animal, they mean that I am (or am not) identical to something that is an animal in the strict sense, not something constituted by an animal or the like. But the identity formulation does not actually say this. It *could* — we could rewrite it to say explicitly that we are numerically identical to things that are animals in the strict sense of the word *are*. But that would be no advance over saying simply that we are animals in that strict sense.

So the identity formulation cannot distinguish animalism from its rivals any better than the simple statement that we are animals can. It needs to specify that the thing to which I am identical is an animal in the strict sense. But if we could do that, we could just as well say that we are animals in that sense and leave identity out of it. Bringing in identity is no help; what does the work is the right sense of the word 'is' or 'are'. I will return to this sense in the next section.

On this point the other proposed statements that I will consider shortly are no better. Some state animalism as the thesis that we are animals *fundamentally* (see §6). But if the plain statement 'we are animals' could mean that we are constituted by animals, then the statement that we are animals fundamentally could mean that we are constituted by things that are animals fundamentally, which is again inconsistent with animalism. We could rule that out only by specifying that the second occurrence of the word 'are' is not an 'is' of constitution or the like. But if we could do that, there would be no need to speak of fundamentality. Stating animalism as the view that we are animals *essentially* (see §7) is unhelpful for the same reason.

I wish I could banish the 'is' of constitution from metaphysics. 'Being' an animal in the sense of being constituted by one is not a way of being an animal. It is, rather, a way of being a non-animal. The most perspicuous statement of the constitution view is that each of us is a non-animal constituted by an animal.[6] For a constitutionalist to say that we are animals is just as misleading as it would be for a Cartesian dualist (one who takes us to be wholly immaterial) to say that we are material things — to say, paraphrasing Shoemaker, that a person 'is' a material thing, not in the sense of being identical to one, but in the sense of being embodied in one.

Although I doubt whether constitutionalists have deliberately attempted to mislead their readers by saying that we are animals, this statement *has* misled, by disguising the implication that we are something other than animals. It gives the appearance that constitutionalists and animalists disagree only over a subtle point, namely the manner in which we are animals. It encourages the thought: 'I am an animal; I'm just not identical to an animal.' That sounds far more comforting than the thought: 'I am a non-animal sharing its matter with an animal.' But this comfort is an illusion. It's like saying that dualists and materialists disagree only about the manner in which we are material things. No dualist would take comfort in thinking, 'I am a material thing; I'm just not identical to a material thing', rather than 'I am an immaterial thing embodied in a material thing'. Dualists understand

---

6 Shoemaker (2011) has recently proposed that there are both 'psychological animals' with psychological persistence conditions and 'biological animals' with brute-physical ones. He says that we are psychological animals constituted by biological animals. So we are constituted by animals, yet we really are animals. But he denies that we are biological animals, which is what animalists and most of their opponents mean by 'animals'. This differs only verbally from the view that we are non-animals constituted by animals: Shoemaker calls the things constituted by biological organisms 'animals' (so that there are two animals sitting in your chair); most other constitutionalists don't. Johnston says the same, but refuses to call the biological animal an animal at all (2007, p. 55).

perfectly well that on their view we are not material things. Those attracted to constitutionalism do not always understand perfectly well that on that view we are not animals. Yet we are no more animals according to constitutionalism than we are according to dualism.

We can see the dangers of the 'is' of constitution in another way by noting its implication that every person is something other than herself. Suppose I am an animal in the sense of being constituted by one. Since nothing can constitute itself, that animal is something other than me. It follows that in whatever sense I am an animal, I am something other than myself. More generally, anything constituted by something is something other than itself. This is no contradiction: it does not imply that every person is something other than herself in the strict sense of the word 'is', or that one thing is numerically identical to another thing. But it shows that the 'is' of constitution needs careful handling. It doesn't always get it. Confusion is inevitable.

And in so far as the statement that x is an animal could mean that x is constituted by an animal, *any* statement of the form 'x is an F' could mean that x is constituted by an F — implying, in most cases, that strictly speaking x is *not* an F. Thus, if animalism needs to be stated in a way that rules out the 'is' of constitution, so do the alternative views. Those who say that we are temporal parts of animals will need to ensure that this is not read 'we are constituted by temporal parts of animals'. Even constitutionalists need to ensure that their statement 'we are things constituted by animals' is not read 'we are things constituted by things constituted by animals'. All parties can avoid this trouble by sticking to the strict use of the word 'is'.

5. How the Identity Formulation is Misleading

Quite apart from its failure to disambiguate the phrase 'we are animals', the identity formulation can be seriously misleading.

Animalism has the virtue of being an intuitively attractive answer to the question of what sort of things we are. Given the choice, most people find it easier to believe that we are animals than to believe that we are things constituted by animals, temporal or spatial parts of animals, immaterial substances, or non-animals of any other sort. But some of this intuitive attraction is lost if animalism has to be stated by saying that we are identical to animals. That we are animals sounds right; that we are *identical to* animals sounds complicated and technical. It's like saying that 5 is identical to a prime number. We all know, without having to think, that 5 is a prime number. But is it *identical to* a prime number? We may be unsure. The technical phrase 'identical to' puts us on our guard. This is unfortunate because there is nothing complicated or technical about animalism. At any rate it's far less complicated and technical than any of its rivals. Nor is the immediate plausibility of our being animals merely the plausibility of our being animals in some loose sense of the word 'are' that is consistent with the alternatives to animalism. That we are animals sounds attractive compared to those alternatives. Stating animalism by saying that we are identical to animals makes a simple and intuitive claim sound complicated and difficult.

The identity formulation is misleading in another way too. Suppose someone said that I was identical to a philosopher, or to a parent, or to a music lover. These statements sound not just complicated and technical, but wrong. (They are in fact true, as we shall see. But no one would ever *say* that I was identical to a parent, as opposed to simply being a parent, because no one ever supposed that I 'was' a parent in a loose sense that is incompatible with my being identical to one: that I was constituted by a parent, say.)[7]

For this reason, saying that I am identical to an animal is bound to suggest that I am an animal in a different and less familiar sense than that in which I am a philosopher, a parent, and a music lover. If being an animal in the strict sense amounts to being identical to an animal, then I must be a philosopher, a parent, and so on in some looser sense. My only genuine properties — those I have strictly speaking — are being an animal and those that follow from it: being a material thing, having a metabolism, and so on. I am *nothing but* an animal. My character, way of thinking, goals, memories, interests, interpersonal relationships — all the things I care most about — are at best superficial features of me. I have them only at arm's length. Whatever exactly this amounts to, it sounds deeply troubling.

But there is no reason for animalists to say any of this. They can say that I am an animal in exactly the same sense that I am a philosopher, a parent, and indeed a person. I am identical to an animal; I am also identical to a person, to a philosopher, and to a parent. And this is what every animalist that I know of does say. That's because being an

---

7   Or almost no one: Matthews (1982) ascribes to Aristotle the view that a person's temporary properties — being musical, for instance, or being a parent — are always borne in the strict sense by something distinct from the person, existing only as long as the person can be loosely said to have the property.

F, for any value of 'F', is logically equivalent to being identical to an F. Nothing could be an F without being identical to an F, or be identical to an F without being an F. This fact is expressed in a theorem of standard predicate logic with identity: $(x)(Fx \equiv \exists y(Fy \& x=y))$.

It may sound paradoxical to say that I am identical to a parent. I wasn't always a parent. I was once a non-parent. I was once identical to a non-parent. Since things cannot be one at one time and two at another, would it not follow that I am both identical to a parent and identical to a non-parent? And given the equivalence between being identical to an F and being an F, doesn't that amount to my being both a parent and a non-parent?

But none of this follows. Nothing is a parent *simpliciter*. To be a parent is to be a parent at a particular time: now, say. My now being a parent is not my now being identical to a parent — identity is not a relation that can hold temporarily — but rather my being identical to something that is a parent now. And my being a non-parent 20 years ago is my being identical to something that was a non-parent then. So something that is a parent now is identical to something that was not a parent 20 years ago. There is no paradox here: being a parent now is perfectly compatible with being a non-parent at some other time. Or at least it is if it's possible for anything to have a property at one time and exist without having that property at another — that is, to change. And animalism does nothing to suggest otherwise.

We can see now why the claim that we are animals does not employ the 'is' (or 'are') of identity. Animalism says that I am an animal in the same ordinary sense in which I am a parent and a music lover. But clearly the statement 'Olson is a parent' does not employ the 'is' of identity. Nor does the statement 'Olson is standing'. This is so even though being a parent is equivalent to being identical to a parent, and standing is equivalent to being identical to something standing. None of these are instances of the 'is' of identity because that expression can only occur between two singular terms, as in 'Superman is Clark Kent' or 'water is H_2O'. The 'is' of identity is a notational variant of the identity sign: 'Superman = Clark Kent' is a grammatical sentence; 'Olson = an animal' is not.[8]

---

[8] This means that the phrase 'is identical to' is sometimes equivalent to the 'is' of identity and sometimes not, depending on whether it is followed by a singular term such as 'Clark Kent' or an indefinite description such as 'an animal'.

The word 'is' in 'Olson is an animal' is the ordinary copula, otherwise known as the 'is' of predication — the same 'is' that features in 'Olson is standing'. And so is the word 'are' in the animalist's claim that we are animals, and in the anti-animalist's claim that we are not animals. I said that according to animalism each of us is an animal in a stricter sense of 'is' than merely being constituted by or embodied in or sharing stages with an animal. This strict sense is simply the most ordinary sense of the word.

So it may be no mistake to state animalism as the view that we are identical to animals, since that formulation is equivalent to the simpler one. But it encourages a number of thoughts that *are* mistaken: that the identity formulation is clearer than saying simply that we are animals, that it implies that we are animals in a stricter sense than we are people or parents, and that it employs the 'is' of identity.

6. The Fundamentality Formulation

Another common formulation of animalism is that we are animals *fundamentally* (or 'fundamentally animals'), where a thing's being fundamentally F is roughly its being F as part of its most basic nature. My being an animal fundamentally implies that I have my identity conditions by virtue of being an animal, rather than by virtue of being a person or a thinking being or a parent, so that what it takes for me to persist is what it takes for an animal to persist. It is also taken to imply that what determines how many people there are at any one time — or at least how many human people — is what determines how many animals at that time qualify as people.

The fundamentality formulation is inspired by the Aristotelian thought that of all the kinds I belong to — *animal, material thing, parent, music lover*, and so on — one is special. It is the most metaphysically rich and important such kind, and tells us more about my nature than any other. If I ask, in a metaphysical tone of voice, what I am, this kind will be the best answer (Aristotle called it a *substance* kind or sort). That we are animals is a candidate for being this answer; that we are essentially rational beings constituted by animals, temporal parts of animals, or simple immaterial substances are others.

But animalism is not committed to this Aristotelian thought. It may be that no answer to the question *What am I?* is metaphysically privileged in this way. Yet it may still be the case that we are animals. Or it may be that we're not animals, but rather brains or immaterial substances or what have you. In the first case animalism is true; in the second it's false.

Even if the Aristotelian thought is right, the fundamentality formulation of animalism can be just as misleading as the identity formulation. The phrase 'fundamentally F' suggests that a thing can be F in two ways: it can be either fundamentally F or non-fundamentally F. And being non-fundamentally F can sound like a loose or second-rate way of being F. Since no one thinks that we are fundamentally philosophers, parents, or music lovers, this suggests that according to animalism we are animals in a stricter sense than we are philosophers, parents, or music lovers. Once more, my true nature consists simply in being an animal, and I have my other properties at arm's length.

But this again is a mistake. My being an animal fundamentally and a parent non-fundamentally does not entail that I am a parent in a looser or weaker sense than I am an animal. Being F fundamentally is not a different way of being F from being F non-fundamentally, or from simply being F.[9] I am no less a parent than I am an animal. I bear exactly the same relation to both properties: having, exemplifying, or instantiating.

Despite appearances, to say that something is fundamentally F is not to say that it is F in some special sense. It is, rather, to say two things: that the thing is F (in the ordinary sense of 'is'), and that being F is a special sort of property, namely a fundamental kind — roughly one that determines the metaphysical nature of the things that have it, including their identity conditions. So the view that we are animals fundamentally is the conjunction of the claim that we are animals with the claim that *animal* is a fundamental kind. (To say that I am a parent fundamentally would be to say that I am a parent and that *parent* is a fundamental kind.) But these two claims are entirely independent: whether we are animals or non-animals is independent of whether *animal* is a fundamental or a non-fundamental kind. More generally, the view that we are animals says nothing about the metaphysical nature of animals, other than that they are capable of thought. As it happens, most of those who think we are animals think that *animal is* a fundamental kind; but then so do most of those who think we're not animals. Both sides agree that animals are animals fundamentally, and

---

9   Not unless 'being non-fundamentally F' means 'being constituted by a thing that is F'. But that would make being non-fundamentally F a way of not being F: another confusing use of the 'is' of constitution.

that we are animals (in the ordinary sense) if and only if we are animals fundamentally.

Here, then, is another reason not to state animalism as the view that we are animals fundamentally. Either animals are animals fundamentally or they're not.[10] If not, then *we* are not animals fundamentally. On the fundamentality formulation, this would make animalism false. Animalism would be false even if we were animals. Yet the animalists' only mistake would be in taking *animal* to be a fundamental kind — something their opponents also believe. The mistake would be incidental to claim that they accept and their opponents deny. To say that this would make animalism false is like saying that someone who believed falsely that being a parent was a fundamental kind would be wrong to say that I was a parent.

What if *animal* really is a fundamental kind? Then nothing could be an animal without being an animal fundamentally. Being an animal and being an animal fundamentally would be logically equivalent, making the qualification 'fundamentally' superfluous. The only reason to say that we are animals fundamentally would be to rule out the view that we are animals *non*-fundamentally. But, for the reasons we have seen, that point is better made by first saying that we are animals and then saying separately that *animal* is a fundamental kind.

Stating animalism by saying that we are animals fundamentally is thus a mistake if *animal* is not a fundamental kind and superfluous if it is. The fundamentality formulation obscures the real point of contention between animalists and their opponents — whether we are animals — by tying it to the entirely independent matter of whether *animal* is a fundamental kind. It gives the false impression that animalists and their opponents agree that we are animals, and disagree only over a fine point to do with fundamentality. It is better to contrast the view that we are animals with the view that we're not, and leave fundamentality out of it.

7. The Essentialist Formulation

Some take animalism to be the view that we are animals essentially and not merely accidentally: we could not exist without being animals. This is no better than the fundamentality formulation. The view that

---

10   If some are and some aren't, consider those that we should be if we were animals at all: the animals that animalists think we are.

we are animals essentially is really a conjunction of two claims: that we are animals, and that animals are animals essentially.[11] These two claims are independent: we could be animals whether or not animals are animals essentially, and animals could be animals essentially whether or not we are animals. Most animalists probably accept the second claim; but so do most of their opponents. Stating animalism as the conjunction of the two makes it controversial for reasons that have nothing to do with whether we are animals. It obscures the central point of disagreement between animalists and their opponents — whether we are animals — by tying it to the unrelated matter of whether animals are animals essentially. It gives the false impression that animalists and their opponents agree that we are animals and disagree only about the modal status of this claim. Whether we are animals has nothing to do with essentialism.

We can illustrate this by noting that someone could be sceptical about modality in general but still have a view about whether we are animals. Suppose I doubt whether there are any modal properties at all, and thus reject both the claim that animals are animals essentially and the claim that they are animals accidentally. Yet I might still take us to be animals, or to be spatial or temporal parts of animals, bundles of perceptions, or what have you. That would make me an animalist or an anti-animalist, depending on which of these views I held.

8. Weak Animalism

There are other claims often combined with the view that we are animals. One is that animals do not have psychological persistence conditions: no psychological relation, even 'non-branching', continuously physically realized psychological continuity, is either necessary or sufficient for an animal to persist through time. Another is the more specific claim that animals persist by virtue of some sort of brute-physical continuity. A third is that no animal is a person essentially, where being a person at a given time is having certain special mental capacities then. (A human animal appears to start out as

---

[11] Constitutionalists sometimes say, or appear to say, that some animals are animals essentially and some are animals accidentally, rendering the second clause ambiguous. But their statement that something is an animal accidentally means only that that thing is accidentally constituted by an animal. They take the animal itself to be an animal essentially. Saying that according to constitutionalism we are animals accidentally is like saying that according to substance dualism we are material things accidentally. This is yet another misleading use of the 'is' of constitution.

an embryo with no mental capacities at all, and can exist in a vegetative state.) The truth of these further claims is entirely independent of whether we are animals, and anti-animalists are as prone to accept them as animalists are. If they *are* true, then our being animals implies that we don't persist by virtue of psychological continuity, but rather by virtue of some sort of brute-physical continuity, and that we are only accidentally and temporarily people. But even if that is so, the view that we are animals does not actually say any of this, and disputing the implication does nothing to cast doubt on it.

So the simple view that we are animals is frequently combined with further claims such as these:

> Animals are animals fundamentally.
> Animals are animals essentially.
> Animals do not persist by virtue of psychological continuity.
> Animals persist by virtue of some sort of brute-physical continuity.
> No animal is a person (in the Lockean sense) essentially.

This enables us to distinguish several varieties of animalism. We could call the bare claim that we are animals (in the ordinary sense of 'are') *weak animalism*. (This is what I have been calling 'animalism'.) Call its conjunction with the further claims *strong animalism*. There are intermediate versions as well, incorporating some but not all of the further claims. It would help, in debating animalism, if it were clear which version was at stake.

Someone might suspect that weak animalism is *so* weak as to be uninteresting. If it doesn't tell us whether we are animals most fundamentally or essentially, or anything about the metaphysical nature of animals, what does it tell us? Isn't the distinctive position that animalists actually defend one of the stronger versions?

This suspicion may be reinforced by the fact that the main objections to animalism are aimed at strong animalism. The most common is that animalism rules out Lockeanism — any psychological-continuity view of personal identity over time. Thus, animalism is taken, by its friends and enemies alike, to imply that you would not go with your transplanted brain. The operation would not give you a new body, but would give me a new brain. Presumably the resulting person would be psychologically continuous with you: he would have memories of your past, and would be firmly convinced that he was you. But he would be me. Ever since Locke described thought experiments like this more than 300 years ago, philosophers have rejected these consequences. Whatever its merits, this is an objection not to weak animalism as such, but to its conjunction with the further claim that animals persist by virtue of brute-physical continuity — sameness of biological life or the like.[12] This is what implies that the surgeons remove the brain from one animal and make it a part of another, just as they might do with a liver or a kidney. The mere claim that we are animals does not rule out saying that the surgeons transfer an animal from one head to another so that the recipient of the transplant is the same animal as the donor, undercutting the objection.

The same goes for most of the other objections to animalism. One is that *person* (in the sense of being a thing with certain special mental properties) has to be a fundamental kind, so that every person is a person essentially. We could not be only accidentally and temporarily people. When a person appears, this is not merely a thing's gaining a new property, as when I become a parent, but a thing's coming into existence. Nor is a person's disappearance just a matter of her changing by losing a property (Baker, 2000, pp. 219f.). But this again is not strictly an objection to our being animals, but to its conjunction with the claim that human animals are never essentially or fundamentally people. Others say that animalism has unacceptable implications about how many people there are at any one time. In certain cases of conjoined twinning, for instance, they say that there are two people but only one animal, implying that at least some human people are not animals (Campbell and McMahan, 2010). This requires an assumption about what determines how many animals there are at any one time that is independent of whether we are animals.

Without the further claims, few of the contentious consequences of animalism would follow, and the question of whether we are animals or non-animals would lose much of its interest. We may even wonder whether there is any reason to reject weak animalism. Of course, many philosophers do reject it. Weak animalism is incompatible with our being things constituted by animals, spatial or temporal parts of animals, bundles of perceptions, or immaterial substances. It rules out all the anti-animalist answers to the personal-ontology question. But most of those who reject animalism do so because they accept at least one of the further claims. They have no quarrel with weak animalism as such. It's strong animalism they don't like.

---

[12] Van Inwagen (1990, §14) gives a detailed account of this further claim. I have called this version of strong animalism 'the biological approach' (Olson, 1997, pp. 16f.).

Weak animalism is nevertheless an important view, even without the further claims. If it were false — if we were not animals — it would follow almost inexorably that no biological organism could ever have any mental property. Otherwise normal, adult human animals would be conscious and intelligent. They would presumably be psychologically indistinguishable from us. Our not being animals would then imply that there were two conscious, intelligent beings wherever we thought there was just one. I should share my thoughts with an animal distinct from me. In fact that animal would be a person by any familiar definition: it would be 'a thinking intelligent being, that has reason and reflection, and can consider itself as itself, the same thinking thing, in different times and places' (Locke, 1694/1975, p. 335). I could never know, it seems, whether I was the animal person or the non-animal person: whatever grounds I may have for believing that I am the non-animal would equally be grounds for him to believe that *he* was too.

To avoid this absurd picture, most opponents of animalism deny that human animals think or are conscious.[13] But what could prevent a normal, adult human animal from using its brain to think? The only serious answer would seem to be that it is metaphysically impossible for any biological organism to have mental properties. It follows that what appears to be a thinking animal is really two things: an unthinking animal and a non-animal thinker. This could reasonably be described as a sort of substance dualism. It is not Descartes' dualism of mind and matter, but a dualism of mind and life. Psychological properties would be not only distinct from biological properties, but metaphysically incompatible with them.

None of this reasoning relies on the further claims. It is the basis of the most popular argument for animalism, the 'thinking-animal argument' (Olson, 2003): there is an animal writing these words and thinking about philosophy. But *I* am the being here thinking about philosophy. It follows that I am an animal. If I were not an animal, one of three things would have to be the case: (1) there is no animal here — presumably because there are no ordinary material things at all; (2) that animal is not thinking about philosophy — presumably because it has no mental properties; or (3) I am not the only thinker

---

[13] Or at least most of those who consider the metaphysical implications of their view, rather than just thinking about brain transplants. Good examples are Shoemaker (1984, pp. 92–7; 2011) and Hudson (2007).

here — there is a thinking animal and there is a thinking non-animal, me. The case for animalism lies in the repugnance of these alternatives.

This is an argument for weak animalism. It does nothing to support the further claims incorporated in the stronger versions. We can illustrate this by replacing 'animal' with 'person', 'philosopher', or 'parent'. The resulting argument is sound if the thinking-animal argument is sound. And indeed I am a person, a philosopher, and a parent, even if not essentially or fundamentally, and the argument makes no claim about what it takes for me to persist through time or about my metaphysical nature generally. The reason why no one has ever advanced the 'thinking-philosopher argument' is simply that its conclusion is of no philosophical interest.

So the objections to animalism are aimed at strong animalism, and the main argument in its favour supports only weak animalism. For that matter, the fact that we appear to be animals before the arguments are given supports only weak animalism. This suggests a hopeful thought. What if we could reject the further claims and endorse weak but not strong animalism? We might call the conjunction of weak animalism with the denial of the further claims *new animalism*. (Its conjunction with those claims themselves was strong animalism, and weak animalism is neutral with respect to the further claims.) New animalism is the view that we are animals but not fundamentally or essentially, that we have psychological rather than brute-physical persistence conditions, and that we have essentially those special mental properties that make us people (or rather, there are different versions of new animalism, combining weak animalism with the negation of one or more of the further claims). This is because human animals are not animals fundamentally or essentially, and they have psychological persistence conditions and are essentially people in Locke's sense. The hopeful thought is that new animalism would please everyone. The opponents of animalism will be happy because it lacks the implications they object to. And the animalists will be happy because it avoids the dualism of mind and life. It would have all the virtues of animalism without its drawbacks.

I don't know whether anyone has ever actually accepted new animalism.[14] In any event, I will devote the rest of this paper to examining it.

9. New Animalism

I won't consider all the further claims that distinguish strong from weak animalism, but only the most controversial. I take this to be the claim that animals persist by virtue of some sort of brute-physical continuity. Suppose they persist instead by virtue of psychological continuity, or at any rate that some sort of psychological continuity is sufficient for us to persist. Suppose the animalists are right to say that you are a biological organism, and the Lockeans are right to say that you would go with your transplanted brain or cerebrum[15] (supposing that its continued functioning suffices for psychological continuity). The operation does not move an organ from one animal to another, but moves an organism from one head to another. More precisely, it cuts away the peripheral parts of an organism: not merely the arms and legs, but the torso and the vital organs within it, the skull, and even the brainstem. The surgeons pare down an animal to the size of a naked cerebrum, move it across the room, and finally provide it with new parts to replace the ones it lost. So if your cerebrum were transplanted into my head, the resulting person would be exactly who he thought he was: you with a new body, and not me with a new cerebrum and false memories of someone else's past. The transplant objection would not apply. This is the version of new animalism that comes most readily to mind.

It would imply the falsity of several further claims characteristic of strong animalism. Human animals would not be animals essentially. A detached cerebrum is no more an organism than a detached liver or a severed hand is an organism. It is a mere hunk of living tissue — living in that it consists of living cells. The operation would change you from an organism to a non-organism and back again. Nor could *animal* or *organism* be a fundamental kind. The metaphysical nature

---

[14] Wiggins (1980, pp. 160, 180) and McDowell (1997, p. 237) make dark statements that sound a bit like it, but I am unsure how to interpret them.

[15] Van Inwagen (1990, pp. 169–81) thinks a detached brain *would* be an organism. A cerebrum clearly would not be, and the point of the thought experiment is the same either way, as psychology is realized for the most part in the cerebrum. Whether van Inwagen is right is disputed: see Shewmon (2001).

of human animals would not follow from their being animals; they would have a fundamentally different nature from other animals, or at least from some other animals: oysters, for instance.

Whatever its superficial attractions, this proposal is remarkably unpromising. For one thing, it looks unprincipled. No organism would go with its transplanted liver: remove an animal's liver and that organ simply ceases to be a part of it. (So it seems very strongly to me, anyway. If it's wrong, I know nothing about the persistence conditions of organisms and all bets are off.) Why would an animal go with its cerebrum but not with its liver, or heart, or left hand? If anything, an animal looks *less* likely go with its transplanted cerebrum than with its transplanted liver, as it needs a liver to remain alive but not a cerebrum: a human being can survive for years with a non-functioning cerebrum (as in vegetative cases), but liver failure soon causes death by blood poisoning.

Another problem arises from the fact that a human animal can persist without any psychological continuity. This happens in cases of irreversible vegetative state, as well as in ordinary prenatal development. Each human animal begins its life as an embryo with no psychology at all: even the most basic mental capacities do not appear until after mid-gestation. What does the persistence of a human animal consist in in these cases? What makes it the case that the precognitive foetus or human in a vegetative state continues to exist for months or years, rather than existing only for a moment and then being replaced by another momentary organism? It appears to be some sort of brute-physical continuity: perhaps the continuation of the organism's biological life, as Locke and van Inwagen have proposed. But whatever it is, it ought to hold between a normal, adult human animal and the empty-headed animal that would result from removing its cerebrum. That is, whatever enables a human animal to survive without any psychological continuity as a foetus or a human in a vegetative state ought to enable it to survive the loss of its cerebrum if that organ were transplanted. But then new animalism would imply that in such a case you would be both the recipient of that organ and the empty-headed animal left behind. Since these are clearly distinct, one thing would be numerically identical to two, which is impossible.

New animalists could try to avoid this consequence by saying that psychological and brute-physical continuity each suffice for a human animal to persist only in the absence of the other, and the first trumps the second when both are present. But even if this could be stated precisely,[16] it is hard to believe. It implies that if your cerebrum were removed from your head in good condition and then destroyed, you would die: the organism would be cut down to a cerebrum and shortly thereafter cease to exist, even if the resulting brainless animal remained alive. If your cerebrum were destroyed without being removed from your head, however, the organism could survive in a vegetative state. So you could kill an animal by removing its cerebrum and then destroying it, but not by destroying its cerebrum in its head: a completely baffling result.

Another problem arises when we consider the empty-headed thing left behind after your cerebrum is removed. It may still be alive, able to survive indefinitely without artificial life support. In that case it would be a living organism. Would it not be the organism from which the cerebrum was removed? It would apparently have the same *life*, in Locke's sense of the word (Locke, 1694/1975, pp. 330f.), that the original animal had: the original animal's life-sustaining functions would have continued uninterrupted throughout the operation in the brainless remainder. And if an organism's biological life carries on, we should expect it to continue to be the life of that same organism. How could an organism be outlived by its own life? But according to new animalism it cannot be the original animal, since that being goes with its transplanted cerebrum.

This would make it pretty mysterious what the persistence of an organism could consist in. Our usual judgments about what happens to an organism when parts are cut away would be seriously unreliable. Think about how many human animals there would be in the transplant story. Everyone takes there to be two: the donor and the recipient of the cerebrum. But according to new animalism there are four. One animal — you — starts out full-sized, is then pared down to a cerebrum, and later acquires my non-cerebral parts, thereby regaining its previous size. The empty-headed animal left behind

---

[16] The most obvious suggestion is this: if x is a human organism at time t and y exists at time t^*, $x = y$ *iff* x is (uniquely) psychologically continuous, at t, with y as it is at t^* or no being is psychologically continuous at t^* with x as it is at t and y has the appropriate sort of brute-physical continuity, at t^*, with x as it is at t. But this implies that if your cerebrum were removed from your head and then destroyed, while the brainless animal left behind survived in a vegetative state, you would first go with the cerebrum and then discontinuously 'jump' to the brainless organism, even though there would be neither psychological nor biological continuity across the jump.

when your cerebrum is removed is a second organism. I am a third. Removing my cerebrum to make way for yours reduces me to a naked cerebrum, leaving behind a fourth animal, which is then displaced when the surgeons put you into its empty head.

These organisms would come into being and pass away in curious ways. Think about the empty-headed animal that results from removing your cerebrum. It could not be you, the original animal. But there was only one human animal within your skin before the operation, which according to new animalism went with its transplanted cerebrum. (Nor, presumably, did any non-animal become an animal when your cerebrum was removed: you can't make a non-animal into an animal by removing its cerebrum.) It follows that removing your cerebrum from your head creates a new animal. Removing my cerebrum to make way for yours must create a new animal in the same way. But can you really create an animal merely by cutting away an organ belonging to another animal — one not even necessary for life?

Likewise, putting your cerebrum into my head would have to destroy an organism. The resulting being — which according to new animalism would be you — would not be the animal into which your brain was transplanted — the one that previously had an empty head as a result of my cerebrum's being removed to make way for yours. *You* never had an empty head. Nor are there two human animals within your skin after the operation — or two things that are or once were animals. It follows that the empty-headed animal created by removing my cerebrum must perish when your cerebrum is put into its head. But how could you destroy an animal merely by supplying it with the organ — again, not even a vital organ — that it was missing? It would be metaphysically impossible for a human organism to lose or gain a working cerebrum, even though such losses and gains need not disrupt its life-sustaining functions. Whether this would go equally for other animals, and if so which ones, is anyone's guess.

These consequences are completely at odds with any account of the metaphysical nature of biological organisms that I know of. You may reply that this is because everyone assumes that human animals must persist by virtue of some sort of brute-physical continuity. This goes along with the assumption that human animals have their metaphysical nature by virtue of being animals (or organisms), and not by virtue of their being people or thinking beings or the like — that is, that *animal* is a fundamental kind. And that is precisely what new animalism denies. To free ourselves from these dogmas, we need to unlearn everything we thought we knew about what it takes for human animals to persist and what determines how many there are. If it sounds badly wrong to suppose that there must be four human beings in the transplant story, that is because we are in the grip of a false metaphysics of biological organisms. I am unsure what to make of this reply. What new animalists need to do is provide a metaphysics of organisms that makes sense of it. I don't say that this can't be done. But it will be hard to take new animalism seriously until it has been.

There may be other versions of new animalism with more going for them. Or maybe new animalism is a complete loss and animalists should be strong animalists. Either way, it's important to know that there are different animalisms, with weak animalism as their unifying feature.

Acknowledgments

For comments on this paper and related matters I am grateful to Radim Bělohrad, Stephan Blatti, Alex Moran, Marya Schechtman, and two anonymous referees.

References

Ayers, M. (1990) *Locke*, vol. 2, London: Routledge.

Baker, L.R. (2000) *Persons and Bodies*, Cambridge: Cambridge University Press.

Blatti, S. (2014) Animalism, in Zalta, E. (ed.) *The Stanford Encyclopedia of Philosophy*, [Online], http://plato.stanford.edu/archives/sum2014/entries/animalism/.

Campbell, T. & McMahan, J. (2010) Animalism and the varieties of conjoined twinning, *Theoretical Medicine and Bioethics*, **31**, pp. 285–301.

Carter, W.R. (1989) How to change your mind, *Canadian Journal of Philosophy*, **19**, pp. 1–14.

Hudson, H. (2007) I am not an animal!, in van Inwagen, P. & Zimmerman, D. (eds.) *Persons: Human and Divine*, pp. 216–236, Oxford: Oxford University Press.

Johnston, M. (2007) 'Human beings' revisited: My body is not an animal, in Zimmerman, D. (ed.) *Oxford Studies in Metaphysics 3*, pp. 33–74, Oxford: Oxford University Press.

Lewis, D. (1976) Survival and identity, in Rorty, A. (ed.) *The Identities of Persons*, Berkeley, CA: University of California Press.

Locke, J. (1694/1975) *An Essay Concerning Human Understanding*, Nidditch, P. (ed.), Oxford: Oxford University Press.

Luper, S. (2014) Persimals, *Southern Journal of Philosophy*, **52** (Spindel Supplement), pp. 140–162.

Matthews, G. (1982) Accidental unities, in Schofield, M. & Nussbaum, M. (eds.) *Language and Logos*, Cambridge: Cambridge University Press.

McDowell, J. (1997) Reductionism and the first person, in Dancy, J. (ed.) *Reading Parfit*, pp. 230–250, Oxford: Blackwell.

Noonan, H. (1998) Animalism *versus* Lockeanism: A current controversy, *Philosophical Quarterly*, **48**, pp. 302–318.

Olson, E. (1997) *The Human Animal*, New York: Oxford University Press.

Olson, E. (2003) An argument for animalism, in Martin, R. & Barresi, J. (eds.) *Personal Identity*, New York: Blackwell.

Olson, E. (2007) *What Are We?*, New York: Oxford University Press.

Olson, E. (2015) Personal identity, in Zalta, E. (ed.) *The Stanford Encyclopedia of Philosophy*, [Online], http://plato.stanford.edu/archives/fall2015/entries/identity-personal/.

Parfit, D. (2012) We are not human beings, *Philosophy*, **87**, pp. 5–28.

Shewmon, D.A. (2001) The brain and somatic integration, *Journal of Medicine and Philosophy*, **26**, pp. 457–478.

Shoemaker, S. (1984) Personal identity: A materialist's account, in Shoemaker, S. & Swinburne, R., *Personal Identity*, Oxford: Blackwell.

Shoemaker, S. (2011) On what we are, in Gallagher, S. (ed.) *The Oxford Handbook of the Self*, Oxford: Oxford University Press.

Snowdon, P. (2014) *Persons, Animals, Ourselves*, Oxford: Oxford University Press.

Unger, P. (2000) The survival of the sentient, in Tomberlin, J. (ed.) *Philosophical Perspectives*, **14** (*Action and Freedom*), Malden, MA: Blackwell.

Van Inwagen, P. (1980) Philosophers and the words 'human body', in van Inwagen, P. (ed.) *Time and Cause*, Dordrecht: Reidel.

Van Inwagen, P. (1990) *Material Beings*, Ithaca, NY: Cornell University Press.

Wiggins, D. (1980) *Sameness and Substance*, Cambridge, MA: Harvard University Press.

Harold Noonan

Plenitude, Pluralism, and Neo-Lockean Persons

Abstract: *The paper discusses the arguments for and against animalism and concludes that a pluralist position which rejects animalism and embraces a multiplicity of thinkers is the best option.*

1. Introduction

Recently, in the debate about personal identity, neo-Lockean psychological continuity accounts and animalist biological accounts have been main contenders. Animalism may be understood as the weak thesis that we (human persons)[1] are (predicatively) animals. But in the sense in which it is opposed to neo-Lockeanism it is the stronger thesis that this is so *and* that psychology is irrelevant to the persistence conditions of (the kind of) animals (we are).[2] This is 'the Biological View' of Eric Olson (1997). Some neo-Lockeans are animalists in the weak sense. Thus Shoemaker's recently expressed view (2010; see also Shoemaker, forthcoming) is a form of weak animalism. He holds that I am (predicatively) an animal in the sense (which must be a good one) in which dogs are. Dogs are *not* entirely biologically individuated entities, he holds, since Fido goes where his (upper) brain and resultant psychology goes.

We will look at Shoemaker's view later, but for now what I wish to emphasize is merely that the debates I am concerned with are those

Correspondence:
Email: harold.noonan@nottingham.ac.uk

---

[1] I.e. persons related to human beings as I am related to the human being sitting here.

[2] Note (i) that this does not entail that we are essentially or fundamentally (biologically individuated) human beings and (ii) that this thesis is formulated indexically (in fact, animalism has no non-indexical formulation).

Journal of Consciousness Studies, **22**, No. 11–12, 2015, pp. 108–31

between neo-Lockeans and strong animalists. So when I write 'animal' I shall mean 'biologically individuated animal'.

These debates interweave with more general debates about the nature of constitution. In his most recent book, Olson (2007) identifies a generic view he calls 'constitutionalism' and a more specific view about persons he calls 'the constitution view'.

Minimally, Olson's constitutionalism is the view that two things can be made of the same matter at a time. His constitution view of persons is that things so related may be a person (thought of as something whose persistence conditions are psychological) and an animal (whose persistence conditions are entirely biological).

As Olson's terminology is intended to suggest, generic constitutionalism and the constitution view of person go naturally together. Indeed, he suggests that they stand or fall together. I agree, I take them as a package deal and defend both.

But begin by jettisoning Olson's terminology. As Shoemaker noted forty-five years ago (1970b), it is not good English to describe the symmetrical relation of matter-sharing, such as holds, according to the psychological continuity theorist, between a person and a biologically individuated animal, or again, as Shoemaker notes, between a statue a temporarily coincident *piece* (contrast: portion or quantity) of bronze, as 'constitution'. It is increasingly common to describe the defender of constitutionalism as a pluralist, and I shall. Equally, it is common to describe what Olson calls the constitution view as the neo-Lockean psychological continuity account. So I will be defending pluralism in general and the neo-Lockean psychological continuity account in particular.

So I align myself with the views of Lewis (1976), Parfit (1971), and Shoemaker. But I am not wholly in agreement with the latter two, and I proceed in a way that is neutral with respect to the ontological commitments of Lewis to temporal parts and many worlds. Nonetheless, I think what I have to say is entirely Lewisian in spirit.

However, pluralism comes in two forms, strong and weak. Shoemaker and Parfit are examples of strong pluralists. They hold that even all-time material coincidence is not enough for identity: an all-time coincident statue (standardly called Goliath in the literature following Allan Gibbard, 1975) and lump of clay (Lumpl) are numerically distinct. This is because they differ modally: the lump could be rolled into a ball without being destroyed, not so the statue. Weak pluralists (like Lewis, 1986) hold only that numerically distinct things can be *sometime* materially coincident. They explain away the apparent modal difference in Gibbard's example as merely apparent and due to the inconstancy of modal predication, the capacity of modal predicates to shift in reference according to the wider linguistic context in which they are embedded. I accept only weak pluralism.

I reject strong pluralism because it entails that two wholly material things, even if not ever coincident, may differ *macrophysically* in their general modal, dispositional, and counterfactual properties, though *microphysically* indistinguishable in all general respects — non-relational and relational, past and future as well as present, even modal and dispositional. If Goliath and Lumpl are distinct there may be a distant twin of Goliath, Goliath*, permanently coincident with a twin of Lumpl, Lumpl*, on a twin Earth in a symmetrical universe (it would be desperate for a strong pluralist to attempt to defend his position by rejecting the possibility of symmetry). Goliath and Lumpl*, according to the strong pluralist, differ in general modal and dispositional respects just as Goliath and Lumpl do, though alike at the microphysical level in all general respects, including modal and dispositional respects. This is akin to supposing that two in all respects microphysically indistinguishable seeds from the same type of plant, which are never planted, would have developed differently if they had been planted. To believe in such macrophysical dispositional differences in the absence of any microphysical difference at all is to believe in magic. But the strong pluralist cannot explain what is objectionable about it.

Weak pluralism, by contrast, is very plausible. It seems as obvious as anything in philosophy that temporary matter-sharing by numerically distinct things is a possibility. In the case of artefacts this is because they are typically made from pre-existent material and can undergo repair and replacement of parts later. Nevertheless, some philosophers reject even weak pluralism. Typically these philosophers also deny the existence of the complex material things which are the weak pluralist's candidates for temporary matter-sharing. One of the most prominent deniers is van Inwagen (1990), who denies the existence of any complex non-living material things. In the next section I will take the time to defend weak pluralism by criticizing van Inwagen's argument for this denial. Of course, other arguments remain, but it may be of interest to expose the weakness of one of the most well-known, though the noted commonsensical status of weak pluralism should make us suspicious of any arguments against it from the start.[3]

After defending weak pluralism I turn next to the defence of the neo-Lockean view. Two arguments for, and one against, have been the focus of most debate. In support there is the argument from the so-called 'transplant intuition' and the argument from what has been called 'the remnant person problem'. I defend these arguments. Against neo-Lockeanism there is the variously-called 'thinking animal', 'too many minds', or 'too many thinkers' objection, most vigorously explored by Olson. This has ontological, epistemic, and semantic aspects. I shall argue that once these aspects are distinguished the argument can be disarmed.

I think the pluralist, true to his name, should regard the multiplicity as unobjectionable and view the situation as similar to how, with Lewis (1976) and Robinson (1985), I wish to view the situation before the fission in the familiar thought experiment.

2. Pluralism Defended

I start by criticizing van Inwagen's argument against the existence of non-living complex material things. As we shall see, although this argument does not succeed, it makes it clear that a believer in complex material objects must accept that there are many more than one might at first think, that is, that a plenitudinous ontology of complex material things is implicit in ordinary thought.

Van Inwagen's argument, as he presents it, goes as follows. If I shake hands with someone nothing new comes into existence in consequence of our brief contact. If we become momentarily paralysed as we shake still nothing new comes into existence. The same is true if we are glued or tied together, or even if our flesh is melted so that no boundary is discernible between us. In all these cases of contact, or

---

3 Opponents of weak pluralism like van Inwagen, who deny the existence of any complex non-living material things, or the still more extreme opponents (mereological nihilists) who deny the existence of any complex material things at all, are in the same position as the sceptic who denies that even if things are, in fact, as we believe they are we do not *know* that they are. We do not have to listen to the sceptics and the opponents of weak pluralism unless they provide arguments, and their arguments have to have premises which are as initially attractive as the propositions they are attacking. It is not ruled out *a priori* that there can be such arguments, which is to say that our everyday view involves philosophically interesting tensions, but the arguments need to be seen and scrutinized.

various kinds of bonding, of living organisms, nothing new is brought into existence as a result of our coming to be so related.

But if there are any complex non-living things then in some of these cases novel complex things *would* come into being as a result of our coming to be related in the way described. For the relations just identified include all the kinds of causal and spatial relations which are created between bits of wood, for example, when, as we would ordinarily say, a chair is made. And van Inwagen states, 'whether certain things... compose a larger object does not depend on anything besides the spatial and causal relations they bear to one another. For example, nothing outside the region of space containing some bricks is relevant to the question whether there is anything they compose; and, in particular, the attitudes and interests of any persons are irrelevant' (van Inwagen, 1990, p. 12) (this is van Inwagen's tenth numbered constraint on his theorizing).

You may say that it could still be that you and I, however bonded, do not compose a third object, whilst the bits of wood glued together do, because it matters for whether composition takes place not only what relations obtain between the putative parts, but also what *kind* of thing they are — bonding relations sufficient for composition when holding between things of one kind, e.g. bits of wood, may not suffice for composition when holding between things of other kinds, e.g. people. But this rejoinder would be deeply implausible, van Inwagen would say, for as he asks, 'if the operation *fastening* has the power to turn inanimate objects into the parts of a whole, why doesn't it have the same power with respect to living organisms?' (*ibid.*, p. 68). The plausible thought behind the rhetorical question here is that if you can make an artefact out of inanimate components of a certain type, you can make an artefact of that same kind out of animate components, or inanimate components of any other type, so long as they are capable of performing the right functional job.[4]

But if a new thing is *not* brought into existence when bits of wood are bonded together in the sort of way we describe as 'making a chair', there never have been any chairs, and if there never have been

---

[4] These theses of van Inwagen's commit him to the possibility of making composite things out of living organisms, by combining them in the way simples are combined when they compose an organism. But this is consistent with van Inwagen's main claim that there are only simples and living organisms, and his rejection of arbitrary undetatched parts.

any chairs, there never have been any complex non-living material objects at all.

This is van Inwagen's argument. But it is easy to resist. Van Inwagen thinks that nothing new comes into existence when you and I are bonded together because 'it is pretty clear that one cannot bring a composite object into existence by bonding... human beings — or... living things of any sort — to each other' (*ibid.*, p. 62). But it is not pretty clear at all. Van Inwagen adds in a rhetorical endnote, 'Try to imagine bringing something into existence by gluing hamsters or snakes together' (*ibid.*, p. 287).

However, nothing is easier. Van Inwagen himself imagines at one point weaving a very long, thin, snake into a hammock. Imagine instead gluing together two or more shortish, flexible snakes to make a whip. If there are any non-living complex material things at all we can do this — and it is the *conclusion* of van Inwagen's argument, not one of its premises, that there are not. But if something new comes into existence when some snakes are bonded together the same must be true when human beings are bonded together in the same way.

So van Inwagen's argument for the non-existence of non-living complex material objects — which is, when stripped of its surrounding paraphernalia, just the argument outlined — is unconvincing.[5]

However, it appeals to two plausible general principles. These are, to repeat, that whether certain things compose a larger object does not depend on anything besides the spatial and causal relations they bear to one another... in particular, the attitudes and interests of any persons are irrelevant (van Inwagen, 1990, p. 12), and that, if you can make something out of inanimate components of a certain type, you can make a thing of that kind out of animate components, or inanimate components of any other type, so long as they are capable of performing the right functional job.

I think that these principles are implicit in our everyday thought. But if we take them seriously we must either deny, with van Inwagen, the existence of such everyday things as chairs, or acknowledge the existence of many more complex material things than we ordinarily

---

[5] Van Inwagen has another argument (1981) which assumes the rejection of DAUP, the Doctrine of Arbitrary Undetached Parts, and appeals to other assumptions too. But its assumptions have little initial plausibility, certainly less than the initial plausibility of the proposition that there are indeed chairs.

speak of. I think that the right conclusion is that such a plenitudinous ontology is implicit in our ordinary thought.

To see how far down this path we can be led consider some other examples.[6] If there are chairs there are children's toys, and if so I can bring such an object, say, a wooden brick house, into existence merely by bringing some smaller objects into contact. Van Inwagen would argue that I cannot since creating the relevant causal and spatial relations between living things cannot bring anything new into existence. Reversing his reasoning, but retaining his two general principles, we must conclude that whenever two things of any kind or kinds, living or non-living, come into contact, whether or not as a result of intentional activity, in such a way as to create the appropriate internal causal and spatial relations between them, then some new complex material object comes into existence.

Again, it is evidently a part of ordinary thought that there are many complex wholes composed of parts that are not in contact. Rock gardens, bird cages consisting of magnetically suspended and spatially separated bits of wire, space stations with separated living and ablution blocks, the USA — all these consist of disconnected parts. And, of course, as van Inwagen notes, 'it is undoubtedly true that, if there are any composite material objects at all, they are composed of elementary particles and elementary particles that compose a given material object are not in contact' (van Inwagen, 1990, p. 34). Appealing to van Inwagen's general principles, we must suppose that smaller things of many kinds, whether animate or inanimate, can compose wholes whether or not they are in contact and whether or not the relations they stand in are a creation of intentional activity.

It does not follow that whenever there are distinct material objects there is a complex object they compose, i.e. Universalism does not follow.[7] But given the plenitudinous ontology now argued to be implicit in everyday thought it is hard to see a reason to object. But Universalism entails (weak) pluralism when taken together with the

---

[6] Recall also that it is certainly no part of ordinary thought that there can be no artefacts apart from those created by human beings; the notion of an 'alien artefact' is an easy one to grasp.

[7] I see no *deductive* route from, for example, the proposition that children can create toy houses by arranging wooden bricks, together with the two general principles identified in van Inwagen's argument, to the conclusion that something new comes into existence when two people shake hands, or that something existed all along of which they were parts.

implication of the arguments above that whenever two things (e.g. snakes or bricks) come into the appropriate spatial and causal relations something *new*, of which they are parts, comes into existence.

However, as I have already said, weak pluralism does not really need to be argued for; at most it needs to be defended against arguments, like van Inwagen's, that attack its commonsensical presuppositions. That is what I have attempted in this section.

3. The Psychological Continuity
Account of Personal Identity

Pluralists can endorse a psychological continuity account of personal identity and accept the possibility of numerically distinct but (temporarily) coincident persons and biologically individuated animals. But why should they?

The attractiveness of neo-Lockeanism derives from the puzzle cases which seem to make it evident that my history is only contingently coincident with that of a biologically individuated animal.

The standard puzzle case is Shoemaker's case of Brown and Brownson. In this the brain, or just the cerebrum, the upper brain (from now on I shall just say 'brain'), of Brown is transplanted into the skull of Robinson. Let us suppose that the result is a completely healthy being, Brownson, with Robinson's body but in character, memories, and personality indistinguishable from Brown, and this not as a consequence of some freak accident but because of his possession of Brown's brain. Now who is this person?

Most philosophers have found it difficult to deny that Brownson is Brown. As Parfit puts it, they have found it hard to deny that 'receiving a new skull and a new body is just the limiting case of receiving a new heart, new lungs and so on' (Parfit, 1984, p. 253). This belief is the so-called 'transplant intuition'. The first argument for neo-Lockeanism and against animalism is that only the former accords with it.

The second argument for neo-Lockeanism I want to discuss is that it does not face what has come to be called 'the remnant person problem'.

If transplantation of a brain is possible so is the brain-in-a-vat scenario, in which the brain is taken out of a skull and preserved in a vat of nutrients as an intermediate stage. It seems undeniable that if appropriately stimulated such a brain would support a mental life; it would be, or be coincident with, a person.

The neo-Lockean can apparently take this in his stride. The animalist has problems. It can hardly be denied that there is a person in the vat. And, anyway, animalists, who do not deny the existence of (non-human) persons other than animals, would have no business doing so. But there is no animal present, they say. So the animalist must say that when the brain is envatted a conscious being is present who (which?) is not an animal, but came into existence at the time of envatting, or existed beforehand, in either a non-conscious or conscious state (located in a proper part of the conscious animal). Similarly, he must say that when the brain is then transplanted the conscious being present in the vat either ceases to exist or comes to be partly coincident in location with a human animal who has acquired a new brain, but not a new identity, and in doing so either remains conscious or ceases to be conscious.

So the extended process first creates and then destroys a conscious being, or renders a previously non-conscious being conscious, later reducing it to non-consciousness again. Or else, either before being envatted or after transplantation, or both, there are two conscious beings present, one identical with or coincident with a proper part of the other — which is an alternative the animalist must avoid at all costs on pain of losing his best argument against the neo-Lockean, the 'too many thinkers' objection.

Mark Johnston (2007) has identified the problems the animalist has with this scenario, which have been dubbed by Olson (forthcoming) the creation and destruction problems. Animalism requires that you can *create* a person, or at least bring to personal consciousness a non-conscious being, simply by removing a sustaining head and torso. Again, it requires that you can *destroy* a person, or at least reduce one to non-consciousness, simply by adding a sustaining head and torso.

The neo-Lockean apparently faces no such difficulties. He can just say that when the brain is envatted, it is the person who is transferred into the vat, severely mutilated, but still conscious. No other conscious being need be supposed present and no conscious being need be supposed to have ceased to exist. On subsequent rehousing of the brain into the new cranium the person goes where it goes and acquires a new set of kidneys, etc. No conscious being ceases to exist as a result or becomes non-conscious.

In defence of animalism Eric Olson has responded to the transplant intuition by pointing out that in real life where there is psychological continuity there is the same animal. So he says that it is hardly surprising that when we contemplate the brain transplant case we mistakenly conclude on the basis of what is in real life conclusive evidence that the brain recipient is the brain donor, even though he is not, since he is not the same animal.

I think this response unpersuasive for the same reasons as Parfit (2012). In this case standardly used criteria come apart. Yet we find ourselves strongly favouring one rather than the other. This is what needs explaining. A fingerprint criterion of personal identity cannot be defended as giving the right result in thought experiments in which its deliverances come apart from those of the psychological continuity and brain-identity criteria on the ground that in real life cases they coincide.

More interesting is Olson's second response to the transplant intuition, which is to try to explain it away on the basis of Parfit's (1971) thesis that identity is not what matters in survival. The recipient, he says, has what matters in the survival of the brain donor. Therefore the donor has the same reason to care about the welfare of the recipient as you have to care about your own welfare. It is the recipient who should be held morally responsible for the donor's actions and it is the recipient rather than the surviving donor (even if provided with a replacement brain) who should be regarded as for all practical matter the same person. So we do believe mistakenly that the recipient is the donor. This is because we recognize that he is his *Parfitian* survivor (the person who has what matters in his survival) and we mistakenly believe that identity is what matters.

Of course, this explanation is only available if Parfit's conjunctive thesis *that identity is not what matters in survival, but we believe that it is* is correct. But this is far from clear, and it is additionally not clear whether an animalist can endorse Parfit's argument for his thesis.

What Parfit means by his slogan is we do not have a non-derivative concern for our own future existence and well-being (though we believe we do). It is this, if anything, that the argument from fission establishes. The best formulation of the argument goes as follows. Looking forward to an imminent future in which my cerebral hemispheres will be divided and transplanted, so that two future people will be psychologically continuous with me as I am now, I should not think that I have anything to lose that I would preserve if the division were to be prevented by the botching of the transfer of one hemisphere, say the right one. But the correct description of the latter, 'botched', fission is that I continue to exist, albeit with only one hemisphere, and of the former, the successful division, that I cease to exist and two new people, numerically non-identical with me, come into existence. This is how we must describe the cases using the language of identity. So if my continued existence matters to me, I do have something to lose in a successful fission and should reject it if given a choice between these options. So my continued existence does not matter to me.

This argument rests on two claims. The first is that accepting the description of fission as my ceasing to exist, and the description of the 'botched' fission as my continuing to exist, albeit light a cerebral hemisphere, I should, given what I care about, regard myself as having nothing to lose by fissioning. The opposing opinion is nicely expressed by van Inwagen: 'Suppose I were given a choice between being totally destroyed a year from now and being partitioned now. Then I think I would choose to be destroyed in a year' (van Inwagen, 1990, p. 212). Jerome Shaffer expresses the same sentiment: 'psychological continuity is important where there is identity, but not otherwise... returning to our case of the man who splits, we would... say that since identity is not preserved even though psychological continuity is preserved, the man should feel quite differently about it from the way he should feel about single transplantation' (Shaffer, 1977, p. 157).

So the first claim on which Parfit's argument rests is contestable.

The second claim on which it rests, also contestable, is that someone ceases to exist in the fission. An alternative description of the case is that it involves multiple occupancy: there are two conscious beings, coincident before the fission, who continue to exist afterwards and to remain conscious, but are then no longer coincident. Parfit's description of the case requires that one accept a 'best candidate' or 'no rival candidate' account of personal identity according to which whether I continue to exist depends on whether there is anyone *uniquely* best qualified to count as me at the later time. (As will be the case if the fission is 'botched' and will not be if it is successful.) This is a highly contentious form of account. It conflicts with the principle formulated by Bernard Williams that whether a later individual is identical with an earlier one can depend only on facts about them and their relationship; no facts about any other individual can be relevant to whether they are one. This has been called the Only x and y Principle (Noonan, 2003). More immediately relevant, it is not at all obvious that an animalist should endorse a best candidate or no rival candidate of personal identity. I have referred to van Inwagen's fundamental tenth constraint on his theorizing. Rejection of such accounts goes with acceptance of this. Van Inwagen writes:

A similar point [i.e. to his tenth constraint]... applies to identity across time. If object A is at place x at t1, and if object B is at place y at t2, then nothing besides the causal processes or chains of events that connect what is going on at x at t1 with what is going on at y at t2 is relevant to the question whether A and B are the same. Closest continuer and best candidate theories of identity across time provide examples of theories that violate this principle. (van Inwagen, 1990, p. 12)

Eric Olson writes of the 'non-branching' or *Uniqueness Requirement* (that you survive only if you stand in some relation to exactly one future or past being): 'It is a startling claim... but no one accepts the Uniqueness Requirement because it sound right. The transplant intuition has led us into a quandary; and the Uniqueness Requirement is seen as the best way out; it is a theoretical necessity' (Olson, 1997, p. 49). However, if the animalist is to endorse the argument for the thesis that identity is not what matters in survival so he can call on it to explain away the seeming evidence of the transplant intuition, he needs to endorse a best candidate or no rival candidate account of fission and accept the Uniqueness Requirement.

The transplant intuition thus seems to remain a very strong argument for neo-Lockeanism.

The same is true, I think, of the remnant person problem.

The animalist can say nothing about this which is not wholly implausible or commits him to (what he views as) the awful prospect of 'too many minds'. Focus just on the initial envatting of the brain. The animalist says that the original person (= animal) is not involved; no animal ends up in a vat. So either some new conscious being is created, or some pre-existing non-conscious being is rendered conscious by the process, or some conscious being other than the original person (= animal) was already present — too many minds.

The most the animalist can hope to defend is the claim that the remnant person problem is a problem for anyone — even the neo-Lockean.

According to the neo-Lockean, before the procedure begins the person is not a living organism, but is coincident with, that is, shares its matter with, one. After the envatting the person is not a brain, but similarly shares its matter with a brain.

Olson argues that this merely relocates the remnant person problem. 'Although removing your brain from your head would not give it consciousness or the power to think, it would give it the power to constitute a conscious, thinking thing. Your brain is now prevented from constituting a thinker by its fleshy surroundings and putting it back where it belongs after its removal would prevent it from doing so once more... And that seems absurd' (Olson, forthcoming).[8]

He goes on to say that any explanation of why a brain could *constitute* a thinking thing when isolated but not in its natural habitat would serve equally well as an explanation of why a brain could think when isolated but not embodied.

But this is not so. The fact that the neo-Lockean needs to appeal to in order to explain why a brain can be composed of the same matter as a thinking thing when isolated but not embodied is merely the fact that a person can survive mutilation — and thus come to be composed of the same matter as something which was previously one of its proper parts — and remain conscious. If you cut off my foot I do not cease to exist or to be conscious. But I come to be composed of the same matter as, i.e. to be coincident with, something that I was not coincident with before — something that was previously merely a proper part of the two-footed animal I was then coincident with and was, therefore, just because of its fleshly surroundings, not then an animal or conscious being or composed of exactly the same matter as any animal or conscious being. The removal of the brain for the neo-Lockean is merely a more extreme mutilation. What happens is just that a continuously conscious being is reduced in size. This is what the animalist cannot say happens since he cannot say that any conscious being *persists* through the mutilation. Compare the case of the cat on the mat. Tibbles is sitting on the mat. Tib is a proper part of Tibbles (all of Tibbles except its tail = its tail-complement). It is not a cat. Tibbles' tail is amputated. Tibbles does not cease to exist. But now Tib coincides with Tibbles. We are not obliged to say either that Tibbles has ceased to exist and been replaced by a new cat, or that Tibbles has ceased to exist and Tib has become a cat, or even that Tib is now (predicatively) a cat as well as Tibbles — for we can say that whether something is a cat depends on its history as well as its current state. For the neo-Lockean what happens to you when you are reduced to the size of a brain-in-a-vat is logically analogous to what happens to Tibbles when his tail is amputated.

Of course, this leads us on to the problem of too many thinkers. The person coincides with a biologically individuated animal beforehand

---

[8]   Of course, Olson is here using 'constitute' in the minimal symmetrical sense (of which Shoemaker disapproves) of 'be composed of the same matter as'.

and with a brain and perhaps a mutilated biologically individuated animal as well afterwards. Granted that these coincident entities are not (predicatively) persons (just as Tib is not a cat), the questions still remain. Are there two thinkers before or is the animal not a thinker at all? And are there two/three thinkers afterwards?

4. The Too Many Thinkers Objection

The objection, briefly, is that it seems undeniable that normal healthy adult human animals are thinkers. But so, by definition, are persons. However, according to the neo-Lockean, persons are not (biologically individuated) animals. So the neo-Lockean account entails the existence of too many thinkers. Moreover, it creates an irresoluble epistemic problem. How do I know I am the person and not the animal thinking falsely that it is a person? Finally, if normal healthy human animals are thinkers, they are persons, since their thoughts are sufficiently sophisticated, so the neo-Lockean's attempt to identify the persistence conditions of persons collapses, since he must acknowledge the existence of different kinds of person with different persistence conditions.

The too many thinkers problem has various aspects. The first is ontological. The objection is that neo-Lockeanism entails an objectionable multiplicity of coincident thinking things. I think that the neo-Lockean can just respond by saying the multiplicity is not objectionable. Numerically distinct things may coincide, at least temporarily, and hence share many properties. Where the coincident statue and piece of clay is there are two things of the same shape, size, weight, and colour, and where the person and animal are there are two things of the same shape, size, weight, and colour. He must admit that it is odd to say these things. But he can insist that they are true anyway. So the claim that it is *odd* to say that there are two subjects of psychological states, two subjects of pain, for example, where I am, should cut no ice with him.

It is important to keep in mind that persons are not the only subjects of psychological states. So are dogs. Now the transplant intuition is just as powerful as an argument that brain transfer is identity-preserving if we suppose the experiment carried out on dogs instead of human beings. So the neo-Lockean must say — as Shoemaker (2010, and forthcoming) does — that even before the transplant there are two coincident, dog-shaped and dog-sized entities present, one of which goes where the brain goes. This entity, the one that goes with the brain transplant, is a subject of psychological states. Why is the other, which shares so many of its features, not? Sometime in the future, perhaps many dog-years away, these coinciding entities will go their separate ways when the transplant is done. But why is it not true to say *now* that there are two perceiving, desiring, and believing entities present, just as there are, the pluralist neo-Lockean must say, two digesting, breathing, running entities? How can this merely future difference make such a difference *now* in the case of the psychological, but not the non-psychological, predications?

If we think about the case of non-human animals, I think it is obvious that the too many thinkers problem provides no reason to reject neo-Lockeanism unless it provides a reason to reject pluralism in general.

But humans are merely psychologically more sophisticated than dogs, not entities of a completely different ontological category. So the neo-Lockean should feel no more pressure to deny the evident truth that human animals are the subjects of psychological states than to deny that (the animals coincident with) dogs are. He can simply say of the situation in which Mr Brown is going to undergo a transplant exactly what he can say of the situation in which this is true of Fido. Each is currently coincident with an entity with which it currently shares, along with much else, its psychology.

But persons have first-personal thoughts and so we come to the other aspects of the too many thinkers problem. How do I know I am the person and not the animal mistakenly thinking it is a person? Fido does not face this problem.

Now perhaps all persons and certainly only persons are objects of first-person reference. Objects of first-person reference are a sub-class of persons (anything which can think of itself as 'I', that is, is a 'thinking intelligent being with reason and reflection which can think of itself as itself, the same thinking being' (Locke), is a person). Whether or not analytic this is obviously true. So we can define the philosophical topic of personal identity, as it has been discussed since Locke, without using the word 'person'. We need three concepts: first, the concept of a word whose meaning is that of the first-person pronoun, secondly the concept of a token utterance, and thirdly the concept of reference. The class of interest is the class of entities that are the referents of token utterances of first-person pronouns, the class of *selves*, we may say (perhaps, as the word is ordinarily used, there are persons that are not selves, but they are not the focus of the philosophical debate). The philosophical question about the persistence conditions of persons over time is a question about some of the necessary conditions of membership in this class — of selfhood.

Now the neo-Lockean position is that all persons (along with creatures of less complexity) have psychological persistence conditions. So, since it is obviously true that all objects of first-person reference are persons, this entails that all objects of first-person reference have psychological persistence conditions. But some normal adult human animals do not, as everyone agrees. So they are not objects of first-person reference according to the neo-Lockean. But all normal adult human animals are *thinkers* of true first-person thoughts. Or so I have effectively just argued, against e.g. Shoemaker, that the neo-Lockean must accept, on pain of making an unacceptable divide between Fido and Mr Brown, or denying that the biologically individuated animal coincident with Fido shares (albeit temporarily) his psychology. So some normal adult human animals are thinkers of true first-person thoughts of which they are not the objects, i.e. which are not thoughts about them, but about the psychological continuers with which they coincide. They are *thinkers* of first-person thoughts, but not *objects* of first-person reference. This is what the neo-Lockean must say on pain of denying that human animals are subjects of psychological states at all.

But how can a normal adult human being, capable of first-personal thought, be incapable of referring to itself in the first person in thinking such a thought, since the currently psychologically indistinguishable psychological continuer is? How can it lack this capacity?

To ask this is to mistake the commitment of neo-Lockeanism. The claim is just that the following is a *de dicto* necessary truth: 'All objects of first-person reference are psychological continuers.'

It does not follow that if human animal A is not a psychological continuer it is essentially or necessarily something whose first-person thoughts are not about itself. No claim of *de re* necessity follows (though many, unlike me, with natural essentialist intuitions, including many neo-Lockeans, will find it plausible, particularly strong pluralists). To be a psychological continuer is to have a certain history and A could have had a different history. So A is not essentially something whose first-person thoughts are not about itself; it is just something whose first-person thoughts are not, in fact, about itself.

The worry may be re-expressed. According to the neo-Lockean, something that is not a psychological continuer cannot be an object of its own first-personal thoughts. It cannot think that it itself is F, by

thinking a thought it can correctly express in the words 'I am F', even
if it can think the thought. But why should this be?

However, the explanation is simple. To be a psychological continuer
is to have a certain kind of history. It is like being a once and future
king. But whether something has psychological states now and how
sophisticated they are, if so, cannot depend on its indefinitely distant
past or future. So no matter how sophisticated a creature's current
thoughts, they cannot guarantee that it is a psychological continuer.
Consequently, *if* the neo-Lockean thesis that all objects of first-person
reference are psychological continuers is correct, they cannot ensure
that it is an object of its own current first-personal thoughts.

So there is no epistemic problem for neo-Lockeanism. There is no
possibility that I am not the object of self-reference but the animal
mistakenly thinking that it is the object of self-reference. Since I am
thinking that I am an object of self-reference, the animal is thinking
the thought it would express by saying 'I am an object of self-
reference', but in doing so it is not thinking about itself, but about me.

But there is a final worry. Given that I and the human animal temporarily coincident with me are psychologically indistinguishable at
present, it must be that whatever I think, the animal thinks the same.
So the animal must think that it is an object of self-reference, since I
do, so it must be mistaken.

The trouble with the argument is that it ignores an ambiguity in
'thinking the same'. The worry is that I and the animal must be
psychologically indistinguishable, so we must be thinking the same
thoughts, so the animal must be thinking that it is an object of self-
reference if I am.

But if you and I both pronounce the *cogito*, in one sense we think
the same thought, in another sense not. In one sense two thinkers think
the same thoughts only if they think of the same things and think of
them in exactly the same way. In this sense — we may call it the
Fregean sense — I and the animal are thinking exactly the same
thoughts. Each of us is thinking of me in a first-person way and
neither of us is thinking of the animal. So the animal is not thinking of
itself in a first-person way (though, of course, its thought 'I am
thinking about myself in the first-person way' is true).

So the answer to the question 'why is the animal not thinking of
itself since I, coincident with it, am?' is that this must be so given that
we are psychologically indistinguishable in *this* respect: we are
thinking the same Fregean thoughts.

Hence the question facing the neo-Lockean who is not willing, with Shoemaker, to deny that human animals think is not 'How can the animal and I *differ* in what we think, given our coincidence?', but why, given our numerical distinctness, we are cognitively identical, thinkers of the same Fregean thoughts?

But it is not difficult for the neo-Lockean to answer this, given his physicalist stance. I and the animal may be completely micro-physically indistinguishable except in irrelevant long-distant past and future respects; it would be a mystery if we were not so cognitively identical, were thinking about different things, or thinking of them in different ways.

It is often said that the meaning of 'I' can be explained by saying 'it is the word each one uses to speak of himself'. But no word's meaning can be such that any user of it is *guaranteed* to make singular reference to himself when he uses it. A user of 'I' refers to himself if he makes it true that he satisfies the open sentence 'x refers to x' — something the slayer of Laius will do if he begins a sentence 'The slayer of Laius...', whether or not he knows he is the slayer of Laius. But his use of 'I' cannot guarantee that he does refer to himself. The illusion of such guaranteed self-reference is what lies behind the thought that the epistemic and semantic aspects of the too many thinkers problem are objections to neo-Lockeanism.

To see that a guaranteed self-reference for 'I' is an illusion consider the familiar fission case and compare it with the (whole) brain transplant case. In the fission case when the two hemispheres are transplanted, according to the 'no rival candidate' or 'best candidate' neo-Lockean accounts of Shoemaker (1970a) and Parfit (1971), the original person ceases to exist and two new persons come into existence. If we reject these accounts because of their conflict with the Only x and y Principle we must, with Lewis (1976), describe fission as multiple occupancy. Before the fission two persons, two conscious beings, Lefty and Righty, are coincident. They cease to be coincident with the fission, but continue to exist and continue to be conscious. On the neo-Lockean view the whole brain transplant should be understood similarly. Before the transplant two conscious beings are coincident. They cease to be coincident with the transplant, but continue to exist, though only one continues to be conscious. The difference between the cases is just that fission is entirely symmetrical.

Now in the fission cases, if described as cases of multiple occupancy, utterances of 'I' before the transplant are not guaranteed a determinate singular reference. What is Lefty referring to when says (simultaneously with Righty) 'I am hungry'? He cannot be speaking of himself alone since he has no way of uniquely identifying himself — he is a person, hence a psychological continuer, thinking the thought 'I am hungry', but so is Righty. Either he fails to refer or, as Lewis (1976) says, he thinks a plural thought, with the content 'We both...' or 'At least one of us...'. If he does not know what is going to happen most plausibly his thought has the content (to use Lewis's language now) 'the maximal sum of pairwise R-related person-stages tokening this thought...', in which case he fails to refer since there are two such maximal sums.[9] The case is essentially no different from the following: I use 'Tom', as I think, to refer to one of my acquaintances; in fact two identical twins, Dick and Harry, have been fooling me.[10] Hence, if it is known that fission is going to take place there is no intelligible doubt Lefty can express by uttering 'I wonder whether I am Righty or Lefty?'. Lefty faces no epistemic problem.

In the whole brain transplant case, by contrast with the fission case, there is an asymmetry. There is only one maximal sum of R-related stages, only one psychological continuer. So the person, the maximal sum, *can* determinately refer pre-transplant to himself using 'I'. But the animal cannot. It can only refer to the person. (It can, of course, determinately refer to itself using the description 'the animal' and when it does so the person also refers to the animal.) In the fission case, if described consistently with the Only x and y Principle, neither conscious being who pre-exists the fission and (literally) survives it succeeds in making a singular reference to itself at all. In the

---

9   A single token of 'I' may be produced by two speakers with differing intentions so that two singular references take place. Compare the case (Johnston, 2006) in which two people with different intentions together create and put in place the ambiguous road sign 'Begin Highway' — one intending it as the name of the highway ('the (Menachem) Begin Highway') and the other as an instruction ('Start highway'). This makes sense because we can imagine the sign constructed and erected by a single person (Mr Janus) who has both intentions (and gets paid twice). In the fission case, however, the two people do not have two different reference-determining intentions which a single person could have simultaneously had.

10   I am here accepting Lewis's view that 'I' uttered pre-fission when fission is not being envisaged has the status of an improper description. It would serve my purpose equally well to regard it as determinately referring to the current shared stage. What I deny is that in this situation the persisting person Lefty is successfully referring to Lefty alone and the persisting person Righty is simultaneously referring to Righty alone. This has been urged by Saunders and Wallace (2008a,b) and contended by Tappenden (2008; 2010). I am with Tappenden.

transplant case both conscious beings make singular references with 'I', but they do not make singular references to *distinct* individuals. Hence only the person, the maximal sum of pairwise R-related person-stages, makes a singular reference to himself. On the opposing view, which underpins the animalist's objection to neo-Lockeanism, the use of 'I' guarantees a reference, but if so Lefty and Righty determinately refer in the fission case, thought of as involving multiple occupancy, and Lefty is asking a good question if he asks 'Will I be going off to the left or the right?'.

If the fission case is not thought of as involving multiple occupancy, the possibility of singular reference by the single conscious being present before the fission returns. But for the neo-Lockean the brain transplant remains a case of asymmetric multiple occupancy unless it is denied that the biologically individuated human animal is a conscious being. So the person and the animal are not expressing different singular thoughts when they utter 'I' and the too many thinkers problem has an obvious solution. In a sense, we may say, the solution is that they *do* face an epistemic problem, the same epistemic problem that the possibility of fission presents if the Only x and y Principle is accepted. But this is just the 'problem' that even reference with 'I' is not guaranteed.[11]

5. Alternative Solutions to the Too Many Thinkers Problem

Shoemaker and Parfit agree that the too many thinkers problem is not an insuperable objection to neo-Lockeanism, but they differ from me in how they answer it (since they do not wish to say that before the transplant the biologically individuated human animal is a conscious being who cannot refer to himself in the first person).

I want to finish by rejecting their answers.

Shoemaker denies that biologically individuated animals, human or non-human, have psychological states at all. He therefore denies that

---

[11] As well as the fission case there is the possible case of conjoined twins sharing a cerebrum but not a brainstem nor any other vital organs involved in the life-processes thought to individuate organisms (Metz, 2001, pp. 289–90). The animalist must say that these are two thinkers, each of which is thinking a single thought about itself when they simultaneously token 'I' (like, he must say, *pace* Lewis, Lefty and Righty in the fission case). This must be so if an 'I'-thought has a guaranteed reference, as he requires for his argument against the neo-Lockean. But it does not seem plausible to say that in this case either animal will be able to refer to itself or know that it was one rather than the other.

dogs are animals in this sense (and says that in a brain transplant the dog goes with its brain). (So he is able to say, despite his opposition to (strong) animalism, that we are predicatively animals, i.e. animals in the sense in which dogs are.)

He distinguishes thick and thin properties: thin properties can be shared by (temporarily) coincident entities with different persistence conditions; thick properties cannot. Size and shape are thin properties, psychological states are thick. A thick property may be thought of as a conjunction of a thin property with a sortal property which determines a set of persistence conditions. So a person and coinciding bio-logically individuated human animal share all their thin properties but not their thick properties because they differ in their persistence con-ditions. And this is so even if we suppose them to have had the same origin — even if we suppose the animal to have been created fully grown, rather than developing from a foetus. In fact, according to Shoemaker *qua* strong pluralist, even if the person and animal are permanently coincident they will still differ in their persistence con-ditions. So the animal will still lack any psychological properties.

I disagree with Shoemaker. I do so, first, because I reject his strong pluralism. But nor do I accept that whether something is now a possessor of any psychologically properties can depend on its future or, except causally, on its past in the way he requires. Some properties are possessed by things at times partly in virtue of what happens at other times. It is implausible that the matter only momentarily coinciding with a person or animal thereby qualifies as either. It is not implausible that psychological properties can only be possessed by things with careers of non-zero temporal extent. The possession of a psychological property by a thing at a time must cause or be caused by its possession of some psychological property at another time. This is part of Shoemaker's position. But the difficulty is this. I and the ani-mal with which I am currently coincident have been together a long time and, God willing, will continue to be so for a few years yet. So if I am now thinking that it is raining and the animal is not, is this difference inexplicable, or is to be explained by differences in non-actualized potentialities or grounded in some long past or future difference? None of these options is attractive. Although it seems absurd to say that the matter now momentarily coincident with me is thinking that it is raining, it seems far from absurd to say this of the animal with which I have been and will be so long coincident. Granted thinking, like breathing and digesting and running, takes time — which is why it is absurd to think of the momentarily coincident piece of matter as doing any of these things — it does not seem that the period of time need be years long. David Lewis's (1981, p. 76) day-long person-stages can count as thinking and walking and talking, even though, as he notes, they cannot do everything a person can do, since they cannot do what a person can do only over a longish period. The biological animal coincident with me can do at least whatever my current day-long person-stage can do.

Derek Parfit's response to the too many thinkers objection is different. He denies that human animals think in the way that persons do, not because they have merely biological persistence conditions, but because they are too big. They contain parts not required for thought so they do not think. You are, in fact, brain-sized. He calls this view the 'Embodied Parts View'. One version of this is that you are your brain. But Parfit thinks a better version is that the thinking embodied part of an animal, i.e. the part you are, is not the brain, but something related to a brain in a way roughly similar to that in which an animal is related to its whole body. This is the Embodied Persons View. You are an entity distinct from but coincident with the brain contained within your skull. So when the transplant takes place you go where the brain goes and when your brain is envatted so are you. No new conscious being is brought into existence, nor is a previously non-conscious being rendered conscious by the mere removal of fleshly surroundings.

Parfit endorses the Embodied Persons View as a way of defending neo-Lockeanism. He formulates what he defends as follows:

> *The Narrow, Brain-Based Psychological Criterion*: If some future person would be uniquely psychologically continuous with me as I am now, and this continuity would have its normal cause, enough of the same brain, this person would be me. If some future person would neither be uniquely psychologically continuous with me as I am now, nor have enough of the same brain, this person would not be me.

My objection is that the Embodied Persons View is as vulnerable to the too many thinkers objection as the standard neo-Lockean view.

It is, first, obvious why Parfit is not willing to identify persons with their brains. These are biological organs, whose persistence conditions are entirely non-psychological. Like biologically individuated animals, their continued existence does not require any psychological function. So, if I am my brain, I existed before I had any psychological properties and may do so again. And if my brain is transplanted

I will go where it goes regardless of whether it carries any psychology with it. This is not what Parfit wants to say.

But the Embodied Persons View avoids these consequences only if the persistence conditions of the thinking part which is coincident with the brain are at least partly psychological. But then the brain and the thinking part will not necessarily have the same history. They will not come apart in a brain transplant, but they will be capable of coming apart in other circumstances. Indeed, they *will* have different histories, except in science-fiction cases in which human beings come into existence fully developed without any foetal stage.

So Parfit faces the too many thinkers objection. He must say that the brain is not a thinker, though it is coincident with one and has the same surroundings and virtually the same history. He cannot explain this by saying that this is because it is too big, with parts not required for thought. So he is left with the same problem Shoemaker faces.

I conclude that neo-Lockeans should not be denying that biologically individuated animals think. They should acknowledge that these animals think, accept the Only x and y Principle, and celebrate their pluralism by endorsing a multiplicity of thinkers.

References

Gibbard, A. (1975) Contingent identity, *Journal of Philosophical Logic*, **4**, pp. 187–222.

Johnston, M. (2006) Hylomorphism, *Journal of Philosophy*, **103**, pp. 652–698.

Johnston, M. (2007) Human beings revisited: My body is not an animal, *Oxford Studies in Metaphysics*, **3**, pp. 33–74.

Lewis, D. (1976) Survival and identity, in Rorty, A.O. (ed.) *The Identities of Persons*, pp. 17–40, Berkeley, CA: University of California Press.

Lewis, D. (1981) *Philosophical Papers*, vol. 1, New York: Oxford University Press.

Lewis, D. (1986) *On the Plurality of Worlds*, Oxford: Basil Blackwell.

Metz, W. (2001) *Ultrasound in Obstetrics and Gynaceology*, New York: Thieme Medical Publishers.

Noonan, H. (2003) *Personal Identity*, 2nd ed., London: Routledge.

Olson, E. (1997) *The Human Animal: Personal Identity Without Psychology*, Oxford: Oxford University Press.

Olson, E. (2007) *What Are We? A Study in Personal Ontology*, Oxford: Oxford University Press.

Olson, E. (forthcoming) Animalism and the remnant person problem, in Gonçales, J. (ed.) *Metaphysics of the Self*, Instituto de Filosofa da Linguagem, Universidade Nova de Lisboa: Peter Lang.

Parfit, D. (1971) Personal identity, *Philosophical Review*, **80** (January), pp. 3–27.

Parfit, D. (1984) *Reason and Persons*, Oxford: Oxford University Press.

Parfit, D. (2012) We are not human beings, *Philosophy*, **87**, pp. 5–28.

Robinson, D. (1985) Can amoebae divide without multiplying?, *Australasian Journal of Philosophy*, **63**, pp. 299–319.

Saunders, S. & Wallace, D. (2008a) Branching and uncertainty, *British Journal for the Philosophy of Science*, **59** (3), pp. 293–305.

Saunders, S. & Wallace, D. (2008b) Saunders and Wallace reply, *British Journal for the Philosophy of Science*, **59** (3), pp. 315–317.

Shaffer, J.A. (1977) Personal identity: The implications of brain bisections and brain transplants. *Journal of Medicine and Philosophy*, **2** (June), pp. 147–161.

Shoemaker, S. (1970a) Persons and their pasts, *American Philosophical Quarterly*, **7**, pp. 269–285.

Shoemaker, S. (1970b) Wiggins on identity, *Philosophical Review*, **79**, pp. 529–544.

Shoemaker, S. (2010) Reply to my critics, *Philosophical Studies*, **148**, pp. 125–132.

Shoemaker, S. (forthcoming) Thinking animals without animalism, in Blatti, S. & Snowdon, P. (eds.) *New Essays on Animalism: Persons, Animals and Identity*, Oxford: Oxford University Press.

Tappenden, P. (2008) Saunders and Wallace on Everett and Lewis, *British Journal for the Philosophy of Science*, **59** (3), pp. 307–314.

Tappenden, P. (2010) *Varieties of Divergence: A Response to Saunders and Wallace*, [Online], http://philsci-archive.pitt.edu/5384/1/Varieties_of_Divergence.pdf.

Van Inwagen, P. (1981) The doctrine of arbitrary undetached parts, *Pacific Philosophical Quarterly*, **62**, pp. 123–137.

Van Inwagen, P. (1990) *Material Beings*, Ithaca, NY: Cornell University Press.

Olley Pearson

Rationality and the First Person

Abstract: In this paper, I will argue that a prominent theory of rationality could ground an argument for the existence of a self. Specifically, a self that is only captured in first-personal beliefs, and which is hence distinct from the physical body, in so far as the latter can be captured in third-personal beliefs. First-personal beliefs are beliefs characteristically expressed with first-personal utterances. Perry has argued that first-personal beliefs are necessary for certain actions. On closer examination, the appropriate conclusion of Perry's arguments is that first-personal beliefs are necessary for rational actions. If one adopts a popular view of rationality according to which it consists in the coherence of one's attitudes, one can give first-personal beliefs a unique role in rationality without giving them a unique content. However, recently it has been argued that rationality consists in responding appropriately to the world. According to this latter theory of rationality, a belief is only necessary for a rational action in so far as one must have a belief in order to be aware of and respond to the world. On this latter theory, if first-personal beliefs are to have a unique role in rationality, first-personal beliefs must capture something unique about the world. The conclusions of the paper are twofold. Firstly, we ought to see the problems surrounding essential first-personal beliefs as bound up with rationality. Secondly, if we follow current trends in the philosophical study of rationality we could be led into conflict with common responses to these problems and towards the existence of a non-physical self.

Correspondence:
Email: f.o.c.pearson@durham.ac.uk

Journal of Consciousness Studies, **22**, No. 11–12, 2015, pp. 132–48

1. Essential First-Personal Beliefs and the Old Problem

Perry (*cf.* 1979)[1] was once in a supermarket following a trail of sugar. He wanted to find the person with the torn sack that was making the mess in order to stop them. After some time Perry had a moment of realization, and reached into his own trolley to turn over the offending sack of sugar. Perry's behaviour changed, he stopped, and this was the result of his forming a new belief. The belief was one that he would express with a first-personal utterance. It was the first-personal belief 'I am making a mess'. (By 'first-personal beliefs' I mean beliefs best[2] expressed with utterances in the first person. By 'third-personal beliefs' I mean beliefs best expressed with utterances in the third person. And so on.)

A first-personal belief was necessary for Perry's action. Perry could have had any number of related beliefs that were not first-personal and he would not have stopped. For example, Perry could have believed 'JP is making a mess', or 'the person with the torn sack is making a mess', or 'that man is making a mess', and he would not have stopped. He would not have stopped even though he was JP, he was the man with the torn sack, and he was the man demonstrated, precisely because he did not know that he was. That is, the need for a first-personal belief arises, either in the form of a belief such as 'I am making a mess', or else in the form of a belief such as 'I am JP' accompanied by a belief such as 'JP is making a mess'.

According to one possible view of beliefs, a belief is a relationship between a person and a proposition which is its content.[3] When Perry correctly believes 'it is raining', he is related to a proposition which represents the state of affairs of it raining. If one assumes this view, then the question arises as to what the content of Perry's first-personal belief is. This question is made all the more difficult by the fact that Perry's first-personal belief is irreplaceable by any non-first-personal beliefs, because this entails that Perry's first-personal belief must be different from, and hence have a different content from, any of his

---

[1]   All references to Perry will be to this text unless otherwise stated.

[2]   This should not be taken to commit me to the idea that a person will always express such a belief in this way, they might not express the belief at all. One might consider the converse of this, such that when Perry says (honestly, etc.) 'I am X' or 'I believe I am x', we take this to inform us that Perry has the belief 'I am X'. (*Cf.* Kripke's, 1979, disquotational principle.)

[3]   Perry (1979) relates this to Frege.

non-first-personal beliefs. Perry raises this as an example of the problem of the essential indexical, and I shall refer to it as the *old problem*.

In order to avoid the conclusion that first-personal beliefs have a different content to any other beliefs, Perry proposes altering our understanding of beliefs and crucially the role the content of a belief plays. Instead of supposing that a person acts simply in light of the content of their beliefs, we are to recognize the import of the belief state itself. The proposal is that we distinguish the content of a person's belief from the state they are in when they have that belief: the belief state. This enables Perry to say that his first-personal belief 'I am making a mess' does in fact have the same content as some of his non-first-personal beliefs, perhaps such as his belief 'JP is making a mess'. However, these two beliefs will be manifested in different belief states, and it is this that explains why the two beliefs have different effects on Perry's behaviour. In saying this Perry makes it clear that we can hold onto the traditional notion of content as propositional content, whilst still accounting for the old problem.[4]

More generally, if Perry and I both believe 'I am making a mess', we will have beliefs which are tokens of the same belief state type. For this reason we can be expected to act in a similar way, for example, stopping what we are doing. However, our beliefs will have different contents, mine will be about me and Perry's will be about him. Moreover, these contents can be the contents of different beliefs. For example, Perry's 'I am making a mess' belief may have the same content as Perry's 'JP is making a mess' belief and my 'You are making a mess' belief. Though, these last two beliefs will lead to different actions from Perry's first-personal belief, because they are manifested in different belief states.

Perry has thus shown that we need first-personal beliefs in some circumstances. A phenomenon that he explains as the need for beliefs manifested in particular types of belief states, rather than the need for beliefs with particular contents. (In 1979 Perry is not explicit in what he means by 'belief state', one might take a belief state to be a physical state of the believer. In later work — for example, 1998 — Perry says things which offer quite a different understanding of it; believers will have webs of beliefs related to one another in various

---

[4]   Perry (1979) makes this clear, and also likens Perry's view to that of Kaplan's (1989): Perry's distinction between belief state and content, reflecting Kaplan's distinction between the character and propositional content of a belief.

ways (as files share information). A belief state might hence be thought of in terms of the place a belief has in such a web. Whichever way belief states are understood will not affect my argument which is focused on Perry's grounding the role of a belief in something other than its content.)

2. Rationality, Essential First-Personal Beliefs, and the New Problem

The idea that first-personal beliefs are essential for certain actions needs to be clarified and made more precise. Consider the bodily movements that Perry undergoes in the supermarket when he stops: his legs move one beside the other, rather than one in front of the other, and his arms draw his trolley towards him. These movements could easily occur without Perry having a first-personal belief such as 'I am making a mess'. For example, if supermarket security guards grab hold of Perry's arms and legs and start manipulating them.

Actions[5] can be thought of as a particular type of bodily movement. Actions are those movements that a person does quite deliberately and intentionally. They are those movements for which a person can provide reasons for their performing them. Actions are thus distinct from mere movements of one's body, as when it is manipulated by someone else, and also from mere doings, such as one's beating one's heart.[6] The cases highlighted by Perry, and where first-personal beliefs are essential, are specifically cases of actions. Perry needs first-personal beliefs when he is performing certain actions. (From here on I shall use this technical notion of action.)

It is also possible for Perry to perform the action of stopping without a first-personal belief, if he is acting irrationally. For example, Perry might stop as a result of forming the belief 'JP is making a mess', or the belief 'De Gaulle is making a mess', without taking himself to be JP or De Gaulle. He might do this if he irrationally takes JP's or De Gaulle's making a mess to be a reason for him to stop.

The point is that people are often recognized to be acting irrationally, and to be doing things for reasons which in fact do not justify doing those things. This is not to say that a person could be recognized

---

5   Which is not to say that all actions are bodily, as opposed to mental or what have you. I shall also stay quiet on whether remaining still, as opposed to moving, can be thought of as an action. None of what I argue is altered by these points.

6   *Cf.* Alvarez (2005, p. 45) and Anscombe (1957/2000, Section 5, p. 9).

to be irrational in the majority of their actions, but to say that the majority of people can be recognized to be acting irrationally in some of their actions. Examples of this are apparently widespread. For example, people often take the fact that a card is showing an even number to be a reason to turn that card over to prove or disprove the hypothesis that cards with a vowel on one side have an even number on the other. However, such an action is irrational. That a card is showing an even number is no reason to turn it over in this case, because whether or not it has a vowel on the other side we will be none the wiser whether the hypothesis in question is true or false.[7]

In order for Perry's action to be rational, it is essential that he has a first-personal belief.[8] However, it is not essential for Perry to have a first-personal belief if he is acting irrationally, or merely undergoing bodily movements and not acting at all. This raises what I shall refer to as the *new problem*: how should we understand first-personal beliefs, given that they are essential for certain actions to be rational?

3. Rationality as Coherence or Fitting Complex Normative Requirements

If we are going to accept Perry's response to the old problem, we must accept that first-personal beliefs can have the same content as non-first-personal beliefs. This means that if we are going to retain Perry's account, whilst answering the new problem, we must adopt an account of rationality according to which two beliefs can be of differing rational import in a particular context without differing in content. There is a prominent theory of rationality that appears to be compatible with this idea.

According to what I shall refer to as the *CNR account*, rationality consists in one's intentional states having a certain coherence, or more specifically, in one fitting a number of complex normative requirements (or simply *CNRs*). The exact form of these CNRs is disputed, but the view can be elucidated by considering the following examples:

---

[7]   *Cf.* Wason (1966) for a much discussed case of widespread irrationality, *cf.* Evans and Over (1996, p. 7) for an account of irrationality along these lines of acting for bad reasons.

[8]   If one adds a sufficiently complicated context, it might be possible for Perry to act rationally without a first-personal belief. However, such a context is not a normal one, and clearly not one that Perry was presupposing. The point remains, in some circumstances, and plausibly the everyday ones presupposed by Perry, first-personal beliefs are essential for rational actions.

CNR1: One rationally ought, if one believes that p, and believes that p entails q, to believe that q.[9]

CNR2: One rationally ought, if one intends to F, and believes that one must G in order to F, to intend to G.[10]

CNR3: One rationally ought to intend to F, if one believes that there is all things considered reason for one to F.[11]

These CNRs speak of intentions, rather than actions, to allow for the possibility of an intention to be thwarted; one is not irrational for failing to do something one believes one has all things considered reason to, if one is being physically restrained from doing that thing. They speak of all things considered reasons, because the reasons at issue are *pro tanto* reasons, which can be weighed against one another; one might have some reason to go walking, but more reason not to go, in which case the rational thing is not to go.

The relevance of the CNR account of rationality is that it references specific intentional states and defines rationality in terms of these. It is therefore open to such an account to distinguish the rational import of two beliefs in a context, without the two differing in content. In order to do this, one would have to interpret the CNRs in a particular way so that the letters I have used as placeholders in their presentation (i.e. p, q, F, and G) do not simply distinguish beliefs by their content.[12] But this might be possible.

One might account for the fact that first-personal beliefs are essential for rational actions by adopting the prominent CNR theory of rationality. This would enable one to maintain that two beliefs can have the same content and yet be of differing rational import, hence answering the new problem whilst maintaining Perry's answer to the old problem.

---

[9] *Cf.* Broome (2007).

[10] *Cf.* Broome (2007), Korsgaard (1997), and Davidson (2001).

[11] Scanlon (2007) offers the looser: one ought to F if one believes one has an object given reason to F; or Broome (2007) offers: one ought to F if one believes one ought to F.

[12] It is notable that writers are not always sufficiently clear about how we ought to understand these symbols. Broome does say something about the matter, though things are left unclear, as he both focuses on propositional content (*cf.* 2001a), and says that the beliefs at issue must be relevantly first-personal (*cf.* 2008).

4. Doubt that Rationality is Coherence
or Fitting Complex Normative Requirements

There is, however, a problem with using the CNR account of rationality to account for the fact that first-personal beliefs can be necessary for a person to be rational. The problem is that the CNR account is itself problematic. In this section I will not argue that the CNR account is false, though I will sketch some worries with the CNR account to enable readers to see that there might be room for doubt.

The first worry that arises for the CNR account is the issue of bootstrapping obligations or reasons into existence. Suppose that whilst sitting on my sofa I form the false, perhaps patently false, belief that I am sitting on my dog. Given that I am not sitting on my dog, I ought not to believe that I am. Moreover, the fact that I ought not to have this belief is unchanged by my adopting the belief. It was the case that I ought not to believe that I am sitting on my dog before I believed that I was, and it is equally the case that I ought not to have the belief even if I do happen to form it.

Nevertheless, it is true that, if I am sitting on my dog, then I am sitting on my dog, and I am quite aware of this. Therefore, if we accept CNR1, because I believe that I am sitting on my dog [p], and I believe that if I am sitting on my dog [p] then I am sitting on my dog [q], then I ought to believe that I am sitting on my dog [q]. CNR1 thus has the false implication that I ought to believe that I am sitting on my dog, even though I am not sitting on my dog. CNR1 says that I ought to have this false belief, simply as I do have this false belief, but in fact I ought not to have the belief, and the fact that I do have it does not change this. CNR1 is thus false, because it bootstraps rational obligations into existence, when in fact there are no such obligations. Similar remarks hold for the other CNRs. Plausibly I ought not to murder, and I ought not to poison in order to murder, and this remains the case even if I form the intention to murder, or form the belief that I have reason to murder, *contra* CNR2 and CNR3 respectively (*cf.* Bratman, 1987, pp. 24–7).

An answer to the bootstrapping worry has been offered by those who adopt a CNR theory. They point out that the bootstrapping only arises if we take the scope of the 'ought' in the CNRs to be narrow. Specifically, in the case of CNR1, the bootstrapping arises if one supposes that one can infer that one ought to believe that q from the fact that one believes that p, and CNR1 (or the fact that one rationally ought, if one believes that p, and believes that p entails q, to believe that q). However, one can deny the validity of this inference, if one takes the 'ought' in CNR1 to have wide scope, and denies detachment.

CNR1 places an obligation on one to fit a certain conditional: if one believes that p and believes that p entails q, then to believe that q. One can satisfy this conditional in two different ways: not believing that p and that p entails q; or, believing q. If we take the obligation to have wide scope and deny detachment, this means that one can be obliged to fit the conditional, but not obliged to fit it in a particular way. In short, one is not obliged to not believe that p and that p entails q, and, one is not obliged to believe that q, and this is so even if one believes that p and that p entails q and one is under the obligation of CNR1. As a result, we do not get particular obligations bootstrapped into existence, and so the bootstrapping problem does not arise (*cf.* Broome, 1999 and 2001b).

It is at this point that the second worry with the CNR account gains force. The problems here are made most apparent when one bears in mind that rationality, and hence the CNRs, are supposed to guide people in the rational formation of certain actions or beliefs. They do not simply stipulate bad combinations of states for a person to be in, but they are also supposed to guide one to behave rationally.

Imagine that at time t I believe that I have all things considered reason to F, but I do not intend to F. In that case I would fail CNR3, and this should guide me towards rational behaviour to ensure I satisfy CNR3 at the later time t^*. I could do this in two ways, dropping my belief that I have all things considered reason to F, or forming the intention to F. If it is accepted that CNR3 understood with a wide scope applies, then it is rational to do one or the other of these. However, dropping a belief that one has all things considered reason to F, on the basis of the fact that one lacks an intention to F, is not a rational form of behaviour. One shouldn't expect what ought to be the case to bow to one's intentions in this way. Given that the CNR account references nothing beside these intentional states, there is no option to base this behaviour on something besides this lack of intention. The most charitable interpretation of the idea of CNR3 would be to focus on the contents of these intentional states instead of the states themselves. However, this is no help. Even if it is appropriate to move from the content of one's belief that one has reason to F, to intending to F, it is not appropriate to move from the content of one's lack of intention to F (if there be such a thing), to one's abandoning one's belief that one has reason to F. Understood with wide scope, CNR3 thus allows as rational a form of behaviour which is not rational. If CNR3 has any plausibility as a requirement of rationality, it is hence as a narrow-scope requirement, not as a wide-scope one (*cf.* Kolodny, 2007).

Similar problems with wide-scope interpretations arise for CNR1 too. For example, it is inappropriate to drop one's belief that p or that p entails q simply on the basis of one's lacking a belief that q. (Which is not to deny that evidence against q can be evidence against p or p entailing q, because the CNR does not concern such evidence beyond one's lack of a belief that q.) These problems with CNR1 and CNR3 are alone enough to damage any CNR account that includes them.[13]

The CNR account thus appears to be left with a dilemma, either horn of which is problematic. Either it takes CNRs to be narrow-scope, in which case we have a worrying bootstrapping of rational obligations, or it takes CNRs to be wide-scope, in which case it con-dones irrational behaviour. Of course, these comments are too brief to disprove the CNR account, but the point to note is that there has recently been a trend moving away from the CNR account (*cf.* for example, Kolodny, 2005, and Raz, 2005), and hopefully these comments are sufficient to open one's mind to the possibility of such a trend, and to make it clear that the CNR account shouldn't simply be assumed to be correct.

5. Rationality as Appropriate Responsiveness to the World

There is a second prominent account of rationality that provides an alternative to the CNR account. The *reasons-based* account, as I shall

---

[13] It is plausible that any complete CNR account, as a complete account of rationality, will have to include relatives of CNR1 and CNR3. Moreover, it is plausible that the prob-lems raised here in relation to CNR1 and CNR3 would apply equally to various differ-ent interpretations of these and other CNRs. The point of these CNRs appears to be to link justifying beliefs to concluding beliefs or intentions which might be justified by those justifying beliefs, and this appears to be all that is required to raise problems. The bootstrapping criticism applies because these justifying beliefs might be mistaken, and hence of little value, and so detachment is denied. The fact that the justifying beliefs are linked to concluding beliefs in CNRs (and not to external reasons) entails that any change of justifying beliefs is directly linked to the possession or lack thereof of the concluding states (and no other reasons). This last point is, in turn, all that is required in combination with the denial of detachment to apply the above criticism of a wide-scope interpretation, i.e. the inappropriate changing of justifying beliefs on the grounds of concluding states or a lack thereof.

refer to it, takes rationality to consist in responding appropriately to reasons, where these reasons are states of affairs or facts (*cf.* Kolodny, 2005, and Raz, 2011). If one is being approached by a speeding car, then that fact justifies one's stepping out of the road: it is a reason for one to do so. If one steps out of the road because of that reason, then one has responded appropriately to that reason, and one has acted rationally.

We can distinguish a number of different reasons: there are justificatory reasons, motivating reasons, and explanatory reasons. A justificatory reason is a reason that justifies an action or a belief. A motivating reason is a reason that motivates an action or a belief. An explanatory reason is a reason that explains something. The distinction between these reasons should not be thought of as a distinction between different types of entities, but rather as the distinction between different roles that entities might play. One and the same fact might justify, motivate, and explain an action of mine. Though, a fact might justify an action of mine without me noticing it, nor hence being motivated by it. Alternatively, I might be motivated by a fact that does not justify my act, or one might explain my movements without reference to anything that motivates me, for example, with a purely physiological explanation.

The reasons that justify actions are facts. If I am being approached by a speeding car, then I ought to step out of the road, even if I am unaware of that fact. Unsurprisingly, it is also facts that usually motivate us to act (if this were not the case, no one would ever be motivated by something that justified them). It is facts that we consider in deliberating about how to act, and that we cite in order to let someone else know what motivated us. The notion of fact at play here is the notion of something metaphysically real and objective. It is not, however, a notion tied to a particular ontology, that is, a fact might be a fundamental kind, but it could equally be a bundle of tropes or an object instantiating a mode, or what have you.[14]

---

[14] For examples of ontologies fitting these descriptions see Armstrong (1997), Rodriguez-Pereyra (2002), and Lowe (2006), respectively. As an anonymous referee has noted, it is possible to act because, for example, it might rain, or it will probably rain. I am not sure that these are necessarily different reasons from the fact that it will rain, because I do not think it is clear that they rationalize different actions. However, if they are different reasons, perhaps the reasons-based account is committed to possibility or probability being metaphysically real and objective. This is not worrying, as this does not commit the reasons-based account to any particular metaphysics of possibility or probability. For example, possibilities could be sets of possible worlds, compatible sets of entities,

Nevertheless, beliefs are essential in order for a person to be motivated, because one must be aware of a fact to be motivated by it, and beliefs, in the minimal sense at issue here, just are states of awareness. A rational person is thus one who forms the beliefs and performs the acts that the justificatory reasons that they are aware of give them most reason to form and perform, and they do so for those reasons. A rational person is one whose justificatory reasons are their motivating reasons.

The idea that it is facts, rather than intentional states or objects, that are justificatory and motivating reasons might seem dubious when one considers a case of mistaken belief. For example, suppose that I believe that it is raining, and as a result take an umbrella with me. It appears that the fact that it is raining cannot be what justifies or motivates my action, because there is no such fact. One response to this is to say that it is my belief, or some intentional entity or perspectival fact that I am related to in having that belief, that is my reason for acting in this case. However, there is no need to say this. Rather, the more accurate thing to say in such a case is that I simply have no justificatory reason; it is not raining so I shouldn't take an umbrella. I also have no motivating reason; what I cite as motivating me is something that does not exist, it is quite literally nothing (being motivated by something is a matter of taking an attitude towards it, and it is quite possible to take an attitude towards something that does not exist, or, expressing the point differently, to be motivated without being motivated by anything). As I have no justificatory reason and no motivating reason in this case of mistaken belief, there is no need to suppose that the reasons in this case are things other than facts. The point is, whilst it might be necessary that beliefs and intentional entities exist when there are such cases of acting on mistaken beliefs, this does not entail that these beliefs or intentional entities are the reasons in such cases. On the contrary, in such cases there are no reasons precisely because the agent is mistaken in their beliefs. Nevertheless, it remains the case that when the beliefs involved in actions are not mistaken, then they do serve to pick out facts, and these facts can be motivating and justificatory reasons.

This response to the cases of mistaken belief is evinced by our behaviour. For example, if Kate paid money to John because she

---

or what have you, and probabilities could be nothing more than statistics of past occurrences, or proportions of possibilities, or some such.

believed it would enable him to feed his child, and Kate subsequently learns that in fact John has no children, then Kate will regret her action. She will form the opinion that she was misled, and that she in fact had no reason to give John the money, and she will ask to be refunded. She forms the belief that she had no reason to give him the money, despite remaining convinced that she had the mistaken belief, and so the belief (and any intentional entity she was related to in it) cannot have been her reason in this case (*cf.* Alvarez, 2010, Chapter 5.2).[15]

Cases of mistaken beliefs can also raise doubts about the idea that it is a responsiveness to reasons, rather than a conforming to CNRs, that constitutes rationality. Suppose that I mistakenly believe that it is raining, and I believe that if it is raining then there are clouds, but I do not believe that there are clouds. It might seem as if I have made some sort of failing of rationality; and this feeling might linger, even if one notes that there are no clouds and I have no justificatory reason for believing that there are clouds. The bootstrapping worry tells us that it is not CNR1 that grounds my irrationality here, but it seems that it cannot be a failing to respond to reasons either, as I am not aware of any reasons to believe that there are clouds. However, one can look elsewhere for the relevant failing of rationality. Specifically, at my belief that it is raining and my belief that if it is raining then there are clouds. If we suppose that I am aware of sufficient reason for these beliefs, then I am aware of sufficient reason to believe that there are clouds. Reasons can transfer across deduction. In which case, we can say my failing of rationality is failing to adopt a belief I am aware of sufficient reason to have. Alternatively, if we say that I am not aware of sufficient reason to believe that there are clouds, then either I am not aware of sufficient reason to believe that it is raining, or I am not aware of sufficient reason to believe that if it is raining then there are clouds. In which case, I have a belief that I am not aware of sufficient reason to have. Therefore, any failing of rationality in this case can be seen as a failing to accord with reasons in line with the reasons-based account.

---

[15] Beliefs can of course be constituents of facts. For example, the fact that Kate has this mistaken belief can be a reason for me to tell her the truth about John. However, the fact that a belief is had is distinct from the belief itself (perhaps, for example, the former is timeless, whilst the latter occurs at a specific time).

The points of the last paragraph, as brief as they are, indicate the potential for the reasons-based account of rationality to provide an error theory for why the CNR account and the CNRs appeared plausible. This is done by making two moves. Firstly, by saying that what makes the CNRs seem correct is that, if one violates one of them, then one appears to have violated rationality. Secondly, it is argued that it is in going against reasons, rather than in going against the CNRs themselves, that one violates rationality in these cases. For example, if one has sufficient reason to believe p, and that p entails q, then one has sufficient reason to believe q. Failing to match the pattern of CNR1 thus involves failing reasons, either by holding beliefs one does not have sufficient reason to hold, or failing to hold beliefs that one does have sufficient reason to hold. No doubt more detail is needed here, but the point is a simple one. The patterns stipulated by the CNRs might reflect the patterns of reasons, and, if they do, it is understandable why one might mistakenly think that rationality consists in fitting CNRs, rather than responding appropriately to reasons (*cf.* Kolodny, 2007).

If the CNR account of rationality is problematic, this does not leave us bereft of hope for answering the new problem, that is for accounting for our need for first-personal beliefs in rational action. Rather, one can instead look to the reasons-based account of rationality.

6. Perhaps the Need for First-Personal Beliefs is the Need for Beliefs with a Unique Content

If one adopts the reasons-based account of rationality, then reasons and beliefs contact in two ways. Firstly, there are the reasons for which one forms a belief. Secondly, there are the reasons to act (or believe) that one is aware of in those beliefs. In Perry's cases, it is the second issue that is of import. We are considering an action that a person performs, and the beliefs that he must have in order to perform it rationally. In such a case, beliefs are only required in so far as an agent must be aware of a reason that justifies their action, and a belief is such a state of awareness. It follows that, if one belief is required in place of another, then the two beliefs must involve an awareness of different reasons, that is, facts.

Perry's cases tell us that first-personal beliefs are needed for certain rational actions, and no non-first-personal beliefs can take their place. The reasons-based account tells us that two beliefs with different rational import must be about different facts. It follows that, if we adopt the reasons-based account of rationality, then we must accept that first-personal beliefs can capture facts that non-first-personal beliefs cannot capture. If this is right, then Perry is wrong to say that first-personal and non-first-personal beliefs can have the same content. Moreover, any view that allows first-personal and non-first-personal beliefs to differ in content, but denies that non-first-personal beliefs can fail to capture all the facts there are, is also mistaken (*cf.* Lewis, 1979; Stalnaker, 1981; Mellor, 1998). The strength of this claim derives from the nature of the reasons-based account, according to which reasons are real and objective facts. This objectivity itself stems from the fact that beliefs and intentional entities are not the reasons that justify or motivate people, objective facts are.

It is important to be clear here what is meant by content, as the notion might be given various interpretations. As I understand beliefs, a true belief is a state of awareness, by which I mean in having a true belief a person is aware of a fact. I shall refer to the fact one is aware of in having a true belief as the *object* of that belief. According to one interpretation of content, the content of a true belief is the object of that belief. This notion of content, however, is not popular, in part for reasons relating to the old problem. Instead a notion of content is often suggested according to which two beliefs might have the same object, but differ in content. A more accurate portrayal of Perry (1979) is given if all talk of content above fits this latter interpretation. However, the core argument of this paper works equally with either interpretation. If the reasons-based account of rationality is correct, first-personal and non-first-personal beliefs cannot have the same objects. If first-personal and non-first-personal beliefs cannot have the same objects, then they cannot have the same content on many interpretations of content, including Perry's (1979).

If the reasons-based account of rationality is accepted, then, first-personal beliefs capture facts that no non-first-personal beliefs can capture. This is the point established in the preceding sections. However, one might also speculate a little about the nature of these facts. Firstly, it is plausible that each person's first-personal beliefs capture different facts, because they can differ in truth-value. For example, Perry might truly believe 'I am making a mess' whilst I falsely believe 'I am making a mess'. Therefore, if we accept the reasons-based account of rationality, we might conclude that each person's first-personal beliefs can capture something about the world that no one else's can, and that no non-first-personal beliefs can. Secondly, what appears to be unique about one's first-personal beliefs, as opposed to another's first-personal beliefs, or non-first-personal beliefs, is specifically that they are about oneself. One might then suppose that if a person's first-personal beliefs capture something unique, it is something about their self or their self itself. Therefore, this self, or attribute of the self, is unique to that individual, and distinct from anything that can be captured non-first-personally, such as the physical body of the individual. Finally, there appear to be ties between first-personal and non-first-personal beliefs. For example, if Perry can truly believe 'I am making a mess', he can truly believe 'Perry is making a mess'; moreover, one can alter the truth of the one belief, by altering the truth of the other. Therefore, there appear to be ties between the self and the body, ties which suggest a metaphysical link between the self and the body: ties not dissimilar to those found in some emergentist theories of the self, for example (*cf.* O'Connor, 2000, and Hasker, 1999). The points of this paragraph are just speculations, but they do reveal how the arguments of this paper could bear on broader debates.

7. Conclusion

It ought to be noted that the proper conclusion of Perry's arguments for essential first-personal beliefs is that first-personal beliefs are necessary for certain actions to be rational. This refines, and hence makes more accurate, Perry's original conclusion. Furthermore, this reveals that the issues surrounding first-personal beliefs raise questions that take us beyond those considered by Perry. We are led from Perry's old problem to the new problem of the essential first person. Answers that have been given to the old problem will not necessarily be answers to the new problem. Most notably, if one adopts a reasons-based account of rationality, there are grounds for saying that many existing answers to the old problem, including Perry's own, fail to answer the new problem. Moreover, they do so because they fail to recognize that first-personal beliefs capture something about the self which is quite unique. This is because many answers to the old problem take first-personal and non-first-personal beliefs to capture the same facts. However, according to the reasons-based account of rationality, it is only the facts captured by a belief that determine the rational import of that belief.

On the other hand, should one wish to deny these unique first-personal facts, one must be aware of the implications that this has for one's view of rationality. One must adopt a view of rationality, such as the CNR account, that is compatible with the rational import of a belief being determined by something other than the facts one is aware of in having that belief. Further, such a commitment will place one under an obligation to respond to arguments given in support of the reasons-based account.

Finally, it has been argued that taking an individual's first-personal beliefs to capture something that no one else's first-personal or non-first-personal beliefs can capture is itself problematic.[16] If this is right, and if one can respond to the problems raised above for the CNR account, then one has access to a new criticism of the reasons-based account: specifically, that it implies such a problematic private language. This means that even those who wish to hold onto the CNR account of rationality have grounds to take note of the new problem. In short, first-personal beliefs continue to have great import, and deserve continued consideration.

Ackonwledgment

I am grateful to the John Templeton Foundation and the Durham Emergence Project whose funding enabled the writing of this paper.

References

Alvarez, M. (2005) Agents, actions and reasons, *Philosophical Books*, **46**, pp. 45–58.

Alvarez, M. (2010) *Kinds of Reasons: An Essay in the Philosophy of Action*, Oxford: Oxford University Press.

Anscombe, G.E.M. (1957/2000) *Intention*, London: Harvard University Press.

Armstrong, D.M. (1997) *A World of States of Affairs*, Cambridge: Cambridge University Press.

Bratman, M.E. (1987) *Intention, Plans, and Practical Reason*, Cambridge, MA: Harvard University Press.

Broome, J. (1999) Normative requirments, *Ratio*, **12**, pp. 398–419.

Broome, J. (2001a) Normative practical reasoning, *Proceedings of the Aristotelian Society, Supplementary Volume*, **75**, pp. 175–193.

Broome, J. (2001b) Are intentions reasons? And how should we cope with incommensurable values?, in Morris, C. & Ripstein, A. (eds.) *Practical Rationality and Preference: Essays for David Gauthier*, pp. 98–120, Cambridge: Cambridge University Press.

Broome, J. (2007) Does rationality consist in responding correctly to reasons?, *Journal of Moral Philosophy*, **4**, pp. 349–374.

Broome, J. (2008) Is rationality normative?, *Disputatio*, **11**, pp. 153–171.

Davidson, D. (2001) Actions, reasons, and causes, in *Essays on Actions and Events*, pp. 3–19, Oxford: Oxford University Press.

---

[16]   *Cf.* for example Wittgenstein (2001, especially sections 243–71).

Evans, J.St.B.T. & Over, D.E. (1996) *Rationality and Reasoning*, Hove: Psychology Press.

Hasker, W. (1999) *The Emergent Self*, London: Cornell University Press.

Kaplan, D. (1989) Demonstratives, in Almog, J., Perry, J. & Wettstein, H. (eds.) *Themes from Kaplan*, pp. 481–563, Oxford: Oxford University Press.

Kolodny, N. (2005) Why be rational?, *Mind*, **114**, pp. 509–563.

Kolodny, N. (2007) How does coherence matter?, *Proceedings of the Aristotelian Society*, **107**, pp. 229–263.

Korsgaard, C.M. (1997) The normativity of instrumental reason, in Cullity, G. & Gaut, B. (eds.) *Ethics and Practical Reason*, pp. 215–254, Oxford: Oxford University Press.

Kripke, S. (1979) A puzzle about belief, in Margrlit, A. (ed.) *Meaning and Use*, pp. 239–283, Dordrecht, Reidel.

Lewis, D.K. (1979) Attitudes *de dicto* and *de se*, *Philosophical Review*, **88**, pp. 513–543.

Lowe, E.J. (2006) *The Four-Category Ontology: A Metaphysical Foundation for Natural Science*, Oxford: Oxford University Press.

Mellor, D.H. (1998) *Real Time II*, London: Routledge.

O'Connor, T. (2000) *Persons and Causes*, Oxford: Oxford University Press.

Perry, J. (1979) The problem of the essential indexical, *Nous*, **13**, pp. 3–21.

Perry, J. (1998) Myself and I, in Stamm, M. (ed.) *Philosophie in Synthetisher Absicht (A festschrift for Dieter Heinrich)*, pp. 83–103, Stuttgart: Klett-Cotta.

Raz, J. (2005) The myth of instrumental rationality, *Journal of Ethics and Social Philosophy*, **1** (1), (electronic publication).

Raz, J. (2011) *From Normativity to Responsibility*, Oxford: Oxford University Press.

Rodriguez-Pereyra, G. (2002) *Resemblance Nominalism: A Solution to the Problem of Universals*, Oxford: Oxford University Press.

Scanlon, T. (2007) Structural irrationality, in Brennan, G., Goodin, R., Jackson, F. & Smith, M. (eds.) *Common Minds: Themes from the Philosophy of Philip Petit*, pp. 84–103, Oxford: Oxford University Press.

Stalnaker, R.C. (1981) Indexical belief, *Synthese*, **49**, pp. 129–151.

Wason, P.C. (1966) Reasoning, in Foss, B.M. (ed.) *New Horizons in Psychology Volume I*, pp. 135–152, Harmandsworth: Penguin.

Wittgenstein, L. (2001) *Philosophical Investigations*, Anscombe, G.E.M. (trans.), Oxford: Blackwell.

Wolfram Hinzen
and Kristen Schroeder

Is 'the First Person' a Linguistic Concept Essentially?

Abstract: *The notion of 'the first person' is centrally invoked in philosophical discussions of selfhood, subjectivity, and personhood. We ask whether this notion, as invoked in these discussions, is contingently or essentially a grammatical term. While it is logically possible that the linguistic dimensions of self-reference are accidental to this phenomenon, we argue that no explications of such phenomena as 'reference* de se' *or 'essential indexicality' in non-grammatical terms has been or likely can be provided, since grammatical factors uniquely co-vary with the forms of self-reference in question. The role of grammar is reinforced by the fact that species-specific forms of reference are never purely lexical and always have a structural signature involving specific grammatical configurations; and by findings that in cognitive disorders independently characterized as disorders of selfhood, such as autism spectrum conditions, the pronominal system proves to be a particular locus of vulnerability. We conclude that grammar and human-specific forms of selfhood form an inextricable unity, inviting renewed attention to language as a constitutive condition of personhood in at least some of its forms.*

Correspondence:
ICREA (Catalan Institution for Research and Advanced Studies), Universitat Pompeu Fabra, Departament de Traducció i Ciències del Llenguatge, Roc Boronat, 138, 08018 Barcelona, Spain. *Email: hinzen@icrea.cat*

Journal of Consciousness Studies, **22**, No. 11–12, 2015, pp. 149–79

1. Introduction

Linguistics has played very little role in philosophical discussions of
the 'self', the 'first-person perspective', 'consciousness', or 'subjectivity'. To this day, the relation between these non-linguistic
theoretical notions and the grammar of self-reference has remained
unclear and has barely been the subject of systematic investigation.
Somehow the 'linguistics of the self' is not on the theoretical radar.
The contribution of this paper is to address this relation between
language and the self directly and to argue for a novel position in
which human-specific forms of self-reference are inextricably linked
to the grammatical forms used to carry such acts of self-reference out,
whether in 'thought' or 'language'. This is not to deny that there are
forms of selfhood unrelated to language — indeed it seems obvious
that babies, prior to having a fully developed language and pronominal system, have *some* sense of their selves. But selfhood is not a
unitary notion, and it is natural to assume that there are species-
specific forms of reference to the self as well, some of which mature
along with language and never mature without it. The claim we
investigate and ultimately defend is that self-reference in the first
person is an inherently linguistic and more narrowly *grammatical*
phenomenon, which cannot be defined or explicated in non-
grammatical terms.

We clear the ground in Section 2 by distinguishing a non-
grammatical concept of person from the grammatical Person concept,
which as a technical linguistic term we will capitalize. We then note,
in Section 3, that it is the latter that has played an essential role in
philosophical discussions on 'subjectivity', 'personal agency',
'essential indexicality', or 'self-directed' thought ('thought *de se*'), yet
without reflection on how these concepts relate to the human language
capacity and grammar specifically. Choosing the notion of essential
indexicality as our focus, we argue in Section 4 that it co-varies with
grammatical factors, and, in Section 5, that no non-grammatical
factors can be substituted for these. Finally, in Section 6 we discuss an
empirical prediction of our account, namely that in mental health
conditions involving disorders of thought and self-reference we should
see a distinctive reflex of these anomalies in their respective language
profiles, and specifically in the pronominal system. We suggest that
currently available evidence confirms this prediction for the case of

autism spectrum conditions.[1] In fact, the system of pronominal reference, which critically involves grammatical Person distinctions, proves to be a particular locus of vulnerability across what might be termed disturbances of selfhood, including schizophrenia, thereby supporting a link between grammar and human-specific forms of cognition and selfhood.

2. Two Concepts of 'Person'

The phrase 'the first person' is technically a definite description, whose denotation is uncontroversially not as such a grammatical one. Thus we can talk about 'the first person talking or entering the room' and we will mean that the person in question does so before the second, third, etc. Used in this way, 'the first person' has a 'compositional' interpretation: 'first' means FIRST and 'person' means PERSON, where capitals are used to denote the *lexical concepts* that the relevant words encode. The word 'person' is then not a grammatical term, any more than the concept 'woman' or 'face': these are simply words in the English lexicon which capture lexical concepts, which in turn correspond to ways we perceptually categorize the world — some stimuli in our experience are spontaneously perceived as persons, women, faces, etc. while others are not. For example, if we look at a peanut, we could not normally construe this as a person through sheer effort of our will.

The definite description in question, however, also has a reading on which it is a purely grammatical term. In this case, unlike the former, there cannot be a fourth, fifth, or sixth person. Rather, there are essentially three grammatical Persons and they are universally organized in such a way that they co-occur as a system. Thus there is no language in which everyone at all times is a 'you' and no one ever refers to himself as 'I' (whether through the pronoun or grammatical Agreement marked on the verbal inflection). And, in discourse, wherever there is a person addressed as 'you' or referred to as 'he', there is also a person doing this addressing and referencing while referring to himself or herself in the first Person. All three of these grammatical Persons can be present either explicitly (*'I* command *you* to leave *him*'*), or implicitly, as in 'You will leave him!', where the

---

[1]   Throughout this paper we will be preferentially using the term 'autism spectrum conditions' rather than 'autism spectrum disorders' in line with the perspective that autism reflects a set of cognitive differences rather that deficits.

first Person is that of the implicit epistemic subject making this judgment, or in 'Leave!', where the imperative is second-Person-directed,
and put forward by the first Person.[2] The occurrences and co-
occurrences of the different grammatical Persons are governed by
grammatical constraints that are systematic rather than language- or
culture-specific, illustrating that distinctions of Person in this second
sense *are* indeed highly grammaticalized: they are part of the grammatical system of human languages and subject to its intrinsic constraints.[3] Contrary to what a current near-exclusive focus on the
(usually *lexical*) semantics and pragmatics of pronominal reference in
philosophy entails (see Section 4–5), pronouns and the Person
distinctions they paradigmatically involve are *grammatical
phenomena*.

It is independently clear that this second concept of Person is not a
perceptual one. We may look at a person and realize that she is a
person, but this will say nothing about whether we (or she) will refer
to her(-self) in the first, second, or third grammatical Person: perception cannot make these grammatical distinctions. Secondly, what
can be a *grammatical* Person is not *perceptually* or *lexically* con-
strained. Thus although our lexical understanding of the concept
PEANUT clearly does not suggest personhood and neither does a
visual image of a peanut, it is unproblematic for children or adults to

---

[2] The person referring to him/herself in the third Person can overtly make reference to
herself in the grammatical third Person, of course, as in the case of honorifics (e.g. the
queen referring to herself in the third Person: 'Her majesty disapproves...'; German
'Du/Sie') or 'imposters' (Collins and Postal, 2011), where a third Person is grammatically present and yet reference is to the speaker/writer: e.g. 'This reviewer has not found
the argument of this paper convincing.' The person referring to herself in the third
Person is not in these instances confused over the fact that she is a first Person, and
Collins and Postal (2011) provide empirical evidence that the grammatical first Person
is indeed present structurally as well in these cases.

[3] For example, a broad (though not exceptionless) typological generalization is that third-
Person pronouns (he, she, it) carry grammatical Number (Singular, Plural) and Gender
(Male, Female), but no Person, whereas the personal pronouns (first and second) carry
Person but no Gender, and arguably no Number (Benveniste, 1966); secondly, while
definite descriptions and third-Person pronouns can both be anaphoric, the personal pronouns do not lend themselves as easily to such uses (Hinzen and Sheehan, 2013,
Chapter 4); third, pronouns can be non-overt, when and because their meaning is
governed grammatically; fourth, third-Person Romance accusative clitic pronouns lend
themselves to predicative and quantificational interpretations, while Dative ones arguably are always referential and require a personal interpretation (Martin, 2009); fifth,
occurrences of clitic pronouns with different grammatical Persons are governed by the
Person Case Constraint, which says that when Accusative and Dative clitics co-occur,
the latter must occur before ('higher') than the former (Perlmutter, 1971).

understand that someone introduced to them verbally as 'Mr. Peanut' (a well-known advertising mascot and character of American popular culture) is a person, not a peanut, though looking like a peanut.

What is the mechanism behind this understanding of an inanimate object as a person? We could provide help to our cognitive system perceptually by giving Mr. Peanut person features (e.g. arms and legs, or a face and smile) — i.e. by exploiting the non-grammatical Person concept and introducing the perceptual features by which it can be triggered. But this won't be sufficient to give Mr. Peanut grammatical Person features: again, a visual presentation of a person-like peanut will have no implications whatsoever for whether this 'person' will refer to himself or herself in the first, second, or third grammatical Person. A mechanism to accomplish this — and the only one — is grammar. In fact, the very moment that we refer to a peanut-like person as 'Mr. Peanut', the matter of grammatical Person is settled: 'Mr. Peanut' is a third-Person referential expression, and its referent becomes a referent in the grammatical third Person as and when he speaks. It is from the grammar in this case that we know we are dealing with a person, not a peanut, for in the expression 'here is Mr. Peanut' the lexical item PEANUT does not function grammatically as a common noun (as in 'a peanut'), but as a personal proper name.[4] The two person concepts must be carefully distinguished and, as noted above, in what follows 'Person' with a capital will solely denote the grammatical concept.

The proper domain in which Person is interpreted is *speech* (or sign). Thus, in the following dialogue, I am grammatically third when and as long as I speak, while you are second Person when and as long as you speak:

(1)   [me:] I love you.
(2)   [you:] I love you too.

There is strong evidence that these Person distinctions are preserved in *self-talk* (self-directed speech) as well. Thus I can mutter (3) declaratively, in a matter-of-fact sort of way:

---

4   As Nieuwland and van Berkum (2006) have shown in an electrophysiological study, when the linguistic context is set up in such a way that peanuts are persons grammatically and in the linguistic context, the brain finds nothing odd in a statement such as *The peanuts were madly in love*; and pointing to Mr. Peanut while saying 'This is a peanut' or 'I want to eat this peanut' would be positively odd.

(3)   I am an idiot.

The *affective* exclamation in (4), on the other hand, made while looking into a mirror, crucially involves the second Person as distinct from the implicit speech subject (the third Person), and the first and third Persons are illicit in this instance in English (*cf.* 5–6):

(4)   You idiot!
(5)   *I idiot!
(6)   *He idiot!

Similarly, I can utter the affective (7), and in this case (8), with reverses to the two grammatical Persons involved, is again strongly ungrammatical (see Holmberg, 2014):

(7)   I hate you!
(8)   *You hate me!

In short, we need to witness the *speech act* as and when it takes place in order to interpret the grammatical Persons. They reflect a semantic dimension of speech content to which the speech act itself is essential. It is crucially *not* enough to know who **acts** when: an *action*, as such, involves agents and (often) patients, but it implies nothing about Person distinctions. The perception of agency is an evolutionary ancient mechanism, and an agent as such can be referenced in *any* of the grammatical Persons, in none, or in two at the same time (as in the examples above) — this will depend on how (and whether) he is referenced in speech (his own or that of others). Just as it is not enough to know who **acts** when, it is also not enough to know who **speaks** when: what matters is how we **refer**, in speech, on an occasion, to such a speaker — again, a speaker as such can be referred to in any grammatical Person. This choice of Person changes the grammatical meaning: (9) and (10) do not mean the same, even if I am the speaker and am called Tom:

(9)   The speaker/Tom sings.
(10)   I sing.

In my utterance of (9) I could refer to anyone using the definite description 'the speaker', and even if I use 'Tom' and this is my name, I could refer to any other person called 'Tom'. This referential ambiguity disappears in (10), in which the use of the first Person in speech induces a *relational interpretation* that we can paraphrase as follows:

(11) For an event *e* of singing and speech event *e´*, the agents of *e* and of *e´* are the same, as and when *e* and *e´* takes place.

More briefly: the singer (subject of 'sing') and the speaker (subject of the speech act as such) are the same. I could be in a circumstance in which I know that a person referred to as 'Tom' is singing. And yet I may not know that *I* am singing. This illustrates how Person distinctions arise in how we *refer* to Persons on an occasion of speech and that a distinction in Person captures relational information about the world relative to speech acts taking place in it. We note next that it is the concept of the grammatical first Person that has played a fundamental role in philosophical enquiry.

3. Person in Philosophy

As Chalmers (1996, p. 17) puts it, 'both the psychological and the phenomenal are real and distinct aspects of mind. At a first approximation, phenomenal concepts deal with the first-person aspects of mind, and psychological concepts deal with the third-person aspects'; Ninan (2010, p. 551) writes that *de se* thought takes place in the 'first Person way'; and as Shoemaker (1994, p. 7) puts it, 'some would say that the philosophy of mind without the first-person perspective, or the first-person point of view, is like *Hamlet* without the Prince of Denmark… or like *Othello* without Iago. I say both'. It is clear that the notion of 'the first Person' used in all of these quotes is the grammatical one. Yet, this is rarely reflected upon, and the topic of discussion is routinely taken to be something else, such as phenomena referred to under such non-grammatical labels as 'subjectivity', 'consciousness', or a special kind of 'perspective'. None of these notions are, *per se*, grammatical ones. If they capture what matters in this discussion, maybe grammar can therefore be ignored, as can Person distinctions. This conclusion, however, would be premature. In particular, there is nothing *per se* 'subjective' about the thought expressed in (12):

(12) I am depressed.

A person might arrive at this conclusion after long reflection on her experience, perhaps supported by clinical data. It would then capture a fact about this person. Where the self-ascription of properties lacks this feature of objectivity, as in the case of a propositional delusion in schizophrenia of the sort in (13), the very problem is that something *becomes* 'subjective' that, by the nature of its grammatical form, would normally be understood as an objective claim, which as such carried information about the world:

(13) I am Napoleon.

Subjectivity in first-Person thought as expressed in declarative is in this sense an indication of *pathology*, and is far from being an intrinsic *feature* of such a thought. Grammatical Person interacts with subjectivity, but it is not the same thing and the two topics should not be run together. Similar remarks apply to the notion of 'perspective', a notion too generic and unspecific to capture Person distinctions and hence the first Person one. Thus I may have a problem with the empathy required to feel pity for a person who has been insulted. But empathy does not require, nor does it entail, the specific deictic frame in which normal language use takes place, namely the triangle involving the grammatical first Person engaged in a speech act, the second Person being addressed, and the third Person (or non-Person) talked about (the 'he' or 'it').[5] In fact, the notion of 'perspective' as such entails no grammar at all — or else, if it does, the notion of perspective is implicitly understood in a grammatical fashion, and hence not explanatory for such Person distinctions, which have to be *added* to the (lexical) notion of a 'perspective' in order for it to capture the phenomenon in question. The same applies to the generic notion of 'self-reference', which is equally found in some forms in non-humans and which even in humans does not as such entail anything about whether a person referring to herself will do so in the first Person or another one; and to the notion of a 'subject of one's experience', which once again can be referred to in any grammatical Person, and with or without invoking lexical concepts (e.g. 'the person thinking these thoughts' *vs.* 'I' or the first Person marked through grammatical Agreement only). In sum, whatever such generic notions could be useful for, they are of little use in clarifying the first Person and its role in human-specific thought.[6]

Acts of reference in the neurotypical deictic frame involve knowing that another thinking being's thoughts are not my thoughts, and that the thoughts of both him/her and me are to be distinguished from what

---

[5]   Accordingly, a lack of emotional empathy as in the case of a psychopath implies little for his use of pronouns, as one referee correctly notes. According to Baron-Cohen (2012), psychopaths lack emotional empathy but they have cognitive empathy, while the reverse is true for autism spectrum conditions.

[6]   We thank one referee for clarifying this paragraph.

is the case (the 'world' or 'it'). Such thoughts involve lexical concepts, which typically function grammatically as predicates and apply to objects in such a way that their applying to an object is not decided by whether the first or the second Person thinks that they do: I am human or I am not, whether or not I think I am human or I am not human. These species-specific features of our deictic frame — the infrastructure in which human referring and thinking takes place — are not captured by generic notions of 'perspective-taking' or 'mind-reading': chimpanzees and other species can do rudimentary forms of either — if these notions are understood in sufficiently broad senses — yet inhabit a different deictic frame (Heyes, 2014). The need for specificity in characterizing a human-specific deictic frame suggests that we need to invoke the three-fold Person distinction that grammar makes available. We now argue that standard cases of essential indexicality support this perspective.

4. The Essential Indexical

A long tradition in philosophy, linguistics, and formal semantics has centred on the special behaviour of deictic pronouns, identifying the latter as 'indexicals' and understanding these as a special lexical class whose semantic values and/or pragmatic usage suggest their 'essential' indexicality, in the sense that non-indexical forms of reference cannot be substituted for them. Essential indexicality is closely related to what is also normally characterized in non-linguistic terms, namely '*de se* thought': in first approximation, thought about oneself as oneself. To illustrate this distinction, consider the classical case of Rudolf Lingens, the amnesic academic who is lost in the Stanford library after closing hours. Reading books available to him, he reads a lot about an academic called 'Lingens', including (14):

(14) Lingens is at Stanford.

Yet he doesn't know (15), which is because he doesn't realize (16):

(15) I am at Stanford.
(16) I am Lingens.

His thinking about himself is in this sense not *de se*, though it is clearly about him, in a purely semantic sense that ignores grammatical Person distinctions. Relatedly, Kaplan (1977/1989) invented the famous case in which he observes (17), shortly before he realizes (18):

(17) This guy's/His pants are on fire.

(18) My pants are on fire.

Now, purely descriptively speaking, the most obvious difference
between the pairs in (15–16) and (17–18) is one of grammatical
Person, which shifts from third to first Person in both as we observe
the shift from *de re* to *de se* self-reference. Yet it is standardly captured as a case of 'essential indexicality' interpreted as a non-
grammatical phenomenon, as discussed shortly. Could grammatical
Person, whether invoked in thought or language, be the key to understanding essential indexicality and the *de se*?[7]

Consider John, who is intoxicated and sits in his chair watching a
documentary on TV about a war hero. Ironically, this person is himself, though he fails to realize that. In this circumstance, watching this
scene we could comment (19) using a third-Person pronoun to refer to
him:

(19) John thinks that he is a war hero.

It is widely accepted that (19) could seek to attribute a *de se* thought,
but that it need not; indeed, we may conclude (19) from John's
behaviour, and the thought that the guy on TV is a war hero may not
actually have consciously occurred to John, even if it is clear to us
from his behaviour that he would assent to it when prompted. Even if
it has, we could stress 'he' as a deictic pronoun and utter it accompanied by a gesture pointing to the guy seen on the TV, in which case
the reading could clearly be *intended* to be *de re* only. Without such
stress, the attribution of a *de se* thought can be strongly suggested
pragmatically and likely to be inferred, but it is not semantically
enforced, as the fact suggests that we could utter (19) ironically,
exploiting its actual semantic structure: *John thinks that he, John, is a
war hero.* Now note that, while inferentially invited in (19), the option
that John thinks *de se* he is a war hero becomes strictly a non-option
when the thought 'he is a war hero' is attributed to the subject as
identified in the first Person:

(20) I believe that he is a war hero.

---

7   We are not able to address a frequently invoked language–thought dichotomy here,
except for noting that language is always integrated with thought, and that thought, of
the kind relevant here, in turn requires internal articulation — including grammatical
features like first *vs.* third Person, since thought is intensional and thought identity
changes with the parts it contains.

As uttered by John this is *de re* only. When there is grammatical Agreement of this first-Person feature *across* the matrix and embedded subject positions, in turn, the result is *de se* only:

(21) I believe that I am a war hero.

This pattern is as expected on an account of essential indexicality as inherently grammatical and related to Person distinctions as appearing in appropriate grammatical configurations. As *we* might capture the fact in (20):

(22) John doesn't know that he is him.

Here 'him' is infelicitous (incomplete) without an accompanying deictic gesture (which will typically be to the person as seen on screen), while 'he' may or may not come with such a gesture. If it does, the pointing accompanying 'he' is naturally to John as sitting in his *chair* — demonstrating disjointness of reference, similarly as in John's own utterance (23), where the disjointness indicative of the *de re* scenario is enforced by a grammatical Person distinction:

(23) [John:] *I* am not *him*.

The idea that obligatory *de se* and *de re* will co-vary with grammatical factors, on the other hand, is contradicted by the classical claim that so-called 'obligatory control' enforces a *de se* reading, irrespective of Person (see, for example, Hornstein and Pietroski, 2010). This classical claim is illustrated by (24), which *lacks* any first-Person morphology and is often claimed to have an obligatory *de se* reading:

(24) [me:] John expects PRO to get a medal.

Here PRO is the non-overt but implicitly understood grammatical subject of the embedded clause, which in this case necessarily co-refers with the matrix subject 'John' (i.e. it's *John* who expects to get a medal). Fortunately for the present account, however, this claim is arguably incorrect as also noted in Cappelen and Dever (2013). Thus imagine us looking at the scene above with John in his chair, and he says: 'he'll get a medal for sure', pointing to the person on screen. I say: 'How funny! John expects to get a medal!' The *de re* reading is not only available now but intended.[8] By contrast, the *de se* again enforced in (25):

 (25) [John:] I expect PRO to get a medal.

Hence, again, it is the use of the first Person in both the matrix and embedded subject positions which draws the line between the *de re* and the *de se*. Use of the first Person is not only necessary but it also appears sufficient.[9] For putative evidence against sufficiency, let us turn the embedded non-finite clause in (25) into a grammatically more complex finite one, as in (26), in which case an overt embedded subject is now required. If this subject is in the first Person, the *de re* is still not optional:

 (26) [John:] I expect that I will get a medal.

Let us, however, put the matrix verb into the past tense:

 (27) [John:] I expected that I would get a medal.

John could utter (27) in a circumstance where he is reflecting on a past episode where he saw the guy on screen without realizing it was himself. Stunned by his error, he now utters (27), likely with contrastive stress on the second 'I'. Uttered in this exact circumstance, (27) could have a *de re* reading — though it is crucially a '*post hoc*' one, in the sense that John can only formulate it *after* he realized his error and there is a clear psychological distance between him now and the person whose thinking he reports. The *de re* reading is thus not a pure one, and there is, in fact, full cognitive transparency by the time of the utterance. Moreover, we suggest that this *post hoc de re* reading is quite expected given that the matrix past tense shifts temporal reference away from the speech time, and the temporally more independent (finite) embedded clause depicts a fantasy that John imagines his past self to have. That is, the grammatical structure facilitates the self-distance required. The fact that we have two lexically overt subjects,

---

[8] The idea that this is a pragmatic effect is contradicted by the fact that PRO is strictly part of the compositional semantic structure of the utterance in question.

[9] We agree that (24) will often trigger the inference that a *de se* thought is being reported. Our point is that this is not only not necessarily so, but that, to the extent that it is, there is a grammatical explanation for this again: if obligatory control into embedded subject conditions simply is movement, and there is only one referential determiner phrase (DP) of which one is a non-overt copy (Hornstein and Pietroski, 2010), the possibility of some disjointness of reference is not as easily recognized.

unlike in the non-finite case, supports this possibility too: while a non-overt PRO will necessarily be *referentially dependent* on the overt noun phrase that 'controls' its referent, a second overt subject in the embedded clause will allow for *new* referential possibilities. Note further that where there is lack of Person agreement of the two subjects, as in (28) and (29), the option of the *de se* completely disappears, *despite* the presence of the first Person in either the embedded or the matrix position:

(28) John expected that I would get a medal.
(29) I expected that John would get a medal.

This makes it again clear that the phenomenon is not merely one to do with grammatical first Person, but that it is a grammatical one in the further sense that it depends on grammatical Agreement *across* two clausal subjects. The *de se* is not a lexical phenomenon and not a pragmatic one either.

A grammatical signature of self-reference in the relevant *de se* sense can also be seen as we replace a control verb such as 'expect' with a so-called 'raising' verb like 'seem':

(30) **It** seems that **I** am depressed.
(31) **I** seem to be depressed.

(30) easily lends itself to an 'objective' reading: it could be uttered by me when I am confronted with clinical data clearly suggesting a state of clinical depression. 'Oh,' I might state looking at these data, 'it seems that I am depressed.' This reading approximates one where the statement is effectively about 'whoever the guy is' whose data are being contemplated: the *de re* case. (31) lends itself to this reading less easily: the person uttering (31) is more likely in a state of being confronted with the depression itself experientially. A technical grammatical difference between raising and control would explain this. Thus a standard textbook derivation of (31) would be that 'I' is first generated as the subject of the embedded clause:

(32) ... seem [I to be depressed].

Then this same subject moves to the matrix position, yielding a complete sentence:

(33) I seem [__ to be depressed].

Therefore, the two subjects are the exact *same* lexical item, which is identical across the two positions: referentially, the experiencing subject and the one being depressed are the same. In the derivation of (30), on the other hand, there are two distinct grammatical subjects.

In sum, there are four cases, all of which involve first-Person agreement in matrix and embedded positions but differ grammatically otherwise: 1. Finite clausal embedding with two lexically overt subjects (27); 2. Non-finite clausal embedding with a PRO subject whose reference is controlled by the (independent) matrix subject (25); 3. Non-finite clausal embedding with an embedded subject and an expletive matrix subject (30); 4. Non-finite clausal embedding with an embedded subject that has moved to the matrix position (31). The embedded clause proves to be semantically most independent in the first case, as we would expect from the fact that it has its own finite Tense and a lexically overt embedded subject. It is less independent where there is a subject but no finite Tense in it, and the subject has no phonological content (the case of controlled PRO). It is least independent where one of the subjects is an expletive or the subjects of the two clauses are *de facto* the same. We predict on our position that the *de re* option will become less available the less clausal independence there is: in other words, the more dependent the embedded clause is on the matrix clause, the less room is there for referential disjointness in the above sense, which gives rise to the *de re*. This prediction seems to be confirmed by the linguistic data.

Overall, these results make it unlikely that we can credit essential indexicality or *de se* thought to any lexical or pragmatic factors: the phenomena in question are grammatical essentially and co-vary with specific forms of grammatical complexity. We will seek to confirm this conclusion in what follows.

5. Against Non-grammatical Accounts of Essential Indexicality

5.1. Is essential indexicality lexical?

Rather than appealing to grammatical Person and configurations, could we have appealed to some special *lexical* properties of a particular class of words, i.e. 'indexicals'? The immediate problem with a lexicalist view is that in (17)–(18), repeated here as (34)–(35), 'this' and 'his' are indexicals as much as 'my' is:

(34) This guy's/His pants are on fire.
(35) My pants are on fire.

The problem therefore is not one of indexicals as such, but of the grammatical Person specified on them. A second immediate problem is that no so-called indexical lexical item *needs* to be indexically used, and that, if it is so used, we can directly predict this from the *grammar* of its occurrence and cannot predict it from anything else. Thus consider (36)–(40):

(36) John likes **his** pants.
(37) When I hire a manager, **she** must be bilingual.
(38) He is a **she**.
(39) This is so **you**.
(40) I am **me**.

In (36), 'his' is grammatically in a position 'c-commanded' by its possible antecedent, i.e. 'John', and is naturally interpreted anaphorically rather than deictically. In (37), 'she' can have a quantificational rather than referential reading, given that it can act as a bound variable for the noun phrase occurring in the adjoined clause. In (38), 'she' is in the position of a grammatical predicate, which denotes the property of being female. In (39), 'you' is in the position of a sentential predicate, similarly to the way that an adjective would be in the same position, and hence is again not referential. The same applies to (40), which is uttered by Hugh Grant in *American Dreamz* to express the fact that he is not the kind of guy his girlfriend wants him to be, but the kind of guy he is: 'me' is again predicative.

The third problem with the lexicalist view is that there is, in fact, no such class as that of 'indexicals' in any human language, as has long been known in the linguistic literature (Roca, 1992; 1996; Cardinaletti and Starke, 1999; Déchaine and Wiltschko, 2002; or Martin and Hinzen, 2014, among others). Apart from the problem already discussed, i.e. that the term 'indexical' indicates a way in which a particular lexical item can (but need not) semantically *function* depending on its grammatical position, the putative class of 'indexicals' comprises elements of very different *types*, all of which interact with grammatical principles in a number of different ways. Thus, above we have already encountered pronouns without lexical-phonological content (PRO), expletive pronouns with minimal such content (expletive 'it'), and overt pronouns. In addition to that, there are clitic and non-clitic pronouns, which again differ in their lexical 'weight', with the former attaching to words that host them rather than remaining independent words, and being in this sense more grammatical than lexical. Within the domain of clitics, we find clitics with a whole range of interpretations, which range from purely predicative to quantificational forms of reference, to rigid, deictic, and finally to personal ones. *None* of these are lexically given, and *all* of them directly interact with grammatical factors, as e.g. in the case of predicative clitics, which bear no structural case (Nominative, Accusative, Dative), clitics that do bear Accusative Case and can but need not be referential and/or deictic, and Dative clitics, which are always referential, deictic, and personal (Martin and Hinzen, 2014).

The fourth problem with a lexical interpretation of essentially indexical reference is more fundamental: referentiality, of which essentially indexical reference is an instance, is simply *never a lexical fact*. This becomes obvious in the simplest examples:

(41) MAN.
(42) the man.

(41) is a lexical item (concept, word). (42) is no lexical item: it is not listed in the English lexicon. (41) cannot as such be referential, but (42) can be, as in 'the man entered'. More generally, a purely lexical concept such as (41) cannot, by itself, support any such distinctions as whether we refer to a specific man as opposed to any man, this man as opposed to that, the man we met yesterday, manhood, mankind, or men in general. Therefore, referentiality falls on the side of grammar, not the lexicon — even though, crucially, any of the kinds of acts of reference just illustrated involve a lexical item, and indeed the exact same one. Indexical reference cannot possibly be lexical when no word ever is, and when the indexicals in question have less lexical contents than any other words — and lose this content, becoming more grammatical, in the case of clitics and PRO discussed above.[10] We conclude from these four points that essential indexicality is not lexical, any more than it can be purely pragmatic.

---

[10] It is commonly maintained that the claim of this paragraph is falsified by the class of proper names, given the view that these, in and of themselves, are 'rigidly referential'. This claim is clearly false, however, since we can only tell from the grammar whether something is used as a proper name. Thus all proper names can be common nouns, as in 'There are many Maries in my class' or 'I've never been in love with a Mary', and in turn all common nouns can function grammatically as proper names, as in the case of Mr. Peanut or a child named 'Pomme' (apple) (see Hinzen and Sheehan, 2013, Chapter 4, updating the tradition of Longobardi, 1994; see also Hinzen, 2007; Borer, 2005).

5.2. Is essential indexicality semantic?

We have already seen that this cannot be the case: the relevant forms of semantics only arise in the appropriate grammatical configurations, and therefore they are at least not non-grammatically semantic, arising instead in what we may call 'grammatical semantics' (Hinzen and Sheehan, 2013). Moreover, standard textbooks in the philosophy of language make very clear that the basic notion of semantics is word-based, i.e. lexical.[11] In this sense, too, essential indexicality could not be called a semantic phenomenon. Let us specifically consider, however, what is currently the most dominant semantics of indexicals. Kaplan (1977/1989), contradicting the prior Fregean tradition, interprets indexicals as expressions that are directly referential semantically, while lexically encoding a 'character'. The latter is crucially not part of the semantics of the expression but represents its 'cognitive value'. Hence (43) and (44) will have exactly the same semantic content, while differing in character:

(43) Lingens is at Stanford.
(44) I am at Stanford.

Put differently, there is one referent, call it R, and there are these two ways of referring to it, which are cognitively different because of the character involved. Now, what is a character? It is said to be a conventional 'rule' governing an indexical's evaluation with regards to a given context, c. Formally, the 'semantic value' associated with the word 'I' (at a lexical level) is a function c_a, which maps a token of this word to an agent, relative to a world of evaluation, w, as well as a context, c:

(45) $[[\text{ I }]]^{c, w} = c_a$

As Kaplan puts the content of this rule, it specifies that 'I' 'refers to the speaker or writer of the relevant occurrence of the word "I", that is, the agent of the context' (*ibid.*, p. 505). All words have characters lexically associated to them. Indexicals differ simply because their

---

[11] E.g. Lycan (2008) discusses meaning almost exclusively in the context of discussing the meaning of words. These are standardly taken to be devices of reference, directly contradicting the evidence that reference is never lexical. In so far as meaning and reference at a grammatical level are considered, the essential notion is semantic compositionality, which means that the notion of meaning *remains* lexical: sentence meaning arises by 'composing' word meanings.

characters are non-constant functions: they map the relevant words to different referents in different contexts, e.g. Bill in one, John in another, Mary in a third.

If we take the above as an explanatory account of essential indexicals, however, it faces the following objections. Firstly, the particular rule above for the use of 'I' is the wrong one: 'agent of the context' is the wrong notion to have if it's the referent of 'I' that is to be determined. Thus I may well know or inspect who **acts** in a given context (e.g. Lingens), and yet not know who is **me**. In fact, the non-linguistic (external) context *cannot* provide the right distinction: the first-Person self is, by its nature, not an object of my experience that I can empirically discover in such a context. The Lingens case illustrates this, but a clearer case is the clinical symptom of auditory verbal hallucinations (AVH), which affects about 70% of all patients diagnosed with schizophrenia: patients hear speech about or directed at them, even though there is no speaker. While the speech is heard (so there is a speech agent recognized), the patient does not know who is speaking or the speaker is determined to be some third Person. The voice, in other words, is self-generated by the patient, but its source is obscure or in the wrong Person. This illustrates that we can observe speech while not knowing its grammatical Person — a disturbance in the deictic frame in the sense above.[12] Therefore, knowing who the agent of the context is or even who is speaking may not yield the right distinctions or the knowledge we seek. The right distinctions are grammatical ones, and neither Kaplan's semantics nor his level of character substitute for or illuminate these grammatical distinctions. We thus suggest that they are grammatical essentially. By unveiling the grammatical dimension of reference *de se*, we have hit rock bottom. The first Person is a grammatical phenomenon, and this is it.[13]

Kaplan's semantics also makes a wrong prediction, which arises from its crucial stipulation that indexicals are *contextually ambiguous*

---

[12] Note that lexical knowledge/semantic memory is relatively unimpaired in the 'ipseity' disturbance (distortions in the sense and integrity of selfhood) that schizophrenia represents. This is further reason for concluding that essential indexical is not lexical. If it was, there would be no reason why the patients in question could not simply learn the relevant lexical rule/character. Note also that problems with pronominal reference and Person go beyond the symptom of AVH in schizophrenia (McKenna and Oh, 2005).

[13] As a referee notes, this does not prejudge the broader question of whether grammatical organization as such can be explained in more fundamental terms not presupposing grammatical terms. This foundational question concerning the basis for grammar itself falls outside of the scope of this paper.

referential expressions, which are otherwise *like* proper names in terms of their semantics. If so there is a *single referent*, R, and two *ways of referring* to it, one contextually ambiguous, the other not, which differ in the values of the Person feature (Figure 1):

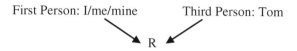

First Person: I/me/mine   Third Person: Tom

R

Figure 1.

The difference between co-referential indexicals and proper names, that is, would be one of context but not of reference, and the semantics (in the sense of the language–world relation) would be exactly the same. Grammatical Person is irrelevant to either the context or the referent, and it is not specified as part of the character either (which is a lexically specified concept or rule, viewed as a non-linguistic, abstract object characterizing an aspect of 'cognition'). The prediction therefore is that if we got rid of Person, nothing relevant in semantics (or even cognition) would change. No object of reference would be missing, and if we only ever used proper names (i.e. third-Person expressions) to refer to any of them, then we would not be missing anything essential to the structure of either meaning (or cognition).

We suggest that this prediction is very unlikely to be true, based not only on evidence for the inherent involvement of the grammar of Person in reference *de se* above, but also on evidence from at least two mental health conditions, autism spectrum conditions (ASC) and schizophrenia. In both of these, the system of pronominal reference, which is paradigmatically sensitive to distinctions of grammatical Person, is often particularly affected. In both syndromes, too, there are fundamental cognitive changes, and a different cognitive phenotype is seen to appear *together* with an altered linguistic profile. These problems with pronominal reference, moreover, may shed light on the aetiology of the cognitive changes in question, if we view them as disturbances of the deictic frame, as independently suggested for the case of schizophrenia by Crow (2010) (see further Hinzen and Rosselló, 2015; for the case of ASC, see Hinzen *et al.*, 2015, and below). The system of grammatical Person is therefore unlikely to be contingent or peripheral to the structure of meaning or how we use language to refer. Eliminating Person would *matter* to the semantics and change our cognitive type.

The significance of Person for the semantics of personal pronouns can be objected to as follows.[14] The Person distinction in our two ways of referring depicted in Figure 1 does not matter to the referent R in question. R, the objection goes, is a *person*, and indeed the exact *same* person in the case of first- and third-Person reference to it. Therefore, the referent R can be identical even if the grammatical Person chosen in referring to R is different, and grammatical Person distinctions do *not* matter to the semantics. This objection fails, however, if nothing could be a person that didn't refer to itself in the first Person. In that case, there only *is* such a thing as R (in the relevant human-specific sense) if we build a grammatical Person distinction in how R refers to itself into our conception of R. But then, in allegedly distinguishing the referent R from the ways of referring to it, we have circularly invoked the grammatical distinction in defining what R is. Therefore, when identifying R we cannot in fact abstract from the distinction of grammatical Person involved in referring to it. A first-Person referent *cannot* be identified with a third-Person referent.[15] The former will be uniquely linguistic and grammatical, in so far as we cannot translate grammatical Person distinctions into any non-linguistic terms. But the latter need not be: we can have perceptual access to third-Person individuated objects as well, and we can investigate them in purely physical rather than linguistic terms.[16]

Even if the crucial factors in essential indexicality are not pragmatic, lexical, or non-grammatically semantic, as we have argued in this section, they could still be 'cognitive' in a non-semantic and non-grammatical sense. That they must be is an entailment of the Kaplanian approach, where the difference between first- and third-

---

[14] The objection was kindly brought to our attention by Lynne Rudder Baker.

[15] A referee worries that, if this were true, 'I could not be able to say "I am [my name]"'. However, although natural language approximates forms of identity that we can state in the languages of logic, copular clauses never encode identities in this sense but retain an asymmetry (see Moro, 1997), with one noun phrase being the grammatical subject and a referential expression, and the other a predicative one. We acknowledge the general desire to keep questions of metaphysics and of language/reference apart, but our argument implies that, at least in the case of the first Person, the form of reference involved is not contingent to the object referenced.

[16] It seems to us that this conclusion is at least consistent with, if it does not indeed support, E.J. Lowe's (2008) conception of personhood, which associates two different 'substances' to selves and their bodies. The technical metaphysical notion of 'substance' does obviously here not mean the same as 'entity' or 'object', and this consequence follows for free from our account, given that selves in this sense are uniquely linguistic entities.

Person forms of reference will essentially lie in the 'character' or 'cognitive value' involved. But we have already challenged the assumption that the relevant rule or character for evaluating the first-Person pronoun can be specified without invoking distinctions of grammatical Person. If so, we achieve nothing by positing a special layer of characters: in specifying them, we will simply have to re-state the grammatical distinctions. Moreover, we have argued that indexicals do affect the semantic structure of natural language and hence do not merely reside at a cognitive level posited as distinct from this semantic one.

There are other objections to a non-grammatical cognitive approach. Thus suppose the special behaviour of personal pronouns would be explained by appeal to particular lexical semantic values associated with them, which would correlate with how they are cognitively processed in a way distinct from other referential expressions. Then the next question would naturally be: why do personal indexicals *have* these special semantic values? Surely this cannot simply be an accident or arbitrary convention that we happen to find in all of the world's languages. So it will need to be *explained*. This need not matter if we are in the business of formal semantics, where we may simply be interested in what the semantics of indexicals *is* and how to state it formally. But if we wish to go beyond semantics as a formal science and ask explanatory questions, the one just raised is fundamental. Martin and Hinzen (2014) offer an account of the forms of reference in which both proper name and indexical reference fall out from the way in which, as grammatical complexity increases in the structure of complex nominals, the relevance of lexical descriptive content in mediating reference decreases, giving rise to rigid and indexical forms of reference (for details that we cannot provide here, see Hinzen and Sheehan, 2013, Chapter 4). Indexicals on this account are not merely contextually sensitive referential expressions, whose referential behaviour is like that of proper names except in a context-sensitive way. They rather instantiate a different form of reference, which is part of an inherent progression towards more grammaticalized forms of reference that we see in the world's languages.

In the final section we follow up on a prediction that our approach makes: in mental health conditions characterized as involving cognitive changes and changes in the integrity of selfhood ('ipseity'), grammar and the system of Person should be distinctly affected. We will focus on the case of ASC, and summarize evidence available today that autism, as an altered cognitive type, involves linguistically specific anomalies, which specifically concern the grammatically mediated referential system.

6. The Linguistics of Autism

The autism spectrum consists of a diverse population of persons who meet threshold-level requirements for communication and social inter-action difficulties as well as repetitive behaviours and restricted inter-ests. Autism is categorized as a pervasive developmental disorder according to international guidelines, including the DSM-V and ICD-10. As such, symptoms are present from early childhood onward and permeate cognition in a broad sense, rather than affecting any one specific aspect. For the past 15 years or so, many researchers in the field have begun to shift away from understanding autism as a series of core deficits to core differences, culminating in a different 'cog-nitive style' (see Happé, 1999, for development of this argument). Indeed, researchers such as Simon Baron-Cohen forgo the clinical term autism spectrum disorders (ASD) for autism spectrum conditions (ASC), the term that we employ here too. However, it has generally been presumed that language problems are not at the core of the symp-tomatology. For example, in diagnosis, autism can be specified with or without accompanying language impairment. By focusing our lens to the linguistic profile of the autism spectrum, we aim to garner greater insight into the linguistic mediation of human-specific person-hood and how cognition may pattern with grammatical distinctions as are involved in the Person system.

The first documented cases of autism were compiled in a series of case studies by psychologist Leo Kanner in 1943. There, Kanner described children who showed what he termed *severe autistic alone-ness*, thereby conceptualizing autism as a kind of separation of the self from others. Kanner interpreted the behavioural symptoms as an *affective* disorder with the root cause possibly attributable to un-warm home environments. However, as more cases of autism were noted, the parental blame subsided and indeed the conception of autism began to shift. By the late 1980s autism was reconceived as a cog-nitive disorder (e.g. Baron-Cohen, 1988) with social and communica-tive deficits primarily grounded in a 'mind-blindness' account, which proposes that individuals with autism have difficulty understanding that the mental states or beliefs of others may be different from their own. Although language abnormalities are cited throughout the litera-ture, including pronominal reference as mentioned above, they have generally been considered to be secondary symptoms of pragmatic deficits that stem from problems understanding the context of speech and which imply understanding mental states and social norms. The clinical basis for diagnosis has also undergone substantial changes over the years, notably in the recent consolidation of the previous symptomatic triad of impairment categories — social deficits, communicative deficits, and restricted interests and repetitive behaviours (RIRBs) — into a duo of (i) social-communicative deficits and (ii) RIRBs. This, in part, was motivated by the systematic patterning together of social and communicative deficits. This is furthered by the sizeable number of cases of 'atypical' autism in which either social-communicative symptoms or RIRBs are not present or are below threshold levels, and in which RIRBs are more likely to be absent (Mandy and Skuse, 2008). Therefore it follows that, while clearly RIRBs are present in a wide percentage of autism cases, the social-communicative deficits are the most widely shared across the entirety of the autism spectrum.

Recently, fine-grained linguistic studies have found syntactic abnormalities across the autism spectrum, which go beyond what one would expect from a pragmatic deficit alone, or a failure to take an interlocutor's 'perspective' into account (see Eigsti, Bennetto and Dadlani, 2007; Durrleman and Zufferey, 2009). If language is relevant to our cognitive development, then it follows that we need to explore different grammatical profiles across cognitively diverse populations including the autism spectrum. In the remainder of this section, we will specifically explore how the grammar of Person is atypical in its use among many individuals on the autism spectrum and how this in turn may pattern with social-communicative challenges.

6.1. Non-standard self-reference

Early works in autism research document atypical language pro-duction, specifically the non-standard use of personal pronouns. As correctly interpreting first- and second-Person pronouns depends on the speech context, the standard interpretation suggests that such pro-noun reversals are symptomatic of a core deficit in pragmatics or broadly-speaking 'context', rather than being due to any problem with pronouns in a narrow sense (e.g. Perovic, Modyanova and Wexler, 2012). Another interpretation attributes pronoun misusage to echo-lalia, such that the child repeats back the pronoun that she or he hears having been directed to them (e.g. Bartak and Rutter, 1974). The most often referenced reversal types are I/you reversals, such that the self is referred to with the pronoun 'you'. For example, a child may request to her or his parent 'you want milk', using 'you' to refer to her/himself (Kanner, 1943). However, although commonly cited in the literature, other kinds of pronominal errors such as third-Person–first-Person reversals may be equally or more robust. Experimental data (which we will explore further below) and corpus data point to an overall shift from the first-Person pronouns to a third-Personal mode of self-reference. Dascalu (2014) analysed the corpora of two French-speaking boys with autism who show problems with pronouns in their spontaneous production. Although there were some you–I reversals, the most dominant pattern was the overuse of third-Person expressions in self-reference. In fact, for one child, the third-Person pronoun 'he' was used like a 'wildcard' to refer to nearly any referent and especially for himself. Could this misusage be due to difficulty managing context in a non-linguistic sense? The answer is open; however, if there are irregularities in production and comprehension that pattern with grammatical distinctions, we would be motivated to set such a pragmatic context account aside. Through a review of the literature, we aim to tease out this question.

Mizuno and colleagues explored deictic shifting of pronouns and visual perspectives in adults on the autism spectrum whose non-verbal IQ were within norms. While pronoun reversals are prevalent in speech of children with autism, many grow out of pronominal difficulties by adulthood. However, although there may be no apparent difficulties, could persons with autism have a different underlying processing? Mizuno *et al.* (2011) targeted this question by testing self-reference comprehension and production via personal pronouns and proper names in an fMRI study. As noted earlier, this is not a distinction of self-reference *per se*, but rather how the person/self grammatically self-references him/herself. The task involved being shown a two-panel image with a picture of a 'house' and a 'carrot' centred in each panel. Then the two panels were folded back in such a way that only one image is visible to the participant, while the other remained visible to examiner. The questions required either the elicitation of pronouns (Q: 'who sees the carrot?', A: I do/me) or the name of the object and hence comprehension of the pronoun (Q: 'what do I see?', A: A house). In the name condition, the pronouns were replaced by the name of the participant and the name of the experimenter.

Interestingly, the authors found that accuracy and response time improved during the proper name condition in relation to the pronoun condition. The imaging results showed a reduction in functional connectivity in comparison to controls for comprehension of questions in which the pronoun 'you' targeted the self's perspective, as in 'What can you see?'. The same was not found in targeting the visual perspective of another. This suggests that the difficulty is neither grounded in reference to the self nor understanding perspective, as the name condition was not problematic. Similarly, it is not merely a lexical problem with a mismatch of the concept of 'I' but rather a more systematic problem of the pronominal and referential system.[17] Furthermore, this study suggests that deictic shifting is residually vulnerable even among persons with autism who no longer present overt pronominal reversals. Therefore we find the foundation of a pattern in the production and comprehension of self-reference — a directional shift of grammatical reference. The shift from first/second Person to names indicates a grammatical change, which can be outlined in the following three points. First, first- and second-Person pronouns lack both Gender and Number, while being specified for grammatical Person. Secondly, they are largely used referentially, in the absence of a lexical description. And thirdly they encompass the grammatical complexity of third- or non-Person descriptions (see Martin and Hinzen, 2014, for the evidence). In contrast to first- and second-Person pronouns, third- or non-Person definite descriptions have reference mediated by a lexical description. Similarly, proper names also have greater lexical weight than pronouns and third-Person pronouns are specified for Gender and Number and easily lend themselves to non-referential (e.g. anaphoric or quantificational) uses.

In sum, the ability to refer to the self is not impaired *per se*, however we find a facilitation of comprehension when personal pronouns are avoided and more third-Person forms of reference such as names are used. This suggests a shift in grammatical complexity affecting the referential system and grammatical Person in particular.

6.2. Non-standard self-reference across modalities

Similar to the findings of proper name facilitation in the Mizuno *et al.* study, photo identification tasks, which elicit first- and second-Person pronouns, further ground the phenomenon that we identify as a

---

[17] As confirmed in a recent study that found autistic children to be at chance with respect to definite but not indefinite determiners (Modyanova, 2009).

grammatical Person shift. This experimental design has been conducted with English-speaking children on the autism spectrum, first by
Jordan (1989) and later by Lee, Hobson and Chiat (1994), and documented a preference to refer to oneself by name rather than pronoun.
Recently, this task was replicated with native signing children of
American Sign Language on the autism spectrum whose non-verbal
IQs were within norms in a study by Shields and Meier (2014). The
task consisted of identifying photos which were either of the participant or the researcher, who they had been acquainted with previously.
They found, similar to Lee and colleagues and Jordan, that children
with autism have a preference to refer to themselves via their name
sign or even finger spell their names rather than pronominally refer to
themselves. This is particularly interesting in that it points to the
robust linguistic nature of the phenomenon as it transcends language
modalities. Furthermore, while the nature of pronouns may still be
debated within sign language, it is generally accepted that the first
Person is indicated by an index finger point to the chest. However, it
appears that this sign, in spite of its iconicity, is avoided in autism in
as much as it is a grammatical pronoun. Independent evidence by
Hobson, García-Perez and Lee (2010) moreover shows that pointing
isn't impaired *per se* in autism. Therefore, this study suggests that
first-Person reference in so much as it is highly grammaticalized is
weakened, while reference to self and other via proper names is
spared.

6.3. Patterning pronoun usage to grammatical distinctions across language diversity

The majority of autism research to date has been conducted in
English, and while we would not predict the specific language to
affect grammatical abilities in autism, cross-linguistic variability may
test whether language anomalies pattern with grammatical differences.
One such instance is a study on syntax among Greek-speaking
children on the autism spectrum by Terzi *et al.* (2014). The children in
this study were on average 5 years old and had non-verbal IQ
measures within norms. This study targeted a range of grammatical
structures including clitic pronouns, which are not present in English.
Clitics are pronouns that may attach to verbs rather than being
lexically independent and therefore are even more stripped of lexical
weight than pronouns in English. Given the preference towards proper
names in elicitation tasks and production, it is interesting to further

explore whether strong lexical over grammatical weight facilitates comprehension in autism.

During a battery of comprehension tasks, only clitics appeared to be problematic for the children with autism, although their comprehension rate was still quite high (88.3%). However, the clitics that were used were third-person only and therefore less complex than first- or second-person clitics which are specified for +Person (Martin and Hinzen, 2014). Furthermore, during elicitation tasks, clitics seen in (46) were often omitted or substituted for a full determiner phrase, however substitutions did not reach significance in relation to their typically developing peers.

(46) Ti filai
      her.cl kisses
      He kisses her

Moreover, although clitics were affected, other pronouns such as reflexives were found to be spared. This contrasted to the findings by Perovic, Modyanova and Wexler (2012) which in part motivated the study in Greek. However, there are two key differences between the two studies. First, the Perovic study was composed of a more heterogeneous group on the autism spectrum, with overall lower IQ, which may contribute to the lower performance; secondly, the grammar involved in reflexive pronouns differs between English and Greek. Greek reflexives act like full lexical noun phrases, in that they are preceded by a determiner and are followed by a possessive pronoun (47):

(47) ton eafto tu
      the self his
      'himself'

Therefore, we find a trend: the higher the lexical weight, the less the pronoun is problematic. Clitics are most stripped of lexical content while English reflexive pronouns have some lexical quality (my + self) and Greek reflexive pronouns are full DPs. Therefore, although heterogeneity of group differences must certainly be taken into consideration, the contrast in performance by Greek- and English-speaking children with autism falls in line with grammatical distinctions.

6.4. Differences in episodic memory

In addition to tasks that specifically elicit pronominal reference, we may also explore self-reference in cognitive domains that may be dependent upon the first-Person perspective, such as episodic memory. Episodic memory, the memory of past events, has been argued to be impaired among persons with autism. While autobiographical memory is intact, such as correctly recalling facts about one's life, individuals with autism may not necessarily recall the events on which the information is based (Lee and Hobson, 1998). Hare, Mellor and Azmi (2007) conducted an experiment in which persons with autism spent the day with researchers doing various activities and were later asked to freely recall what had happened. They found that, unlike in controls, persons with autism did not have any bias for free recall of self-experienced events over observed other-experienced events. This is not a problem of ipseity related to the self in a generic sense, since they did indeed remember events in which they participated. What differed from controls was that they did not show the typical distinction between a first-person and a third-person perspective in the remembered event. Furthermore, memory is indeed not an area of general difficulty, as many persons with autism manifest particular strengths in memory (Happé and Frith, 2009). Rather, when memory evokes the grammatical distinctions of Person, we find differences from peers without autism.

7. Summary

It is not in doubt that 'I' as used in philosophical debates on 'the first person' is intended to be what we have distinguished as the 'grammatical' notion of Person. What is in doubt is whether or not this grammatical notion captures a non-grammatical and independently given distinction. The above evidence from essential indexicality and from language in autism does not suggest that non-grammatical substitutes are available that capture the required distinctions. The meaning of 'I' cannot, we suggest, be explicated in any terms not invoking grammatical distinctions. It is a linguistic and more narrowly grammatical term essentially. Whatever forms of selfhood and self-reference it goes with, therefore, are essentially linguistic. Language is not a contingent extra or mere 'tool' in which independently given forms of selfhood are merely 'expressed'. Nor does there pre-theoretically seem to be any implausibility in the view that grammar, the uncontroversial and essential organizational principle distinctive of human language, allows for forms of self-reference that do not exist in the absence of language. Renewed attention to the cognitive function of grammar in this way promises new insights on language, metaphysics, and cognitive diversity alike.

References

Baron-Cohen, S. (1988) Social and pragmatic deficits in autism: Cognitive or affective?, *Journal of Autism and Developmental Disorders*, **18** (3), pp. 379–402.

Baron-Cohen, S. (2012) *The Science of Evil: On Empathy and the Origins of Cruelty*, New York: Basic Books.

Bartak, L. & Rutter, M. (1974) The use of personal pronouns by autistic children, *Journal of Autism and Childhood Schizophrenia*, **4**, pp. 217–222.

Benveniste, E. (1966) Problèmes de linguistique générale, vol. 1, *Les Etudes Philosophiques*, **21** (3), pp. 403–404.

Borer, H. (2005) *In Name Only: Structuring Sense*, vol. 1, Oxford: Oxford University Press.

Cappelen, H. & Dever, J. (2013) *The Inessential Indexical*, Oxford: Oxford University Press.

Cardinaletti, A. & Starke, M. (1999) The typology of structural deficiency: A case study of three classes of pronouns, in van Riemsdijk, H. (ed.) *Clitics in the Languages of Europe*, pp. 145–233, Berlin: Mouton de Gruyter.

Chalmers, D. (1996) *The Conscious Mind: In Search of a Fundamental Theory*, Oxford: Oxford Unified Press.

Collins, C. & Postal, P. (2011) *Imposters: A Study of Pronominal Agreement*, Cambridge, MA: MIT Press.

Crow, T.J. (2010) The nuclear symptoms of schizophrenia reveal the four quadrant structure of language and its deictic frame, *Journal of Neurolinguistics*, **23**, pp. 1–9.

Dascalu, C.M. (2014) *Self-Reference in Autistic Children: Semantic, Pragmatic and Cognitive Approaches*, Doctoral dissertation, Paris 3 Sorbonne-Nouvelle University.

Déchaine, R.M. & Wiltschko, M. (2002) Decomposing pronouns, *Linguistic Inquiry*, **33** (3), pp. 409–442.

Durrleman, S. & Zufferey, S. (2009) The nature of syntactic impairment in autism, *Rivista di Grammatica Generativa*, **34**, pp. 57–86.

Eigsti, I.M., Bennetto, L. & Dadlani, M.B. (2007) Beyond pragmatics: Morpho-syntactic development in autism, *Journal of Autism and Developmental Disorders*, **37**, pp. 1007–1023.

Happé, F. (1999) Autism: Cognitive deficit or cognitive style?, *Trends in Cognitive Science*, **3** (6), pp. 216–222.

Happé, F. & Frith, U. (2009) The beautiful otherness of the autistic mind, *Philosophical Transactions of the Royal Society of London, Series B: Biological Sciences*, **364** (1522), pp. 1345–1350.

Hare, D.J., Mellor, C. & Azmi, S. (2007) Episodic memory in adults with autistic spectrum disorders: Recall for self- versus other-experienced events, *Research in Developmental Disabilities*, **28** (3), pp. 317–329.

Heyes, C.M. (2014) Animal mindreading: What's the problem?, *Psychonomic Bulletin and Review*, **22** (2), pp. 313–327.

Hinzen, W. (2007) *An Essay on Naming and Truth*, Oxford: Oxford University Press.

Hinzen, W. & Sheehan, M. (2013) *The Philosophy of Universal Grammar*, Oxford: Oxford University Press.

Hinzen, W. & Rosselló, J. (2015) The linguistics of schizophrenia: Thought disturbance as language pathology across positive symptoms, *Frontiers in Psychology*, **6**, p. 971.

Hinzen, W., Rosselló, J., Mattos, O., Schroeder, K. & Vila, E. (2015) The image of mind in the language of children with autism, *Frontiers in Psychology*, **6**, p. 841.

Hobson, R.P., García-Perez, R.M. & Lee, A. (2010) Person centered (deictic) expressions in autism, *Journal of Autism Developmental Disorders*, **40** (4), pp. 403–414.

Holmberg, A. (2014) *Self-Talk*, Manuscript, Department of Linguistics and Language Science, University of Newcastle, UK.

Hornstein, N. & Pietroski, P. (2010) Obligatory control and local reflexives: Copies as vehicles for de se readings, in Hornstein, N. & Polinsky, M. (eds.) *Movement Theory of Control*, pp. 67–88, Amsterdam: John Benjamins.

Jordan, R.R. (1989) An experimental comparison of the understanding and use of speaker–addressee personal pronouns in autistic children, *British Journal of Disorders of Communication*, **24**, pp. 169–179.

Kaplan, D. (1977/1989) Demonstratives, in Almog, J., Perry, J. & Wettstein, H. (eds.) *Themes from Kaplan*, pp. 481–563, New York: Oxford University Press.

Kanner, L. (1943) Autistic disturbances of affective contact, *Nervous Child*, **2**, pp. 217–250.

Lee, A., Hobson, R.P. & Chiat, S. (1994) I, you, me, and autism: An experimental study, *Journal of Autism and Developmental Disorders*, **24** (2), pp. 155–176.

Lee, A. & Hobson, R.P. (1998) On developing self-concepts: A controlled study of children and adolescents with autism, *Journal of Child Psychology and Psychiatry*, **39**, pp. 1131–1144.

Longobardi, G. (1994) Reference and proper names: A theory of N-movement in syntax and logical form, *Linguistic Inquiry*, **25**, pp. 609–665.

Lowe, E.J. (2008) *Personal Agency: The Metaphysics of Mind and Action*, New York: Oxford Unified Press.

Lycan, W.G. (2008) *Philosophy of Language*, London: Routledge.

Mandy, P.L. & Skuse, D. (2008) Research review: What is the association between the social-communication elements of autism and repetitive interests, behaviours and activities?, *Journal of Child Psychology and Psychiatry*, **49** (8), pp. 795–808.

Martin, T. (2009) Deconstructing Catalan object clitics, *NYU Working Papers in Linguistics*, **2**, pp. 1–19.

Martin, T. & Hinzen, W. (2014) The grammar of the essential indexical, *Lingua*, **148**, pp. 95–117.

McKenna, P. & Oh, T. (2005) *Schizophrenic Speech*, Cambridge: Cambridge University Press.

Mizuno, A., Liu, Y., Williams, D., Keller, T., Minshew, N. & Just, M. (2011) The neural basis of deictic shifting in linguistic perspective-taking in high-functioning autism, *Brain*, **134**, pp. 2422–2435.

Modyanova, N. (2009) *Semantic and Pragmatic Language Development in Typical Acquisition, Autism Spectrum Disorders, and Williams Syndrome*, Doctoral dissertation, MIT.

Moro, A. (1997) *The Raising of Predicates*, Cambridge: Cambridge University Press.

Nieuwland, M.S. & van Berkum, J.J.A. (2006) When peanuts fall in love: N400 evidence for the power of discourse, *Journal of Cognitive Neuroscience*, **18** (7), pp. 1098–1111.

Ninan, D. (2010) De se attitudes: Ascription and communication, *Philosophy Compass*, **5** (7), pp. 551–567.

Perlmutter, D. (1971) *Deep Structure and Surface Structure Constraints in Syntax*, New York: Holt, Reinhart and Winston.

Perovic, A., Modyanova, N. & Wexler, K. (2012) Comprehension of reflexive and personal pronouns in children with autism: A syntactic or pragmatic deficit?, *Applied Psycholinguistics*, **34** (4), pp. 813–835.

Roca, F. (1992) *On the Licensing of Pronominal Clitics: The Properties of Object Clitics in Spanish and Catalan*, Master's thesis, Universitat Autònoma de Barcelona, Spain.

Roca, F. (1996) Morfemas objetivos y determinantes: los clíticos del español, *Verba*, **23**, pp. 83–119.

Shield, A. & Meier, R.P. (2014) Personal pronoun avoidance in deaf children with autism, in *Proceedings of the 38th Annual Boston University Conference on Language Development*, pp. 403–415, Somerville, MA: Cascadilla Press.

Shoemaker, S. (1994) The first person perspective, *Proceedings and Addresses of the American Philosophical Association*, **68** (2), pp. 7–22.

Terzi, A., Marinis, T., Francis, K. & Kotsopoulou, A. (2014) Grammatical abilities of Greek-speaking children with autism, *Language Acquisition*, **21**, pp. 4–44.

Lynne Rudder Baker

Autism and 'I'

Abstract: *After summarizing my own (non-Cartesian) views of 'I' and the first-person perspective, I consider a well-known autistic, Temple Grandin, who claims that she thinks only in pictures, not in language. I argue, to the contrary, that Grandin's mental life as she describes it in fact requires language, which, as a writer, she undoubtedly has. Finally, I turn to the question of whether thought as Temple Grandin describes it is independent of language.*

Over the years, I have developed a non-Cartesian view of the first-person perspective and its importance for understanding what a person is. Here, I want to explore how my view can apply to someone with autism. In particular, I'll consider a well-known autistic person, Temple Grandin, who makes it obvious that some autistics (her term) have rich inner lives — albeit inner lives differently organized from the mental lives of people she calls 'neurotypicals': she reports that, unlike neurotypicals, she thinks only in pictures. Grandin says, 'I would be denied the ability to think by scientists who maintain that language is essential for thinking' (Grandin, 2006, p. 186). However, I shall argue, to the contrary, that Grandin's mental life as she describes it in fact *requires* language, which, as a writer, she undoubtedly has. After summarizing my own views on the word 'I' and the first-person perspective, I'll argue that having a first-person perspective is essential to being a person. Then I'll make some remarks about autism, and finally, I'll turn to Temple Grandin and the question of whether thought as she describes it is independent of language.

I am not any kind of scientist, nor any kind of expert on autism. So, you may ask, how dare I undertake this project? Well, according to *Autism Asperberger's Digest*, 2008, autism is 'no longer viewed as a strictly behavioral disorder, but one that affects the whole person on

Correspondence:
Lynne Rudder Baker, University of Massachusetts Amherst, USA.
Email: lrbaker@philos.umass.edu

Journal of Consciousness Studies, **22**, No. 11–12, 2015, pp. 180–93

various fronts: biomedical, cognitive, social, and sensory' (Grandin 2011, p. xxiv). In the first place, as a syndrome that affects the whole person, autism is within the purview of philosophy — one of the few disciplines that focuses on the whole person, as opposed to sub-personal systems, functions, or organs. In her recent book, *The Autistic Brain* (Grandin and Panek, 2013), Temple Grandin empha-sizes the whole person — including education and employment — not just neurological results. As I see it, knowledge of the brain, though important, will always fall short of knowledge of the whole person.

In the second place, important data on autism come from self-reports, first-person reports that scientists typically disparage. About 90% of people with autism suffer from sensory overload: certain sounds or smells (the swish of a skirt or the fragrance of a certain perfume) overwhelm them, and the *only* way to find out what it's like to live in an alternate sensory reality is to ask. The data so obtained are perforce first-personal and not subject to objective verifiability (*ibid.*, p. 76). Unlike many scientific researchers, I do not disparage self-reports. In *The Autistic Brain*, Grandin expresses the hope that 'new technologies [like electronic tablets] might allow for a higher incidence of self-reporting' (*ibid.*, p. 77). Now, let's turn to my views on the pronoun 'I' and the first-person perspective.

1. The Pronoun 'I' and the First-Person Perspective

In the first place, I believe, *pace* Anscombe, that 'I' is a referring expression. It refers to its user — the one who thinks or utters it. It refers to the person, the whole person, constituted by a body. Its referent is not a self, or a soul, or a mind or any non-personal or sub-personal item.

In the second place, I believe that the pronoun 'I' has more than semantic interest. Its role as an indexical doesn't begin to exhaust its significance. A first-person perspective is a dispostional property with two stages: rudimentary and robust. The robust stage, enjoyed by language-using persons, makes possible many characteristic human activities and abilities. Indeed, a robust first-person perspective is the seat of the uniqueness of persons. Without a robust first-person per-spective, one would not be able to know what she was doing; one would not be able to evaluate reasons for acting; one would not be able to own up to what one does. Full mastery of the word 'I' culmi-nates in a robust first-person perspective, and indeed in self-consciousness. A robust first-person perspective requires not only that one can refer to herself in the first person, but also that she can know that it is herself to whom she is referring, that she can conceive of herself as herself in the first person.

Contrast the robust with the rudimentary stage of the first-person perspective. A toddler is a person, who has consciousness and intentionality but not yet language; she is only at the rudimentary stage. She experiences her surroundings from a first-person point of view; but without a language, she cannot yet conceive of herself as herself in the first person. She may use 'Baby wants water' interchangeably with 'I want water' or even just 'want water'. But she cannot reflectively think about herself as herself. She has no self-concept and no robust first-person perspective.

When a person acquires a robust first-person perspective, she acquires the ability to formulate thoughts expressible by complex sentences — like 'I wonder how I'm going to die' or 'I wish that I were a movie star' or 'I promise that I'll stand by you'. In these sentences, the speaker refers to herself with the first occurrence of 'I' and she attributes to herself a first-person reference with the second occurrence of 'I' (Castañeda, 1967; 1966; Baker, 1981). The attribution to oneself of a first-person reference manifests a robust first-person perspective: one cannot attribute to oneself a first-person reference without realizing that it is oneself to whom she attributes the first-person reference. And one needs no name or description to pick out who one is referring to.

We can see this semantically. If I say 'I like spinach', what I say is true if and only if Lynne Baker likes spinach. But if I say 'I'm glad that I like spinach', what I say is not true unless I am able to conceive of myself in the first person. To put it another way, an utterance 'I'm glad that I like spinach' entails that the speaker has a robust first-person perspective, and is able to conceive of herself as herself in the first person. In utterances like 'I'm glad that I like spinach', the first occurrence of 'I' in such sentences can be replaced by a name of the speaker *salva veritate*; but the second occurrence of 'I' cannot be replaced by a name *salva veritate*: it doesn't just refer to the speaker, but atttributes to the speaker a first-person reference.

Even if one could eliminate 'I' from simple sentences like 'I like spinach', one would not be able to eliminate the second occurrence of 'I' in 'I'm glad that I like spinach'. If Jones says 'I regret that I don't like spinach', there is no adequate paraphrase without a first-person attribution ('Jones regrets that Jones doesn't like spinach' won't do as a paraphrase, since the paraphrase can be true when the corresponding

I-utterance is false, and vice versa. Jones's utterance 'I regret that I don't like spinach' is true only if Jones can conceive of himself in the first person).

In order to attribute to oneself a first-person reference, one must have a self-concept, and a self-concept is not a stand-alone concept. A self-concept is linked to natural language in the following way: one acquires concepts generally by learning the meanings of words, and one needs a sizeable store of concepts — e.g. *toy, water, ball, mummy* — in order to acquire a self-concept. To acquire a self-concept — a concept that allows the speaker to conceive of herself without the possibility of being mistaken about who she is referring to — one must have learned a natural language.

The second occurrence of 'I' in an utterance — the one that directly manifests a robust first-person perspective (e.g. 'I'm glad that I like spinach') — expresses a self-concept. Once one has a robust first-person perspective and has mastered complex first-person sentences whose main verbs are psychological or linguistic, and which have subordinate first-person 'that'-clauses (as in 'I'm sorry that I misled you'), then her use of 'I' in simple sentences ('I misled you') also expresses a self-concept and manifests a robust first-person perspective. The robust first-person perspective is a conceptual dispositional property that can be manifested in indefinitely many ways, each of which is an occasion of conceiving of oneself *as* oneself, in the first person.

2. Persons as Essentially First-Personal

Persons, on my view, are essentially embodied (constituted by bodies with which they are not identical) and are essentially first-personal.

Let's begin by asking: 'Are autistics persons?' My answer is an unequivocal yes, but other philosophers may give a more guarded answer. John Locke, for example, took 'person' to stand for 'a thinking intelligent Being, that has reason and reflection, and can consider itself as itself, the same thinking thing in different times and places' (Locke, 1690). On this definition, perhaps not all autistics are Lockean persons. But my view is not Locke's — despite the fact that I, like Locke, distinguish persons from animals, and also despite the fact that I take what I call a 'first-person perspective' to be essential to being a person.

As I mentioned, I take the first-person perspective to be a two-stage dispositional property. The rudimentary stage is shared by human infants and many non-human animals. At the rudimentary stage, a first-person perspective is a non-conceptual capacity: it is the capacity of a conscious subject to perceive and interact with entities in the world, from a first-personal 'origin'. What is required for a rudimentary first-person perspective — exemplified by human or beast or anything else — are consciousness and intentionality. At the robust stage, a first-person perspective is a conceptual capacity: it is the capacity to conceive of oneself as oneself from the first person. What is required for the robust stage is a degree of mastery of a natural language (throughout, by 'language' I am talking about spoken and written language, the stuff of speech acts — not an abstract symbol system).

Metaphysically speaking, a person essentially has a first-person perspective, rudimentary or robust. When a human organism develops to the point of being able to support a first-person perspective, the organism comes to constitute a new entity, a person who has a first-person perspective essentially (Baker, 2007; 2013). (Contrast a chimpanzee; when a chimpanzee is able to support a (rudimentary) first-person perspective, no new entity comes into existence; the chimpanzee just gains a new contingent property.)

The new person, who has a first-person perspective essentially, comes into existence with a rudimentary first-person perspective and a remote capacity (or a second-order capacity) to develop a robust first-person perspective. The remote capacity to develop a robust first-person perspective is a capacity to develop a capacity — a capacity which may never be realized. So, some persons may never have a robust first-person perspective. For most persons, the stage of the rudimentary first-person perspective at the beginning of existence is but a prelude to the robust stage of the first-person perspective. Indeed, what distinguishes persons from entities of every other sort is that only persons are of a kind that typically develops the robust stage of the first-person perspective.

Let me emphasize that a person is a single individual throughout her existence. She continues to manifest her first-person perspective in different ways as she learns a language and gets to the robust stage of the first-person perspective. What makes you the same person that you were when you were an infant is that there is a single exemplification of the dispositional property of having a first-person perspective both then and now — regardless of the vast differences in its manifestations over the years. For example, an infant may manifest a first-person perspective (at the rudimentary stage) by drawing back from a looming figure, and an adult may manifest a first-person perspective (at the robust stage) by making a will. A human person from infancy through maturity until death (and perhaps beyond) is a single exemplifier of a first-person perspective — whether rudimentary or robust.

So, born with a rudimentary first-person perspective and a remote capacity to develop a robust first-person perspective, a neurotypical person gets to the robust stage in the natural course of development. As she learns a language, a person acquires numerous concepts, among which is a self-concept that she can use to conceive of herself as herself in the first person. On acquiring a self-concept, a person gains a robust first-person perspective — an in-hand capacity to conceive of herself as herself in the first person, without identifying herself by a name, description, or third-person demonstrative. For example, if I say or think 'I'm afraid that I won't live up to my ideals', I directly manifest a robust first-person perspective — the capacity to conceive of myself as myself in the first person. This capacity is exhibited throughout one's life in characteristically human activities — from making contracts to celebrating anniversaries to seeking fame by entering beauty contests.

Moreover, a robust first-person perspective makes possible an inner life. Oliver Sacks noted that there was a time when the autistic mind was supposed to be 'incapable of self-understanding and understanding others and therefore of authentic introspection and retrospection' (Sacks, 1995, p. 253). That conception of autism has been proved wrong, especially by writers like Temple Grandin. Nevertheless, some with very severe autism may be unable to enjoy a robust first-person perspective. But such individuals, even though they have only rudimentary first-person perspectives, are nonetheless persons. Remember that, unlike Locke, I do not take a person to be defined by an ability to 'consider itself as itself, the same thinking thing in different times and places'.

Now, I hope, we can see why I say that autistics, even severe autistics, even autistics who do not speak, are persons: they have first-person perspectives essentially — whether or not they develop robust first-person perspectives, as neurotypicals do.

3. Some Remarks about Autism

Autism is a confusing condition. Although autism is considered to be a disability, sometimes autistics exhibit extraordinary abilities — e.g.

prodigious memory, perfect pitch, amazing calendar calculation —
even as they display the more usual symptoms of autism. As I mentioned, autism is a spectrum of disorders, with a great variety of
symptoms — such as frequent tantrums, lack of empathy, 'destructive
behavior, inability to speak, a sensitivity to physical contact, a fixation
on spinning object', inability to make eye contact, poor short-term
memory, obsessive repetitive behaviour, sensitivity to noise and confusion, appearance of deafness, and more (Grandin and Panek, 2013,
pp. 3, 5; Grandin and Scariano, 1986/2005, p. 153).

These symptoms are exhibited in different combinations and to
different degrees. This is further complicated by the fact that recent
brain research has shown that researchers 'can't be sure that someone
else manifesting the same behavior would have the same anomaly [in
the brain]'. And conversely, researchers 'can't be sure that that
anomaly [in the brain] will have the same behavioral effect in a
different brain' (Grandin and Panek, 2013, p. 37). So, although neuroimaging techniques have revealed a variety of neural patterns that
correspond to a variety of autistic behaviours, there's no single clear
picture. For example, sensory difficulties are correlated with both
overconnectivity and underconnectivity between cortical regions in
the brain.

Interestingly, one researcher has suggested that 'Impaired social
interactions and withdrawal may not be the result of a lack of com-
passion, incapability to put oneself into someone else's position or
lack of emotionality, but quite to the contrary a result of an intensely if
not painfully aversively perceived environment' (Grandin and Panek,
2013, p. 87, quoting Markram, 2007). Even if autism is *caused* by
anomalous 'wiring' in the brain, as Temple Grandin sometimes
suggests, what autism *is* is a spectrum of complex syndromes. Neural
causes aside, scientists generally define autism by several behavioural
conditions: 'impaired social interaction, impaired communication, and
restricted and repetitive interests and activities' (Happé, Ronald and
Plomin, 2006, p. 1218). I'll now turn to a remarkable person with
autism, Temple Grandin.

4. Temple Grandin

Temple Grandin, despite serious autism, is a scientist and an articulate
reporter of her own mental life and the challenges that she has overcome. With a PhD in animal science, she has a particular interest in
cattle chutes. But what really makes her unusual is that she has a

serious form of autism. She had a wonderful mother, who took her to a neurologist rather than a psychiatrist when she was three years old, and she ended up in a pre-school with a talented speech therapist (Sacks, 1995, p. 271; Grandin and Panek, 2013, p. 3).[1] She has regarded her deficits as challenges to be overcome or worked around, and now has high-functioning autism or Asperger's.

One autism researcher described Grandin as 'growing from an extremely handicapped child who appeared to be destined for permanent institutionalization to a vigorous, productive, and respected adult who is a world-authority in her field' (Grandin and Scariano, 1986, p. 6). And, despite the fact that she writes unabashedly in the first person, Jerome Groopman called her 'one of our most astute interpreters of autism' (Groopman, 2013, p. 40).

Wonderfully articulate, Temple Grandin conveys her immediate intuitive sympathy with cattle: she knows how they feel, whereas she has to 'compute' how people feel. She told Sacks that she felt like 'an anthropologist from Mars' trying to interpret the natives.

5. Grandin and the Robust First-Person Perspective

As I explained, on my view, personhood does not require having a *robust* first-person perspective. But no matter. Grandin most assuredly has one. Oliver Sacks said in his Foreward to her book, *Thinking in Pictures,* that there had never been an 'inside narrative' of autism before Grandin's; for forty years it had been medical dogma that 'there *was* no "inside," no inner life, in the autistic, or if there was it would be forever denied access or expression' (Grandin, 2006, p. xiii).

An example from Sacks's *An Anthropologist from Mars* gives conclusive evidence of Grandin's robust first-person perspective. Grandin didn't know that she could draw until she was 28 and watched a draftsman drawing plans. 'I saw how he did it', she told Sacks.

> 'I went out and got exactly the same instruments and pencils as he used — a point-five-millimeter HB pentel — and then I started pretending I was him. The drawing did itself, and when it was all done I couldn't believe I'd done it. I didn't have to learn how to draw or design, I pretended I was David — I appropriated him, drawing and all.' (Sacks, 1995, p. 266)

---

[1] 'I was able to learn to speak because I could understand speech, but low-functioning autistics may never learn to speak because their brains cannot discriminate among speech sounds' (Grandin, 2006, p. 42).

'I pretended I was David' is direct manifestation of a robust first-person perspective. That same thought cannot be formulated or expressed without Grandin's being able to conceive of herself as herself in the first person. Grandin did not just distinguish Grandin from David; she distinguished *herself* from David.

Grandin's books also give ample evidence of a robust first-person perspective. The last chapter of one of her books is 'My Self-Identity', based on her teenaged fixation on science, horses, and the projects that she built (Grandin, 2011, p. 311). Anyone who talks about her self-identity is manifesting a robust first-person perspective.

Here's a final example of Grandin's sense of herself in the first person. When she started out designing cattle chutes, she needed concrete representations of advancement in the cattle industry. In her words, 'I wore a green work uniform with cattle pins on the collar like a soldier's rank insignia. I started out as a private, with bronze cattle pins, and as I became recognized in the industry I awarded myself high-ranking silver or gold cattle pins. I was totally oblivious to the fact that other people regarded my uniform as ridiculous' (Grandin, 2006, p. 112).

After Grandin's boss had 'his secretaries take [her] shopping for nicer clothes and teach [her] better grooming', she reports, 'Now I wear a more appropriate western shirt, but I still award myself an advancement in cattle rank and put two silver cattle pins on my collar' (*ibid.*, p. 112). She wasn't just conferring awards on Temple Grandin, but on herself — herself in the first person. I don't know of any more conclusive evidence of a robust first-person perspective than this touching story.

As Grandin describes her mental life, she engages in visual or picture thinking almost exclusively. She starts with details, she says, and looks for unifying principles. The common denominator of all autistic thinking, she says, 'is that details are associated into categories to form a concept. Details are assembled into concepts like putting a jigsaw puzzle together' (*ibid.*, p. 32).

Grandin describes herself as a bottom-up thinker: get the visual details and try to figure out how they fit together. She forms a concept, she says, by assembling many images that exemplify the concept and looking to see what they have in common. 'Being autistic,' she says, 'I don't naturally assimilate information that most people take for granted. Instead, I store information in my head as if it were on a CD-ROM disc.' She goes on:

When I recall something I have learned, I replay the video in my imagination. The videos in my memory are always specific; for example, I remember handling cattle at the veterinary chute at Producer's Feedlot or McElhaney Cattle Company. I remember exactly how the animals behaved in that specific situation and how the chutes and other equipment were built... I can run these images over and over and study them to solve design problems. (*ibid.*, pp. 8–9)

Her thinking, Grandin says, is imagistic; it is associative and non-sequential. When she reads, she converts 'words into pictures'. She says that her mind is similar to a computer's search engine, 'set to locate photos'. 'All my thoughts are in photo-realistic pictures, which flash up on the "computer monitor" in my imagination', Grandin says. 'Words just narrate the picture.'

I don't want to take issue with Grandin's claim to think in pictures rather than in words. Rather, I want to argue that the kinds of complex thinking that Grandin expresses requires language. I want to show that, even on Grandin's description of how she thinks, language plays an essential role in thinking: not that she thinks *in* language, but that language *is presupposed* by the way that she thinks in pictures.

Grandin, like the rest of us, thinks in concepts; the difference between Grandin and neurotypicals is that her concepts derive, not directly from words, but from large series of specific examples. Fortunately, Grandin has a photographic memory. She has visual images for everything she has seen, heard, or read. There are no generic objects, or pictures of generic objects. When asked on a spatial test to build a fence, she exploded: 'A fence for what? A cattle fence? A fence along a highway? A privacy fence at a house? A barbed wire fence? A wrought-iron fence?' 'There is no *fence*', she concluded (Grandin and Panek, 2013, p. 164).

Grandin insists that 'both animals and people with autism can think without language. They think by associating sensory-based memories such as smells, sounds, or visual images into categories' (Grandin, 2006, p. 201). However, Grandin's thinking goes far beyond associating smells, sounds, or visual images into categories. For example, as a child Grandin categorized dogs so that they were distinguished from cats by size. Then a neighbour bought a Dachshund. 'I remember looking at the small dog', Grandin reports, 'and trying to figure out why she was not a cat' (*ibid.*, p. 30).

My question is this: if Grandin did not already have a modicum of natural language when she encountered the Dachshund, why didn't she blithely go on, and simply think that the Dachshund was an odd-shaped cat?[2] I can accept Grandin's view that her concepts are imagistic and still claim that in a world without language there would be no miscategorization; she couldn't even suspect that she was putting an image in the wrong category (e.g. 'cat') unless she had some way of understanding the category apart from what she put in it. No array of particular images can tell you the use of a particular word or concept.[3] With nothing but images to go on, one might follow Wittegenstein when he averred: 'One would like to say: whatever is going to seem right to me is right. And that only means that here we can't talk about "right"' (Wittgenstein, 1958, par. 258).

Whatever one's view of concepts — whether they are all linguistic or not, whether they are mental representations or not — it seems indisputable to me that the kinds of thoughts one can have are limited by the concepts that one possesses. For example, one cannot have universal beliefs, or past-tense beliefs, or counterfactual beliefs, or modal beliefs, or beliefs that express logically complex facts ('Every girl loves some boy'), or beliefs expressible in terms of some symbol system ('2 + 3 = 5'), or higher-order beliefs that one is in such-and-such a mental state — one can not have beliefs of any of these kinds without having a language. And Grandin's books are studded with many beliefs of these kinds.

So my hypothesis is this: Grandin already had enough natural language to allow her to know that a Dachshund is not a cat. Without someone to tell her that the Dachshund was a dog, and not a cat, it is difficult to see why she would have felt a need to 'create a new category in my mind to differentiate [between dogs and cats]'.

Even if language played a role in her re-categorization of dogs, her concept may still have been 'sensory based, not word based'. Her new concept was also visual: she noticed that all dogs, large and small, had similar-shaped noses. She notes that she could have had other ways to

---

2   My own view is that natural language is the vehicle for conscious thought. It is a phenomenological fact that I think and reason and deliberate in a language that I understand. Otherwise I would not know what I think. My thoughts are in words — English words, words that express concepts. I do not a have a theory of concepts, but if pressed, I'd compare concepts to Fregean senses.

3   'Imagine a picture representing a boxer in a particular stance', says Wittgenstein. 'Now this picture can be used to tell someone how he should stand, should hold himself; or how he should not hold himself; or how a particular man did stand in such-and-such a place and so on' (Wittgenstein, 1958, p. 11).

categorize dogs — e.g. by sound (barking as opposed to meowing) or by smell.

While agreeing that Grandin's concept *dog* was sensory-based, not language-based, language still seems to have played two roles in her acquisition of the concept. First, she had to know which specific images to use for the categorization, and second, she had to find out that an image of a new object that fit the criterion for the old category did not belong in the category (*dog*). I do not believe that she could have found out either of these facts without the help of language.

To put the point more generally: Grandin reports that she acquires concepts by sorting many 'specific photo-realistic pictures... into categories'. So, one wonders, how does she decide which specific images to include in her sorting? She speculates about what the images have in common. In a world without language, how would one know which sensory-based images to speculate about? Indeed, even the distinction between objects and images is a sophisticated distinction, itself apparently requiring language.

From what she said, Grandin had sufficient linguistic skill when she got to the point of categorizing. By age three-and-a-half, Grandin was making meaningful sounds, and before that (she doesn't say when) she could understand what was being said, but was unable to respond except by screaming and flapping her arms. Early on, she could follow instructions (Grandin and Scariano, 1986, p. 25). When she did start speaking, it was one word at a time, without voice inflection. So, when she started categorizing, she already had the rudiments of language.

What seems to me to be probably true is that Grandin's phenomenology is photographic rather than propositional. But even if Grandin thinks in pictures, it does not follow that she could have the thoughts that she has without language. And I don't believe that she could.

But Grandin may not disagree. She uses the term 'non-verbal' differently from the way that I use it. She calls autistic individuals who can type but not speak 'non-verbal'. Indeed, she even speaks of 'self-reports from nonverbal individuals who can type' (Grandin and Panek, 2013, p. 78). I use the term 'non-verbal' to refer to individuals who do not have language at all, but clearly individuals who can type do have language. What they may not have is the ability to speak. So I would use a term like 'non-oral' (if that's a word) or 'non-speaking', not 'non-verbal', to refer to people who communicate by typing. Since Grandin takes 'non-verbal' to apply to typists who cannot speak, she may or may not take issue with what I say about language and thought. However, she clearly describes her own thinking in terms of 'photo-realistic pictures that pop up in [her] imagination' — pictures that she suggests are independent of language.

6. Conclusion

Using Temple Grandin as a test case, I have tried to show two things: first, that autistics may have a rich inner life, even if an atypical one (hence, she is a person); and second, that Temple Grandin's claim that she only thinks in pictures does not conflict with the claim that the concepts and thoughts that she has require language.

As I mentioned earlier, Grandin says, 'I would be denied the ability to think by scientists who maintain that language is essential for thinking' (Grandin, 2006, p. 186). However, nothing that she says diminishes my conviction that language is essential for thinking of the kind that Grandin reports. Certainly, Grandin does not lack language or a robust first-person perspective. Indeed, she describes herself as an avid reader, and she lectures worldwide. Although she processes information in very different ways from neurotypical people, she has figured out ways to make those differences almost invisible. Her writings make a convincing case that she is, as she says, 'different, not less' (Grandin, 2011, p. 296).

References

Baker, L.R. (1981) Why computers can't act, *American Philosophical Quarterly*, **18**, pp. 157–163.

Baker, L.R. (2007) *The Metaphysics of Everyday Life*, Cambridge: Cambridge University Press.

Baker, L.R. (2013) *Naturalism and the First-Person Perspective*, New York: Oxford University Press.

Castañeda, H.N. (1966) He: A study in the logic of self-consciousness, *Ratio*, **8**, pp. 130–57.

Castañeda, H.N. (1967) Indicators and quasi-indicators, *American Philosophical Quarterly*, **4**, pp. 85–100.

Grandin, T. (2006) *Thinking in Pictures: My Life with Autism*, 2nd ed., New York: Vintage Books.

Grandin, T. (2011) *The Way I See It: A Personal Look at Autism and Asperger's*, 2nd ed., Arlington, TX: Future Horizons.

Grandin, T. & Scariano, M.M. (1986/2005) *Emergence: Labeled Autistic — A True Story*, New York: Grand Central Publishing.

Grandin, T. & Panek, R. (2013) *The Autistic Brain: Thinking Across the Spectrum*, Boston, MA: Houghton Mifflin Harcourt.

Groopman, J. (2013) What is autism?, *The New York Review of Books*, June 6.

Happé, F., Ronald, A. & Plomin, R. (2006) Time to give up on a single explanation for autism, *Nature Neuroscience*, **9** (10), pp. 1218–1220.

Locke, J. (1690) *Essay Concerning Human Understanding*, Vol. Book II, Chapter XXVII, Section 9, Pringle-Pattison, A.S. (ed.), Oxford: Clarendon Press.

Markram, H. (2007) The intense world syndrome: An alternative hypothesis for autism, *Frontiers of Neuroscience*, **1** (1), pp. 77–96.

Sacks, O. (1995) *An Anthropologist from Mars*, New York: Vintage Books.

Wittgenstein, L. (1958) *Philosophical Investigations. Third*, New York: The Macmillan Company.

Angela J. Guta

First-Person and Third-Person Perspectives and Autism

Abstract: The difficulties children with autism have in their use of personal pronouns, in understanding the perspectives of others, and in their imitation skills have all been well documented in the literature. It can be argued that each of these relate to the social impairment evidenced in autism. In light of the aforementioned challenges, this paper will focus on an educational approach to facilitate the development of social skills in primary school children with autism in relation to first- and third-person perspectives. Specifically, to identify whether video modelling filmed from the first-person perspective or the third-person perspective is more effective in increasing the verbal and action imitation skills of the participants with autism. Results from this paper suggest that, of the two approaches, point-of-view video modelling filmed from the first-person perspective was more effective in increasing the verbal and action imitation skills for two out of the three groups in the study, and for maintaining skills at a three-week follow-up for one of the groups.

1. Introduction

Individuals with autism often demonstrate pronoun reversals. This can be seen when a child says 'you' rather than 'I' or 'me'. For example, a child might say 'You want milk' instead of 'I want milk'. Similarly, a child might ask a question in place of a request, such as 'Do you want juice?' instead of 'I want juice'. Reversal errors for children with autism occur not only in their speech, but also in their imitation of

Correspondence:
Email: ajguta@aol.com

Journal of Consciousness Studies, **22**, No. 11–12, 2015, pp. 194–217

actions. It can be argued that pronoun reversals are a reflection of the difficulties children with autism have in their concept of 'self' and 'others'. The difficulties children with autism have in their use of personal pronouns, in understanding the perspectives of others, and in their imitation skills have all been well documented in the literature. It can be argued that each of these relate to the social impairment evidenced in autism. In light of the aforementioned challenges, this paper will focus on an educational approach to facilitate the development of social skills in primary school children with autism in relation to first- and third-person perspectives. Specifically, the following research questions set the foundation for the implementation of this study: *1) Will video modelling or point-of-view video modelling be more effective in increasing the verbal and action imitation skills of the participants with autism? and 2) Will video modelling or point-of-view video modelling result in maintenance of skills at a three-week follow-up?* Results from this paper suggest that, of the two approaches, point-of-view video modelling filmed from the first-person perspective was more effective in increasing the verbal and action imitation skills for two out of the three groups of participants in the study, and maintaining skills at a three-week follow-up for one of the groups.

2. Concept of Self and Others

It is well documented in the literature that individuals with autism have challenges with a concept of self and a concept of others, whether this be fragmented or atypical. It was Leo Kanner, a child psychiatrist, who first described autism in 1943. In his clinical account, Kanner described features of autism in a group of children which are commensurate with the current diagnostic descriptions of the condition. Kanner himself, in 1943, documented the challenges children with autism face with respect to the concept of self and of others. However, it should be pointed out that some elements of self-concept may appear to be intact in individuals with autism. Indicators of a problem with self-concept include, but are not limited to, a lack of responding to one's own name, marked impairments in joint attention, difficulty understanding one's role in a social world, and seeing how one can be similar yet at the same time different than others in this social world (Frith, 1989/2003; Baron-Cohen, 2005; Hobson and Meyer, 2005; Hobson *et al.*, 2006, as reported in Lombardo *et al.*,

2009). Each of these indicators has been established as a characteristic of the social impairment of autism.

The formation of a self-concept and a concept of others occurs at an early age which depends largely on the development of language (Lyons and Fitzgerald, 2013). At around the age of 18 months, children begin to refer to themselves by using the word 'I', while they refer to others with the word 'you'. The personal pronoun 'I' is a symbolic representation of the self in the form of language (Kircher and David, 2003, as reported in Lombardo *et al.*, 2009). The use of personal pronouns 'I' and 'you' is considered to be a form of self-expression (Hobson, 1993). Personal pronoun comprehension occurs at the end of the second year into the third year. According to Hobson (1993), personal pronouns occur at around the same time as children make references to mental states such as feelings. To form a concept of mental states entails the ability to form a concept of what it means for a subject to experience something, i.e. what it means to be a 'self' (*ibid.*, p. 95). Children with autism have been known to use pronoun reversals (*I*, *me*, and *you*) which demonstrates their difficulties with an awareness of self and of others.

In this case, Peeters *et al.* (2003) suggest that the reason why children with autism communicate from a third-person perspective, instead of first- and second-person perspectives, is that they have a non-social basis of categorizing self and others. Furthermore, Bosch (1970, as reported in Hobson, 1993) observed that children with autism sometimes refer to themselves in the third-person by using 'he' or a personal name. This is suggestive of a difficulty in how the child perceives himself/herself and others. Different reasons are given as to why this happens. For example, Charney (1981, as reported in Hobson, 1993) suggests that children with autism adopt speech forms that relate to their own experiences and repeat what they have heard. This is done in contrast to relating to what has been said to oneself and then identifying with the person's statement (Hobson, 1993). In contrast, Kanner (1943) proposed that children with autism simply repeat personal pronouns as they are heard, such as in an echo response. Furthermore, studies by Jordan (1989) and Tager-Flusberg (1989) show that difficulties with personal pronouns are due to 'abnormal forms of self- and other-reference, not merely echoing' (as reported in Hobson, 1993, p. 97).

Northoff and Heinzel (2003) indicate that the use of third-person perspective specifies a disjointed image of self and other. Hans Asperger, himself, would refer to himself from a third-person

perspective (Lyons and Fitzgerald, 2007). The mere fact that children
with autism have difficulty using the personal pronouns 'me' to label
self and 'you' to label others demonstrates their difficulty in
distinguishing themselves from other selves (Jordan, 1989, as reported
in Hobson, 1993; Kanner, 1943; Lee, Hobson and Chiat, 1994, as
reported in Lind and Bowler, 2009). Studies by Loveland and Landry
(1986, as reported in Hobson, 1993) have shown that the ability to use
personal pronouns appropriately by children with autism in their study
was directly related to their spontaneous initiations of joint attention.
However, not all children with autism demonstrate pronoun reversals.

3. Autism and Social Skills

Autism is a neurodevelopmental disorder characterized by deficits in
social communication and social interaction, and restricted, repetitive
patterns of behaviour, interests, or activities (American Psychiatric
Association, 2013). The deficit in social relatedness is considered the
most pervasive and *troubling*. Many argue that social deficits can be
considered a 'core feature' of the more general syndrome (Carter *et
al.*, 2005; Rogers, 2000; Sigman, 1994). Wing (1988), in referring to
the impairments in autism, suggests that each area of impairment will
have a marked impact on all areas of social skills throughout the life-
span. Similarly, Ozonoff and Miller (1995) stress the importance of
the development and improvement of social skills for overall long-
term adjustment. As children with autism improve in the area of social
skills, they will be better equipped to adjust to all other aspects of life.
This illustrates the importance of interventions that address the core
deficit of social skills in individuals with autism. Social skills encompass play skills such as initiating play, joining in on existing play,
turn-taking, sharing, reciprocal play, imaginative play, and coopera-
tive play. It is through the development and mastery of social skills
that a person is deemed as socially competent.

Social impairment in students with autism is characterized by a lack
of seeking to share enjoyment and interest with others; by a lack of
showing, bringing, or pointing out an object of interest; and a lack of
social and emotional reciprocity (American Psychiatric Association,
2000; 2013). Individuals with autism demonstrate impairments in
turn-taking skills, joint attention, pretend play, and maintaining social
interactions. This is rooted in the difficulty they face in understanding,
predicting, and responding to the social, emotional, and communication behaviours of others. These difficulties can be linked to deficits

with theory of mind, mind-blindness, weak central coherence, and executive function (Baron-Cohen, 1997; Baron-Cohen, Tager-Flusberg and Cohen, 2000; Baron-Cohen, Leslie and Frith, 1985; Frith, 1989/2003; Happé and Frith, 2006; Semrud-Clikeman, 2007). Social interactions require an ability to process ever-changing input from context, language, and emotions. Individuals with autism often interpret situations literally, or from their own set of beliefs, which often leads to improperly understanding the social situation at hand (Semrud-Clikeman, 2007).

In any social situation, a great deal of information is available at one time. But what determines what one chooses to pay attention to? For example, in a typical social play situation, a child may recognize that his friend begins to sigh loudly and look away as he is talking to him. He begins to realize, or sense, that the friend is either disinterested in his conversation or wants to move on to another topic. This can be tied to one's understanding of non-verbal social cues (i.e. facial expressions and body gestures). However, individuals with autism often miss out on these social cues. They may focus on certain aspects of a situation, while missing out on the big picture (Frith, 1989/2003; Happé and Frith, 2006). For example, in this same situation, the child with autism might continue talking because the friend is still playing with his cars, while he is playing with his own. The child with autism is not aware of the other person's perspective, as he is not under-standing the subtle social cues from his friend. The child with autism is not able to interpret the friend's behaviour as an indication that he may need to adjust his own behaviour. For example, as Klin *et al.* (2002) point out, people with autism can become distracted with irrelevant items, such as objects, and ignore the more essential aspects of the interaction such as facial and body gestures of people. This is because these same social cues can be subtle at times and can be missed by the average individual in any given social situation. So it is important to point out that subtle social cues (facial expressions, body gestures, tone of voice, etc.) are a major component of social inter-actions. Social cues help a person modify his own behaviour based on the social expectations of his/her social partner. A lot could be said in this regard, but for now that is not the focus of this paper.

Having briefly described some of the challenges individuals with autism face with respect to social interactions, I now take an in-depth look at imitation skills, which can be considered a subset of social skills, social relatedness, and joint attention skills (Wetherby and Prizant, 2000; Hogan, n.d.). Imitation skills can include toy/object imitation, motor imitation, verbal imitation, and the imitation of gestures. This study specifically looks at verbal and action imitation skills within a play sequence. In regards to object imitation, Hogan (n.d.) suggests that children first learn to imitate simple actions using objects before they move on to imitation of body movements. Object imitation first involves actions that are intended for that object (e.g. pushing a car across the table), followed by actions that the object is not intended for (e.g. rolling a drum stick across the table rather than hitting it on a drum). In addition to object imitation, children also imitate body movements. According to Hogen, imitation is a more difficult skill, since it requires the child to remember what he/she observes and then make that action. Granpeesheh *et al.* (2014) describe non-vocal imitation skills as part of a critical foundation for the development of more advanced social skills (p. 290). Moreover, they note that imitation skills are among the first skills to emerge in child development. Through non-vocal imitation, an individual can observe and copy the behaviours of others. In doing so, he/she can learn ways to engage with his/her surroundings (*ibid.*, p. 290).

Whether imitating language or actions, the learner must determine 'what' it is that he/she is attempting to imitate. In this regard, Carpenter (2006) pointed out several important factors to be considered when deciding what to imitate. They include the goals and intentions of the communicator/model, the goals and intentions towards the object, communicative intentions, and shared knowledge. Similarly, Rogers and Bennetto (2000) describe the various components involved in imitation. They include visually perceiving the movement, encoding the movement into working memory, mapping the change from a visual stimulus to a proprioceptive stimulus in one's body, creating a movement plan, performing it, and comparing their movement to what was originally perceived.

Imitation skills play an important role in language development, play skills, and joint attention (Carpenter and Tomasello, 2000; Rogers and Pennington, 1991). In typical infant development, imitation serves two functions — a learning function and a social function (Uzgiris, 1981). Through imitation, infants gain new skills and knowledge (i.e. learning function). Through imitation, they participate in social and emotional interactions with others (i.e. social function). For example, infants participate in interactions with caregivers where they engage in mutual and reciprocal imitation of vocalizations and facial expressions (Ingersoll, 2008). These reciprocal, give-and-take imitation interactions play an important role in the development of future early peer interactions (*ibid.*). Further expanding on this idea, Carpenter (2006) emphasized that either the learning function ('instrumental function' as Carpenter refers to it) or the social function can be important to the learner at the moment of demonstration. In light of this, the component that is more interesting to the learner — instrumental or social — is more likely to be imitated.[1]

As already discussed, it is suggested that individuals with autism process information in a disconnected way. As a result, individuals with autism focus on certain details while missing out on the big picture (see Frith, 1989/2003, and Happé and Frith, 2006). In the context of social interactions, this can be seen when an individual with autism focuses on things of high interest to him, rather than on a social interaction, possibly at the expense of that social interaction. For example, a child with autism may focus on lining up cars during a play time at school, while at the same time taking them away from two boys who were playing with those same cars next to him. Another example might be a child who joins a board game activity, focusing on only one aspect of the game while missing out on the sequence of steps involved in that game, at the expense of upsetting the peers involved and missing out on the intent of the game.

When we look at imitation skills, individuals with autism may focus on erroneous details in what is being modelled, as opposed to focusing on the relevant details that should be imitated. For example, in a study conducted by Ohta (1987), children with autism copied an action according to their own perspective, rather than the perspective of the model. That is, when shown a palm facing towards them, children with autism held their hand so that it faced them, rather than turning it to face away from them. Similarly, in the study conducted by Shield and Meier (2012), children with autism, who had native exposure to a sign language such as American Sign Language (ASL), demonstrated a reverse palm orientation on signs that are intended to be either inward or outward in orientation. The reverse palm orientation supports the notion that individuals with autism imitate gestures as they appear from their own perspective. This demonstrates the difficulty in understanding the perspective of the model giving the

---

[1] For an extensive look at imitation in relation to autism and typical development, see Rogers and Williams (2006). Also see Rogers and Bennetto (2000); Charman *et al.* (1997); Dawson *et al.* (1998); Loveland *et al.* (1994); Rogers *et al.* (1996); Smith and Bryson (1998); Stone and Hogan (1993); Stone and Lemanek (1991).

demonstration.[2] This is a major area of deficit for individuals with autism.

4. Video Modelling

A relatively new area of research in social skills interventions for individuals with autism is that of video-based interventions (Rayner, Denholm and Sigafoos, 2009). This is the focus of the present article. Specifically, this has to do with the use of video modelling filmed from either the first-person perspective or the third-person perspective in relation to the social skills of children with autism.

Video-based instruction taps into a relative strength of individuals with autism in how they process visual stimuli (Ayres and Langone, 2007; McCoy and Hermansen, 2007; Nikopoulos and Keenan, 2006; Plimley and Bowen, 2007; Sigafoos, O'Reilly and de la Cruz, 2007). As pointed out by Bellini and Akullian (2007), video-based instructions can be seen as socially valid, as watching videos is a socially acceptable activity for typically developing individuals. Furthermore, video-based instruction can be seen as a non-invasive form of intervention for individuals with autism (*ibid.*). Although video-based interventions for students with autism is a relatively new area of research, the concept behind this type of learning is related to the work of Albert Bandura and his 'social learning theory' (Bandura, 1969; 1971; 1976; 1977). The social learning theory is based on an individual learning a new behaviour by observing a model performing that behaviour. Observational learning involves four steps: attention, remembering what has been seen, producing the behaviour, and responding to reinforcement (Semrud-Clikeman, 2007). Bandura proposed that observational learning happens through three models: by watching other people perform a behaviour (a live model), verbal instruction on how to perform a behaviour, and through a real or fictional character that demonstrates the behaviour through the media, a video, etc.

In what follows, I will explain how the use of video-based instruction is described in some of the literature. In a study by Sturmey (2003), video was described as a tool to draw one's attention to the behaviours being modelled, and at the same time provide

---

2   For similar studies involving reproducing actions from one's own perspective, see Hobson and Lee (1999); Meyer and Hobson (2004); Smith and Bryson (1998).

stimulus control. In another study, Klin *et al.* (2002) found that people with autism can become distracted with irrelevant items in a situation, such as objects, and ignore the more essential aspects of the interaction, such as facial and body gestures. Individuals with autism are also known to have difficulty attending to relevant details in their environment. Rather than scanning their environment as a whole to identify and focus on important details, they focus on smaller details which may not be the most important ones to attend to. This often leads to missing out on other important things that are happening in their environment. This is often referred to as 'overselectivity'. At times, overselectivity is due to distractions in the environment or a heightened sensitivity to one of the senses (i.e. auditory, tactile, olfactory, and visual). In this case, video-based interventions help address the challenges individuals with autism face when they do not attend to the most salient details in their environment. For example, video presentations, such as those filmed from the first-person perspective, can present information that is most important for the individual with autism to focus on, while at the same time removing extraneous details: for example, a video that shows a play sequence filmed from the first-person perspective while removing background distractions such as children playing in the background with a different toy that is not the focus of instruction.

Here I will briefly describe the various forms of video modelling. First, video modelling is a process where a person is first asked to watch a video containing a target skill modelled by either an adult or a peer, followed by an opportunity to imitate the behaviour modelled (Bellini and Akullian, 2007; Graetz, Mastropieri and Scruggs, 2006; Sigafoos, O'Reilly and de la Cruz, 2007). Second, video self-modelling uses the individual being instructed as the model in the videotape. Similar to video modelling, video self-modelling is a process where the individual is asked to watch the video of the target behaviour being modelled, followed by an opportunity to imitate that behaviour (Bellini, Akullian and Hopf, 2007; Graetz, Mastropieri and Scruggs, 2006). Third, point-of-view video modelling is very different from video modelling and video self-modelling in that it is filmed in the context of an activity from the visual perspective (at eye level) of the individual who is being instructed, i.e. first-person perspective (Hine and Wolery, 2006; Schreibman, Whalen and Stahmer, 2000). The video provides a picture of what they are supposed to do from the initial step until the completion of the task. This method promotes visual comprehension and allows for familiarity with the materials or settings in the video (Shukla-Mehta, Miller and Callahan, 2010).

As stated earlier, video-based interventions help address the challenges individuals with autism face when they attend to details which are not the most salient details in their environment, otherwise known as 'overselectivity'. Video modelling provides an opportunity to break down a certain skill into isolated steps while providing accurate demonstrations of a targeted skill. Additionally, video modelling allows for the modelled targeted behaviour to be presented in a repetitive fashion. This serves several purposes: reducing the demand for the teacher or staff to provide this level of repetition, providing a routine which is a preferred learning style for individuals with autism, and increasing the likelihood of skill acquisition through multiple repetitions.

5. Educational Approach to Address Social Skills Deficit in Autism

In light of the difficulties that children with autism face in understanding perspectives, a study was conducted to identify whether video modelling filmed from the first-person perspective or the third-person perspective would be more effective in increasing the verbal and action imitation skills of the participants with autism. What follows is a brief summary of the study conducted.

Study

Two studies were conducted at primary schools located in North East England. At the first school, five students with autism (Liam, age 4 yrs 10 mths; Esther, age 5 yrs 0 mths; Joseph, age 5 yrs 2 mths; David, age 5 yrs 9mths; and John, age 6 yrs 7 mths)[3] and three mainstream students (two boys, ages 6 yrs 1 mth and 6 yrs 4 mths; and one girl, age 5 yrs 5 mths) participated in the study. At the second school, two students with autism (Eli, age 6 yrs 3 mths; and Zac, age 7 yrs 5 mths) and two mainstream students (both boys, ages 10 yrs 3 mths and 9 yrs 11 mths) participated in the study. The study took place 5 days per week at each school site, with a total of 32 sessions at School 1 and 29 sessions at School 2.

---

[3]   Please note that the names of all participants have been changed to remain anonymous.

The setting for all sessions was held within the school that the participants attended, rather than in a clinical setting. Three play sets were used in the study. At School 1, a farm play set, a town play set, and a playground play set were used. At School 2, a knights and castle play set, a pirate play set, and a space play set were used.

In addition to the play sets, videotapes were created. Prior to creating the videos, mainstream children were observed playing with each toy set. These sessions were videotaped for later viewing. Information was gathered from these observations for possible use in the scripts for the videotapes. Scripts were developed to be used with the play sets. The same script created for one play set was used for both videotapes filmed from the two different perspectives — the first-person perspective and the third-person perspective. No script was developed for the play sets used in the control sessions.

Videos filmed from the first-person perspective are referred to as *point-of-view video modelling (POVM)*. POVM videos are filmed from the eye-level perspective of the individual being instructed. POVM videos show a targeted behaviour from the initial step until completion. Body parts such as the hands or feet are shown in the video rather than the whole person (i.e. eye-level perspective) (Hine and Wolery, 2006; Schreibman, Whalen and Stahmer, 2000). First-person relations can be understood by the following model 'I → X,' where 'I' represents the perceiver, '→' represents directional activity, and 'X' represents an object (Gomez, 1996, p. 130). When a person is looking at something from the first-person perspective, the person observes an activity directed at an object by the perceiver itself (i.e. the perceiver picks up object X).

Videos filmed from the third-person perspective are referred to as *video modelling (VM)*. VM videos show the whole person, whether an adult or child, modelling a particular action. Video modelling is described as a process where a person is first asked to watch a video of a peer or adult modelling a target skill, followed by an opportunity to imitate the behaviour (Bellini and Akullian, 2007; Graetz, Mastropieri and Scruggs, 2006; Sigafoos, O'Reilly and de la Cruz, 2007). Third-person relations can be understood by the following model 'O → X,' where 'O' is a person different than the perceiver, '→' represents directional activity, and 'X' is the object of the other person's activity (Gomez, 1996, p. 130). With this model in mind, when a person is looking at something from the third-person perspective, the person observes another person acting on an object (i.e. person O picks up object X).

All sessions (baseline, intervention, and probes) were videotaped and later transcribed for future analysis. Data were scored from these videotapes on the occurrence of the following responses: *Scripted verbalizations*: verbalizations that matched the script of the model. In addition, statements that were similar to the modelled response but not identical were also scored. This included a substitution or omission of a word (MacDonald *et al.*, 2009). *Unscripted verbalizations*: verbalizations that were not modelled in the videotape but were appropriate to the context of play (*ibid.*). *Scripted play actions*: motor actions that matched the actions of the video model and the same change to the environment occurred (*ibid.*). And finally, *Unscripted play actions*: play action that was not modelled in the video but was appropriate to the context of the play (*ibid.*).

The research process involved both quantitative and qualitative methods. A single-subject, multiple-baseline design across participants (N = 7) and three treatment conditions (video modelling from the third-person perspective, point-of-view video modelling from the first-person perspective, and a control group) was implemented. For the purposes of this article, information on the control group will not be described in depth.

Baseline: Prior to the participants entering the room, the table and chairs were set up. Chairs were placed facing the rectangular table on each of the longer sides of the table. The play set materials were placed centrally on the rectangular table. Once the participants entered the room and were seated around the rectangular table, they were provided with a visual and verbal prompt. The visual prompt was in the form of a picture of each play set. For example, as the researcher stated 'First, we're going to play with farm', the picture was pointed to. Followed by 'Then play with town' while pointing to the picture of the town play set. And finally, 'Then play with fairground' as the picture of the fairground play set was pointed to. Prior to beginning play with the first play set, a timer was set and then the participants were prompted, 'It's time to play'. The participants were then given four minutes to play with the toys. The three mainstream participants were in the room playing alongside the participants with autism.

Intervention: During intervention sessions, the participants with autism were prompted to sit in front of a laptop. The visual schedule was modified with the addition of a picture of the laptop. The participants were prompted, 'First, we're going to watch a movie, then play farm. Then we are going to play town and fairground'. The video was then started with a prompt, 'Let's watch'. If a participant looked away from the video while it was presented, he/she was prompted visually to look at the video. If needed, a verbal prompt was added. Following the video, the children were then directed to the table to play with the materials. As in baseline, the participants were given four minutes to play with the toys. The three mainstream participants were in the room playing alongside the participants with autism.

Presentation of videos

In order to reduce the possibility of order effects within groups, counterbalancing of order treatments was implemented (McLeod, 2007). By this, I mean that each group of participants was presented with a different order of treatment conditions for School 1. At School 1, for example, with the farm play set, Group 1 was presented with the video filmed from the third-person perspective, while Group 2 was presented with the video filmed from the first-person perspective. With the town play set, Group 2 was presented with the video filmed from the third-person perspective, while Group 1 was presented with the video filmed from the first-person perspective. For School 2, as there was only one group of participants, the group viewed the video filmed from the third-person perspective for the pirates play set, while the group viewed the video filmed from the first-person perspective for the knights and castle play set.

Control group: During the control group phase involving the third play set, just as in the baseline phase, a timer was set and the participants were prompted, 'It's time to play'. The participants were then given four minutes to play with the toys. The three mainstream participants were in the room playing alongside the participants with autism. Throughout this phase, the participants were not presented with any video as in the intervention phase. As this play set did not have a video presentation, a script was not developed. However, a list of functional play actions for this play set was created.

Follow-up probes: Three weeks following the completion of the study, a one-time follow-up probe was conducted. In this probe, the videotapes were not presented. The participants were presented with the play sets and the same visual and verbal prompts as in baseline. As in previous sessions, the participants were given four minutes to play with the toys. The three mainstream participants were in the room playing alongside the participants with autism.

Results

When looking at the data for each participant at School 1, within groups, participants in both groups imitated behaviours from the video modelling and the point-of-view video modelling interventions. Specifically, two out of five participants increased the range of their scripted actions and verbalizations following the video modelling intervention (third-person perspective). In contrast, five out of five participants increased the range of their scripted actions following the point-of-view video modelling intervention (first-person perspective), while three out of five participants increased the range of their scripted verbalizations following the point-of-view video modelling intervention. Data were then presented in a multiple-baseline format to allow comparison of the video modelling intervention to the point-of-view video modelling intervention. In doing so, any levels, patterns, trends, or variability could be identified. Using the method suggested by Nugent (2001), by drawing a line from the lowest data point in the intervention to the last data point, an upward trend of scripted behaviours following the point-of-view video modelling intervention was identified for two participants in Group 2. This upward trend was to a higher degree than the trend identified following the video modelling intervention for these same participants.

When looking at the data at School 2, participants in this group imitated behaviours from the video modelling and the point-of-view video modelling interventions. Specifically, both participants increased the range of their scripted actions and verbalizations following the video modelling intervention (third-person perspective). In contrast, only one increased the range of his scripted actions following the point-of-view video modelling intervention (first-person perspective), while both of the participants increased the range of their scripted verbalizations following the point-of-view video modelling intervention. Further, by analysing the data presented in a multiple-baseline format, an upward trend of scripted behaviours following the point-of-view video modelling intervention was identified for both participants in this group. This upward trend was to a higher degree than the trend identified following the video modelling intervention for both participants. The above findings from both schools directly answer the first research question, *Will video modelling or point-of-view video modelling be more effective in increasing the verbal and action imitation skills of the participants with autism?* Based on the outcome of the study, it is point-of-view video modelling.

6. Discussion

This study suggests that point-of-view video modelling (first-person perspective) was more effective than video modelling (third-person perspective) in increasing the verbal and action imitation skills of the participants with autism. Specifically, all three groups of participants increased their verbal and action imitation skills following both intervention models. However, point-of-view video modelling elicited the higher level of imitation from the three groups than with video modelling. For example, the change in mean level of scripted actions and scripted verbalizations from baseline to the intervention phase nearly doubled for four out of the seven participants (Esther, Liam, Zac, and Eli) following the point-of-view video modelling intervention. This was at a higher level of increase than that observed following the video modelling intervention. It is important to point out that findings need to be interpreted with caution in light of several factors, such as the variability within the data points for each of the participants. This and other factors need to be taken into consideration when evaluating the results of this study.

Moreover, the two participants from the second school were both able to maintain scripted actions and verbalizations at the follow-up session following the point-of-view video modelling procedure. Additionally, one of the two participants demonstrated a higher level of imitation during the follow-up probe than during the intervention phases. These results are significant because these participants were able to maintain skills three weeks following the last intervention session. These additional findings indicate that point-of-view video modelling resulted in a maintenance of skills at a three-week follow-up. These additional findings answer the second research question, *Will video modelling or point-of-view video modelling result in maintenance of skills at a three-week follow-up?* The answer is, point-of-view video modelling.

Results obtained from this study are consistent with the results of Hine and Wolery's (2006) and Tetreault and Lerman's (2010) studies in that both participants increased their play skills following the POVM procedure. In addition, the findings are consistent with the results of Sancho *et al.*'s (2010) study in that both participants maintained their skills following the POVM procedure. Furthermore, this study adds to the current body of knowledge of POVM procedures, since a very small number of studies have been conducted to date in this area.

The outcome of this study has many implications for educators and professionals working with individuals with autism. Keeping in mind that individuals with autism can focus on certain details while missing out on relevant details, as well as the challenges they face with perspective-taking, clinicians and educators alike may want to explore further the presentation of material in the first-person perspective. It is often natural for educators in a social classroom setting to ask their students to watch someone perform a behaviour from the third-person perspective, whether live or in a video. With the understanding that some individuals with autism may imitate better when presented with a task to learn or imitate from the first-person perspective, educators may want to change how information is presented to them. This can have other implications regarding how hand motions such as sign language are used in the classroom, or how gestures are used to support sound development or other academic tasks presented. The same can be said for professionals working in a clinical setting. If a client is presented with a task to learn or imitate from the third-person perspective, whether live or in a video, it would also be beneficial to present information from the first-person perspective to see if better results could be gained. Removing extraneous details from the presentation, and focusing on the relevant details (e.g. as in point-of-view videos), educators and clinicians may see a more rapid response and understanding to the presentation.

7. Limitations

Results of this study should be interpreted with the following limitations in mind. Limitations which the researcher did not have control over included limitations due to the number of participants, obtaining consent for the participants, and scheduling issues at the school sites. Due to space limitations, it is not be possible to go into detail. However, two additional limitations will be briefly described here.

First, a criterion performance for each participant to achieve prior to transferring from one condition to the next was included in the planning phases of this research study. Due to limitations set by the school administration at School 1 in regards to the amount of time the participants were made available daily for the study, this criterion was not met. The second condition was introduced with the anticipation that the participants would continue to increase their imitation skills throughout the intervention phase. With the time constraints raised at the first school site in mind, the intervention conditions at the second school were introduced in a similar manner. Had the criterion performance been established at both school sites, it is anticipated that the results would have shown less variability and more stable trends than identified in this study. The issues raised with time constraints speak to the types of challenges researchers face in conducting research in a real-life setting.

Second, whether the possibility of order effects of the two interventions, within subjects, was actually controlled. An order effect is a change in the participants' behaviour due to the order in which the treatment conditions are presented. In order to reduce the possibility of order effects within groups in this study, counterbalancing of order treatments was implemented (McLeod, 2007). By this I mean that each group of participants was presented with a different order of treatment conditions. For example, one group viewed the video filmed from the third-person perspective, while the second group viewed the video filmed from the first-person perspective for the same play set. The results of this study suggest that the two groups which displayed a higher level of imitation following the POVM treatment received the treatment in a different order from each other. Yet it is still difficult to say conclusively how much the participants' interest in a particular play set had a factor in the results. Therefore, a degree of caution must be taken in considering the results. This is due to the possibility that the results would have been much different had each group only been exposed to one treatment condition.

Third, limitations involving the control group. During the planning phases of this study, the intention was to have three groups of participants. For each play set, one group would receive the first-person perspective treatment, the second group the third-person perspective, and the final group would be a control group, receiving no treatment. With this in mind, the control group would have provided more experimental control and comparisons. If there had been a control group receiving no treatment for the first two play sets at both schools, a better comparison would be provided to see whether the treatment itself promoted higher levels of imitation than other factors such as the play set or the mainstream peers that were involved in the intervention. However, due to the small number of participants available which met the criteria for this study this was not possible. Despite this, some beneficial data were obtained from the analysis of their functional play skills during the control group sessions, which could be used for future instruction and intervention.

8. Application

As this study focused on the social skill of imitation, it was important to address both the learning function of imitation as well as the social function of imitation. This study provided a platform where children with autism could be taught the skill of imitation by viewing the video, followed by an opportunity to practise the skill(s) among mainstream peers. This addressed both the learning function and the social function of imitation (Uzgiris, 1981). This intervention was implemented in a natural setting among mainstream peers, where other social communicative behaviours occur (Ingersoll, 2008). It did not occur in isolation or in a clinical setting. Yes one can learn in isolation, but in order to generalize you need exposure to naturalistic social settings. In the literature, it is recognized that individuals with autism have great difficulty connecting what they have learned in one situation in relation to another. Additionally, this study incorporated mainstream peers into all phases of the intervention. For example, Bellini (2006) emphasized the importance of rich social opportunities and experiences that the natural environment provides, rather than a clinical setting or a specific social skills instruction that ends the moment the child leaves the therapy room (p. 198). Elliot and Gresham (1991), as cited by Bellini (2006), stress that the 'lack of opportunity to interact socially and lack of opportunity to practice social skills are two factors that contribute to the development of social skills deficits' (p. 198). Similarly, Bellini stated, 'in any formal social skills training, children need opportunities to practice their newly learned skills with other children in natural settings' (*ibid.*, p. 198).

Another practical application of this study is that it reinforces the comments from adults with autism in Müller, Schuler and Yates's (2008) study when they spoke about their own social experiences. Several participants commented on observing the social behaviours of 'non-autistic individuals' in order to learn from them (p. 183). One participant in their study talked about copying other people. It is through this type of exposure to social situations where one practises, watches, interprets, and begins to understand social norms and rules that one can learn and acquire new social skills. Without these experiences, children with autism will be at a disadvantage.

For a moment, imagine the following scenario from a classroom:

Imagine a child who is overwhelmed when he enters his classroom. Further, the child approaches some children playing a game that the

A.J. GUTA

child has never seen before. The child wants very much to play, but is confused by the intricacies. The children appear to be adept at playing this game but the child feels lost. What can be done? Imagine further that the teacher notices the child's interest in the game. She provides the child with an opportunity to watch a video that she has made of the children playing the game. Further, in the video, the intricate steps of the game are broken down for the child. After watching the video, the child has a chance to imitate the actions observed. The next time the child enters the classroom and sees the same peers playing the game, the child feels more confident in playing now that he has had an opportunity to practise what was learned through the video. This example illustrates how easily video modelling can be incorporated into the supports available in a classroom for children with autism. Further, the same strategies are applicable to all children. This example also confirms Bandura's statement:

> Learning would be exceedingly laborious, not to mention hazardous, if people had to rely solely on the effects of their own actions to inform them what to do. Fortunately, most human behaviour is learned observationally through modelling: from observing others one forms an idea of how new behaviours are performed, and on later occasions this coded information serves as a guide for action. (Bandura, 1977, p. 22)

9. Conclusion and Recommendations

In light of the findings from this study, I conclude that video modelling filmed from the first-person perspective is clearly an effective educational approach for children with autism, specifically their imitation skills. Videos filmed from the first-person perspective present information that is most important for the individual with autism to focus on, while at the same time removing extraneous details.

In light of what I have presented in this paper, there are five areas that I would recommend further research in in the area of video modelling filmed from the first-person perspective. First, to replicate this study with different groups of children with autism based on age, cognitive skills, and language levels. Second, scaffolding could be embedded in the videos (i.e. breaking down a task into manageable units for a child who may have difficulty imitating). Third, include subtitles throughout the video. This would tap into an area of strength for individuals with autism in how they process visual information that is coupled with auditory information. Fourth, it would be beneficial for participants to be part of the selection process of what is included in the intervention. Children with autism could be asked what set of toys or game they would like to learn how to play. This information could be used to develop the video modelling procedure specifically for those children. Further, it would be interesting to allow children with higher functioning autism to help develop the videos to be used in the procedure. Finally, future research using a larger number of participants and with statistical analyses would greatly contribute to the current body of literature on video modelling from the first-person perspective.

Acknowledgments

This research was completed as part of the requirements for a Doctorate of Philosophy in Autism by the author. A special thanks to the children, families, and teachers who participated in this study. Finally, I thank the anonymous referees for their comments.

References

American Psychiatric Association (2000) *Diagnostic and Statistical Manual of Mental Disorders*, 4th ed., text revision, Washington, DC: American Psychiatric Association.

American Psychiatric Association (2013) *Diagnostic and Statistical Manual of Mental Disorders*, 5th ed., Arlington, VA: American Psychiatric Association.

Ayres, K. & Langone, J. (2007) Intervention and instruction with video for students with autism: A review of the literature, *Education and Training in Developmental Disabilities*, **40**, pp. 183–196.

Bandura, A. (1969) *Principles of Behavior Modification*, New York: Holt, Reinhart and Winston.

Bandura, A. (1971) *Social Learning Theory*, New York: General Learning Press.

Bandura, A. (1976) Effecting change through participant modeling, in Krumboltz, J.D. & Thorensen, C.E. (eds.) *Counseling Methods*, pp. 248–265, New York: Holt, Reinhart Winston.

Bandura, A. (1977) *Social Learning Theory*, Englewoods Cliffs, NJ: Prentice-Hall.

Baron-Cohen, S. (1997) *Mindblindness: An Essay on Autism and Theory of Mind*, Cambridge, MA: MIT Press.

Baron-Cohen, S. (2005) Autism — 'autos': Literally, a total focus on the self?, in Feinberg, T.E. & Keenan J.P. (eds.) *The Lost Self: Pathologies of the Brain and Identity*, Oxford: Oxford University Press.

Baron-Cohen, S., Leslie, A.M. & Frith, U. (1985) Does the autistic child have a 'theory of mind'?, *Cognition*, **21**, pp. 37–46.

Baron-Cohen, S., Tager-Flusberg, H. & Cohen, D.J. (eds.) (2000) *Understanding Other Minds: Perspectives from Developmental Cognitive Neuroscience*, Oxford: Oxford University Press.

Bellini, S. (2006) *Building Social Relationships: A Systematic Approach to Teaching Social Interaction Skills to Children and Adolescents with Autism*

Spectrum Disorders and Other Social Difficulties, Shawnee Mission, KS: Autism Asperger Publishing Company (APC).

Bellini, S. & Akullian, J. (2007) A meta-analysis of video modeling and video self-modeling interventions for children and adolescents with autism spectrum disorders, *Exceptional Children*, **73**, pp. 264–287.

Bellini, S., Akullian, J. & Hopf, A. (2007) Increasing social engagement in young children with autism spectrum disorders using video self-modeling, *School Psychology Review*, **36**, pp. 80–90.

Bosch, G. (1970) *Infantile Autism*, Jordan, D. & Jordan, I. (trans.), New York: Springer-Verlag.

Carpenter, M. (2006) Instrumental, social, and shared goals and intentions in imitation, in Rogers, S.J. & Williams, H.G. (eds.) *Imitation and the Social Mind: Autism and Typical Development*, pp. 48–70, New York: Guilford Press.

Carpenter, M. & Tomasello, M. (2000) Joint attention, cultural learning, and language acquisition: Implications for children with autism, in Wetherby, A.M. & Prizant, B.M. (eds.) *Autism Spectrum Disorders: A Transactional Developmental Perspective*, Vol. 9, pp. 31–54, Baltimore, MD: Paul H. Brookes Publishing Co.

Carter, A.S., Davis, N.O., Klin, A. & Volkmar, F.R. (2005) Social development in autism, in Volkmar, F.R., Klin, A., Paul, R. & Cohen, D.J. (eds.) *Handbook of Autism and Pervasive Developmental Disorders*, 3rd ed., pp. 312–334, Hoboken, NJ: Wiley.

Charman, T., Swettenham, J., Baron-Cohen, S., Cox, A., Baird, G. & Drew, A. (1997) Infants with autism: An investigation of empathy, pretend play, joint attention, and imitation, *Developmental Psychology*, **33** (5), pp. 781–789.

Charney, R. (1981) Pronoun errors in autistic children: Support for a social explanation, *British Journal of Disorders of Communication*, **15**, pp. 39–43.

Dawson, G., Meltzoff, A.N., Osterling, J. & Rinaldi, J. (1998) Neuropsychological correlates of early symptoms of autism, *Child Development*, **69** (5), pp. 1276–1285.

Elliot, S. & Gresham, F. (1991) *Social Skills Intervention Guide*, Circle Pines, MN: American Guidance.

Frith, U. (1989/2003) *Autism: Explaining the Enigma*, Oxford: Blackwell.

Gomez, J.C. (1996) Second person intentional relations and the evolution of social understanding, *Behavioural and Brain Sciences*, **19** (1), pp. 129–130.

Graetz, J.E., Mastropieri, M.A. & Scruggs, T.E. (2006) Show time: Using video self-modeling to decrease inappropriate behavior, *Teaching Exceptional Children*, **38**, pp. 43–48.

Granpeesheh, D., Tarbox, J., Najdowski, A. & Kornack, J. (2014) *Evidence-based Treatment for Children with Autism: The CARD Model*, Oxford: Academic Press.

Happé, F. & Frith, U. (2006) The weak coherence account: Detail-focused cognitive style in autism spectrum disorders, *Journal of Autism and Developmental Disorders*, **36** (1), pp. 5–25.

Hine, J.F. & Wolery, M. (2006) Using point-of-view video modeling to teach play to preschoolers with autism, *Topics in Early Childhood Special Education*, **26**, pp. 83–93.

Hobson, R.P. (1993) *Autism and the Development of Mind*, Hove: Lawrence Erlbaum Associates.

Hobson, R.P. & Lee, A. (1999) Imitation and identification in autism, *Journal of Child Psychology and Psychiatry*, **40**, pp. 649–659.

Hobson, R.P. & Meyer, J.A. (2005) Foundations for self and other: A study in autism, *Developmental Science*, **8**, pp. 481–491.

Hobson, R.P., Chidambi, G., Lee, A., Meyer, J., Müller, U., Carpendale, J.I.M., Bibok, M. & Racine, T.P. (2006) Foundations for self-awareness: An exploration through autism, *Monographs of the Society for Research in Child Development*, pp. i–166.

Hogan, T. (n.d.) Nonverbal thinking, communication, imitation, and play skills with some things to remember, *TEACCH Autism Program*, [Online], http://teacch.com/communication-approaches-2/nonverbal-thinking-communication-imitation-and-play-skills-with-some-things-to-remember [24 November 2014].

Ingersoll, B. (2008) The social role of imitation in autism: Implications for the treatment of imitation deficits, *Infants and Young Children*, **21** (2), pp. 107–119.

Jordan, R.R. (1989) An experimental comparison of the understanding and use of speaker addressee personal pronouns in autistic children, *British Journal of Disorders of Communication*, **24**, pp. 169–172.

Kanner, L. (1943) Autistic disturbances of affective contact, *Nervous Child*, **2**, pp. 217–250.

Kircher, T. & David, A.S. (2003) Introduction: The self and neuroscience, in Kircher, T. & David, A.S. (eds.) *The Self in Neuroscience and Psychiatry*, Cambridge: Cambridge University Press.

Klin, A., Jones, W., Schultz, R., Volkmar, F. & Cohen, D. (2002) Visual fixation patterns during viewing of naturalistic social situations as predictors of social competence in individuals with autism, *Archives of General Psychiatry*, **59** (9), pp. 809–816.

Lee, A., Hobson, R.P. & Chiat, S. (1994) I, you, me, and autism: An experimental study, *Journal of Autism and Developmental Disorders*, **24**, pp. 155–176.

Lind, S.E. & Bowler, D.M. (2009) Delayed self-recognition in children with autism spectrum disorder, *Journal of Autism and Developmental Disorders*, **39** (4), pp. 643–650.

Lombardo, M.V., *et al.* (2009) Atypical neural self-representation in autism, *Brain*, **133**, pp. 611–624.

Loveland, K. & Landry, S.H. (1986) Joint attention and language in autism and developmental language delay, *Journal of Autism and Developmental Disorders*, **16**, pp. 335–349.

Loveland, K., Tunali-Kotoski, B., Pearson, D., Brelsford, K., Ortegon, J. & Chen, R. (1994) Imitation and expression of facial affect in autism, *Development and Psychopathology*, **6**, pp. 433–444.

Lyons, V. & Fitzgerald, M. (2007) *Asperger Syndrome — A Gift or a Curse?*, New York: Nova Science Publishers.

Lyons, V. & Fitzgerald, M. (2013) *Atypical Sense of Self in Autism Spectrum Disorders: A Neuro-Cognitive Perspective, Recent Advances in Autism Spectrum Disorders — Volume I*, Fitzgerald, M. (ed.), [Online], http://www.intechopen.com/books/recent-advances-in-autism-spectrum-disorders-volume-i/atypical-sense-of-self-in-autism-spectrum-disorders-a-neuro-cognitive-perspective [1 June 2015].

MacDonald, R., Sacramone, S., Mansfield, R., Wiltz, K. & Ahearn, W.H. (2009) Using video modeling to teach reciprocal pretend play to children with autism, *Journal of Applied Behavior Analysis*, **42** (1), pp. 43–55.

McCoy, K. & Hermansen, E. (2007) Video modeling for individuals with autism: A review of model types and effects, *Education and Treatment of Children*, **30**, pp. 183–213.

McLeod, S.A. (2007) *Experimental Design*, [Online], http://www.simplypsychology.org/experimental-designs.html [16 February 2015].

Meyer, J.A. & Hobson, R.P. (2004) Orientation in relation to self and other, *Interaction Studies*, **5**, pp. 221–244.

Müller, E., Schuler, A. & Yates, G.B. (2008) Social challenges and supports from the perspective of individuals with Asperger syndrome and other autism spectrum disabilities, *Autism*, **12** (2), pp. 173–190.

Nikopoulos, C.K. & Keenan, M. (2006) *Video Modeling and Behavior Analysis: A Guide for Teaching Social Skills to Children with Autism*, London: Jessica Kingsley Publishers.

Northoff, G. & Heinzel, A. (2003) The self in philosophy, neuroscience and psychiatry: An epistemic approach, in Kircher, T. & David, A. (eds.) *The Self in Neuroscience and Psychiatry*, pp. 40–55, Cambridge: Cambridge University Press.

Nugent, W.R. (2001) Single case design visual analysis procedures for use in practice evaluation, *Journal of Social Service Research*, **27** (2), pp. 39–75.

Ohta, M. (1987) Cognitive disorders of infantile autism: A study employing the WISC, spatial relationship conceptualization, and gesture imitations, *Journal of Autism and Developmental Disorders*, **17**, pp. 45–62.

Ozonoff, S. & Miller, J.N. (1995) Teaching theory of mind: A new approach to social skills training for individuals with autism, *Journal of Autism and Developmental Disorders*, **25**, pp. 415–433.

Peeters, G., *et al.* (2003) Self-other and third-person categorization in normal and autistic children, *Developmental Science*, **6**, pp. 166–172.

Plimley, L. & Bowen, M. (2007) *Social Skills and Autistic Spectrum Disorders*, London: SAGE Publications.

Rayner, C., Denholm, C. & Sigafoos, J. (2009) Video-based intervention for individuals with autism: Key questions that remain unanswered, *Research in Autism Spectrum Disorders*, **3**, pp. 291–303.

Rogers, S.J. (2000) Interventions that facilitate socialization in children with autism, *Journal of Autism and Developmental Disorders*, **30** (5), pp. 399–409.

Rogers, S.J. & Pennington, B.F. (1991) A theoretical approach to the deficits in infantile autism, *Developmental and Psychopathology*, **3**, pp. 137–162.

Rogers, S.J., Bennetto, L., McEvoy, R. & Pennington, B.F. (1996) Imitation and pantomime in high-functioning adolescents with autism spectrum disorders, *Child Development*, **67**, pp. 2060–2073.

Rogers, S.J. & Bennetto, L. (2000) Intersubjectivity in autism: The roles of imitation and executive function, in Wetherby, A.M. & Prizant, B.M. (eds.) *Autism Spectrum Disorders: A Transactional Developmental Perspective*, Vol. 9, pp. 79–107, Baltimore, MD: Paul H. Brookes Publishing Co.

Rogers, S.J. & Williams, H.G. (eds.) (2006) *Imitation and the Social Mind: Autism and Typical Development*, New York: Guilford Press.

Sancho, K., Sidener, T.M., Reeve, S.A. & Sidener, D.W. (2010) Two variations of video modeling interventions for teaching play skills to children with autism, *Education and Treatment of Children*, **33** (3), pp. 421–442.

Schreibman, L., Whalen, C. & Stahmer, A.C. (2000) The use of video priming to reduce disruptive transition behavior in children with autism, *Journal of Positive Behavior Interventions*, **2**, pp. 3–11.

Semrud-Clikeman, M. (2007) *Social Competence in Children*, East Lansing, MI: Springer Science + Business Media, LLC.

Shield, A. & Meier, R.P. (2012) Palm reversal errors in native-signing children with autism, *Journal of Communication Disorders*, **45** (6), pp. 439–454.

Shukla-Mehta, S., Miller, T. & Callahan, K.J. (2010) Evaluating the effectiveness of video instruction on social and communication skills training for children with autism spectrum disorders: A review of the literature, *Focus on Autism and Other Developmental Disabilities*, **25** (1), pp. 23–36.

Sigafoos, J., O'Reilly, M. & de la Cruz, B. (2007) *PRO-ED Series on Autism Spectrum Disorders: How to Use Video Modeling and Video Prompting*, Austin, TX: PRO-ED.

Sigman, M. (1994) What ARE the core deficits in autism?, in Broman, S.H. & Grafman, J. (eds.) *Atypical Cognitive Deficits in Developmental Disorders: Implications for Brain Function*, pp. 139–157, Hillsdale, NJ: Lawrence Erlbaum Associates.

Smith, I. & Bryson, S. (1998) Gestures imitation in autism: Nonsymbolic postures and sequences, *Cognitive Neuropsychology*, **15** (6), pp. 747–770.

Stone, W.L. & Lemanek, K.L. (1991) Parental report of social behaviours in autistic pre-schoolers, *Journal of Autism and Developmental Disorders*, **20**, pp. 513–522.

Stone, W.L. & Hogan, K.L. (1993) A structured parent interview for identifying young children with autism, *Journal of Autism and Developmental Disorders*, **23**, pp. 639–652.

Sturmey, P. (2003) Video technology and persons with autism and other developmental disabilities: An emerging technology for PBS, *Journal of Positive Behavior Interventions*, **5**, pp. 3–4.

Tager-Flusberg, H. (1989) An analysis of discourse ability and internal state lexicons in a longitudinal study of autistic children, presented at the *Biennial Meeting of the Society for Research in Child Development*, Kansas City, MO, April 1989.

Tetreault, A.S. & Lerman, D.C. (2010) Teaching social skills to children with autism using point-of-view video modeling, *Education and Treatment of Children*, **33** (3), pp. 395–419.

Uzgiris, I. (1981) The social context of imitation in infancy, *International Journal of Behavioral Development*, **4**, pp. 1–12.

Wetherby, A.M. & Prizant, B.M. (eds.) (2000) *Autism Spectrum Disorders: A Transactional Developmental Perspective*, Vol. 9, Baltimore, MD: Paul H. Brookes Publishing Co.

Wing, L. (1988) The continuum of autistic characteristics, in Schopler, E. & Mesibov, G. (eds.) *Diagnosis and Assessment in Autism*, New York: Plenum Press.

Mihretu P. Guta

Consciousness, First-Person Perspective, and Neuroimaging

Abstract: In this paper, my main goal is to discuss two incompatible answers proposed to what I shall call the objectivity seeking question (OSQ). The first answer is what I shall call the primacy thesis, according to which the third-person perspective is superior to that of the first-person perspective. Ultimately I will reject this answer. The second answer is what I shall call the scepticism thesis, according to which the distinction between the first-person perspective and the third-person perspective can be maintained without reducing to/ explaining away the former in terms of the latter. This is the answer I will defend albeit with some qualification. In this case, I will advance my discussion by appealing to the metaphysics of conscious experience/phenomenal consciousness. Third and finally, I will consider some empirically motivated objections against the scepticism thesis. In this case, my focus will be on modern neuroimaging techniques such as fMRI, EEG, and PET, and seeing whether or not they pose a serious threat against the scepticism thesis. My overall conclusion will be that science and subjectivity, which is rooted in the first-person perspective, can coexist in the sense of complementing each other.

Correspondence:
Email: mihretup@aol.com

Journal of Consciousness Studies, **22**, No. 11–12, 2015, pp. 218–45

1. Introduction

The notion of the first-person perspective is intimately linked with subjective/conscious experience (e.g. sensation of pain).[1] The connection between the first-person perspective and subjectivity has to be taken seriously if we are to make sense of the very nature of subjectivity. Yet it has been said that, both in the case of the first-person perspective and subjectivity, our view of the world could be tainted owing to our personal biases/prejudices thereby preventing us from attaining an objective knowledge of things.[2] By contrast, the third-person perspective is said to be a source of an objective or what is sometimes described as 'scientific knowledge', which is said to be publicly accessible and impartial as opposed to being private, as often seems to be the case with subjective experience.[3] But the question remains: can we achieve objectivity which is devoid of subjectivity? Let us call this the *objectivity seeking question* (OSQ). As I see it, OSQ can be answered in at least two ways: (1) affirmatively either by reducing or eliminating the first-person perspective in favour of the third-person perspective (e.g. Dennett, 1991; Metzinger, 2003; Churchland, in Shear, 1995–7, pp. 197–215; Churchland, 1988); and (2) negatively by arguing that the first-person and the third-person perspectives are intimately intertwined in the sense of complementing each other (e.g. Nagel, 1986; Chalmers, 2010; Velmans, 1994; also *cf.* Shoemaker, 1996; Searle, 1992). Those who embrace (1) often argue that for subjective experience to have any bite, i.e. in the sense of being scientifically respectable, it should be analysable from the third-person perspective. Taken this way, proponents of (1) want to establish the primacy of the third-person perspective over that of the first-person perspective. Let us call this the thesis about the *primacy of the third-person perspective* (the *primacy thesis*, for short). By contrast, proponents of (2) argue that a complete analysis of subjective experience purely in terms of third-person language essentially leaves out the qualitative aspect(s) of one's experience.[4] So, for proponents

---

[1] I will give more precise characterization of conscious experience in Section 3.

[2] Here by things I mean, quite broadly, anything that is the object of one's enquiry.

[3] For an informative discussion on objectivity in science (see Couvalis, 1997).

[4] This is one of the central points in philosophy of mind over which physicalists and dualists of various persuasions often debate (see, for example, some of the references in footnote #5). For present purposes, I am not interested in engaging with these debates, nor am I interested in developing my discussion along these lines.

of (2), the alleged primacy of the third-person perspective over that of the first-person perspective remains very much an open question, to say the least. Let us call this the thesis about *serious scepticism about the primacy of the third-person perspective* (the *scepticism thesis*, for short). In this essay, my goal is to develop my own answer to the OSQ by aguing why the reasons given in defence of (1) are often based on a questionable conception of the relation between subjective experience and science on the one hand, and a mistaken conception of the distinction between the first-person and the third-person perspectives on the other. By contrast, I will argue that (2) allows us to construct the most plausible answer(s) to OSQ, which I also take to be the best alternative to adopt.

In the course of developing my answer(s) to OSQ, I will use consciousness as a test case throughout my discussion. In this case, however, my primary aim is not to discuss the familiar objections, problems, and solutions contemporary consciousness theorists grapple with.[5] Instead my focus will be on the notion of subjectivity often linked to the first-person perspective which in turn is firmly rooted in consciousness. Consciousness is an ambiguous term. For instance, Baruss (1990) lists some twenty-nine distinct definitions of the term consciousness. In his own way, Chalmers (1996) also makes eight distinctions when spelling out the term consciousness. But Chalmers' well-known and exhaustively debated distinctions are the *easy problem* and the *hard problem* of consciousness (see, for example, Shear, 1995–7). For Chalmers, both on philosophical and scientific levels, it is the hard problem of consciousness that presents a serious challenge for anyone who tries to understand the nature of conscious experience.[6] This is the aspect of consciousness I also would like to focus on in developing my case for the *scepticism thesis*. This aspect of consciousness is characterized by Nagel's famous phrase, 'what it is like to be such and such' (Nagel, 1974). Moreover, in this paper, I will consider some empirically based objections against the reasons I will be giving in defence of the *scepticism thesis*. The objections I

---

5   See, for example, Block, Flanagan and Güzeldere (1997); Rosenberg (2004); Rosenthal (2005); Kim (2006); Moreland (2008); and Chalmers (2010).

6   Whether or not Chalmers' bifurcation of the problem of consciousness into 'easy' and 'hard' is the right way to think about the nature of consciousness, nothing I will say in this essay would hang on it. For critical discussions on Chalmers' bifurcation, see the essays by E.J. Lowe, David Hodgson, Bernard J. Baars, Benjamin Libet, and Eugene O. Mills in Shear (1995–7).

have in mind come from modern neuro-/brain-imaging methods and the purported support they are said to lend in establishing the *primacy thesis*. In this case, I will discuss briefly neuroimaging techniques such as functional magnetic resonance imaging (fMRI), electro-encephalography (EEG), and positron emission tomography (PET). I will conclude this essay by claiming that science, which often adopts the third-personal approach, and subjective experience, which is rooted in the first-person perspective, can coexist, and therefore there is no good reason to reduce or eliminate the latter in favour of the former.

2. The Primacy Thesis and the OSQ

Earlier I had given a somewhat vague characterization of the *primacy thesis* according to which the third-person perspective has primacy over that of the first-person perspective. As it stands, this characterization is far from adequate. For example, it does not tell us the sense of the notion of the primacy of the third-person perspective over that of the first-person perspective. Nor does it shed light on what we mean by first-person and third-person perspectives. To get clear on these and other related issues, it is crucial to figure out first the underlying core assumptions of the *primacy thesis*. Here the core assumptions I have in mind are well captured by Baker's characterization of what she calls the *Master Argument*.

2.1. The Master Argument

In her essay entitled 'Science and the First-Person',[7] Baker argues that there are irreducible first-personal phenomena of both 'subjective' and 'non-subjective' kinds. By first-personal subjective phenomena, Baker has in mind states of awareness of the contents of one's own mind. Here an example would be conscious experiences such as a particular greenness of grass, or a particular taste of chocolate.[8] By non-subjective first-personal phenomena, Baker has in mind states of awareness of oneself from the first-person point of view as an entity in the world, which she claims are expressed in first-personal language such as 'I'm the one in the red dress'.[9] Baker claims that if irreducible

---

[7]   Baker (n.d) http://people.umass.edu/~lrb/files/bak08sciM.pdf, accessed April 2015.

[8]   I will say more on this in Section 3.

[9]   Baker (n.d, p. 1); see also Baker (2000, Chapter 3).

first-personal phenomena exist, then the only way we can discern them is from a first-person point of view. However, as Baker further points out, irreducible first-personal phenomena stand in sharp conflict with two other claims that make up the heart of the *Master Argument*, namely (i) the claim that all phenomena can be described and explained by science, which Baker calls *scientific naturalism*; and (ii) the claim that everything within the purview of science is intersubjectively accessible, which in turn is said to show that all science is constructed exclusively from the third-personal point of view. Based on (i) and (ii) Baker formulates the *Master Argument* as follows:[10]

> 1. All phenomena can be described and explained by science.
> 2. All science is constructed exclusively from a third-personal point of view.
> Therefore, 3. All phenomena can be described and explained from a third-personal point of view.

In evaluating the *Master Argument*, Baker's main aim is to show why, if there are irreducible first-personal phenomena (which can only be discerned from the first-person point of view), the conclusion of the *Master Argument* cannot be true. But the *Master Argument* is valid (as Baker herself recognizes).[11] So in order to establish the falsity of the conclusion of the *Master Argument*, one has to show which one of its premises is false. The question then is: which premise of the *Master Argument* should be deemed false? Baker's own strategy in dealing with this question is to remain neutral/undecided (though she argues that at least one premise is false). Instead Baker argues against the conclusion of the *Master Argument* by pointing out a class of phenomena that the third-personal sciences ultimately fail to explain. In this case, irreducible first-personal phenomena of both subjective and non-subjective varieties are paradigm cases of those phenomena for which a purely third-personal explanation, as Baker claims, is unavailable.[12] However, my own approach in assessing the *Master Argument* will be based on singling out a specific premise which I think should be rejected. In fact, with closer scrutiny, it can be shown

---

[10] Baker (n.d., p. 1). In the *Master Argument*, I assume that by 'science' Baker means natural sciences often taken to consist of mainly physics, biology, and chemistry.

[11] Baker (n.d., p. 1).

[12] *Ibid.* There is a lot to be said about Baker's arguments, although for lack of space I won't discuss them any further.

that the ground for endorsing either one of the premises of the *Master Argument* turns out to be very shaky indeed, to say that least. Let me then begin my discussion by looking briefly at the first premise. But, for reasons that will be evident in due course, much of what I have to say in defence of the *scepticism thesis* as the best answer to the OSQ comes from my critique of premise 2.

2.2. The Primacy Thesis and the Master Argument

2.2.1. Premise 1

Premise 1 of the *Master Argument* seems to crown science with both actual and potential ability to describe and explain all phenomena. Here I introduce the terms 'actual' and 'potential' mainly because the phrase 'can be' in premise 1 could be spelled out in terms of what science has actually described/explained so far on the one hand and what science is capable of describing/explaining at some point in the future on the other. Understood this way, to say that all *X can be* explained by *Y* is to say that, given *Y*'s past track record of explaining some aspect of *X*, all there is to be explained about *X* potentially can be explained at some point in the future. For example, modern science's significant past achievements include: Galileo's astronomical observations which confirmed Copernicus's hypothesis regarding heliocentrism (see, for example, Machamer, 1998), Galileo's and Newton's classical mechanics (Taylor, 2005), Einstein's special and general relativity (Einstein, 1916), quantum mechanics with all its known but not fully understood complexities and microscopic weirdness (Greene, 1999/2003, Chapters 4–5), and the discovery of the double helix, i.e. the structure of the DNA molecule,[13] and the discovery of the chemical elements on the periodic table. Despite our knowledge being expanded in each of these areas, there are also many unresolved issues.[14] So, for the not-yet-resolved issues in these and other areas of scientific enquiry, it could always be argued that science's past track record (as briefly pointed out above) provides one with confidence to hope that whatever leftover

---

[13] See, for example, one of its discoverers, Francis Crick's papers: http://profiles.nlm.nih.gov/SC/Views/Exhibit/narrative/doublehelix.html, accessed June 2015.

[14] For example, general relativity and quantum mechanics are two important theories in theoretical physics. Yet they still need to be brought under one umbrella, see e.g. Smolin (2006) and Mauldin (1994/2002). We can also add to the list here the problem of the origin of consciousness (see, for example, Chalmers, 2010).

anomalies there are in the natural world they will also be explained by science. That is, the past achievements of science play a crucial role in terms of setting the tone for future scientific pursuits.[15]

In light of this, as we shall see, the main motivation for those who defend the *primacy thesis* comes from an epistemic advantage science is said to enjoy over other domains of enquiry, say philosophy or religion. Of course, from this it does not follow that other domains of enquiry lack any status as a source of knowledge. Yet, given premise 1 of the *Master Argument*, other domains of enquiry could still be denied being sources of knowledge concerning phenomena of which science can tell us nothing. This seems to be the spirit in which Quine (1969), for example, argued for his well-known *naturalized epistemology*, which rules out traditional (i.e. Cartesian) epistemology in favour of an epistemology that is guided by natural science and psychology.[16] In a similar tone, Ladyman and Ross (along with Spurrett and Collier) advocated for the abandonement of analytic/ traditional metaphysics in favour of what they call a 'naturalized metaphysics', which is said to be firmly rooted in contemporary science (Ladyman and Ross, 2007, Chapter 1). In his own way, Jackson (1998) also argued that the picture of the world/reality that must be taken seriously is the one that is dictated by modern science (e.g. physics). In a nutshell, the conception of science advocated by these philosophers can be summed up in Ladyman's and Ross's own words. That is, 'input for philosophizing must come from science' (Ladyman and Ross, 2007, p. viii).

Problem

But why should we adopt such a conception of science? One general problem is that it is very unclear just what such a conception of science amounts to. For one thing, such references in the singular to science or to the scientific world-picture are radically underspecified. A main lesson of history and philosophy of science of the last thirty years has been its pluralistic, disunified character, and the further fact,

---

[15] *Cf.* Kuhn (1962, p. 10). Here, following Salmon (1998), we can understand scientific explanations as having to do primarily with the question of 'why something occurs' as opposed to 'what something means' or 'how to do something'.

[16] It should be noted that *naturalized epistemology* comes in many different forms, although emphasis on empirical science is what underlies all of them. See, for example, Kornblith's approach based on the Darwinian argument (1985/1994). For a nice introduction and critical discussion on this issue, see Lemos (2007, Chapter 10) and Kim (1988). For a more advanced survey, see Feldman (2001).

noted by Dupré (1993) among others, that broad references to 'science' and its methods therefore cease to be legitimate.[17] Despite modern science's ongoing empirical discoveries in general and technological advancement in particular, it hardly seems to be the case that philosophizing (even in principle) must always come from science (*cf.* Cartwright, in Stone and Wolfe, 2000, Chapter 11). As it stands, the conception of science advocated by the philosophers mentioned above, namely Quine, Ladyman, Ross, and Jackson, entails a strong form of scientism, one of whose most common forms is *epistemic scientism*, the view that all forms of knowledge have to be empirically based (see Stenmark, 2001, Chapter 1; and Peels, 2015).

There is a serious problem here though. That is, the very claim that 'all forms of knowledge have to be empirically based' is not itself a scientific claim, but rather is a philosophical claim about what sort of limit science sets with respect to what counts as knowledge and what does not. So here there is a clear conflation of a first-order discipline (e.g. science) with the second-order philosophical claim about science (Guta, 2011, p. 57). Such conflation gets even deeper, as Bennett and Hacker (2003) point out, when one fails to maintain the distinction between empirical questions (e.g. about the nervous system) which belong to the domain of science on the one hand, and conceptual questions (e.g. about the concept of mind, memory, thought, imagination) which fall within the purview of philosophy on the other. If this distinction is taken seriously, then, as Bennett and Hacker further argue, a complete understanding say of the nature of conscious experience will not be possible on the basis of only what science says. In this case, the only promising way to guard against the problem of scientism seems to be to allow science and philosophy to work in synergy. We should do this for the simple (but important) reason that philosophical presuppositions are inescapable in any scientific enquiry. Here Lowe's remarks hit home:

> Devotees of scientism… fail to see that science *presupposes* metaphysics and that the role of philosophy is quite as much normative as descriptive — with everything, including science, coming within its critical purview. Scientists inevitably make metaphysical assumptions, whether explicitly or implicitly, in proposing and testing their theories — assumptions which go beyond anything that science itself can

---

[17] On the limitations of science, see Dupré (2001). On the plurality and disunity of science, see Galison and Stump (1996) and Kellert, Longino and Waters (2006).

legitimate. These assumptions need to be examined critically, whether by scientists themselves or by philosophers — either way, the critical philosophical thinking that must be done cannot look to the methods and objects of empirical science for its model. Empirical science at the most tells us what is the case, not what must or may be (but happens not to be) the case. (Lowe, 1998, p. 5; see also Lowe, 2006)[18]

If the foregoing discussion has any truth to it, which I believe that it does, then we have good reasons to remain unconvinced by premise 1.

2.2.2. Premise 2

Premise 2 of the *Master Argument* underscores under what sort of methodological constraint science is said to operate. In this case, all science is said to be constructed strictly from a third-personal point of view/perspective. Confining the practice of science to the third-person perspective seems to have, *prima facie*, some compelling reasons in its favour. More importantly, as we shall see, these reasons are taken to be the backbone of the *primacy thesis*. The reasons I have in mind here have to do with the things that are believed to be central for the justification of scientific theories. Regarding this, for example, Couvalis remarks:

> It is widely believed that many scientific theories have been justified objectively and that we know they give us a true picture of the world. In contrast, the claims of philosophers and the pronouncements of religions, no matter how plausible, are widely believed to be speculative and dubitable. The belief that many scientific theories have been justified objectively is allied to the view that scientific theories can be justified by observation because observation gives us direct access to the world. Taking this view, science provides an ideal method for acquiring knowledge which should be emulated whenever possible — the answer to the central problem of epistemology, 'how can we get knowledge?', is 'follow the methods of science as much as possible'. (Couvalis, 1997, p. 11)[19]

From the above passage we can extract the three most important things that are said to justify the third-person approach in doing science, namely (i) objectivity in science; (ii) observation in science;

---

[18] For other problems that beset scientism, see Williams and Robinson (2015). Scientism has its roots in 1930s logical positivists' verificationist theory, according to which the only form of genuine knowledge about the world is the one that is empirically verifiable.

[19] For sophisticated meta-analysis of the notion of scientific theories, see Vickers (2013).

and (iii) methodology in science.[20] In Section 4 my focus will be on (ii), where I will attempt to show, *inter alia*, how the notion of observation and the notion of subjectivity are closely related. In this section I will concentrate on (i), which is taken to be something that science ultimately aims to achieve. On the other hand, both (ii) and (iii) can be taken as mechanisms by which science strives to ensure (i). Here *objectivity* is often contrasted with *subjectivity*. But what precisely is (in the present context) this *objectivity* that is said to be so central for scientific enquiry? Notice that, in raising this question, one is basically asking what constitutes an objective knowledge (presumably as it pertains to every aspect of scientific enquiry). In this case, for example, Tiles (1984, pp. 49–50) distinguishes between two senses of non-subjective, i.e. objective, knowledge. That is: (a) objective knowledge is such that the object of knowledge, i.e. what is known, whether this be a particular thing, phenomena, or fact, is supposed to be distinct from the knowing subject, at least allowing a cognitive gap between them; and (b) objective knowledge is independent of the individual, non-cognitive constitution of the subject, so that it is possible knowledge of a depersonalized, rational subject. In light of (a) and (b), one's scientific pursuit must aim at eliminating possible sources of error in one's cognitive judgments, thereby also conforming as much as possible to the theoretical ideal of a purely rational subject. The upshot of bringing (a) and (b) together, as Tiles sees it, is what allows us to understand the notion of objective knowledge as the product of critical rationality (*ibid.*). In a nutshell, Tiles' analysis of scientific objectivity captures the essence of what is asserted by premise 2 of the *Master Argument.* That is, the third-person perspective is the only effective mode of enquiry that allows us to attain an objective knowledge.

Problem

However, Tiles' analysis of scientific objectivity as laid out above in (a) and (b) will inevitably elicit some reactions. On the one hand, there seems to be nothing problematic in assuming that there is a cognitive gap between a knowing subject on the one hand and an object of what

---

[20] Yet each of the things mentioned in (i)–(iii) has been and still is contentious in the philosophy and history of science (see, for example, Papineau, 1996; Lange, 2007; Hempel, 1966; and Kuhn, 1962). For now, I am only interested in discussing them from the standpoint of their relation to the notion of the first-person and the third-person perspectives.

that knowing subject attempts to enquire into on the other. In fact, this is to be expected if we want to make sense of the very enterprise of scientific practice. So, in light of this, (a) can be taken as portraying scientific objectivity as an attempt to grasp a mind-independent reality.[21] On the other hand, the most controversial and, perhaps, even outrightly questionable assumption is the one that is suggested in (b). That is, the assumption that *objective knowledge* is (or must be) devoid of a subjective dimension. What seems to be implicitly presupposed in (b), therefore, is the susceptibility of the first-person approach to errors that pertain to one's subjective experience(s). Echoing such concerns, for instance, Dennett proposed what he calls 'heterophenomenology', which is supposed to be 'the neutral path leading from objective physical science and its insistence on the third-person point of view, to a method of phenomenological description that can... do justice to the most private and ineffable subjective experiences, while never abandoning the methodological scruples of science' (Dennett, 1991, p. 72). Dennett's heterophenomenology reduces first-person phenomena to a third-person description, which he says exhausts everything that can be said with respect to the former (see further 'The Fantasy of First-Person Science', 2001).[22] Churchland also argues that, although first-person phenomena exist, their true nature is yet to be explained by mature future neuroscience (in Shear, 1995–7, pp. 37–44). For his part, Metzinger (2003) claims that first-person phenomena do not count as scientific data. Alternatively, Metzinger suggests that only third-person data obtained, say, via neuroimaging techniques such as fMRI count as scientific data. The common thread we can pull from Dennett-Chuchland-

---

21 Here, following Warner, we can describe 'mind-independent reality' as follows: 'an item is mind-independent just in case its being the way it is does not, in any essential way, depend either on our beliefs about it, or on the way in which we form those beliefs' (in Shear, 1995–7, p. 140; see also Heil, 2012; Lowe, 1998). Yet whether or not human enquirers like us eventually will be able to get to the bottom of the nature of a mind-independent reality, as too well-known, is a highly contentious matter. Here debates on *realism* vs. *anti-realism* in metaphysics (see, for example, Loux, 1998, Chapter 7) as well as debates on the implication of quantum mechanics for the true nature of the fabric of the universe (see, for example, Heisenberg, 1958; *cf.* Kosso, 1998) are two good cases in point. Yet, in my view, such controversies would do nothing to mitigate against the plausibility of (a).

22 In her article 'Science and the First-Person' (mentioned in Section 1), Baker has raised, to my mind, decisive objections against Dennett's heterophenomenology. Baker shows why Dennett's method ultimately fails to reduce first-person phenomena to the third-person description.

Metzinger's claims is that they are all committed to the *primacy thesis* as described in Section 1.

Where does embracing (b) as discussed so far leave us? One thing we can say is that by embracing (b) one is committed to reducing the first-person phenomenon to a third-person description or eliminating it altogether from the scientific domain. In fact, this is precisely what is implied by Dennett-Churchland-Metzinger's approach as briefly discussed above. In response to such moves, one standard counter-move in the literature is to appeal to quantum mechanics. In this case, particularly given the Copenhagen interpretation of quantum mechanics, the role of an observer is said to have introduced sub-jectivity back into a scientific domain (for details see Stapp, in Shear, 1995–7, pp. 197–215; Heisenberg, 1958).[23] Most importantly, sub-jectivity discussed in this regard is often linked directly to conscious-ness, which is a paradigm example of it (see, for example, Shear, Clarke, Hameroff and Penrose, Stapp, and Bilodeau in Shear, 1995–7; see also Smith, Lockwood, Page and Loewer, in Smith and Jokic, 2003). In this case, the discussions that are advanced in defence of the existence of subjectivity within a scientific domain severely under-mine the contrary views advanced along the lines of Dennett-Churchland-Metzinger. However, for now, I will not rehearse these familiar arguments and counterarguments. Instead, in what follows I want to briefly sketch out what I take to be rarely explicitly articulated aspects of the distinction between first-person and third-person per-spectives. In doing so, my aim is to raise significant problems against the *primacy thesis*, thereby also giving reasons why I think premise 2 of the *Master Argument* is false; and, hence, it must be rejected. All of this will pave the way for my defence of the *scepticism thesis* (Section 3).

---

[23] In light of the fact that many these days do not embrace the Copenhagen interpretation, it could be said that the subjectivity it is said to have introduced into the scientific domain turns out to be hardly established. But this objection is hardly decisive for the simple reason that, even if one rejects a Copenhagen interpretation, subjectivity can still be defended with a different interpretation of quantum mechanics (see, for example, Lockwood, 1989).

2.3. The Distinction between First-Person and Third-Person Perspectives

The distinction between first-person and third-person perspectives is often taken to be straightforwardly a clear-cut matter. Instead, much emphasis has been given to trying to tackle philosophical problems that arise due to a strong conceptual link between the first-person perspective and the first-person pronoun 'I'. The semantics of the indexical term 'I' remains to be the source of much debate, as can be seen in as diverse fields as linguistics,[24] philosophy of language, philosophical logic, philosophy of mind, and metaphysics. For example, discussions besetting self-consciousness, self-awareness, self-knowledge, self-reference, self-identification, one's own exist-ence or what Tallis calls 'existential intuition', etc. are all directly linked with the term 'I' (see, for example, Hamilton, 2013; Brinck, 1997; Cassam, 1994; Campbell, 1994, Chapters 3–4; Tallis, 2004). Moreover, debates on dualism and physicalism make explicit as well as implicit references to 'I' (see, for example, Kim, 2006; Lowe, 2000). In short, from an ontological point of view, the outstanding difficulty we face is, as Ryle once famously put it, 'the systematic elusiveness of "I"' (in Cassam, 1994, p. 31). That is, what 'I' actually stands for. For present purposes I remain neutral on the question of what the referent of 'I' is supposed to be. That said, whatever the term 'I' happens to refer to (i.e. immaterial substance of a Cartesian sort or simply a physical substance such as a body/brain), it must be pre-supposed if we want to make sense of the very notion of the first-person perspective.

Although expressions such as 'from my perspective', 'from my point of view', and 'from my standpoint' in relation to the notion of the *first person* appear to be unproblematic, that is not always the case. The problem arises when it comes to *first-person knowledge*. For example, Mellor (1991) claims that first-person knowledge is commonly and naturally called 'subjective', i.e. in the sense of being relative to the subject or the person who has the knowledge. Mellor also notes that there is another sense in which to be 'subjective' is said to be a mere matter of opinion. By this Mellor means that validating any belief as good as any other thereby implies that there is no fact of

---

24 In the case of linguistics, see, for example, the discussion by Hinzen and Schroeder in this special issue.

the matter to determine some belief as true and contrary ones as false. But Mellor claims that first-person knowledge, say knowledge about oneself, is not subjective in the latter sense, i.e. being a matter of opinion. This is because, as Mellor claims, there are observable facts about who one is, which are as knowable to oneself as the shape of the Earth, or the fact that $2 + 2 = 4$. In light of such considerations, Mellor rightly cautions us against erroneously understanding the above expressions (i.e. point of view) in their mundane sense, such as, 'as I see it' or 'in my opinion', etc. (*ibid.*, pp. 5–6).[25]

But what precisely is the notion of the first-person perspective supposed to be? Here, following Baker's lead, I want to introduce a *capacity-based* notion of the first-person perspective. Baker argues that the first-person perspective underlies all forms of self-consciousness, which, on her view, ultimately constitutes personhood, i.e. what it is to be a person (Baker, 2000, Chapter 3).[26] On Baker's view, a conscious being becomes self-conscious when such a being acquires a first-person perspective. This is a capacity that enables a conscious being to be able to think of himself/herself as an individual facing a world. Moreover, a first-person perspective enables one to distinguish himself/herself from everything else. Although all sentient beings are subjects of experience (i.e. are conscious), Baker thinks that not all sentient beings have first-person concepts of themselves. So, for Baker, only those sentient beings with first-person perspectives are fully self-conscious (Baker, 2000, p. 60).

In spelling out the first-person perspective in terms of capacity, I do not mean to imply a sort of second-order capacity that can be acquired through some sort of training. For example, when I claim to have a capacity to read, it is understood that I acquired it through learning. I do not just become a reader by virtue of being a human being. To be a reader, I have to learn or get the necessary training for it. Yet, being human, I do have a first-order capacity (or natural disposition) to read, whether or not I exercise it. If it were not for the first-order capacity, I

---

[25] A mundane sense of these expressions simply makes them a matter of opinion.

[26] My own official view of what constitutes personhood differs significantly from that of Baker's. But, for now, nothing hangs on such differences. Moreover, since 2000, Baker has refined her conception of the first-person perspective. Now she says that it is a two-stage dispositional property that comprises a *rudimentary stage* (conciousness and intentionality) and a *robust stage* (the ability to have a self-concept). For details see Baker's discussion in the present special issue. But Baker still maintains a capacity-based notion of first-person perspective.

would never be able to learn how to read or exercise the second-order capacity in the first place. That means that it is always the case that the first-order capacity is prior to that of the second-order capacity not just conceptually but, more so, ontologically. That is, it takes being a certain kind of entity such that certain capacities are possessed and certain others aren't. For example, we may teach a dog how to ride on a scooter (second-order capacity) but, no matter how hard we try, we will never be able to teach a dog how to speak a language in the sense that human beings do, since in this case a dog entirely lacks a natural disposition (*cf.* Davidson, 2001, Chapter 7).

   If I am right about all this, then fundamentally a first-person perspective is not a second-order capacity. Taken this way, the notion of the first-person perspective has an important implication with respect to the nature of knowledge one can be said to have of, *inter alia*, one's conscious experience(s). In this case, the type of knowledge that is directly linked to the notion of the first-person perspective is what the early Russell (in his classic *The Problem of Philosophy*) introduced as *knowledge by acquaintance*. This is a sort of knowledge in which we are directly aware without the intermediary of any process of inference (Russell, 1912, pp. 25ff.).[27] In this case, conscious experience, as Rosenberg remarks, 'does not necessarily involve language or self-understanding. For example, when a newborn infant cries on first experiencing the world, it must be *feeling* something, even though it has not yet developed language or self-understanding. Because it feels, it is phenomenally conscious. We identify phenomenal consciousness by being acquainted with it, not by looking up a scientific definition' (Rosenberg, 2004, p. 4).[28] In light of such considerations, a first-person perspective can be summed up as a first-order capacity that certain conscious beings (e.g. humans) exercise, via which they have direct access to *first-person data* such as conscious experience(s) as well as perceive external entities.

   On the other hand, the notion of the third-person perspective, as we saw in Section 1, makes the heart of the *Master Argument*. But what often seems to be lacking whenever we talk about the notion of the third-person perspective is some sort of story being told with respect

---

[27] This is often contrasted with 'propositional' and 'know-how' knowledge (see, for example, Feldman, 2003).

[28] Elsewhere, I explain in more detail this and other related issues (see Guta, 2011, pp. 35–58).

to what its very source is, on the one hand, and in what precise sense its distinction from the first-person perspective should be understood, on the other. In each of these cases, the notion of *intersubjectivity* takes centre stage since it forms the background assumption of premise 2 of the *Master Argument* (i.e. a third-person approach underlying the practice of science).[29] Here my main claim is that, unlike the first-person perspective (which as I argued is a first-order capacity), the notion of the third-person perspective is an *abstraction* mainly from an intersubjective undertaking. Of course, as we shall see, the notion of the third-person perspective could also be abstracted via non-intersubjectivity-involving ways. In each of these cases, the concept of 'abstraction' has a key role. Here I understand the concept of 'abstraction' in a Lockean sense, which is to say that it is a mental process via which, *inter alia*, one forms ideas (see, for example, Locke, 1975, *Essay* II, XI. 9; also see Guta, 2013, Chapter 1). Taken this way, to abstract a particular notion N_2 from another notion N_1 is to say that there is a person P such that P is capable of exercising a second-order capacity to form N_2. That means that, no matter what form the second-order capacity takes, ultimately it is *parasitic* on the first-order capacity. This is all to say that the notion of the third-person perspective is entirely *parasitic* on the first-person perspective. One way we can make sense of this is by getting clear on what underlies intersubjectivity.

We can illustrate this, for example, via what Davidson calls *triangulation*. In his *Subjective, Intersubjective, Objective* (2001), Davidson uses the term 'triangulation' to explain a three-way relation among two speakers (i.e. the first person and the second person/'I-and-you') and a shared/common world (*ibid.*, p. xv). In this case, for two people to know of each other, Davidson claims that they must be in communication. That is, each must speak to the other and be understood by the other (*ibid.*, p. 121). This is for the very reason that 'communication depends on each communicator having, and correctly thinking that the other has, the concept of a shared world, an intersubjective world' (*ibid.*, p. 105). On Davidson's view, it is the knowledge we have of a shared/intersubjective world which eventually gives rise to objectivity (*ibid.*, p. 83; see also Popper, 1959, pp. 22–6). Based on such a Davidsonian conception of intersubjectivity, we can

---

[29] It must be noted that intersubjectivity is a complex notion, since it could be understood in various ways (see Crossley, 1996).

see that the source of intersubjectivity is the collaboration among a
group (or groups) of people in a shared world. In this case, notice that
a group is made up of individual human persons, each of whom has
strictly speaking only the first-person perspective in a sense discussed
earlier. That means that other perspectives (i.e. second-person and
third-person) each depend upon and can only exist given a more fundamental first-person perspective. Even more precisely, we can say
that the source of intersubjectivity is what I shall call the 'coming
togetherness' of particular token/individual first-person perspectives.
Although far from being complete/exhaustive, this idea can be
visually represented as follows:

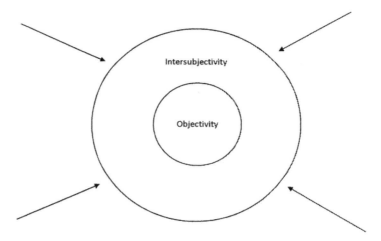

Figure 1.

The arrows pointing towards the centre of the circle in Figure 1 above
represent token first-person perspectives. The big circle represents
what happens when token first-person perspectives come together,
which is to say that they give rise to *intersubjectivity*. This in turn
leads to an intersubjective collaboration among a group (or groups) of
people with the aim in mind (as indicated inside the small circle) to
achieve *objectivity*.[30] Notice that, as explained so far, the source of

---

[30] The objectivity invoked here has an epistemological as well as a metaphysical/
ontological dimension to it. In the case of the former, the focus is on the extent of our
knowledge of the things that we investigate whereas, in the case of the latter, the

'objectivity' is intersubjectivity. If so, this has an important implication for the OSQ (i.e. objectivity seeking question) which was introduced in Section 1. What this means is that, *inter alia,* scientific objectivity arises from a subjective base. As Shear insightfully remarks, 'insofar as it is observation-dependent, science is also to a degree dependent on the subjectivity of the observing scientific investigators. Conseqently philosophers of science came up with the notions of *intersubjectivity* and *intersubjective corroboration* to recognize the role of subjectivity in empirical science' (Shear, 1995–7, p. 3).[31]

In light of the foregoing considerations, I now explain how we get the notion of the third-person perspective as well as the sense in which it can be said to be distinct from that of the first-person perspective. When someone says that science is done from the third-person perspective, all that should mean is that someone approaches the object of his/her enquiry, as it were, from outside, i.e. relative to that particular object. For example, when a neuroscientist peers into my brain using fMRI, it is right for me to say that 'my brain has been peered into by someone', which is to say by a third person. Yet the converse is not true. That is, if a neuroscientist were to say that 'she is peering into my brain from the third-person point of view', that would literally be false. This is because a neuroscientist can only peer into my brain from her own first-person perspective. That means that the third-person language comes into the picture only relative to the object of one's enquiry — in this case, my brain. It is then precisely in the relativized sense of the term as indicated in the above example that we can talk about the third-person perspective. Taken in that sense, the third-person perspective is once again an abstraction from an intersubjective undertaking. The same thing is true in non-intersubjectivity-involving cases. For example, I can refer to myself in the third person without using the first-person pronoun 'I' or 'me'. I can simply say that 'Mihretu is bored'. Or, standing in front of a mirror looking at my own reflection, I can say that 'that person is smart or stupid' (of course, depending on the mood of the day!). If I am right about all of this, it follows that the first-person perspective is not only

---

emphasis is on mind-independent reality (see again footnote #22). The former is always rooted in the latter.

[31] One could always argue that science being observation-dependent means that it is theory laden, which in turn affects the objectivity of science. But this is hardly the case (see, for example, Couvalis, 1997, Chapter 1).

basic compared to that of the third-person perspective; but, more importantly, it is a *primitive* notion. That is, it is not further analysable into a more basic perspective than itself. Hence, no matter what we do, it must be presupposed.

If the foregoing account is correct, then the distinction that exists between the first-person perspective and the third-person perspective turns out to be merely *conceptual* or a *'distinction of reason'* as opposed to being a *real* distinction. The former kind of distinction, as both Descartes and Suarez[32] noted, holds between two entities that can be distinguished in thought or mentally (e.g. substance and property). In this case, the distinction does not hold between two independently existing entities. By contrast, the latter sort of distinction holds between two independent entities which can exist separately (e.g. table and chair). So my earlier claim that the third-person perspective is *parasitic* on the first-person perspective is entirely reflective of the former kind of distinction. However, notice that even if the first-person perspective can be said to exist in the absence of the third-person perspective, the converse is not the case at all. If so, we can only talk about the notion of the third-person perspective in its abstracted sense.

In light of such considerations, two significant problems arise for premise 2 of the *Master Argument*. First, premise 2 of the *Master Argument* seriously equivocates on the notion of the third-person perspective. That is, how are we supposed to understand the distinction between this perspective and the first-person perspective, i.e. in terms of the *conceptual* sense or in terms of the *real* sense? Premise 2 does not settle the nature of this distinction. Second, strictly speaking (as already argued) science is not constructed exclusively from the third-person perspective after all. At this point, however, one may voice an objection claiming that premise 2 is arguably ambiguous between at least two readings. On the one reading, the claim made in premise 2 could be taken to mean that science does not require any perspective other than the third-person perspective. On the second reading, it could be understood to mean that science does not make claims from any perspective other than the third-person perpective. In light of this, my objector may claim that the hitherto argument I gave, if successful, only undermines the first reading of premise 2 but not the second

---

32   For details see Francis Suarez (1947) in *Disputation VII, Disputationes Metaphysicae*; Descartes, Vol. 1 (1985, pp. 29–30); and Moreland (2001, pp. 21–2).

reading. My objector may even go further, claiming that, to undermine the *Master Argument*, it is the second reading of premise 2 that needs to be targeted. The immediate problem with this objection has to do with the misinterpretation of premise 2. As I already indicated in §2.2.2, the focus of premise 2 is exclusively on how science is supposed to be practised (i.e. the methodology of science). So it seems very hard to see what motivates the second reading of premise 2 as suggested in the objection considered above. Even if for the sake of argument the second reading of premise 2 is granted, it will raise more questions than it answers. For example, since science is being practised by human subjects who often make claims from a first-person perspective, how can science be said to make claims that are only third-personal? I see no satisfactory answer forthcoming for such a question. If am right about this, then my original claim against the prospect of science being practised from a purely third-person perspective still stands.

So premise 2 of the *Master Argument* is false and, thus, must be rejected. The upshot of all of this is that the *primacy thesis* is unsustainable. But from such considerations it hardly follows that we should stop 'talk of the third-person methodology'. As is well-known, the notion of the third-person approach plays an important theoretical as well as methodological role, be it within or outside of science. Therefore, my discussion in this regard has not been aimed at convincing anyone to stop using 'talk of the third-person approach/ method'. I have only attempted to get clear on what the notion of the third person amounts to, at least given the reasons we saw in this paper. So, in so far as we guard against making a mistake of putting the notion of the third-person perspective on par with the notion of the first-person perspective, there is nothing wrong in utilizing the former as we always do. Where does all this leave us then? In Section 3, I will briefly explain the sense in which the notion of the first-person perspective and the notion of the third-person perspective can be said to complement each other.

3. The Scepticism Thesis

In this case, *contra* the *primacy thesis*, the notion of the first-person perspective and the notion of the third-person perspective can be integrated. Advocating for such an integration is what lies at the heart of the *scepticism thesis*. In this case, for the most part, I will be arguing in the spirit of both Nagel (*cf.* 1986, Chapter 1) and Chalmers

(2010, Chapter 2), each of whom has also championed for integration. That said, it must be noted that the term 'scepticism' here should not be confused with a well-known *Cartesian epistemological/methodic scepticism* about the external world and one's own existence (see, for example, *First Meditations*). The *scepticism thesis* as I am using it in this paper is intended to show why the *primacy thesis* is unsustainable. In this case, at least three reasons stand out:

(1) Conscious experience is rooted in the first-person perspective and thus it cannot be reduced to or analysed in terms of the third-person perspective without the loss of content, i.e. leaving out an intrinsic feature of a given experience. For example, this issue has been argued in detail by Nagel (1974; also *cf.* 1986, Chapter 1), Chalmers (1996; 2010), Moreland (2008), and Searle (1992), just to mention a few; (2) the first-person perspective has features which are unique to each person. Here both 'first-person authority' and 'first-person ascriptions' take centre stage. These are two related notions which presuppose each other. For example, as Gallois remarks, 'each one of us has first-person authority over his or her consciously held beliefs, desires, intentions, wishes, hopes, fears, and the like' (Gallois, 1996, pp. 2–3). That means that, when particular consciously held mental states are ascribed from one's own first-person perspective, they enjoy a certain epistemic immediacy as well as authority (Bar-On, 2004, p. 128). Instances of 'utterances' which ascribe states of mind a particular speaker happens to be in at any given time are called 'avowals' (see for details Bar On, 2004). One of the distinguishing features of *avowals* is that they are non-evidence-based. Here an example would be an utterance such as 'I have a splitting headache'. When I am in this particular mental state, I have an immediate knowledge of being in such a state. That means that first-person ascriptions (i.e. reports of one's mental states), as Shoemaker claims, are not grounded on any evidence of any kind (Shoemaker, 1996, p. 158). And (3) there is strict asymmetry between the first-person perspective and the third-person perspective. For example, the former is private whilst the latter is public. As Chalmers points out, the data for the former come from such sources as visual experiences (e.g. colour and depth), other perceptual experiences (e.g. auditory and tactile), bodily experiences (e.g. pain), mental imagery (e.g. recalled visual images), emotional experiences (e.g. anger), and occurent thought (e.g. reflecting). By contrast, the data for the latter come from the behaviour and the brain processes of conscious systems (Chalmers, 2010, p. 38). Defenders of the *primacy thesis* (e.g.

Jackson, 1998, Chapter 1) often attempt to get around (1)–(3) by adopting some sort of reductive or eliminative strategies which forces them to leave out an intrinsic aspect of conscious experience. But, as I have extensively argued elsewhere, such strategies are almost always guaranteed to be inadequate, to say the least. The main reason for this is that qualitative features of, say, a pain, that it is *hurtful*, are hardly amenable to any sort of reductive descriptions (see for details Guta, 2011, pp. 35–58).[33]

The question then is: where does a motivation for defenders of the *scepticism thesis* come from for proposing an integration between first-person and third-person perspectives? The answer lies in the asymmetry as stated in (3). Such asymmetry is responsible for two related things, namely *constraints* and the *explanatory gap problem*. In case of the former, since conscious experience is rooted in a first-person perspective, it places practical constraints on the third person's ability to access the content of the conscious experience of another person. That means that without the cooperation of the first person, the third person cannot directly capture what it is like to undergo a particular sort of subjective experience for that person. This in turn leads us to an explanatory gap problem between the first-person data and the third-person data. This is one of the reasons why neuro-scientists (not to mention psychologists) cannot ignore first-person data. So the only solution to bring subjectivity (i.e. first-person experi-ence) and objectivity (i.e. third-person observation) together is integration as advocated here (also *cf.* Shear, 1995–7, pp. 325–74). If my claims are on the right track, then ultimately we have no good reason to embrace the *primacy thesis*. So the best answer to the OSQ turns out to be the *scepticism thesis*. No doubt each of these claims could be challenged in so many ways. But, due to a lack of space, I cannot raise them here. However, in Section 4 I will briefly consider some possible objections from the domain of neuroscience.

4. Objections: Neuroimaging

One way a defender of the *primacy thesis* could challenge the defence I gave for the primitiveness of the notion of the first-person

---

[33] Here I also give a detailed critique of Jackson's proposal in regards to reducing *de se* (first-personal) claims to those of *de dicto* (non-first-personal) claims.

perspective is by appealing to modern neuroimaging techniques.[34] My
objector could claim that what we already know and continue to
discover about the structure and the function of the human brain is
more in line with the *primacy thesis* as opposed to being, say, with the
scepticism thesis. My objector's main reason in saying this has to do
with the fact that neuroimaging is done from a third-person stance.
This method allows neuroscientists, *inter alia*, to understand the brain
both on the spatial scale which ranges from neurons to systems on the
one hand, and the temporal scale which ranges from miliseconds to
decades on the other (Bandettini, 2009, p. 260). The benefit of good
spatial resolution is that it allows neuroscientists to locate where in the
brain neuronal activity happens. Similarly, by having a good temporal
resolution, neuroscientists can know when neuronal activity occurs
(Medin, Ross and Markman, 2005, p. 24).[35] Most importantly, in a
clinical environment, neuroimaging plays a crucial role in terms of
revealing abnormal changes in brain structure and processes which
could be implicated, for instance, in neurodegenerative diseases. For
example, Parkinson's disease affects the region of the brain known as
the *substantia nigra*, located in the mid-brain, which leads to a problem of motor coordination. Similarly, Alzheimer's disease damages
neurons in different regions of the brain, such as the neocortex, limbic
system structures, and reticular formation nuclei (see Nordan, 2007,
pp. 19–33). The clinical application of neuroimaging techniques is
hardly disputable. However, the controversy immediately kicks in
when it comes to utilizing these techniques to infer certain conclusions
with respect to someone's first-person conscious experience(s).

Take, for example, popular imaging techniques such as EEG, PET,
and fMRI mentioned in Section 1. Details aside, EEG is used to detect
electrical activity in the brain. It has good temporal resolution but poor
spatial resolution. On the other hand, PET is used to detect the
increase in the amount of blood flow. Compared to EEG, PET has
good spatial resolution which is in the order of millimetres, but its
temporal resolution is poor (see further Medin, Ross and Markman,
2005, pp. 24–5; see also Toga and Mazziotta, 1996). Similarly, fMRI
is used, *inter alia*, to detect blood flow, metabolic activity, blood

---

[34] For a survey of these techniques, see Bandettini (2009) and for a detailed account, see
Toga and Mazziotta (1996).

[35] That said, however, having good spatial as well as temporal resolutions concurrently
remains a problem, mainly owing to lack of imaging techniques that could carry out
both functions (*ibid.*).

volume, blood oxygen level, as well as to correlate brain activity with specific mental tasks (Bandettini, 2009, p. 260). The question remains: what are these techniques good for? Clearly they are good for retrieving third-person data having to do with, *inter alia*, complex neuronal, chemical, electrical activities that take place in the brain. But the knowledge we gather in this regard, no matter how detailed it may turn out to be, offers no help whatsoever in and of itself by way of giving us access to the first-person data. To retrieve the latter data, the right thing to do would be to directly engage with subjects of experience, that is, with people. The imaging techniques scan brains but not people's thoughts/intentions/plans/regrets, and the list goes on and on (*cf.* Bennett and Hacker, 2003, pp. 399ff.). First-person data and third-person data are not equivalent. To think otherwise would be a clear sign of conceptual confusion. In short, these techniques cannot pick out first-person data (*cf.* Chalmers, 2010, Chapter 2). In saying all this, however, I am not denying that correlations can be drawn between brain activities and particular mental tasks. But it should be noted that such correlations still do not imply causation (Jones, 2010, p. 125).

Furthermore, there is an epistemic challenge brought about by such imaging techniques. For example, Bechtel and Stufflebeam (2001) argue that even if most scientific evidence is procured via instruments and research techniques, still it is not obvious whether purported evidence is rather an artefact. This is because purported evidence is often extremely variable as new instruments are being introduced. Even granting that the same instruments are used by different researchers who use similar procedures, small-scale variations often result in significantly different outcomes. Moreover, researchers do not always have a good grip on why applying new instruments lead to different phenomena, which in turn complicates researchers' analysis of purported evidence. So, researchers often face serious difficulties of identifying whether purported evidence is an artefact or genuine evidence (*ibid.*, pp. 55–7; also see Bandettini, 2009). It seems, then, that appealing to neuroimaging does not seem to help us turn our back against the asymmetry between the first-person perspective and the third-person perspective we saw in Section 3. Hence, the *scepticism thesis* still stands.

5. Conclusion

In this paper I discussed two incompatible answers to what I called the *objectivity seeking question* (OSQ), namely the *primacy thesis* and the *scepticism thesis*. I gave reasons why the *primacy thesis* is inadequate. I then defended the *scepticism thesis* that attempts to bring subjective experience and objective, i.e. scientific, data together. In light of this, *contra* the *primacy thesis*, I conclude that science and subjectivity can coexist.

Acknowledgments

I am grateful to the John Templeton Foundation for funding this research via the Durham Emergence Project. I would also like to thank Nancy Cartwright, Lynne Baker, Ian Kidd, Matthew Tugby, Olley Pearson, audiences at the *Metaphysics of Consciousness* workshop at Durham University (2015), Ustinov College Annual Conference at Durham University (2015), University of Vienna (2015), and the referees for very helpful comments.

References

Baker, L.R. (n.d.) *Science and First Person*, [Online], http://people.umass.edu/~lrb/files/bak08sciM.pdf [April 2015].

Baker, L.R. (2000) *Persons and Bodies: A Constitution View*, Cambridge: Cambridge University Press.

Bandettini, P.A. (2009) What's new in neuroimaging methods?, The Year in Cognitive Neuroscience, *Annals of the New York Academy of Sciences*, **11** (56), pp. 260–293.

Bar-On, D. (2004) *Speaking My Mind: Expression*, Oxford: Oxford University Press.

Baruss, I. (1990) *The Personal Nature of Notions of Consciousness*, New York: University of Press America.

Bechtel, W. & Stufflebeam, R.S. (2001) Epistemic issues in procuring evidence about the brain: The importance of research instruments and techniques, in Bechtel, W., Mandik, P., *et al.* (eds.) *Philosophy and the Neurosciences: A Reader*, Oxford: Blackwell.

Bennett, M.R. & Hacker, P.M.S. (2003) *Philosophical Foundation of Neuroscience*, Oxford: Blackwell.

Block, N., Flanagan, O.J. & Güzeldere, G. (eds.) (1997) *The Nature of Consciousness*, Cambridge, MA: MIT Press.

Brink, I. (1997) *The Indexical 'I': The First Person in Thought and Language*, Dordrecht: Kluwer Academic Publishers.

Campbell, J. (1994) *Past, Space, and Self*, Cambridge, MA:MIT Press.

Cassam, Q. (1994) *Self-Knowledge*, Oxford: Oxford University Press.

Chalmers, D.J. (1996) *The Conscious Mind: In Search of a Fundamental Theory*, Oxford: Oxford University Press.

Chalmers, D.J. (2010) *The Character of Consciousness*, Oxford: Oxford University Press.

Churchland, P.M. (1988) *Matter and Consciousness*, Cambridge, MA: MIT Press.

Couvalis, G. (1997) *The Philosophy of Science: Science and Objectivity*, London: SAGE.

Crossley, N. (1996) *Intersubjectivity: The Fabric of Social Becoming*, London: SAGE.

Davidson, D. (2001) *Subjective, Intersubjective, Objective*, Oxford: Clarendon Press.

Dennett, D. (1991) *Consciousness Explained*, London: Penguin Books.

Dennett, D. (2001) *The Fantasy of First-Person Science*, [Online], http://ase.tufts.edu/cogstud/dennett/papers/chalmersdeb3dft.htm [8 June 2015].

Descartes, R. (1985) *The Philosophical Writings of Descartes*, Vol. I, Cottingham, J., Stoothoff, R. & Murdoch, D. (eds.), Cambridge: Cambridge University Press.

Dupré, J. (1993) *The Disorder of Things: Metaphysical Foundations of the Disunity of Science*, Cambridge, MA: Harvard University Press.

Dupré, J. (2001) *Human Nature and the Limits of Science*, Oxford: Oxford University Press.

Einstein, A. (1916) *Relativity: The Special and the General Theory*, Lawson, R.W. (trans.), London: Routledge.

Feldman, R. (2001) Naturalized epistemology, in Zalta, E.N. (ed.) *The Stanford Encyclopedia of Philosophy (Summer 2012 Edition)*, [Online], http://plato.stanford.edu/archives/sum2012/entries/epistemology-naturalized/.

Feldman, R. (2003) *Epistemology*, Upper Saddle River, NJ: Prentice Hall.

Galison, P. & Stump, D.J. (eds.) (1996) *The Disunity of Science: Boundaries, Contexts, and Power*, Satnford, CA: Stanford University Press.

Gallois, A. (1996) *The World Without the Mind Within: An Essay on First Person Authority*, Cambridge: Cambridge University Press.

Greene, B. (1999/2003) *The Elegant Universe*, New York: Vintage Books.

Guta, M.P. (2011) Frank Jackson's location problem and argument from the self, *Philosophia Christi*, **13** (1), pp. 35–58.

Guta, M.P. (2013) John Locke's contemporaries' reaction against the theory of substratum, in Baumgartner, S., Heisenberg, T. & Krebs, S. (eds.) *Metaphysics or Modernity*, Nurenberg: University of Bamberg Press.

Hamilton, A. (2013) *The Self in Question: Memory, the Body and Self-Consciousness*, London: Palgrave Macmillan.

Heil, J. (2012) *The Universe As We Know It*, Oxford: Oxford University Press.

Heisenberg, W. (1958) *Physics and Philosophy*, London: Penguin Books.

Hempel, C.G. (1966) *Philosophy of Natural Science*. Englewood Cliffs, NJ: Prentice Hall.

Jackson, F. (1998) *From Metaphysics to Ethics*, Oxford: Oxford University Press.

Jones, D.G. (2010) Peering into people's brains: Neuroscience's intrusion into our inner sanctum, *Journal of the American Scientific Affiliation*, **62** (2), pp. 122–132.

Kellert, H.S., Longino, E.H. & Waters, C.K. (eds.) (2006) *Scientific Pluralism*, vol. XIX, Minneapolis, MN: University of Minnesota Press.

Kim, J. (1988) What is naturalized epistemology?, in Tomberlin, J.E. (ed.) *Philosophical Perspectives*, 2, pp. 381–406, Asascadero, CA: Ridgeview Publishing Co.

Kim, J. (2006) *Philosophy of Mind*, Cambridge, MA: Westview.

Kornblith, H. (ed.) (1985/1994) *Naturalizing Epistemology*, Cambridge, MA: MIT Press.

Kosso, P. (1998) *Appearance and Reality: An Introduction to the Philosophy of Physics*, Oxford: Oxford University Press.

Kuhn, T. (1962) *The Structure of Scientific Revolutions*, Chicago, IL: University of Chicago Press.

Ladyman, J. & Ross, D. (2007) *Every Thing Must Go: Metaphysics Naturalized*, Oxford: Oxford University Press.

Lange, M. (2007) *Philosophy of Science: An Anthology*, Oxford: Blackwell.

Lemos, N. (2007) *An Introduction to the Theory of Knowledge*, Cambridge: Cambridge University Press.

Locke, J. (1975) *An Essay Concerning Human Understanding*, Nidditch, P.H. (ed.), Oxford: Clarendon Press.

Lockwood, M. (1989) *Mind, Brain and the Quantum*, Oxford: Basil Blackwell.

Loux, M. (1998) *Metaphysics: A Contemporary Introduction*, 2nd ed., London: Routledge.

Lowe, E.J. (1998) *The Possibility of Metaphysics*, Oxford: Oxford University Press.

Lowe, E.J. (2000) *Introduction to Philosophy of Mind*, Cambridge: Cambridge University Press.

Lowe, E.J. (2006) *The Four Category Ontology: A Metaphysical Foundation for Natural Science*, Oxford: Oxford University Press.

Machamer, P. (ed.) (1998) *The Cambridge Companion to Galileo*, Cambridge: Cambridge University Press.

Maudlin, T. (1994/2002) *Quantum Non-Locality and Relativity*, Oxford: Blackwell.

Medin, D.L., Ross, B.H. & Markman, A.B. (2005) *Cognitive Psychology*, 4th ed., Hoboken, NJ: John Wiley & Sons.

Mellor, D.H. (1991) *Matters in Metaphysics*, Cambridge: Cambridge University Press.

Metzinger, T. (2003) *Being No One: The Self-Model Theory of Subjectivity*, Cambridge, MA: MIT Press.

Moreland, J.P. (2001) *Universals*, London: McGill-Queen's University Press.

Moreland, J.P. (2008) *Consciousness and the Existence of God: A Theistic Argument*, London: Routledge.

Nagel, T. (1974) What it is like to be a bat?, *Philosophical Review*, **83** (4), pp. 435–450.

Nagel. T. (1986) *The View from Nowhere*, Oxford: Oxford University Press.

Nordon, J. (2007) *Understanding the Brain*, Chantilly, VA: The Teaching Company.

Papineau, D. (ed.) (1996) *The Philosophy of Science*, Oxford: Oxford University Press.

Peels, R. (2015) A conceptual map of scientism, in de Ridder, J., Peels, R. & Woudenberg, R.V. (eds.) *Scientism: Problems and Prospects*, Oxford: Oxford University Press.

Popper, K. (1959) *The Logic of Scientific Discovery*, London: Routledge.

Quine, W.V. (1969) *Ontological Relativity and Other Essays*, New York: Columbia University Press.

Rosenberg, G. (2004) *A Place for Consciousness*, Oxford: Oxford University Press.

Rosenthal, D. (2005) *Consciousness and Mind*, Oxford: Oxford University Press.

Russell, B. (1912) *The Problem of Philosophy*, Oxford: Oxford University Press.

Salmon, W.C. (1998) *Causality and Explanation*, Oxford: Oxford University Press.

Searle, J. (1992) *The Rediscovery of the Mind*, Cambridge, MA: MIT Press.

Shear, J. (ed.) (1995–7) *Explaining Consciousness: The 'Hard Problem'*, Cambridge, MA: MIT Press.

Shoemaker, S. (1996) *The First-Person Perspective and Other Essays*, Cambridge: Cambridge University Press.

Smith, Q. & Jokic, A. (2003) *Consciousness: New Philosophical Perspectives*, Oxford: Oxford University Press.

Smolin, L. (2006) *The Trouble with Physics*, New York: A Mariner Book.

Stenmark, M. (2001) *Scientism, Ethics and Religion*, Farnham: Ashgate Publishing.

Stone, M.W.F. & Wolff, J. (2000) *The Proper Ambition of Science*, London: Routledge.

Suarez, F. (1947) *Disputation VII: On the Various Kinds of Distinctions*, Vollert, C. (trans.), Milwaukee, WI: Marquette University Press.

Tallis, R. (2004) *I Am: A Philosophical Inquiry into First-Person Being*, Edinburgh: Edinburgh University Press.

Taylor, J.R. (2005) *Classical Mechanics*, Herndon, VA: University Science Books.

Tiles, M. (1984) *Bachelard, Science and Objectivity*, Cambridge: Cambridge University Press.

Toga, A.W. & Mazziotta, J.C. (1996) *Brain Mapping*, San Diego, CA: Academic Press.

Velmans, M. (1994) A thoroughly empirical first-person approach to consciousness: Commentary on Baars on contrastive analysis, [Online], http://www.theassc.org/files/assc/2281.pdf [1 August 2015].

Vickers, P. (2013) *Understanding Inconsistent Science*, Oxford: Oxford University Press.

Williams, R.N. & Robinson, D.N. (eds.) (2015) *Scientism: The New Orthodoxy*, New York: Bloomsbury.

Matthew Ratcliffe
and Sam Wilkinson

Thought Insertion Clarified

Abstract: *'Thought insertion' in schizophrenia involves somehow experiencing one's own thoughts as someone else's. Some philosophers try to make sense of this by distinguishing between ownership and agency: one still experiences oneself as the owner of an inserted thought but attributes it to another agency. In this paper, we propose that thought insertion involves experiencing <u>thought contents</u> as alien, rather than <u>episodes of thinking</u>. To make our case, we compare thought insertion to certain experiences of 'verbal hallucination' and show that they amount to different descriptions of the same phenomenon: a quasi-perceptual experience of thought content. We add that the agency/ownership distinction is unhelpful here. What requires explanation is not why a person experiences a type of intentional state without the usual sense of agency, but why she experiences herself as the agent of one type of intentional state rather than another. We conclude by sketching an account of how this might happen.*

1. Introduction

First-person reports of 'thought insertion' in schizophrenia (hereafter TI) suggest that it is possible to experience one's own thoughts as emanating from someone else. On one interpretation, TI involves an error of identification: you recognize the thought but fail to recognize it as your own. If this is right, it overturns the assumption that you can be 'wrong about which psychological state you are in' but not about 'whose psychological state it is' (Campbell, 1999, p. 609). In phenomenological terms, it challenges the view that, if you experience psychological state x, then you experience x as yours. A comprehensive explanation of TI needs to include an account of (a) what a TI

Correspondence:
Email: matthew.ratcliffe@univie.ac.at

Journal of Consciousness Studies, **22**, No. 11–12, 2015, pp. 246–69

experience consists of and (b) how TI is generated, where (a) is concerned solely with clarifying the relevant phenomenology, while (b) also addresses non-conscious or 'subpersonal' mechanisms. In this paper, we focus upon (a), but there are also implications for (b). Suppose TI is taken to be an experience of type x when it is in fact an experience of type y, and that an account is then offered of x-generating mechanisms, where x-generating mechanisms are not involved in generating y. Such an account would not merely be false but also irrelevant. Hence it is crucial to get the phenomenology broadly right, and that is what we seek to do here.

One way to make sense of TI without accepting that it involves a radical error of identification is to distinguish between our experiences of 'subjectivity' and 'agency' (Stephens and Graham, 2000), or 'ownership' and 'agency' (Gallagher, 2005). We experience ourselves as the owners of our thoughts; they arise *within* the boundaries of our subjectivity. We also experience ourselves as the agents of our thoughts; we *think them*. The 'inserted thought' is experienced as produced by another agency, one that uses one's own mind as a medium to think. So one owns the thought but is not the agent behind it.[1] In what follows, we will argue that this distinction does not illuminate the nature of TI (although we do not seek to reject the distinction outright; it may well be informative in other contexts), and we will offer an account of the phenomenology of TI that does not appeal to retention of ownership and loss of agency.

We begin by suggesting that the standard illustrations of TI are ambiguous, in failing to distinguish alien *thought contents* from alien acts or episodes of *thinking*. This ambiguity is then carried through to philosophical accounts of TI. We then argue that TI involves experiencing thought contents as somehow alien, rather than episodes of thinking. Our approach is to show that TI experiences are no different from certain 'verbal hallucinations'. Both involve an unfamiliar way of experiencing content p that lies somewhere between 'having the thought that p' and 'perceiving that p'. One's experience of p is perception-like, in that p appears non-self-produced. But it also remains thought-like, in that p continues to resemble thought content

---

[1] This move defuses an apparent contradiction: 'it is my thought, but it is not my thought.' The first 'my' is the 'my' of ownership (the thought occurs within my psychological boundaries) and the second 'my' is the 'my' of agency (the thought is not of my doing).

more so than sensory perceptual content. Hence it might be described in terms of a perception with an unusual content or a thought that one has not produced.

We go on to argue that the agency/ownership distinction fails to illuminate the nature of TI. It is not a matter of experiencing 'state y without agency' rather than 'state y with agency'. What requires explanation is why p is experienced as the content of an unfamiliar type of intentional state, x, rather than a familiar type of intentional state, y. Then we offer a tentative phenomenological account of how this could happen in at least some cases: anxious anticipation of one's own thought contents as they form leads to an experience of them as alien and strange. We conclude by noting that TI therefore involves a profound change in one's experience of self and world. The sense of being a coherent locus of experience and agency, distinct from one's surroundings, is inseparable from the capacity to experience perceiving that p and thinking that p as distinct. That capacity is, to varying degrees, compromised in TI.

2. Verbal Hallucinations and Inserted Thoughts

The philosophical literature on TI is over-reliant on a few choice examples, which frequently serve as the principal or sole basis for discussion. Here are the two most popular ones:

> I look out of the window and I think that the garden looks nice and the grass looks cool, but the thoughts of Eamonn Andrews come into my mind. There are no other thoughts there, only his… He treats my mind like a screen and flashes his thoughts into it like you flash a picture. (Mellor, 1970, p. 17)

> Thoughts are put into my mind like 'Kill God.' It's just like my mind working, but it isn't. They come from this chap, Chris. They are his thoughts. (Frith, 1992, p. 66)

Both are ambiguous in failing to distinguish encountering the *content* of a thought as alien from encountering an *act of thinking* as alien. Of course, the phenomenology of 'thinking' is heterogeneous. For instance, thinking is active and effortful to varying degrees. However, although it is unclear what exactly the various experiences of thinking consist of, we suggest that a general distinction can be drawn between acts or episodes of thinking and the thought contents that are generated through them. Hence it can be asked: is Chris's *thinking* experienced as going on in one's own 'mind' or, alternatively, the *thought contents* that his thinking produces? Is Eamonn Andrews 'flashing' his *thought processes* onto a screen or just the contents of his thoughts? This lack of clarity remains in many philosophical accounts of TI. For example, Stephens and Graham (2000, p. 4) state that '[in TI] the experience of thinking is not "I think" but "Someone else is putting their thoughts in my head"'. Does one experience the thoughts as having been put in one's head, and thus as originating elsewhere? Alternatively does one experience the act of their being 'put there', which would be more akin to experiencing someone else's thinking?[2]

We propose that TI involves experiencing thought contents as alien, rather than thinking. B is not mistaken about whether she is the owner and/or the agent of her thinking. What happens is that she experiences p as the content of an unfamiliar, quasi-perceptual experience, rather than one of thinking that p. The experience is perception-like, in so far as B experiences something as present (rather than as remembered, anticipated, or imagined) and as emanating from elsewhere. However, it remains thought-like, in so far as the content of the experience continues to resemble that of an act of thinking. This interpretation has the advantage of rendering the phenomenon more tractable, given that such mistakes are perhaps not so unfamiliar. On one interpretation of dreaming, we take ourselves to perceive or believe that p when we actually dream or imagine that p. And we often lack insight into the nature of our emotions: we take ourselves to be happy for someone when we resent their achievements, or we fail to recognize how upset we are about something. Occasionally, we might take ourselves to remember something when we actually imagine it, or feel uncertain about whether we are remembering or imagining it. Nevertheless, our account of TI does not render it mundane or detract from its philosophical interest. As will be made clear in the concluding section, TI — as we have characterized it — involves a profound disruption of self-experience, of a kind that is not limited to the sense of agency.

Why adopt the content-interpretation? There is no evidence in the TI literature for the view that it concerns thinking rather than thought contents; stock examples are compatible with both interpretations. Furthermore, there is a positive case to be made for our view. To

---

2 However, Graham (2004, p. 96) states more clearly that TI concerns the 'phenomenology of thinking'. See also Roessler (2013, p. 661) for the observation that discussions of TI often fail to differentiate the content of an 'episode of thinking' from the thought produced.

make that case, we turn to verbal hallucinations (hereafter, VHs).[3] According to orthodox conceptions, an hallucination is a perceptual experience that arises in the absence of appropriate external stimuli (e.g. Frith, 1992, p. 68). Thus, if the 'act of thinking' interpretation of TI is adopted, VHs turn out to be very different from TI: VH involves experiencing p in the absence of p, while TI involves thinking that p but experiencing one's thinking as someone else's. In one case, there is an anomalous experiential content. In the other, one's own intentionality is misattributed to someone else. So, while VH involves a familiar kind of experience (albeit a non-veridical one), TI involves an experience that is intrinsically anomalous and strange — a thought process that one does not think. Given this difference, it is puzzling that many authors attempt to account for them both in the same way, often by appealing to the agency/ownership distinction (e.g. Stephens and Graham, 2000; Gallagher, 2005).

The content view has the virtue of dissolving this tension. It is sometimes suggested that VH and TI are actually different descriptions of the same phenomenon (e.g. Langland-Hassan, 2008, p. 373). The content view makes clear how this could be so. If TI involves experiencing thought contents as (a) present and (b) emanating from elsewhere, then it shares these characteristics with perceptual experiences. Hence it might equally be described in terms of a perception with an unfamiliar content. Conversely, if VH content is not perceived to originate in a localized external source and does not have the full range of auditory characteristics, it could equally be described in terms of experiencing an alien thought.

So far, this is rather speculative. We have argued that (a) TI could involve thought content rather than episodes of thinking; (b) this would bring it closer to various familiar phenomena and thus make it easier to understand; and (c) the content view also accommodates the alleged similarity or even identity between VH and TI. But is there any evidence for the view? In order to address that question, we first need to constrain the scope of our enquiry to certain kinds of VH. VHs are heterogeneous; variables include number of voices, degree of personification, the content of what is said, mode of address (second- or third-person), and presence or absence of auditory qualities (Nayani

---

[3] The more usual term is '*auditory* verbal hallucination' (AVH). We use the term 'verbal hallucination' (VH) instead, as not all 'voice hearing' experiences are genuinely auditory, and it is the non-auditory ones that we focus upon here.

and David, 1996; Larøi, 2006; McCarthy-Jones *et al.*, 2014). Sometimes, VHs are said to be auditory and external. For example, Leudar *et al.* (1997, p. 888) describe them as 'verbal and with phenomenal properties like hearing another person speaking, but in the absence of anyone who could have produced it'; Garrett and Silva (2003, p. 445) similarly state that 'the subjective quality of sensation is a near-universal feature of auditory hallucinations'; and Wu (2012, p. 90) premises his model on the fact that VHs *'sound* like voices'. However, others describe them as predominantly internal and lacking in auditory properties. Stephens and Graham (2000) argue at length that most 'voice-hearers' do not actually hear voices at all; Frith (1992, p. 73) maintains that a VH can involve something more abstract than hearing a voice, 'an experience of receiving a communication without any sensory component'; and Moritz and Larøi (2008, p. 104) suggest that the term 'voice-hearing' may well be a 'misnomer', an 'inaccurate term to express that their cognitions are *not their own'*.

In fact, it seems clear that VHs come in both guises. David (1994) states that most but not all subjects experience voices as arising 'inside the head', while Nayani and David (1996) report that 49% of their subjects heard voices through their ears, 38% internally, and 12% in both ways. Leudar *et al.* (1997, p. 889) state that 71% of their subjects heard only internal voices, 18% heard voices 'through their ears', and 11% heard both. Some or all external VHs might well have properties much like those of veridical auditory perceptions, but internal VHs do not. Although they are not always described as *wholly* bereft of auditory properties, first-person accounts suggest that they are quite different from those VHs that are experienced as audition-like and as originating in externally located events. This is readily apparent when we scrutinize the testimonies of individuals who experience both kinds, where the two are explicitly contrasted:

'I feel like I have other people's thoughts in my head and also hear other people having conversations outside my head.'(#3)

'They are inside my head. I do sometimes hear voices that are indistinguishable, but it's shorter and much less frequent.' (#15)

'There are two kinds — one indistinguishable from actual voices or noises (I hear them like physical noises), and only the point of origin (for voices) or checking with other people who are present (for sounds) lets me know when they aren't actually real. The second is like hearing someone else's voice in my head, generally saying something that doesn't "sound" like my own thoughts or interior monologue.' (#17)

'The voice is inside my head at times appears to come from within my brain. But at other times, specifically when my name is called, it seems that it comes from outside, almost like someone is trying to catch my attention.' (#27)

Neither 'internal' nor 'external' VHs are exclusive to schizophrenia diagnoses. The above quotations (and all other numbered quotations in this paper) were obtained via a questionnaire study on 'voices and voice-like experiences', and respondents listed several different diagnoses. So, while we aim to say something about the nature of TI and VH experiences, we remain non-committal about (a) the reliability of diagnostic categories such as 'schizophrenia' and (b) whether certain kinds of experience are specific to certain diagnostic categories.[4]

Some internal VHs are described as having no auditory qualities at all.[5] Hence we might wonder whether their sensory qualities differ in any way from those of some or all thought contents. If they do not, then what we would have is a perception-like experience of thought content, an unfamiliar kind of experience that could equally be communicated in either of two ways:

- I experience content p as a thought content that I did not think.
- I experience content p as a perceptual content, but one that is anomalous in lacking certain properties.

And this, we suggest, is exactly what happens. Internal VHs are not experiences of a familiar kind that are regarded as strange only because they are non-veridical. Like TI, they are intrinsically strange. They involve an unfamiliar kind of 'perception-like' intentional state, a view that is supported by the observation that people frequently struggle to convey them.[6] They are often said to be 'almost like'

---

[4]   Quotations were obtained via a 2013 internet questionnaire study, which we conducted with several colleagues as part of the Wellcome Trust funded project 'Hearing the Voice'. The study received ethical approval from the Durham University Philosophy Department Research Committee. Participants were asked to provide free text responses to several questions about voices and voice-like experiences. Study design was closely based on earlier work addressing the phenomenology of depression (for details, see Ratcliffe, 2015). All respondents quoted in this paper had psychiatric diagnoses: schizophrenia (#8, #32); schizoaffective disorder (#33); borderline personality disorder (#1, #3, #4); dissociative identity disorder (#2, #5); post-traumatic stress disorder (#22); psychosis (unspecified) (#7, #15); bipolar disorder (#17); major depression (#18, #27).

[5]   This is consistent with reports of 'voices' in congenitally deaf subjects (e.g. Aleman and Larøi, 2008, pp. 48–9).

[6]   See also Langland-Hassan (2008, p. 373) for the view that VHs are difficult to describe, given that they do not fit into familiar psychological categories.

something — it is 'as though' something were the case. For instance, they are sometimes described as 'like' telepathy:

> 'The commentary and the violent voices I heard as though someone was talking to me inside my brain, but not my own thoughts. Almost like how telepathy would sound if it were real. I don't know how else to explain it.' (#4)

> '...there are things I "hear" that aren't as much like truly hearing a voice or voices. [...] Instead, these are more like telepathy or hearing without hearing exactly, but knowing that content has been exchanged and feeling that happen.' (#7)

> 'Telepathic conversations between me and most other people.' (#8)

> 'The best way to describe it is telepathy, in different grades of vividness, from bearable to intrusive.' (#33)

It might be objected that what we have said conflicts with the observation that even internal VHs are usually reported in terms of audition, rather than other kinds of perceptual experience. However, information of the relevant kind is usually received via auditory channels, at least in the absence of visual stimuli such as reading materials. So, even when it is bereft of the usual sensory qualities, it lends itself to description in those terms. Furthermore, talk of hearing and sounds is often qualified, and auditory terms may appear in scare quotes (as in quotation #7 above). In fact, an internal VH that lacked auditory properties could equally be compared to an experience of reading, but in the absence of any perceived text. As one questionnaire respondent remarks: 'When you read a book, you hear it in the voice of the author or the narrator, but you know that voice isn't yours. It's a lot like that' (#5). Importantly, internal VHs can also be described in terms of TI. That this is the case is made clear by first-person reports that straddle TI and VH, referring to the same phenomenon both as a voice and as an alien thought:

> 'The voice inside my head sounds nothing like a real person talking to me, but rather like another person's thoughts in my head.' (#1)

> 'The voices inside my head are like thoughts, only they are not my own...' (#2)

> '...it definitely sounds like it is from inside my head. It's at some kind of border between thinking and hearing.' (#18)

Of course, phenomenology cannot simply be read off first-person reports. Such reports are often vague and amenable to a range of interpretations. So we have not offered a conclusive case. Nevertheless, the interchangeability of TI and VH descriptions constitutes evidence in support of the thought content view; people *do* describe the same experience in terms of perceiving that *p* and experiencing the thought that *p* as alien. Furthermore, our account makes sense of such reports, by postulating an unfamiliar kind of experience that falls somewhere in between thinking and perceiving. Hence, in the absence of conflicting evidence in support of the thought process view, the content view is to be preferred.

It is plausible to suggest that some internal VHs do have auditory or audition-like properties, and thus further lend themselves to description in terms of 'hearing voices'. However, this need not conflict with our claim that they are TI under another description. The view that thought is sometimes or always *wholly* bereft of auditory properties is far from uncontroversial.[7] Most approaches to VHs take them to involve misattributed 'inner speech' rather than simply 'thought', where inner speech is only one form that our thoughts can take. And Hoffman (1986), amongst others, maintains that inner speech incorporates 'auditory imagery'. We should add that, in suggesting that internal VHs resemble perceptions, we do not wish to imply an exclusive resemblance to sensory perceptions of the external environment. They are experienced as falling within one's bodily boundaries and — in this respect — more closely resemble interoception or proprioception. However, as meaningful communications are ordinarily received through external sensory channels, internal VHs differ from bodily experiences as well. This further emphasizes the point that TI/VH involves an unusual kind of experience, something that is not quite like thinking, externally directed perception, or perception of one's bodily states.

The more general phenomenon sometimes referred to as 'double bookkeeping' serves as further evidence for our view that TI/VH involves an unfamiliar kind of intentional state. Many who express delusional beliefs and describe hallucinatory experiences also speak and act in ways that distinguish their delusions from other beliefs, and their 'hallucinations' from veridical perceptions (Sass, 1994, p. 3).

---

[7]   See, for example, Prinz (2011) for the stronger claim that conscious cognitive episodes never lack sensory qualities. This is one of various views adopted in the context of the current 'cognitive phenomenology debate'. See Bayne and Montague (2011) for a good anthology on this.

Consider this passage from *Autobiography of a Schizophrenic Girl*, where the author, 'Renee', describes the cries in her head:

> I did not hear them as I heard real cries uttered by real people. The noises, localized on the right side, drove me to stop up my ears. But I readily distinguished them from the noises of reality. I heard them without hearing them, and recognized that they arose within me. (Sechehaye, 1970, p. 59)

Descriptions like this again suggest a kind of experience that does not fit neatly into established intentional state categories. Indeed, J.H. van den Berg (1982, p. 105) observes how 'voices' are often given a 'special name' to set them apart from perceptual experiences, due to their having a 'recognizable character of their own which distinguishes them from *perception* and also from *imagination*'. This would also explain why the majority of clinical and non-clinical 'voice-hearers' are readily able to distinguish their 'voices' from veridical auditory perceptions (Moritz and Larøi, 2008).

3. Distinguishing Types of Intentional State

The position we have defended complements an approach to delusions proposed by Currie (2000) and Currie and Jureidini (2001), according to which a delusion is not a recalcitrant false belief but an imagining that is mistaken for a belief. In the case of VH/TI, there is similarly confusion between two kinds of intentional state: perceiving and thinking. Currie and Jureidini (2001) construe this as an epistemic problem: one actually imagines that p but mistakes one's imagining that p for the belief that p. However, they later reject a categorical distinction between imagination and belief, allowing for the possibility of intentional states that fall between the two (Currie and Jureidini, 2004).

Whether our account is to be construed in epistemic or constitutive terms depends on which definitions of 'perception' and 'thought' are adopted. It could be maintained that perception — by definition — involves receipt of information from an external source, whereas thinking does not. Perception is to be defined in terms of its success conditions: one perceives that p only where the experience of p is produced by an external source in an appropriate way. So an hallucination — in the orthodox sense of the term — is not a perception but an experience that resembles a perception. And the same applies to TI/VH. Alternatively, we could appeal to perception-specific neurobiological processes. An hallucination would qualify as a perception if those same processes were involved in its production. But TI/VH would not, assuming it involved processes associated with thinking rather than perceiving. If it involved a combination of the two, there might be no fact of the matter. Another option is to adopt a wholly phenomenological conception of perception and thought: if one is in a phenomenological state that is like believing or perceiving, then one is *ipso facto* in a state of that kind (e.g. Horgan and Tienson, 2002).[8] Hence TI/VH would not involve mistaken identity but a blurring of the distinction between thinking and perceiving, a type of intentionality that is neither one nor the other.

For current purposes, we do not wish to insist on any particular definition of perception. Our claim is that, whether or not 'perceiving or thinking that *p*' is to be identified with 'experiencing oneself as perceiving or thinking that *p*', what we have in the case of TI/VH is 'an experience of being in a certain kind of intentional state', which differs in character from mundane experiences of thinking that *p* or perceiving that *p*.[9] Hence, regardless of how perception is defined, it is clear that TI/VH departs from the orthodox conception of hallucination. In phenomenological terms, orthodox hallucination involves a perceptual experience of *p* (or an experience that closely resembles one of perception in a given sensory modality), but in the absence of *p*. Although certain VH experiences may take this form, those that are also describable in TI terms involve an intrinsically strange, quasi-perceptual experience of something that otherwise resembles thought content.

One might also wonder how our account relates to the widespread view that TI is a 'delusion'. It cannot simply be the case that VH is an 'hallucination' and TI a 'delusion', given that they can amount to different descriptions of a common phenomenon. The 'voice hearer' may or may not take her experience of VH/TI to be veridical. It feels *as if* the content comes from elsewhere, and whether or not this either constitutes or gives rise to a delusion depends on whether or not the

---

[8] As Horgan and Tienson (2002, pp. 522–3) put it: 'In addition [to the phenomenology of intentional content], there is also a specific what-it's-likeness that goes with the attitude type as such. There is a phenomenological *difference* between wondering whether rabbits have tails on one hand and thinking that rabbits have tails on the other. This aspect is *the phenomenology of attitude type*.'

[9] Garrett and Silva (2003, p. 453) also suggest that VHs involve 'a new category of experience that blends elements of perception and thought but remains distinct from both'. However, they emphasize the sensory qualities of VHs in a way that we do not.

subject accepts that it comes from elsewhere. It is debatable whether a sense of the content's coming from a personal source is intrinsic to the experience or whether it involves the embellishment of a core experience. However, the latter is plausible, given that VHs are personified to varying degrees (Bell, 2013). And, as noted by Hoerl (2001, p. 189), patients 'seem much more unequivocal that the thoughts in question do not belong to them than they are about possible ways in which others might be implicated in their occurrence'. A high degree of personification may also be linked to delusion-formation, in so far as it involves an increasingly elaborate attempt to *make sense of* the experience in terms of another agent, who may have specific characteristics and intentions. In addition, it is likely that the description 'TI' lends itself to a delusional interpretation more so than that of 'hearing a voice'. Saying that one 'hears a voice' serves to express an anomalous experience but does not operate as an explanation of it (unless one further insists that the experience is a veridical one). However, TI includes more specific reference to causes. Hence it is less likely to be used as a non-committal description of an experience, and also more likely to operate as an explanation: I have the anomalous experience *because* B is inserting thoughts in my head. That said, the same delusion could equally be construed in terms of other people 'really speaking in my head', and a TI description does not *imply* endorsement of a TI explanation. So the distinction between an internal VH and a 'delusion of TI' is not a clear one, and the underlying experience can be the same in both cases.

4. Agency and Ownership Revisited

Given the account we have sketched, we do not find the agency/ownership distinction helpful in this context. That distinction could be applied to an intentional state, its content, or both: I am the agent and/or owner of intentional state x and/or its content p. In one sense, experienced ownership of an intentional state implies ownership of its content. In short, if I experience myself as perceiving, then I experience myself as having a perception of something. And, if I experience myself as thinking, I experience myself as having a thought with some content. Even in the case of TI, one takes oneself to be having an experience with some content. What is anomalous is not that the content 'fails to belong to me' but that it is experienced as non-self-generated, when contents of that kind usually are self-generated. However, there is another sense in which one does not experience oneself as the 'owner' of *p*. As Bortolotti and Broome (2009, p. 208) ask, do you really 'own' something that you feel so 'radically alienated' from? The answer to this question is that you do not experience yourself as owning the inserted *thought* any more than you experience yourself as owning a chair as you look at it (where 'ownership' is understood in terms of something's falling within one's psychological boundaries). What you *do* own, though, is an experience of that thought content, an experience of its originating from elsewhere. By analogy, when you hear someone say 'I hate you', you have an experience that includes the content 'I hate you', a content that you might be said to 'own'. But, just as the experience of a chair can be distinguished from the chair itself, experience of the utterance can be distinguished from the utterance. In both cases, there is a sense that what one experiences is non-self-produced. This is all that talk of continued ownership expresses: one has an experience of *p*, but an experience of *p's* originating in an external source. 'I still own *p*' is just another way of saying 'I am not the agent that produced *p*'. It therefore adds nothing to the view that TI involves lack of experienced agency.[10]

Should we say, then, that TI involves experiencing content *p* with no associated sense of agency, resulting in a perception-like experience? That's not really helpful either. It can be maintained that perception, like thought, involves a sense of agency. Perception is not a wholly passive process. We actively look, we listen, we interact with our surroundings, and we physically manipulate objects in order to reveal their hidden features. As various enactivist approaches to perception have emphasized, perception is a matter of exploratory activity rather than the passive receipt of information (e.g. Noë, 2004). And one need not endorse one or another enactivist position in order to accept the less committal view that perceptual experience involves varying degree of agency, rather than passive receipt of sensory

---

[10] See also Sousa and Swiney (2013, p. 644) for a 'deflationary' account of 'ownership' along these same lines. Talk of 'ownership', they note, can have all sorts of different connotations. In the context of TI, it is just another way of saying that one is not the agent of the thought. 'The patient is simply emphasizing via the language of thought ownership that she does not have the sense of being the producer ("source") of the thoughts.' See Gallagher (in press) for a response to several criticisms of the agency/ownership distinction and for further clarification of his own view. His various responses and refinements do not — so far as we can see — pose a challenge to our own concerns about the agency/ownership distinction as applied to TI, although they do amount to a plausible case for its more general applicability.

information. It should of course be added that we do not experience
ourselves as wholly responsible for the *contents* of our perceptions.
Whatever theory of perception one might adopt, it seems fair to say
that we experience the contents of our perceptions *as* largely determined by things that are external to ourselves. So perceptual experience might involve some sense of agency, but we don't attribute our
perceptual contents to our own agency. Whether or not one sees a
table or a window depends on where one turns one's head, but it is the
presence of a table that determines whether one sees a table when one
does turn one's head in a given direction. Thought contents, unlike
perceptual contents, are not experienced as environmentally dependent
in this way.

However, it is unclear what the relevant experience of agency is
supposed to consist of. One might struggle to think through a
philosophical problem and, in so doing, experience a coherent stream
of thought as self-generated and effortful. However, the song that
suddenly, unexpectedly, and effortlessly pops into one's head is quite
different, as are occasional and uncomfortable thoughts that do not
cohere with one's own values, such as 'why not punch him on the
nose to see how he reacts?'. Such thoughts can arise unannounced and
even be surprising, but this does not prevent their being experienced
unproblematically as episodes of thought. So the experience of
'having the thought that *p*' is not a singular one, and encompasses
various cases that seem to involve little or no awareness of agency.
Hence it is not clear that the *phenomenological* difference between
having the thought that *p* and having an experience of *p* as non-self-
produced can be attributed to the presence or absence of a sense of
agency. All we have so far is the following:

- When one experiences oneself as the agent of mental state type
  x, the content of *x* is experienced as self-produced.
- When one experiences oneself as the agent of mental state *y*, the
  content of *y* is experienced as non-self-produced.

Why, then, is the content of thought ordinarily experienced as self-
produced while the content of perception is not? The answer might
seem simple enough: non-self-produced contents have certain properties that distinguish them from self-produced contents. For
example, a voice that emanates from somewhere else has a perceived
location and various distinctively auditory characteristics. But one of
the most interesting things about TI/VH is that it challenges such a
view. The phenomenological difference between thinking that *p* and

perceiving that p cannot be wholly attributed to different contents, given that TI involves something that retains the properties of thought content but at the same time seems to come from elsewhere. So what we need to account for is this:

> One experiences a content of the kind ordinarily associated with a state of type x, but in such a way that it is experienced as non-self-produced. In virtue of the content's seeming to be non-self-produced, the experience resembles a state of type y, even though its content differs from those ordinarily associated with y.

We will now sketch a tentative account of how such an experience might arise, an account that does not appeal to the sense of agency.

5. Reformulating the Question

We have suggested that the question to ask is not 'why is there a sense of ownership but no sense of agency for an intentional state of a given type?' but, rather, 'why is there an erosion of the phenomenological distinction between two intentional state types?'. As already noted, we doubt that appeals to conscious agency will assist in distinguishing quasi-perceptual experiences of thought content from seemingly passive but quite unproblematic 'episodes' of thought. But one could instead appeal to a breakdown of non-conscious processes. Even when a thought seems to come unannounced, that thought (and — to some degree — its content) might still be anticipated in a non-conscious way. It is when such anticipatory processes break down that the thought is experienced in an anomalous way.

That said, we should not be too hasty in ruling out a role for conscious *anticipation*. Even if we do not experience a sense of effort, agency, or intention in relation to all thought contents, perhaps they are at least *anticipated*. So it could be that the phenomenological difference between TI and thinking is that the content of TI arises without any conscious anticipation and is therefore more like perceptual content. However, there are two problems with that view. First of all, perceptual contents are not always unanticipated. Indeed, it has been argued that perceptual experience is riddled with anticipation, as exemplified by moments of surprise when things do not appear as anticipated but where anticipation did not involve consciously entertaining a propositional attitude with the content 'x is behind the door' or 'y has property p and not property q' (Husserl, 1948/1973; Noë, 2004; Ratcliffe, 2008; 2015; Madary, 2013). Furthermore, what we perceive is often partly attributable to our own activities, which we expect to have certain, often quite specific, effects. If I hurl a glass at a wall, it comes as no surprise to me when it makes a loud crash and shatters into pieces. The second problem is that many 'voice hearers' *do anticipate* when they will 'hear' a voice, and they also anticipate, to varying degrees, *what* they will 'hear'. Some report being able to communicate with their 'voices' (e.g. Garrett and Silva, 2003, p. 449), and 38% of the subjects who participated in a study by Nayani and David (1996, p. 183) reported being able to initiate a voice. This also poses problems for the view that VH/TI is to be accounted for in terms of non-conscious prediction mechanisms. It could well be that some such mechanism fails. Even so, where there is conscious anticipation, some kind of non-conscious prediction mechanism is surely at work too.

Another consideration to keep in mind is the content-specificity of many TI/VH experiences. Where a non-conscious mechanism breaks down, it might do so only sporadically, but this does not account for the fact that many TI/VH experiences have consistent thematic contents. More often than not, the contents of 'voices' are insults and simple terms of abuse, an observation that applies to several different psychiatric diagnoses and also to some of the VH experiences reported in non-clinical populations (Nayani and David, 1996; Leudar *et al.*, 1997; Aleman and Larøi, 2008). Given this, it is unsurprising that VHs are often associated with heightened anxiety (Allen *et al.*, 2005; Kuipers *et al.*, 2006; Paulik, Badcock and Maybery, 2006). What is of particular interest to us, though, is the observation that generalized social anxiety often *precedes* the onset of VHs and that anxiety may be especially pronounced immediately before the onset of a voice. It has therefore been suggested that anxiety acts as a trigger (Freeman and Garety, 2003, p. 923).

We will now briefly sketch an account of how anxiety might generate the kind of experience described here. (A more detailed account is offered in Ratcliffe and Wilkinson, in preparation.) We do not wish to insist that this account applies to every case of TI/VH; such experiences could well arise in a number of different ways. Rather, our claim is that on the basis of (a) our account of VH/TI, and (b) available empirical evidence, there is a plausible hypothesis that applies to at least a subset of cases. Our proposal is that VH/TI is not a matter of lacking anticipation, conscious or otherwise, but of antici- pating the arrival of thought contents in a distinctive *way*. It is about *how* one anticipates. Anxiety, we suggest, alienates a person from the object of anxiety: when one is anxious about p, one experiences p as something that impedes one's agency — something that one may seek to avoid but feel helpless in the face of. By implication, p is experienced as distinct from oneself. It need not be experienced as *physically* external. Serious illness can involve losing an implicit 'trust' in the body's ability to perform its various functions and, along with this, a curious sense of estrangement from one's body (Carel, 2013). With this, bodily experiences may themselves be objects of anxiety; they are experienced as impinging upon the self, threatening the self. We can also feel anxious about our own abilities to perform various tasks. However, we are seldom anxious about our own thought contents. When we are anxious about the prospect of messing up something important, we are anxious about a state of affairs that may or may not arise, not about 'the thought that a state of affairs might arise'.

But suppose that you became anxious about the arrival of thoughts with contents such as 'you are a worthless piece of filth and everyone is laughing at you'. It might be objected that you cannot feel anxious about a thought with the content p before you have that thought; the thought must have formed already. However, thought contents do not always form instantaneously. Often, there is a short period during which they coalesce and their content becomes more determinate. Take the experience of realizing that you have forgotten something important. It can start with an inchoate sense of anxiety which might be expressed by the indeterminate content 'something is wrong', followed by 'I've forgotten something' and, finally, 'I've not brought my passport to the airport', after which the repercussions of this omission increasingly sink in.

That thoughts take shape in some such way is also consistent with the commonplace assumption that VHs involves misidentified 'inner speech', as distinct from thought more generally, where inner speech is a form that only some thoughts take on. As Stephens and Graham (2000, p. 82) remark, talking to oneself is one 'way of thinking'. This suggests a process whereby thought contents become inner speech contents (Hoffman, 1986; Fernyhough, 2004). We can add that, when a thought takes on an explicitly linguistic form (which is not to imply that thought more generally is bereft of linguistic structure), its content gains greater determinacy. This view gains further plausibility from the observation that many VH/TI contents are emotionally charged. In fact, they might be regarded as more determinate linguistic expressions of emotional attitudes towards oneself, involving feelings of shame, worthlessness, and social estrangement. The person might resist such emotional states, try to avoid them, and thus feel a sense of dread as they coalesce into a more determinate linguistic judgment.[11]

So, one way in which a VH/TI experience could occur is that the person anxiously anticipates the arrival of thought content *p* as it coalesces. Given that anxiety alienates, *p* is then experienced as something she confronts, something that threatens, which she feels helpless in the face of. This sense of alienation from *p* amounts to a perception-like experience of it: *p* is the object of an emotional experience that is not ordinarily associated with thought contents, an experience that is more usually associated with what we encounter through external sensory perception or through interoception. By analogy, consider the experience of reading a letter with a consistently abusive and insulting content. What would such an experience be like if the text were absent and if one could not avoid the content by averting one's gaze? One would dread what is coming next, feel increasingly alienated from it, and yet continue to anticipate it.[12] Certain first-person reports indicate something much like this:

> 'It's very difficult to describe the experience. Words seem to come into my mind from another source than through my own conscious effort. I find myself straining sometimes to make out the word or words, and my own anxiety about what I hear or may have heard makes it a fearful experience. I seem pulled into the experience and fear itself may shape some of the words I hear.' (#32)

If something along these lines is right, then the difference between TI and more mundane experiences of thinking is not that TI involves a *lack* of something (for example, a sense of agency). Rather, a certain affectively charged way of anticipating is *present* in TI. Hence it may not be that some positive characteristic is required in order to identify thought content as self-generated. Perhaps it does not require any

---

[11] Colombetti (2009) suggests that expression and, more specifically, linguistic expression serves to individuate or even partly constitute certain emotions, a point that may apply to inner speech as much as to overt linguistic expression.

[12] Billon (2013, p. 16) similarly offers an analogy between TI and being perceptually presented with a sentence, but offers an account according to which inserted thoughts, unlike thoughts more generally, are not 'phenomenally conscious'. Hence TI involves having a conscious experience of something that is not itself part of one's consciousness and thus appears alien to it. We similarly maintain that TI involves experiencing one's thoughts in a perception-like way, but we do not attribute this to a lack of 'first-order phenomenology'. Rather, it is a matter of taking oneself to be in intentional state *x*, rather than *y*, something that can be accounted for without appealing to the distinction between phenomenally conscious and unconscious thoughts.

anticipation at all, conscious or otherwise. Many thoughts could well be just what they seem to be, unanticipated and quite mundane — the song that starts in one's head, the irrelevant thought that disrupts one's concentration while writing. Self-attribution could be the default way of experiencing thought contents. It takes an anomalous mode of anticipation, such as anxious anticipation, to transform an episode of thought into a quasi-perceptual encounter with something.[13]

What we are proposing is, in one respect, consistent with accounts that appeal to lack of endorsement; a thought appears alien when — for whatever reason — one fails to endorse its content (Stephens and Graham, 2000; Bortolotti and Broome, 2009). The difference is that, according to our account, lack of endorsement does not follow formation of thought content. Rather, one seeks to avoid the content as it arises but feels helpless before it. One might say that the experience is one of ineffectively resisting the arrival of a negative emotional judgment regarding oneself:

'...it's mocking me, I hate that one [...] I am left in a state of fear [...] They don't sound like me. They are angry most of the time. I don't like to think of mean things, I try hard not to, but the more I try not to think the more the voices get nasty.' (#22)

It can be added that this generally occurs in the context of a more general susceptibility to blurring of the phenomenological boundaries between intentional state types. Subjects with a range of different psychiatric diagnoses report pervasive feelings of anxiety and estrangement, which would render one more vulnerable to TI in those cases where thought contents are especially troubling. There may also be more specific phenomenological changes associated with the pro-dromal stages of schizophrenia, which can involve thoughts in general being experienced as more perception-like, thus weakening the phenomenological boundaries between intentional state types in a way that increases vulnerability to more pronounced, content-specific disturbances (e.g. Raballo and Larøi, 2011).

This type of account could be extended from the thinking/perceiving distinction to intentional states more generally. For instance, the alienating role of anxiety could apply equally to the anticipation of

---

[13] Our account thus differs from that of Gallagher (2005), who suggests that anxiety may explain why thoughts appear alien but suggests that anxiety disrupts anticipation such that thoughts arrive unannounced and fully formed, rather than coalescing in a way that is consistent with what was anticipated.

distressing memories and imaginings, both of which may have more pronounced auditory qualities. Indeed, Michie *et al.* (2005) propose that VHs involve memory intrusions, rather than misplaced inner speech, although McCarthy-Jones *et al.* (2014) report that only 39% of their subjects acknowledged VH contents resembling memories and even fewer said that their VH contents were memories. It could well be that internal VHs are heterogeneous, involving experiences of inner speech, memories, and imaginings, as well as some contents that blend memories with imaginings. And the predominance of one form or another may reflect individual differences, different life histories, and different diagnostic categories. To speculate, we might find a pre-dominance of alienated memory contents in cases where there is past trauma. However, inner speech VHs with less pronounced auditory phenomenology may be more often associated with schizophrenia diagnoses, thus accounting for more frequent reports of TI in schizophrenia.[14]

6. Conclusion

It might seem that we have offered a rather deflationary view of TI. One does not experience an episode of thinking while failing to identify oneself as the agent. Rather, one experiences *p* as the content of an unfamiliar type of intentional state. Although still puzzling, this is closer to more familiar experiences where we take ourselves to be in state *x* in relation to *p* when we are actually in state *y*. However, what we in fact end up with is a version of the view that TI involves an erosion of ego boundaries, an experienced blurring of the distinction between self and non-self (see, for example, Hoerl, 2001, for a

---

[14] As noted earlier, other 'subtypes' of VH are not captured by our account, including many that more closely resemble veridical auditory experiences in character. However, certain kinds of 'external VH' can also be understood in terms of social anxiety, thus accounting for why internal and external VHs often occur together. Dodgson and Gordon (2009, p. 326) observe that anxiety and hyper-vigilance generate false positives, especially in 'noisy' environments where stimuli are susceptible to multiple interpreta-tions. This, they suggest, accounts for a 'substantial subset of externally located voices'. This is also consistent with the 'neural diathesis-stress' model of schizophrenia (Walker and Diforio, 1997), especially a more recent version of it that places the emphasis on responses to situations involving an 'uncontrollable, social-evaluative threat' (Jones and Fernyhough, 2007, p. 1174). If something along these lines is right, the phenomenology and underlying mechanisms in the internal and external cases would be quite different, but they could be attributable to a common underlying cause — pronounced and pervasive social anxiety.

discussion of that view). It is not that one fails to distinguish self from non-self by experiencing a state of type *x* while failing to self-attribute it. Rather, one lacks an ability to distinguish type *x* from type *y*, where the distinction between them is partly constitutive of the self/non-self distinction.

Suppose one were completely unable to distinguish perceiving that *p* from entertaining the thought that *p* or remembering that *p*, and that this applied to all cases of *p*. One would lack any sense of the distinction between one's own consciousness and things external to it. More specifically, if the distinction between thinking that *p* and receiving the communication that *p* from someone else were lacking, one would not be able to distinguish one's own thought contents from those of others. The 'I think' would be gone from experience. Now, TI does not involve anything quite so extreme. Even so, to have frequent experiences that do not respect the phenomenological distinctions between types of intentional state (distinctions that the self/other/ world distinction depends upon for its intelligibility) would challenge — to varying degrees — the sense of being a singular subject of experience, distinct from the surrounding world and from other subjects. This would be exacerbated by a less extreme but more pervasive erosion of the experienced distinctions between intentional state types. Consider the following first-person account, by someone with a schizophrenia diagnosis:

> ...the real 'me' is not here any more. I am disconnected, disintegrated, diminished. Everything I experience is through a dense fog, created by my own mind, yet it also resides outside my mind. I feel that my real self has left me, seeping through the fog toward a separate reality, which engulfs and dissolves this self. (Kean, 2009, p. 1034)[15]

Talk of disintegration and diminishment, and of things being experienced as self-created and at the same time 'outside', can be plausibly interpreted in terms of the erosion of phenomenological differences between familiar intentional state categories. Without those distinctions, one is no longer a 'real self', situated in a world that is not of one's own making. The sense of being a coherent locus of experience and agency, distinct from what it experiences, is thus compromised and the self is 'diminished'. Hence TI does, after all, point to a profound disturbance of first-person experience.

---

[15] Sass (e.g. 1992; 1994) describes such experiences in great detail, in a way that is consistent with much of what we have proposed.

Acknowledgments

We are grateful to the Wellcome Trust for funding the research that led to this paper (grant number WT098455). We would also like to thank Shaun Gallagher, audiences at the Universities of Durham and Warwick, and two anonymous referees for their helpful comments and suggestions.

References

Aleman, A. & Larøi, F. (2008) *Hallucinations: The Science of Idiosyncratic Perception*, Washington, DC: American Psychological Association.

Allen, P., Freeman, D., McGuire, P., Garety, P, Kuipers, E., Fowler, D., Bebbington, P., Green, C., Dunn, G. &d Ray, K. (2005) The prediction of hallucinatory predisposition in non-clinical individuals: Examining the contribution of emotion and reasoning, *British Journal of Clinical Psychology*, **44**, pp. 127–132.

Bayne, T. & Montague, M. (eds.) (2011) *Cognitive Phenomenology*, Oxford: Oxford University Press.

Bell, V. (2013) A community of one: Social cognition and auditory verbal hallucinations, *PLOS Biology*, **11** (12), pp. 1–4.

Billon, A. (2013) Does consciousness entail subjectivity? The puzzle of thought insertion, *Philosophical Psychology*, **26**, pp. 291–314.

Bortolotti, L. & Broome, M. (2009) A role for ownership and authorship in the analysis of thought insertion, *Phenomenology and the Cognitive Sciences*, **8**, pp. 205–224.

Campbell, J. (1999) Schizophrenia, the space of reasons, and thinking as a motor process, *The Monist*, **82**, pp. 609–625.

Carel, H. (2013) Bodily doubt, *Journal of Consciousness Studies*, **20** (7–8), pp. 178–197.

Colombetti, G. (2009) What language does to feelings, *Journal of Consciousness Studies*, **16** (9), pp. 4–26.

Currie, G. (2000) Imagination, delusion and hallucinations, in Coltheart, M. & Davies, M. (eds.) *Pathologies of Belief*, pp. 167–182, Oxford: Blackwell.

Currie, G. & Jureidini, J. (2001) Delusion, rationality, empathy: Commentary on Davies et al., *Philosophy, Psychiatry & Psychology*, **8**, pp. 159–162.

Currie, G. & Jureidini, J. (2004) Narrative and coherence, *Mind & Language*, **19**, pp. 409–427.

David, A.S. (1994) The neuropsychological origin of auditory hallucinations, in David, A.S. & Cutting. J.C. (eds.) *The Neuropsychology of Schizophrenia*, pp. 269–313, Hove: Psychology Press.

Dodgson, G. & Gordon, S. (2009) Avoiding false negatives: Are some auditory hallucinations an evolved design flaw?, *Behavioural and Cognitive Psychotherapy*, **37**, pp. 325–334.

Fernyhough, C. (2004) Alien voices and inner dialogue: Towards a developmental account of auditory verbal hallucinations, *New Ideas in Psychology*, **22**, pp. 49–68.

Freeman, D. & Garety, A. (2003) Connecting neurosis and psychosis: The direct influence of emotion on delusions and hallucinations, *Behaviour Research and Therapy*, **41**, pp. 923–947.

Frith, C. (1992) *The Cognitive Neuropsychology of Schizophrenia*, Hove: Psychology Press.

Gallagher, S. (2005) *How the Body Shapes the Mind*, Oxford: Oxford University Press.

Gallagher, S. (in press) Relations between agency and ownership in the case of schizophrenic thought insertion and delusions of control, *Review of Philosophy and Psychology*.

Garrett, M. & Silva, R. (2003) Auditory hallucinations, source monitoring, and the belief that 'voices' are real, *Schizophrenia Bulletin*, **29**, pp. 445–457.

Graham, G. (2004) Self-ascription: Thought insertion, in Radden, J. (ed.) *The Philosophy of Psychiatry: A Companion*, pp. 89–105, Oxford: Oxford University Press.

Hoerl, C. (2001) On thought insertion, *Philosophy, Psychiatry & Psychology*, **8**, pp. 189–200.

Hoffman, R.E. (1986) Verbal hallucinations and language production processes in schizophrenia, *Behavioral and Brain Sciences*, **9**, pp. 503–548.

Horgan, T. & Tienson, J. (2002) The intentionality of phenomenology and the phenomenology of intentionality, in Chalmers, D.J. (ed.) *Philosophy of Mind: Classical and Contemporary Readings*, pp. 520–533, Oxford: Oxford University Press.

Husserl, E. (1948/1973) *Experience and Judgment*, Churchill, J.S. & Ameriks, K. (trans.), London: Routledge.

Jones, S.R. & Fernyhough, C. (2007) A new look at the neural diathesis-stress model of schizophrenia: The primacy of social-evaluative and uncontrollable situations, *Schizophrenia Bulletin*, **33**, pp. 1171–1177.

Kean, C. (2009) Silencing the self: Schizophrenia as a self-disturbance, *Schizophrenia Bulletin*, **35**, pp. 1034–1036.

Kuipers, E., Garety, P., Fowler, D., Freeman, D., Dunn, G. & Bebbington, P. (2006) Cognitive, emotional, and social processes in psychosis: Refining cognitive behavioral therapy for persistent positive symptoms, *Schizophrenia Bulletin*, **32** (S1), pp. 24–31.

Langland-Hassan, P. (2008) Fractured phenomenologies: Thought insertion, inner speech, and the puzzle of extraneity, *Mind & Language*, **23**, pp. 369–401.

Larøi, F. (2006) The phenomenological diversity of hallucinations: Some theoretical and clinical implications, *Psychologia Belgica*, **46**, pp. 163–183.

Leudar, I, Thomas, P., McNally, D. & Glinski, A. (1997) What voices can do with words: Pragmatics of verbal hallucinations, *Psychological Medicine*, **27**, pp. 885–898.

Madary, M. (2013) Anticipation and variation in visual content, *Philosophical Studies*, **165**, pp. 335–347.

McCarthy-Jones, S., Trauer, T., Mackinnin, A., Sims, E., Thomas, N. & Copolov, D.L. (2014) A new phenomenological survey of auditory hallucinations: Evidence for subtypes and implications for theory and practice, *Schizophrenia Bulletin*, **40**, pp. 231–235.

Mellor, C.H. (1970) First rank symptoms of schizophrenia, *British Journal of Psychiatry*, **117**, pp. 15–23.

Michie, P.T., Badcock, J.C., Waters, F.A.V. & Maybery, M.T. (2005) Auditory hallucinations: Failure to inhibit irrelevant memories, *Cognitive Neuropsychiatry*, **10**, pp. 125–136.

Moritz, S. & Larøi, F. (2008) Differences and similarities in the sensory and cognitive signatures of voice-hearing, intrusions and thoughts, *Schizophrenia Research*, **102**, pp. 96–107.

Nayani, T.H. & David, A.S. (1996) The auditory hallucination: A phenomenological survey, *Psychological Medicine*, **26**, pp. 177–189.

Noë, A. (2004) *Action in Perception*, Cambridge MA: MIT Press.

Paulik, G., Badcock, J.C. & Maybery, M.T. (2006) The multifactorial structure of the predisposition to hallucinate and associations with anxiety, depression and stress, *Personality and Individual Differences*, **41**, pp. 1067–1076.

Prinz, J. (2011) The sensory basis of cognitive phenomenology, in Bayne, T. & Montague, M. (eds.) *Cognitive Phenomenology*, pp. 174–196, Oxford: Oxford University Press.

Raballo, A. & Larøi, F. (2011) Murmurs of thought: Phenomenology of hallucinating consciousness in impending psychosis, *Psychosis*, **3**, pp. 163–166.

Ratcliffe, M. (2008) *Feelings of Being: Phenomenology, Psychiatry and the Sense of Reality*, Oxford: Oxford University Press.

Ratcliffe, M. (2015) *Experiences of Depression: A Study in Phenomenology*, Oxford: Oxford University Press.

Ratcliffe, M. & Wilkinson, S. (in preparation) How anxiety induces verbal hallucinations.

Roessler, J. (2013) Thought insertion, self-awareness, and rationality, in Fulford, K.W.M., Davies, M., Gipps, R.G.T., Graham, G., Sadler, J.Z., Stanghellini, G. & Thornton, T. (eds.) *The Oxford Handbook of Philosophy and Psychiatry*, pp. 658–672, Oxford: Oxford University Press.

Sass, L.A. (1992) *Madness and Modernism: Insanity in the Light of Modern Art, Literature and Thought*, New York: Basic Books.

Sass, L.A. (1994) *The Paradoxes of Delusion: Wittgenstein, Schreber, and the Schizophrenic Mind*, Ithaca, NY: Cornell University Press.

Sechehaye, M. (1970) *Autobiography of a Schizophrenic Girl*, New York: Signet.

Sousa, P. & Swiney, L. (2013) Thought insertion: Abnormal sense of thought agency or thought endorsement?, *Phenomenology and the Cognitive Sciences*, **12**, pp. 637–654.

Stephens, G.L. & Graham, G. (2000) *When Self-Consciousness Breaks: Alien Voices and Inserted Thoughts*, Cambridge, MA: MIT Press.

Van den Berg, J.H. (1982) On hallucinating: Critical-historical overview and guidelines for further study, in de Koning, A.J.J. & Jenner, F.A. (eds.) *Phenomenology and Psychiatry*, pp. 97–110, London: Academic Press.

Walker, E.F. & Diforio, D. (1997) Schizophrenia: A neural diathesis-stress model, *Psychological Review*, **104**, pp. 667–685.

Wu, W. (2012) Explaining schizophrenia: Auditory verbal hallucination and self-monitoring, *Mind & Language*, **27**, pp. 86–107.

Thomas Metzinger

M-Autonomy

Abstract: What we traditionally call 'conscious thought' actually is a subpersonal process, and only rarely a form of mental action. The paradigmatic, standard form of conscious thought is non-agentive, because it lacks veto-control and involves an unnoticed loss of epistemic agency and goal-directed causal self-determination at the level of mental content. Conceptually, it must be described as an unintentional form of inner behaviour. Empirical research shows that we are not mentally autonomous subjects for about two thirds of our conscious lifetime, because while conscious cognition is unfolding, it often cannot be inhibited, suspended, or terminated. The instantiation of a stable first-person perspective as well as of certain necessary conditions of personhood turn out to be rare, graded, and dynamically variable properties of human beings. I argue that individual representational events only become part of a personal-level process by being functionally integrated into a specific form of transparent conscious self-representation, the 'epistemic agent model' (EAM). The EAM may be the true origin of our consciously experienced first-person perspective.

1. M-Autonomy

The two main claims of this contribution are, first, that for roughly two thirds of their conscious lives human beings are not mentally autonomous subjects, and, second, that what we traditionally call 'conscious thought' primarily and predominantly is a subpersonal process. The argument is partly based on recent empirical research demonstrating the ubiquitous occurrence of 'mind-wandering', or spontaneous, task-unrelated thought. Examples of mind-wandering are daydreams, automatic planning, the sudden occurrence of unbidden

Correspondence:
Email: metzinge@uni-mainz.de

Journal of Consciousness Studies, **22**, No. 11–12, 2015, pp. 270–302

memories, or depressive rumination.[1] Methods like externally cued experience sampling show how unnoticed attentional lapses leading to uncontrolled mental activity of this kind are much more frequent than most of us intuitively think. Mind-wandering is interesting for philosophy of mind because its phenomenology as well as new empirical data bear direct relevance on our theoretical notion of 'mental autonomy' (M-autonomy). As it were, mind-wandering is the opposite of M-autonomy, because it involves a loss of self-control at the level of conscious thought. My epistemic goal in this paper is to find out how a more careful look at the phenomenology and novel empirical data can help to improve our conceptual understanding of what it means to be a mentally autonomous subject.

Mental autonomy includes the capacity to impose rules on one's own mental behaviour, to explicitly select goals for mental action, the ability for rational guidance and, most importantly, for the intentional inhibition, suspension, or termination of an ongoing mental process. M-autonomy is a functional property,[2] which any given self-conscious system can either possess or lack. Its instantiation goes along with new epistemic abilities, a specific phenomenological profile, and the appearance of a new layer of representational content in the phenomenal self-model (Metzinger, 2003a). In humans, first insights into its neuronal realization are now beginning to emerge. From a philosophical perspective, this functional property is interesting for a whole range of different reasons. One of them is that it is directly

---

[1] This paper is based on an earlier and more comprehensive publication of mine, which offers a first philosophical perspective on the recent surge of scientific work related to the phenomenon of 'mind-wandering' (Metzinger, 2013a). It aims at further developing only a few of its central ideas and leaves out as much empirical detail as possible, including my own empirical hypothesis that mind-wandering can be characterized by unnoticed switches in what I have called the phenomenal 'unit of identification' (UI) and an experimentally detectable 'self-representational blink' (SRB). In terms of recent references on the topic since my earlier publication, I recommend Smallwood and Schooler (2015) for a recent empirical review; Carruthers (2015, Chapter 6.5), Dorsch (2014), Irving (2015), and Pliushch and Metzinger (2015) are philosophical discussions. I am also extremely grateful to two anonymous reviewers, who have both offered very helpful, constructive, and substantial criticism, as well as to Carsten Korth and Wanja Wiese for additional comments.

[2] Functional properties are abstract properties referring to the *causal role* of a state (the set of its causal relations to input, output, and other internal states), without implying anything about the properties of its physical realization. Just like states described in a Turing machine table or computer software, they are multi-realizable. For example, as M-autonomy is a functional property, it could in principle also be implemented in a machine.

relevant to both our traditional notions of a 'first-person perspective' and of 'personhood'. If one cannot control the focus of one's attention, then one cannot sustain a stable first-person perspective, and for as long as one cannot control one's own thought one cannot count as a rational individual.

This paper is composed of three parts. First, I will briefly introduce the concept of 'M-autonomy'. Part 2 will connect this new idea with the two notions of 'possessing a first-person perspective' and of 'personhood', by enriching the functionalist concept with a dynamic, representationalist account: M-autonomy consists in the possession of an 'epistemic agent model' (EAM). Here, one central point is that the transition from subpersonal to personal-level cognition is enabled by a specific form of conscious self-representation, namely, a global model of the cognitive system as an entity that *actively* constructs, sustains, and controls knowledge relations to the world and itself. In Part 3, I will show that for the largest part of our conscious lives we are not mentally autonomous cognitive systems in this sense and conclude that what we traditionally call 'conscious thought' actually is a subpersonal process.

Let us begin by pointing out how biological systems produce different kinds of observable output, which can in turn be characterized by different degrees of autonomy and self-control. For the purposes of this paper, let us say that there are actions and behaviours. Both kinds of output are conceptually individuated by their satisfaction conditions; they are directed at goal states. However, for actions, conscious goal-representation plays a central causal role, actions can be terminated, suspended, intentionally inhibited, and they exhibit a distinct phenomenological profile involving subjective qualities like agency, a sense of effort, goal-directedness, global self-control, and ownership. Behaviours, on the other hand, are purposeful, but possess no explicit form of conscious goal-representation. They are functionally characterized by automaticity, decreased context-sensitivity, and low self-control, we may not even notice their intitiation, but they can be faster than actions. While their phenomenological profile can at times be completely absent, behaviours typically involve the subjective experience of ownership without agency, whereas the introspective availability of goal-directedness varies and there frequently is a complete lack of meta-awareness.

There are not only bodily actions, but also mental actions. Deliberately focusing one's attention on a perceptual object or consciously drawing a logical conclusion are examples of mental actions.

Just like physical actions, mental actions possess satisfaction conditions (i.e. they are directed at a goal state). Although they mostly lack overt behavioural correlates, they can be intentionally inhibited, suspended, or terminated, just like bodily actions can. In addition, they are interestingly characterized by their temporally extended phenomenology of ownership, goal-directedness, a subjective sense of effort, and the concomitant conscious experience of agency and *mental* self-control.

Let me distinguish the two most important types of mental action:

- **Attentional agency** (AA), the ability to control one's focus of attention.
- **Cognitive agency** (CA), the ability to control goal/task-related, deliberate thought.

AA and CA are not only functional properties that are gradually acquired in childhood, can be lost in old age or due to brain lesions, and whose incidence, variance, robustness, etc. can be scientifically investigated. They also have a subjective side: attentional agency (Metzinger, 2003a, 6.4.3; 2006, Section 4) is also a phenomenal property, as is the case for pain or the subjective quality of 'blueness' in a visual colour experience (Metzinger, 1995). AA is the conscious experience of actually initiating a shift of attention, of controlling and fixing its focus on a certain aspect of reality. AA involves a sense of effort, and it is the phenomenal signature of our functional ability to actively influence what we will come to know, and what, for now, we will ignore. Consciously experienced AA is theoretically important, because it is probably the earliest and simplest form of experiencing oneself as a knowing self, as an epistemic agent. To consciously enjoy AA means that you (the cognitive system as a whole) currently identify with the content of a particular self-representation, an 'epistemic agent model' (EAM; see Section 2 and Metzinger, 2013a,b) currently active in your brain. AA is fully transparent:[3] the

---

[3] 'Transparency' is a property of conscious representations, namely, that they are not experienced *as* representations. Therefore, the subject of experience has the feeling of being in direct and immediate contact with their content. Transparent conscious representations create the phenomenology of naïve realism. An opaque phenomenal representation is one that is experienced *as* a representation, for example in pseudo-hallucinations or lucid dreams. Importantly, a transparent self-model creates the phenomenology of identification (Section 3; Metzinger, 2003a; 2008). There exists a graded spectrum between transparency and opacity, determining the variable

content of your conscious experience is not one of self-representation or of an ongoing process of self-modelling, of depicting yourself as a causal agent in certain shifts of 'zoom factor', 'resolving power', or 'resource allocation', and so on. Rather, you directly experience *yourself* as, for example, actively selecting a new object for attention. During mind-wandering episodes we do not have AA, although these episodes can of course be *about* having been an attentional agent in the past, or *about* planning to control one's attention in the future. Other examples of situations in which this property is selectively missing are non-lucid dreaming and NREM-sleep mentation (Metzinger, 2013b; Windt, 2015), but also infancy, dementia, or severe intoxication syndromes.

An analogous point can be made for CA. Conceptually, cognitive agency is not only a complex set of functional abilities, like the capacity of mental calculation, consciously drawing logical conclusions, engaging in rational, symbolic thought, and so on. Again, there is a distinct phenomenology of currently being a cognitive *agent*, which can lead to experiential self-reports like 'I am a thinking self in the act of grasping a concept', 'I have just actively arrived at a specific conclusion', etc. What AA and CA have in common is that in both cases we consciously represent ourselves as epistemic agents: according to subjective experience, we are entities that actively construct and search for new epistemic relations to the world and ourselves.

There are, however, not only mental actions, but also mental behaviours. 'Mind-wandering', or spontaneous, task-unrelated thought, is a paradigm example of unintentional mental behaviour. It may often be purposeful, but exhibits no conscious goal-representation, no overt behavioural correlates, it is characterized by an unnoticed loss of mental self-control and high degrees of automaticity, plus a lack of sensitivity to the situational context, while the phenomenological profile is characterized by ownership without agency, variable or absent introspective availability of goal-directedness, and frequently by a complete lack of meta-awareness (Schooler *et al.*, 2011). Empirically, it is plausible to assume that unconscious mind-wandering, instantiating no phenomenal properties whatsoever, exists as well (Horovitz *et al.*, 2009; Pliushch and Metzinger, 2015; Samann *et al.*, 2011; Vanhaudenhuyse *et al.*, 2010).

---

phenomenology of 'mind-independence' or 'realness'. Unconscious representations are neither transparent nor opaque. See Metzinger (2003b) for a concise introduction.

What we can consciously access as daydreaming, inner thoughts, fantasies, unbidden memories and feelings may rather be just the tip of the iceberg, a small partition of a much larger state space in which the continuous cognitive dynamics unfolds. Conscious mind-wandering would then be characterized by a higher degree of coherence, but still emerge out of a larger unconscious background of activity. Mind-wandering and nocturnal dreaming (*cf.* Metzinger, 2013a,b; Fox *et al.*, 2013; Wamsley, 2013; Windt and Metzinger, 2007; Windt, 2015) are both interesting to philosophers of mind, because both involve sudden shifts in mechanisms of self-identification, rationality deficits, and a cyclically recurring decrease in mental autonomy that is not self-initiated and frequently unnoticed.

Some mental activities are not autonomously controllable, because one centrally important defining characteristic does not hold: they cannot be inhibited, suspended, or terminated. Let us call these activities 'unintentional mental behaviours'. Mind-wandering can therefore be conceptualized as a form of unintentional behaviour, as an involuntary form of mental activity. Of course, the fact that a given behaviour, be it mental or bodily, is unintentional in no way implies that this behaviour is unintelligent or even maladaptive. For example, low-level, saliency-driven shifts in attentional focus are unintentional mental behaviours, and not inner actions. In standard situations, they cannot be inhibited. They are initiated by unconscious mechanisms, but may well result in a stable, perceptually coupled first-person perspective as their final stage. Stimulus-independent, task-independent thought, however, normally begins as a form of uncontrolled mental behaviour, a breakdown of consciously guided epistemic auto-regulation, which is the active control of one's own epistemic states at the level of high-level cognition. Just like an automatic, saliency-driven shift in the focus of attention, it may be caused by unconscious factors like introspectively inaccessible goal representations that drive the high-level phenomenology of mind-wandering (Klinger, 2013), for example by representations of postponed goal-states which have been environmentally cued by goal-related stimuli under high cognitive load (Cohen, 2013; McVay and Kane, 2013). Both low-level attention and uncontrolled, automatic thinking will frequently count as intelligent, an adaptive type of inner behaviour. But as long as it is going on, we seem to lack the ability to terminate or suspend it — we are fully immersed in an inner narrative and cannot deliberately 'snap out of it' (see below and note #9). Perhaps the most relevant and hitherto neglected phenomenological constraint for a theory of mental autonomy is that, subjectively, we do not notice this fact.

But what exactly is autonomy? Very generally speaking, autonomy would be the capacity for rational self-control, whereas the term 'mental autonomy' refers to the specific ability to control one's own mental functions, like attention, episodic memory, planning, concept formation, rational deliberation, or decision making, etc. Let us begin by looking at the contrast class of our target phenomenon, at cases where some of these functions would selectively operate *without* the decisive ability to wilfully terminate or suspend them. How can one better describe the missing element? As it turns out, the contrast class is very large. A second highly relevant fact that has been almost completely overlooked by philosophers, or so I will claim in Section 3, is that a recurring *loss* of mental autonomy is one major characteristic of our cognitive phenomenology,[4] and that both research on dreaming and mind-wandering have already developed important research tools to investigate this hitherto neglected aspect further (like external probing, or systematic questions after sleep lab awakenings; *cf.* Smallwood, 2013; Windt, 2015). However, in this case, empirical and conceptual questions are so deeply intertwined that we need a stronger form of cooperation between the disciplines. Therefore, what is now needed is a first set of conceptual instruments that opens the field for fruitful interdisciplinary collaboration.

One way of providing a richer conceptual analysis of what a loss of mental autonomy actually amounts to is by describing it as losing the ability for *second-order mental action*. This ability can be decomposed into the following capacities:

- The imposing of rules on one's own mental behaviour;
- explicit goal-selection, goal-commitment, goal-permanence;
- satisfaction of rationality constraints or rational guidance;
- intentional inhibition, suspension, or termination of an ongoing process.

---

[4] 'Cognitive phenomenology' is a new subfield of research in philosophy of mind that focuses on the phenomenal character of occurrent non-sensory mental states like thoughts or wishes, and on the distinct subjective quality that goes along with thinking (see Bayne and Montague, 2011, for a good overview). Some philosophers claim that there is a *proprietary*, *distinctive*, and *individuative* phenomenology of higher cognitive processing that cannot be derived from sensory phenomenology, others deny this claim. For present purposes, I leave this controversial issue to the side (but see the point about predictive horizons in Section 3).

Let us introduce a working concept of 'second-order mental action'. The satisfaction conditions of second-order mental actions are constituted by successfully influencing other mental actions or mental behaviours, first-order mental processes are the targets of second-order mental action. Examples of second-order mental action are the termination of an ongoing violent fantasy, but also the deliberate strengthening and sustaining of a spontaneously arising pleasant daydream, the effortful attempt to make an ongoing process of visual perception more precise by selectively controlling the focus of attention, or — as in mental calculation and logical thought — the process of imposing a very specific abstract *structure* on a temporal sequence of inner events, of 'conducting' a symbolic train of thought (McVay and Kane, 2009). Philosophically, it is interesting to note how second-order mental actions are essential tools for achieving higher degrees of mental autonomy and self-determination; and also how many of them can be described as processes of computational resource allocation in the brain — for example, in the case of attentional agency, as an active optimization of precision expectations (Friston, 2010; Hohwy, 2013; Clark, 2015). However, an important distinction is the difference between *possessing* an ability (for example, the 'tool' of second-order mental action) and having an explicit *knowledge* that oneself possesses this ability. What Schooler and colleagues have provisionally termed 'meta-awareness' (Schooler *et al.*, 2011) is a necessary precondition for second-order mental action.

We may treat the preceding discussion as a first set of empirical, phenomenological, and conceptual constraints that any good philosophical theory should satisfy, and then ask: What exactly is autonomy at the mental level? First, because developmentally as well as phenomenologically AA clearly is the more basic form of epistemic mental agency, we need a subdoxastic account of autonomy here, one that does not presuppose rationality constraints, propositional attitudes, or access to some Sellarsian or other kind of 'logical space of reasons'. Please recall how, above, I already pointed out that consciously experienced AA is theoretically important, because it is probably the earliest and simplest form of experiencing oneself as an autonomous epistemic agent. A second point of interest is that, at least in human beings, it not only causally enables high-level rational thought, but helps to constitute it: AA can exist without CA, but it is a necessary condition for CA. If we cannot control our attention, we cannot engage in rational, logically structured thought, but on the other hand there are many self-conscious biological systems that, while not having the capacity for high-level rationality, can actively control and even become the object of their own attention (think of mirror-self-recognition in chimpanzees, bottlenose dolphins, or the Eurasian magpie). Second, we want a working concept of M-autonomy that facilitates interdisciplinary cooperation by being open to fine-grained functional analysis, yielding testable empirical predictions (e.g. the existence of a 'self-representational blink' following every single loss of autonomy, see Metzinger, 2013a).

'Veto control', or the capacity for intentional inhibition, may have to be the central semantic element in our new working concept of M-autonomy — simply because if you cannot terminate your very own activity, then you cannot be said to be autonomous in any interesting sense. This element can be empirically grounded, gradually refined, and may prove heuristically fruitful in guiding future research. Veto control is a manifestation of the capacity to voluntarily suspend or inhibit an action, and from a logical point of view it is a functional property which we do not ascribe to the brain, but to the person as a whole. Let us call the capacity in question 'intentional inhibition'.[5] During a mind-wandering episode, we do not have this capacity, because we cannot actively suspend or inhibit our own mental activity. Recent empirical work reveals the dorsal fronto-median cortex (dFMC) as a candidate region for the physical realization of this very special form of purely mental second-order action.[6] It does not overlap with known networks for external inhibition, and its computational function may lie in predicting the social and more long-term individual consequences of a currently unfolding action, that is, in representing the action's socially and temporally more distant implications for the organism.[7] There is a considerable amount of valuable neurobiological data on the physical substrates of intentional inhibition in human beings, and a number of them have already led to more abstract computational models of volitional control, action

---

[5]   In adopting this terminological convention, I follow Marcel Brass (Brass and Haggard, (2007); an excellent and helpful recent review is Filevich, Kühn and Haggard (2012).

[6]   See Kühn, Haggard and Brass (2009), Brass and Haggard (2007), Campbell-Meiklejohn *et al.* (2008). A helpful recent review of negative motor effects following direct cortical stimulation, listing the main sites of arrest responses and offering interesting discussion is Filevich, Kühn and Haggard (2012).

[7]   This passage draws on Metzinger (2013a). See also Filevich, Kühn and Haggard (2012; 2013).

selection, and intention inhibition itself (Filevich, Kühn and Haggard, 2012; 2013; Campbell-Meiklejohn *et al.*, 2008; Kühn, Haggard and Brass, 2009; Brass and Haggard, 2007). These data are valuable not only for understanding the 'back end' of many mind-wandering episodes, but also for a more comprehensive theory of mental autonomy (for more, see Metzinger 2013a, Section 3.3).

Conceptually, many forms of mental self-control — like AA — presuppose exactly this ability for veto control, but are not directly guided by consciously represented reasons, explicit logical inferences, or arguments. Indeed, there is no need or even conceptual necessity to specify autonomy as *rational* self-control, because our capacity for rational self-control is only a special case of a more comprehensive, fundamental set of functional properties. First, rationality does not have to express itself in terms of explicit, symbolic reasoning processes using propositional data-formats (e.g. a Fodorian 'language of thought'), but can be operationally defined as a property of some global input-output-function maximizing a specific fitness criterion. Second, there are more operational and empirically grounded models of autonomy, combining the notion of causal self-determination with independence from alternative causes, both inner and outer (see Seth, 2010, for the notion of 'G-autonomy' based on a formal analysis of Granger causality). For empirical research programmes on mind-wandering, such operational concepts are more likely to yield specific, testable hypotheses. Nevertheless, the notion of 'rational mental self-control' in the traditional sense remains important if we want to understand the *phenomenology* of high-level cognition and the normative components of our concept of 'personhood'. Explicit rational self-control at the mental level cannot be reduced to veto control — on the contrary, the capacity for veto autonomy is only one of its centrally relevant constitutive conditions. Clearly, the capacity for inhibiting mental processes via second-order acts of vetoing without the involvement of quasi-conceptual or quasi-propositional representations is the more frequent and also more basic phenomenon, and hence also the more fundamentally relevant target for research. You can only be rational if you have the capacity for mental veto control, but you can achieve a high degree of mental autonomy without rational self-control.

This yields a working concept of M-autonomy as the ability to control the conscious contents of one's mind in a goal-directed way, by means of attentional or cognitive agency. This ability can be a form of rational self-control, which is based on reasons, beliefs, and conceptual thought, but it does not have to be. What is crucial is the 'veto component': being mentally autonomous means that all currently ongoing processes can in principle be suspended or terminated. Importantly, this does not mean that they actually *are* terminated, it just means that the ability, the functional potential, is given and that the person has knowledge of this fact. This point provides us with a third and equally important phenomenological constraint: if we only 'tune out', but do not 'zone out' — for example if we observe the spontaneous arising of memories or the beginning stages of a day-dream, or if we even voluntarily indulge in a fantasy while all the time knowing that we could terminate this inner activity at any instant — then we possess M-autonomy (see note #9). Call this the principle of 'Autonomy by Phenomenal Self-Representation': one can only deliberately and autonomously exert an ability if that ability is explicitly represented in one's phenomenal self-model. Terminating a train of thought is one example of such an ability, detaching the focus of attention from a perceptual object is another. In sum, M-autonomy is the capacity for causal self-determination at the mental level. It is based on a complex and graded functional property, which comes in three major degrees: the phenomenally represented *knowledge* that *oneself* currently possesses this specific ability, executed *attentional* self-control, and *cognitive* self-control.

2. M-Autonomy, the First-Person Perspective, and Personhood

For a human being, to possess a consciously experienced first-person perspective means to have acquired a very specific functional profile and a distinctive level of representational content in one's currently active phenomenal self-model: it has, episodically, become a dynamic inner model of a *knowing self*. Representing facts under such a model creates a new epistemic modality. All knowledge is now accessed under a new internal mode of presentation, namely, as knowledge possessed by a self-conscious entity intentionally directed at the world. Therefore, it is *subjective* knowledge. This notion of a con-scious model of oneself as an individual entity actively trying to estab-lish epistemic relations to the world and to oneself, I think, comes very close to what we traditionally mean by notions like 'subjectivity' or 'possession of a first-person perspective'. If we combine this observation with the concept of M-autonomy, then we can perhaps gain a fresh, empirically grounded, and conceptually enriched perspective on traditional philosophical puzzles related to concepts like 'perspectivalness' and 'personhood'.

Let us introduce a second conceptual instrument. The concept of an 'epistemic agent model', or EAM, refers to a specific type of conscious self-representation, a small subset of phenomenal self-models (PSMs).[8] This simply means that, at the level of conscious experience, the self is represented as something that either currently stands in an epistemic relation to the world, in the relation of knowing, thinking, actively guiding attention, or actively trying to understand what is going on in its environment; or, more abstractly, as an entity that has the *ability* to do so.[9] For any information processing system, to possess a first-person perspective means to operate under a specific kind of conscious self-representation, a PSM that portrays the system as an epistemic agent, as an entity that is actively searching for and optimizing its knowledge, for example by controlling its own high-level, quasi-symbolic processing as a cognitive agent (CA) or by actively sustaining and controlling the focus of attention (AA). This is what I call an EAM.[10] Again, having an EAM is a special case of

---

8   A useful conceptual instrument to develop more fine-grained descriptions of the phenomenology of mind-wandering and the episodic reappearance of M-autonomy is the notion of a 'phenomenal self-model' (PSM; Metzinger, 2003a; 2006; 2008). A PSM is a conscious representation of the system as a whole, including not only global body representation (Metzinger, 2014; Blanke and Metzinger, 2009), but also psychological, social, and other potential personal-level properties. One central idea of the self-model theory (Metzinger, 2003a) is that, under standard conditions, a large part of the human PSM is 'transparent', because we are not able to experience it *as* a model and therefore fully identify with its representational content. Having an EAM is a special case of having a PSM.

9   This is not to say that we never purposefully engage in daydreams or that there are never situations in which we are mind-wandering while being passively aware of this fact. This is only to say that intentional episodes of daydreaming, to the extent that they do involve the phenomenology of AA and CA, thereby do not count as episodes of mind-wandering, which refer only to unintentional episodes of stimulus-independent thought. One advantage of the terminological solution proposed here is exactly that it enables a continuous description of real-world cases: as long as the EAM still represents the *ability* to become an active attentional or cognitive agent, we have M-autonomy. What has been termed 'zoning out' (unaware mind-wandering) and 'tuning out' (mind-wandering with awareness) in the empirical literature (Smallwood, McSpadden and Schooler, 2007, p. 524; 2008; Schooler *et al.*, 2011, p. 323) can be nicely captured by this conceptual distinction.

10   For details, see Metzinger (2003a, and 2006, Section 4). The philosophical notion of a 'phenomenal model of the intentionality relation' (PMIR) is directly related to the idea of dynamically integrating top-down control (e.g. by the fronto-parietal control network) with subpersonal, bottom-up components (e.g. a subset of activity in the default mode network) by creating an internal model of the whole organism as currently *being*

having a PSM, not all PSMs are EAMs. Empirically, it has been
shown that human beings can enjoy a minimal form of self-
consciousness without possessing an EAM (Blanke and Metzinger,
2009; Limanowski and Blankenburg, 2013). The transition from
simple, bodily self-identification to the relevant, stronger form takes
place when a system phenomenally represents itself as an entity
capable of epistemic agency, or even as one currently exerting
epistemic agency. If such a specific kind of self-model is in place,
ongoing processes can be *embedded* into it, thereby creating the
phenomenology of ownership (*my* thought, *my own* autobiographical
memory, *my own* future planning). If these processes are additionally
represented as control processes, as successful acts of exerting causal
influence, they can now be consciously experienced as processes of
self-control or instances of successful mental *self*-determination. An
EAM is an instrument in what one might call 'epistemic autoregulation': it helps a self-conscious system in selecting and determining
what it will know, and what it will not know. Yet, an epistemic agent
model of this kind is not a little man in the head, but itself an entirely
subpersonal process. During full-blown episodes of mind-wandering,
we are not epistemic agents, neither as controllers of attentional focus
nor as deliberate thinkers of thoughts, and we have forgotten about our
agentive abilities. A first interim conclusion then is that what really
takes place at the onset of a mind-wandering episode must be a
collapse of the EAM.

It would perhaps be tempting to say that during such periods we
have altogether lost the functional ability to control our own thought. I
want to defend a more moderate, nuanced position: what we have lost
is a specific form of *knowledge*, and not the ability itself, namely,
conscious knowledge of our potential for second-order mental action.
We are still persons, because we have the relevant potential. But we
currently lack an explicit and globally available *representation* of an
existing functional ability for active epistemic self-control — because
we have not epistemically appropriated it. And that is exactly what an
EAM does for us. But why do we then have the feeling that all of this
cannot be an accurate phenomenological description of a very large
portion of our conscious lives? Because we confuse our abstract,

---

directed at an object component, for example, by means of a well-ordered train of
thought; see Smallwood *et al.* (2012). The PMIR would then be the conscious correlate
of this process, the phenomenal experience of what was termed CA in the main text.

retrospective, and purely intellectual knowledge that, in principle, we had the critical mental ability all along with what actually was the case on the level of concrete, inner phenomenology: the absence of an EAM. As Franz Brentano (1874/1973, pp. 165f.) and much later Daniel Dennett (1991, p. 359) have pointed out, the representation of absence is not the same as the absence of representation.

It follows that in most cases the re-emergence of an EAM will have to be caused by an unconscious event, perhaps by chance, perhaps based on an *implicit* knowledge about the relevant potential, about an already existing ability. Whenever the dynamic process of creating and sustaining an EAM takes place, we also have a first-person perspective. AA is one specific example of having a consciously experienced first-person perspective. Its theoretical relevance consists in the fact that it is plausibly the simplest form of an EAM human beings can have. We still lack an empirically grounded theory of subjectivity, a model of the first-person perspective as a naturally evolved phenomenon (Metzinger, 2003a). But it is clear that having a first-person perspective is not a unitary but a graded phenomenon, and research on mind-wandering can make decisive contributions by functionally dissociating different levels. For example, we can see more clearly how attentional control is a necessary condition of personhood: you cannot engage in rational thought if you cannot control your own attention, because high-level epistemic autoregulation functionally presupposes low-level epistemic autoregulation.

Originally, the concept of a 'first-person perspective' is not much more than a visuo-grammatical metaphor. It has two different semantic components: the specific logic of the self-ascription of psychological properties using the first-person pronoun 'I', and the entirely contingent spatial geometry of our dominant sensory modality. Conscious vision of the human kind has a 'perspectival' geometrical structure, because it involves a single point of origin, namely, behind our eyes as phenomenally experienced. On a more abstract level, we may connect this phenomenological notion of an 'origin' constituting the centre of our internal model of reality with the origin of multimodal perceptual space ('here'), with self-location in a temporal order ('now'), and with the sensorimotor origins of *action* space, i.e. with the physical body ('embodiment'). Arguably, however, all of this only leads to a more or less minimal sense of selfhood (see Blanke and Metzinger, 2009), in which the subjectivity and perspectivalness of experience are mostly captured in an implicit or spatial sense. I think the concept of an EAM is interesting for any non-trivial notion of subjectivity, because it isolates the origin of our *inner* space of action.

What about personhood? Clearly, an animal or artificial cognitive system could have a first-person perspective in this sense without counting as a person. On the other hand the potential for M-autonomy and the functional ability to (at least sometimes) operate under a conscious EAM are excellent candidates for criteria of personhood, which have the advantage of empirical grounding and hardware-independence at the same time. For the purposes of this paper, let us say that 'personhood' is a concept of social ontology. Personhood is constituted not in brains, but in societies — via a process in which human beings acknowledge each other as rational individuals possessing the capacity for moral thought and action. This makes the two concepts of M-autonomy and an EAM even more interesting: they potentially allow us to describe not only necessary conditions of personhood, but also the *transition* to personhood in a more fine-grained way. Human beings only *become* persons exactly by having the potential to phenomenologically identify with the content of an EAM, a step which on the sociocultural level causally enables relevant practices like linguistically ascribing person-status to themselves and mutually acknowledging each other as subjects of experience, as epistemic agents, and as morally sensitive, rational individuals. This led to a major expansion of our culturally structured cognitive niche and enabled the evolution of new forms of intelligence via a mutual scaffolding between all those individuals immersed in it. But why do we subjectively experience some of our cognitive processes *as* personal-level properties? There is a long story to be told here (Metzinger, 2003a; 2006; 2007; 2008), but the short answer is this: because they have been embedded into an EAM, which is currently active in our brain; and because we live in a normative sociocultural context in which we are now able to folk-psychologically describe and reciprocally acknowledge each other as rational individuals — a fact which then in turn influences introspective experience itself, turning the self-model into a person-model. From a functional perspective, M-autonomy dramatically expands our inner and outer space of possible behaviours, and one may speculate that perhaps it was exactly the emergence of an EAM which causally triggered the transition from biological to cultural evolution in our ancestors.

3. Conscious Thought is a Subpersonal Process

Before I present a simple, quantitative argument for the main claim of this paper, please follow me in considering an introductory example. It may help to further clarify and illustrate what has been said above. Imagine you are participating in a Buddhist-style silent retreat, an intensive course in mindfulness meditation. During the first three days your teacher instructs you to very precisely observe your breath as it comes and goes, but without in any way interfering with the respiratory process itself. Your task is to, whenever you have noticed an incoming thought or any other sort of distraction, gently bring back your attention to the bodily sensations going along with the rise and fall of your chest or abdomen, and to the sensation of the breath at the nostrils and the internal flow of air. Whenever you notice another attentional lapse, you simply return to your breath. But later, as the retreat progresses, you are instructed to become non-judgmentally aware of those incoming thoughts themselves, as they come and go, not identifying with or reacting to them. Now your task is to simply be present with whatever arises in your conscious mind.

We have two different tasks, and, at least initially, two different kinds of mental action, leading to two different inner situations. Given these two situations — what exactly is it that you are phenomenally representing? Let us ask: what is your conscious experience an experience *of*? I claim that in both cases you are representing physical processes in the body, you are experiencing not actions, but events, namely, chains of *subpersonal* events. The properties instantiated during these processes are not properties of the person as a whole. Let us first look at the intentional object of your introspective experience from a metaphysical perspective.

From the perspective of metaphysics, to gain meta-awareness of ongoing mind-wandering really is almost exactly like gaining meta-awareness of your breath. The introspective experience of breathing, as well as seemingly task-unrelated, phenomenologically spontaneous thoughts, are not personal-level psychological processes that are mysteriously correlated with or caused by some physical chain of events. The most parsimonious metaphysical interpretation of the relevant scientific data is that they are *identical* with functionally complex, but sub-global physiological processes in the biological body. In the case of mind-wandering, this physiological process is a specific, widely distributed pattern of neural activity, and it is now empirically plausible to assume that large parts of this pattern overlap with activity in the default mode network (DMN; Buckner, Andrews-Hanna and Schacter, 2008; Christoff, 2012, Christoff *et al.*, 2009; Weissman *et al.*, 2006; Stawarczyk *et al.*, 2011; Andrews-Hanna *et al.*, 2010; Mantini and Vanduffel, 2012; Buckner and Carroll, 2007; Mason *et al.*, 2007; Spreng, Mar and Kim, 2009), but that it also extends to other functional structures like the rostrolateral prefrontal cortex, dorsal anterior cingulate cortex, insula, temporopolar cortex, secondary somatosensory cortex, and lingual gyrus (for a recent meta-analysis, see Fox *et al.*, 2015). What we introspectively represent are specific, as yet unknown abstract properties of the physical dynamics characterizing this pattern.

'Sub-global' or 'local', however, does not automatically imply 'sub-personal'. A sub-global physiological process in the brain can *become* a personal-level process by being functionally integrated and repre-sented within an EAM. Conversely, simply being identical with a 'global' process in the brain does not automatically imply being attributable to the person as a whole. What is required for the relevant shift from the subpersonal to the personal level is an epistemic appro-priation at a specific level of phenomenal self-consciousness, the functional integration into an EAM (as explained in Section 2). The wandering mind does not meet this criterion, it is therefore sub-global *and* subpersonal. As the brain is a part of our body, any rational research heuristics targeting the neural correlates for the introspective phenomenology of breathing, or alternatively the critical subset of neural activity underlying mind-wandering, will therefore treat them as subpersonal, bodily processes. They have a long evolutionary history (Corballis, 2013; Lu *et al.*, 2012; Mantini and Vanduffel, 2012), and both of them clearly are constituted by dynamic, self-organizing chains of neural events that continuously and automatically unfold over time. They are not agentive processes implying explicit goal-selection, rationality constraints, etc. The postulation of a local, domain-specific identity is a tenable, coherent metaphysical inter-pretation of this fact. Whatever will figure as the *explanans* in a future scientific theory of mind-wandering or the phenomenology of breathing will therefore not be global properties of 'the mind' or the person as a whole, but specific microfunctional properties realized by the local physical dynamics underlying each episode of consciously experienced subpersonal cognitive processing. Therefore, if one adds the straightforward metaphysical assumption of a domain-specific identity (Bickle, 2013; McCauley and Bechtel, 2001) holding between the phenomenal states constituting episodes of mind-wandering and what we are currently beginning to discover and incrementally isolate as their local, minimally sufficient neural 'correlates' (NCCs; e.g. Chalmers, 2000), then it seems obvious that mind-wandering simply is the phenomenal awareness of a local bodily process. What the Buddhist meditator attends to is activity in the NCC for mind-wandering, the dynamics of a local physical process.

But what then explains the marked phenomenological difference between those two different inner situations? On a more abstract, representationalist level of description we would say that attention has been directed to two different content levels in the conscious self-model, to certain aspects of the *body-model* and to the internal dynamics of the *cognitive self-model*. The crucial difference between the phenomenological profile of mindfully observing the breath and that of 'being present with whatever arises in the mind' can now be explained by the fact that only in the first case we find the functional property of information being made globally available through an interoceptive *receptor system*. Therefore, what Buddhists call 'Anapanasati' (or mindfulness of breathing) generates a *sensory* phenomenology of bodily self-representation. By contrast, as the human brain is devoid of any self-directed sensory channels or receptor systems, the relevant subset of neural activity in the NCC for mind-wandering cannot be informationally accessed through any perception-like causal links — although it, too, is a bodily process. Consequently, the phenomenology of cognition must necessarily be a *non-sensory* phenomenology — although it can of course be *about* possible sensory perceptions, fantasy worlds, linked to motor simulations, affectively toned, etc.

Put differently, what the cognitive self-model continuously *predicts* (Friston, 2010; Hohwy, 2013; Clark, 2015) are just much more abstract aspects of reality, in a wider temporal frame of reference, and not ongoing events on the sensory sheet. The PSM can be seen as an integrated global hypothesis about the state of the system in which it appears, constituted by a large number of individual predictions or sub-hypotheses, which are hierarchically structured and optimized at different timescales. A conscious self-model is therefore composed of different layers of expectations, in a continuous attempt of minimizing uncertainty and prediction error related to the system itself. Some layers continuously target causal regularities in shorter time-windows, some extract regularities relative to larger time-windows. In the words of Jakob Hohwy:

...the difference between percepts and concepts comes out in terms of a gradual movement from variance to invariance, via spatiotemporal scales of causal regularities. There is thus no categorical difference between them; percepts are maintained in detail-rich internal models with a short prediction horizon and concepts in more detail-poor models with longer prediction horizons. (Hohwy, 2013, p. 72)

What, then, determines the two different introspective phenomenologies of breathing and thinking? First, there will necessarily be different internal data-formats corresponding to either direct perceptual coupling sustained by receptor-driven input or to its absence, as we are clearly dealing with very different hierarchical levels in the self-model. Second, the different prediction horizons functionally characterizing these levels will lead to an embodied, fully situated, and perceptually coupled sense of presence in the first case, and to an 'unextended', much more disembodied (and potentially 'absent-minded') phenomenology in which the temporal succession of inner events is more salient, while at the same time spatial qualities as well their deep sensorimotor origins have become almost unnoticeable. With regard to these more abstract content-layers of the human self-model, the facts that philosophers have frequently overlooked are, first, that non-agentive cognitive phenomenology is much more widespread than intuitively assumed, and second, that, conceptually, it often is not a personal-level process at all.

Before presenting some empirical evidence, let us remain with the illustrative example of mindfulness meditation to see a second, equally relevant, point more clearly. It is not about the metaphysics, but about the epistemology of conscious self-knowledge. One advantage of the concept of 'M-autonomy' is that it also offers a new understanding of what classical mindfulness meditation is: it is a systematic and formal mental practice of cultivating M-autonomy. Because mindfulness and mind-wandering are opposing constructs (Mrazek, Smallwood and Schooler, 2012), the process of losing and regaining meta-awareness can be most closely studied in different stages of classical mindfulness meditation (Hölzel et al., 2011; Slagter, Davidson and Lutz, 2011). In the early stages of object-orientated meditation, there will typically be cyclically recurring losses of M-autonomy (see Hasenkamp et al., 2012, fig. 1; Metzinger, 2013a), plus an equally recurring second-order mental action, namely the decision to gently but firmly bring the focus of attention back to the formal object of meditation, for example to interoceptive sensations associated with the respiratory process. Here, the phenomenology will often be one of mental agency, goal-directedness, and a mild sense of effort. In advanced stages of so-called 'open monitoring' meditation, however, the aperture of attention has gradually widened, typically resulting in an effortless and choiceless awareness of the present moment as a whole. Whereas in beginning stages of object-orientated mindfulness practice the meditator identifies with an internal model of a mental agent directed at a certain goal-state ('the meditative self'), meta-awareness of the second kind is typically described as having an effortless and non-agentive quality. In the first case an EAM is present, leading to a process that would still count as personal-level, whereas in the second case we have meta-awareness without an EAM. It is important to understand that these are distinct phenomenological state-classes. Interestingly, even the neural correlates pertaining to this difference between 'trying to meditate' and 'meditation effortlessly taking place' are already beginning to emerge (Garrison et al., 2013).

From an epistemological point of view it is now interesting to note how the conceptual distinction between AA and CA either as functional or as phenomenal properties allows for the possibility of *hallucinating* epistemic agency. We might experience ourselves as autonomous mental subjects, but in some cases this might be an adaptive form of self-deception or confabulation (Hippel and Trivers, 2011; Pliushch and Metzinger, 2015). For example, if a subject during an experimental design involving mindfulness-based stress reduction regains meta-awareness (Hölzel et al., 2011; Mrazek, Smallwood and Schooler, 2012) and describes the experience as 'I have just realized that I was daydreaming and redirected my attention to the current moment and the physical sensations caused by the process of breathing!', it may be false to assume that, functionally, the 'realization' was actually a form of AA or CA (see Schooler et al., 2011, and Metzinger, 2013a, Section 3.3). What is subjectively described or experienced as a form of second-order mental action may sometimes not be a personal-level event at all, but a shift in the subpersonal self-model that is then misdescribed on the level of self-report, an auto-phenomenological *post hoc*-confabulation.[11] To consciously represent

---

[11] Let me point to a structural commonality with well-known problems in dream research, which may shed further light on the issue of what exactly it means that a mind-wandering episode *ends*. First, there is the phenomenon of 'false awakening', that is of realistic dreams of waking up (Windt, 2015; Windt and Metzinger, 2007; Green, 1994); second, current research interestingly shows that there are different levels of stages of

oneself as just having exerted a certain mental ability does not mean that one actually *had* this ability; the phenomenology of M-autonomy does not justify the claim that the functional property of M-autonomy was actually present. Claiming so would be a category mistake in which epistemic properties are ascribed to something that does not intrinsically possess them (Metzinger and Windt, 2014, p. 287; 2015, p. 7).

Regaining M-autonomy — a functional transition that in healthy people probably takes place many hundred times every day — seems to be a form of mental self-constitution, because a new type of conscious self-model is created, an EAM, which may later change global properties of the system as a whole (e.g. turning it into a subject of experience, or being recognized as a rational individual by other cognitive systems). You can certainly own the thoughts generated by a wandering mind without an EAM (phenomenologically they are still yours) even if the knowledge that you have the causal capacity for self-control is not consciously available, not represented on the level of your PSM. But representing yourself as a cognitive agent leads to the instantiation of a new phenomenal property. Let us call it 'epistemic self-causation': according to subjective experience — at the very moment of 'coming to' as it were — you actively constitute yourself as a thinker of thoughts. You are now consciously representing yourself *as currently representing*, as an individual entity creating new states of itself that are not just 'real' or bodily states, but states that might be true or false. You have intentional properties. As I have said in earlier work, having a first-person perspective means to dynamically co-represent the intentional relation itself *while* you represent, to operate under a model of reality containing the 'arrow of intentionality', which includes a conscious model of the self as directed at the world. The conscious experience of epistemic self-causation would then be a result of exactly such a continuous process of dynamical self-organization, a non-agentive process leading to a new functional level in the PSM. Importantly, this also suggests that rationalizing the immediately preceding, earlier episode as having *been* under one's control may be a functionally necessary way of re-

becoming lucid in a dream (Noreika *et al.*, 2010; Voss *et al.*, 2013; Metzinger, 2013b). If there is an additional awareness of meta-awareness as just having been regained (i.e. a third-order meta-representation or second-order EAM), then the point made in the previous paragraph also applies: as such, this is just phenomenal experience, and not necessarily knowledge — we might always be introspectively self-deceived.

establishing and preserving internal coherence of the new conscious self-model, even if this process involves a retrospective confabulation.

Leading empirical researchers come to the same conclusion. Schooler and colleagues, referring to work by the late Daniel Wegner, point out that regaining meta-awareness may be accompanied by an illusion of control (Schooler *et al.*, 2011, Box 1; Wegner, 2002). Whenever we have this case, it seems that a specific new self-model has appeared: an autobiographical self-representation falsely depicting the last mental event as something that was self-controlled, an instance of deliberate causal self-determination at the mental level. This form of control is often described as an *auto-epistemic* form of self-control, as an instance of actively acquired self-knowledge or a sudden insight. Thus, a typical auto-phenomenological report may claim 'I have just regained meta-awareness, because I just intro-spectively realized that I was lost in mind-wandering!'. Do we have reason to believe such claims? Is the reappearance of meta-awareness a subpersonal event or is it something in which global control and the conscious EAM actually played a decisive causal role?

Here, my positive proposal would be that we may actually be con-fronted with a functionally adequate form of self-deception, at least in many such cases: the re-emergence of an EAM, really triggered by unconscious events, may necessarily involve a confabulatory element ('I generated this insight myself!') in order to ensure the coherence of the *autobiographical* self-model over time. In order to be able to con-ceive of myself as an autonomous mental agent again, I simply must have been a mental agent in the preceding conscious moment too, because I had the ability, the potential, all the time. The transition must have been self-caused, because a 'representational bridge' has to be built to earlier instances of M-autonomy, thereby preserving the (virtual) transtemporal identity of the conscious, thinking self. I cannot *consciously* simulate myself as having *unconsciously* known about my ability for epistemic agency in the past. The onset of every fresh period of M-autonomous cognition may therefore, necessarily, involve an element of misrepresentation: if I want to consciously represent myself as *just now* having acquired the capability of causal self-determination, I need to integrate the (subpersonal) event of transition into the currently active PSM, endowing it with the phenomenal property of ownership and connecting it with earlier such events. If this is true, an illusory phenomenology of self-causation will be a necessary neurocomputational fiction in the construction of any new EAM, terminating the mind-wandering episode which preceded it.

The onset of a mind-wandering episode, on the other hand, can be understood as a loss of M-autonomy, because it involves an unnoticed loss of mental self-control and epistemic agency, either on the level of attention or of cognition. As an unintentional form of mental behaviour it is not rationally guided, and while it is unfolding it cannot be terminated at will. Mind-wandering is a failure of causal self-determination at the level of mental content, and although it clearly has aspects that can be described as functionally adaptive, its overall performance costs and its negative effects on general, subjective well-being are obvious and have been well documented (for example, in terms of reading comprehension, memory, sustained attention, or working memory, *cf.* Mooneyham and Schooler, 2013, Table 1). It is an important and philosophically relevant contribution of research on mind-wandering to have demonstrated the ubiquity of the phenomenon and its effects (Smallwood and Schooler, 2015).

Let us therefore look at some empirical constraints, which any convincing philosophical theory of what, today, we still call 'conscious thought' must satisfy. We know that conscious mind-wandering is a process that can get completely out of control (Schupak and Rosenthal, 2009; Bigelsen and Schupak, 2011), but that can also come completely to rest, either in practitioners of mindfulness meditation (Mrazek, Smallwood and Schooler, 2012; Slagter, Davidson and Lutz, 2011) or following lesions to the medial frontal cortex (Damasio and van Hoesen, 1983). Under normal conditions, we spend 30–50% of our conscious waking lives mind-wandering (Kane *et al.*, 2007; Killingsworth and Gilbert, 2010; Schooler *et al.*, 2011). During these times we do not possess M-autonomy. If we assume a 16-hour day period, 40% of waking mind-wandering would amount to an average of 384 minutes, a period during which we are not autonomous mental subjects. NREM-sleep mentation and non-lucid dreaming clearly are also periods during which the functional property of M-autonomy is absent, although complex cognitive processes are taking place across all sleep stages (Windt, 2014; Wamsley, 2013; Fox *et al.*, 2013; Nielsen, 2000; Fosse, Stickgold and Hobson, 2001). They can be sampled and statistically evaluated, for example using a serial awakening paradigm (Noreika *et al.*, 2009; Siclari *et al.*, 2013). Although great progress has recently been made in isolating the neural correlates of dream lucidity (Dresler *et al.*, 2012; Voss *et al.*, 2009) and developing a more fine-grained conceptual taxonomy for different kinds of lucidity (Noreika *et al.*, 2010; Voss *et al.*, 2013; Voss and Hobson, 2015), it remains clear that M-autonomy during the dream state is a very rare, and therefore negligible, phenomenon.

Adults spend approximately 1.5 to 2 hours per night in REM sleep (Hobson, 2002, pp. 77–79f.). NREM sleep yields similar reports during stage 1, other stages of NREM sleep are characterized by more purely cognitive/symbolic mentation. Clearly conscious thought during NREM sleep also lacks M-autonomy, because it is mostly confused, non-progressive, and perseverative. Whereas 81.9% of awakenings from REM sleep yield mentation reports, the incidence of reports following NREM awakenings lies at only 43% percent (Nielsen, 2000, p. 855). If we assume an average REM-time of 105 minutes, there will be an average of 86 minutes characterized by phenomenally represented, but subpersonal cognitive processing; 375 minutes of NREM sleep will yield roughly 161 minutes of conscious mentation, again, without M-autonomy. Assuming a waking period of 960 minutes, a very rough, first-order approximation is that human beings enjoy one sort of phenomenology or another for about 20 hours a day (1207 minutes; or about 84% of their daytime).

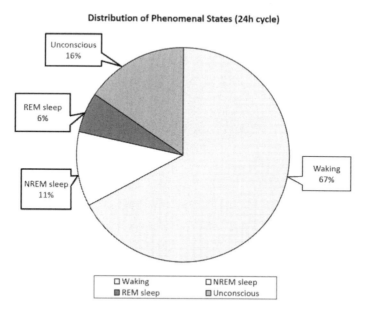

Figure 1. Distribution of conscious experience over the 24-hour-cycle.

However, healthy adults are only M-autonomous for 9.6 hours (576 minutes; or 40% of an average day). These are very conservative estimates. For example, they also exclude lifetime periods of illness, intoxication, or anaesthesia. In addition, there is evidence for extended periods in which human beings lose M-autonomy altogether. These episodes may often not be remembered and also frequently escape detection by external observers, as in 'mind-blanking' (Ward and Wegner, 2013). The same may also be true of periods of insomnia, in which people are plagued by intrusive thoughts, feelings of regret, shame, and guilt while suffering from dysfunctional forms of cognitive control, such as thought suppression, worry, depressive rumination, and counterfactual imagery (Schmidt, Harvey and van der Linden, 2011; Schmidt and van der Linden, 2009; Gay, Schmidt and van der Linden, 2011). We do not know when and how children actually acquire the necessary changes in their conscious self-model (Redshaw and Suddendorf, 2013), but we may certainly add the empirically plausible assumption that children only gradually acquire M-autonomy and that most of us likely lose it towards the ends of our lives.

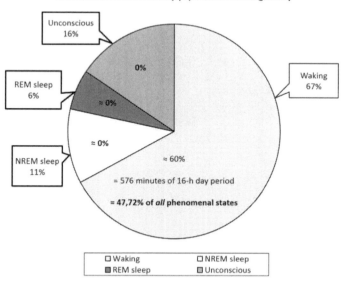

Figure 2. Distribution of M-autonomy over the 24-hour-cycle.

The first conclusion to be drawn from this first-order approximation is that, according to our preliminary working concept of M-autonomy, human beings, although phenomenally conscious, are not autonomous mental subjects for roughly two thirds of their conscious lifetime. A second, related conclusion is that conscious thought primarily and predominantly is an automatic subpersonal process, like respiration, heartbeat, or immune autoregulation — and that, at the conceptual level, we should do justice to this fact. It is empirically plausible to assume that a considerable part of our own cognitive phenomenology simply results from a frequent failure of executive control (McVay and Kane, 2009; 2010). I would claim that this actually is one of the most important functional and phenomenological characteristics of human self-consciousness, as a matter of fact, one of its most general, principal features: the almost constant presence of subpersonal and automatically generated mental activity (as generated by certain parts of the extended default mode network; Raichle *et al.*, 2001; Buckner, Andrews-Hanna and Schacter, 2008; Mantini and Vanduffel, 2012), in combination with a frequent inability of the executive-control system to shield primary-task performance off against interference from these subpersonal thought processes (Smallwood *et al.*, 2012). If I am right, autonomous cognitive self-control is an exception, not the rule.

To conclude, we may have to conceive the instantiation of a first-person perspective and certain necessary conditions of personhood as rare, graded, and dynamically variable properties of self-conscious cognitive systems — at least in our own case. I have proposed a background model of subjectivity as autonomous epistemic goal-selection at the mental level, with the EAM as the true origin of our consciously experienced first-person perspective. As the large majority of our mental activity is not driven by explicit, consciously available goal-representations and cannot, while it is unfolding, be inhibited, suspended, or terminated, we are not mentally autonomous subjects for about two thirds of our conscious lifetime. At the level of conscious mental activity, epistemic agency is the exception, not the rule. For human beings, epistemic agency can be differentiated into cognitive agency (CA; the ability to control goal-directed/task-related, deliberate thought) and attentional agency (AA; the ability to control the focus of attention). For most of their conscious lifetime, human beings are neither cognitive nor attentional agents, and they also lack an explicit phenomenal self-representation of themselves as currently *possessing* these abilities. Conceptually, most of our conscious activity must be characterized as a form of unintentional mental behaviour. Therefore, two thirds of conscious thought can be described as a subpersonal process that functionally results from a continuously recurring loss of M-autonomy. However, I argued for a moderate interpretation of this fact, not in terms of a complete loss of the relevant ability, but only as an epistemic deficit, a lack of conscious self-knowledge: an absence of representation that is not represented as an absence.

From a philosophical perspective, mind-wandering is not a property of the person as a whole, but a local dynamics that is determined by a set of functional properties physically realized by a specific part of the brain. If it is in accordance with our theoretical interests, we may choose to describe this dynamics as a *representational* kind of dynamics. Then we can say that, internally, an individual representational token or event only *becomes* part of a personal-level process by being functionally integrated into and actively controlled with the help of a specific form of transparent conscious self-representation, the 'epistemic agent model' (EAM), and by being embedded into a highly specific sociocultural context. This context may be thought of as providing an external scaffolding for the stabilization of the EAM — for example, by enabling normative practices of mutually ascribing personhood to each other, or by realizing a linguistically structured cognitive niche in which the concept of a 'person' is continuously present as an instrument for social as well as mental self-representation. Here, one important conceptual distinction is the one between conscious self-representation of ongoing cognitive or attentional agency and a more implicit, passive representation of the *ability* to act as an epistemic agent, involving the more subtle phenomenology of knowing about the potential for mental action without actually realizing it. Being aware of this ability, also in others, suffices for the appearance of a first-person perspective.

In interdisciplinary discourse, it has now become a standard, and at times tiring, job for philosophers to tell neuroscientists that it is the *person* who thinks, and not the brain — a perennial job, it seems, because most neuroscientists never seem to really learn. The omnipresent and all too well-known mistake is the ascription of psychological predicates to parts of a person's brain (e.g. 'The prefrontal cortex plans actions'; 'The premotor cortex decides on the initiation and organization of own movement sequences'; and so on). The conceptual error of ascribing a property that can only be ascribed to the whole entity to a part of it (called the 'mereological fallacy'; see Bennett and Hacker, 2003, p. 72) often, but not necessarily, accompanies the explanatory error of ascribing mental properties to subpersonal *explananda* (the 'homunculus fallacy'; for a lucid discussion, see Drayson 2012, Section 2.2). Ironically, if what I have said above is correct, then at least some neuroscientists, in all their slightly indocile stubbornness, may actually have had a better intuition than philosophers: if for more than two thirds of our conscious lifetime 'thought' should better be described as an unintentional, subpersonal process, then most of the time it really is the *brain* that thinks — and not us.

References

Andrews-Hanna, J.R., Reidler, J.S., Huang, C. & Buckner, R.L. (2010) Evidence for the default network's role in spontaneous cognition, *Journal of Neurophysiology*, **104**, pp. 322–335.

Bayne, T. & Montague, M. (eds.) (2011) *Cognitive Phenomenology*, Oxford: Oxford University Press.

Bennett, M.R. & Hacker, P.M.S. (2003) *Philosophical Foundations of Neuroscience*, Oxford: Blackwell.

Bickle, J. (2013) Multiple realizability, in Zalta, E.N. (ed.) *The Stanford Encyclopedia of Philosophy, Spring 2013 Edition*, [Online], http://plato.stanford.edu/archives/spr2013/entries/multiple-realizability/.

Bigelsen, J. & Schupak, C. (2011) Compulsive fantasy: Proposed evidence of an under-reported syndrome through a systematic study of 90 self-identified non-normative fantasizers, *Consciousness & Cognition*, **20**, pp. 1634–1648.

Blanke, O. & Metzinger, T. (2009) Full-body illusions and minimal phenomenal selfhood, *Trends in Cognitive Sciences*, **13**, pp. 7–13.

Brass, M. & Haggard, P. (2007) To do or not to do: The neural signature of self-control, *Journal of Neuroscience*, **27**, pp. 9141–9145.

Brentano, F. (1874/1973) *Psychology from an Empirical Standpoint*, McAlister, L. (ed.), London: Routledge and Kegan Paul.

Buckner, R.L. & Carroll, D.C. (2007) Self-projection and the brain, *Trends in Cognitive Sciences*, **11**, pp. 49–57.

Buckner, R.L., Andrews-Hanna, J.R. & Schacter, D.L. (2008) The brain's default network, *Annals of the New York Academy of Sciences*, **1124**, pp. 1–38.

Campbell-Meiklejohn, D.K., Woolrich, M.W., Passingham, R.E. & Rogers, R.D. (2008) Knowing when to stop: The brain mechanisms of chasing losses, *Biological Psychiatry*, **63**, pp. 293–300.

Carruthers, P. (2015) *The Centered Mind*, New York: Oxford University Press.

Chalmers, D.J. (2000) What is a neural correlate of consciousness?, in Metzinger, T. (ed.) *Neural Correlates of Consciousness: Empirical and Conceptual Questions*, pp. 17–39, Cambridge, MA: MIT Press.

Christoff, K. (2012) Undirected thought: Neural determinants and correlates, *Brain Research*, **1428**, pp. 51–59.

Christoff, K., Gordon, A.M., Smallwood, J., Smith, R. & Schooler, J.W. (2009) Experience sampling during fMRI reveals default network and executive system contributions to mind wandering,. *Proceedings of the National Academy of Sciences*, **106**, pp. 8719–8724.

Clarke, A. (2015) *Surfing Uncertainty: Prediction, Action, and the Embodied Mind*, Oxford: Oxford University Press.

Cohen, A.-L. (2013) Attentional decoupling while pursuing intentions: A form of mind wandering?, *Frontiers in Psychology*, **4**, p. 693.

Corballis, M.C. (2013) Wandering tales: Evolutionary origins of mental time travel and language, *Frontiers in Psychology*, **4**, p. 485.

Damasio, A.R. & van Hoesen, G.W. (1983) Emotional disturbances associated with focal lesions of the limbic frontal lobe, *Neuropsychology of Humam Emotion*, **1**, pp. 85–110.

Dennett, D.C. (1991) *Consciousness Explained*, Boston, MA: Little Brown.

Dorsch, F. (2014) Focused daydreaming and mind-wandering, *Review of Philosophy and Psychology*, pp. 1–23, [Online], http://link.springer.com/article/10.1007%2Fs13164-014-0221-4.

Drayson, Z. (2012) The uses and abuses of the personal/subpersonal distinction, *Philosophical Perspectives*, **26**, pp. 1–18.

Dresler, M., Wehrle, R., Spoormaker, V.I., Koch, S.P., Holsboer, F., Steiger, A., *et al*. (2012) Neural correlates of dream lucidity obtained from contrasting lucid versus non-lucid REM sleep: A combined EEG/fMRI case study, *SLEEP*, **35**, pp. 1017–1020.

Filevich, E., Kühn, S. & Haggard, P. (2012) Intentional inhibition in human action: The power of 'no', *Neuroscience and Biobehavioral Reviews*, **36**, pp. 1107–1118.

Filevich, E., Kühn, S. & Haggard, P. (2013) There is no free won't: Antecedent brain activity predicts decisions to inhibit, *PLoSONE*, **8**, e53053.

Fosse, R., Stickgold, R. & Hobson, J.A. (2001) Brain-mind states: Reciprocal variation in thoughts and hallucinations, *Psychological Science*, **12**, pp. 30–36.

Fox, K.C.R., Nijeboer, S., Solomonova, E., Domhoff, G.W. & Christoff, K. (2013) Dreaming as mind wandering: Evidence from functional neuroimaging and first-person content reports, *Frontiers in Human Neuroscience*, **7**, p. 412.

Fox, K.C.R., Spreng, R.N., Ellamil, M., Andrews-Hanna, J.R. & Christoff, K. (2015) The wandering brain: Meta-analysis of functional neuroimaging studies of mind-wandering and related spontaneous thought processes, *Neuroimage*, **111**, pp. 611–621.

Friston, K. (2010) The free-energy principle: A unified brain theory?, *Nature Reviews Neuroscience*, **11**, pp. 127–138.

Garrison, K.A., Santoyo, J.F., Davis, J.H., Thornhill, I.V., Thomas, A., Kerr, C.E. & Brewer, J.A. (2013) Effortless awareness: Using real time neurofeedback to investigate correlates of posterior cingulate cortex activity in meditators' self-report, *Frontiers in Human Neuroscience*, **7** (440), pp. 1–9.

Gay, P., Schmidt, R.E. & van der Linden, M. (2011) Impulsivity and intrusive thoughts: Related manifestations of self-control difficulties?, *Cognitive Therapy and Research*, **35**, pp. 293–303.

Green, C.E. (1994) *Lucid Dreaming: The Paradox of Consciousness During Sleep*, Hove: PsychologyPress.

Hasenkamp, W., Wilson-Mendenhall, C.D., Duncan, E. & Barsalou, L.W. (2012) Mind wandering and attention during focused meditation: A fine-grained temporal analysis of fluctuating cognitive states, *Neuroimage*, **59** (1), pp. 750–760.

Hippel, W. von & Trivers, R. (2011) The evolution and psychology of self-deception, *Behavioral and Brain Sciences*, **34** (1), pp. 1–56.

Hobson, J.A. (2002) *Dreaming: An Introduction to the Science of Sleep*, Oxford: Oxford University Press.

Hohwy, J. (2013) *The Predictive Mind*, Oxford: Oxford University Press.

Hölzel, B.K., Lazar, S.W., Gard, T., Schuman-Olivier, Z., Vago, D.R. & Ott, U. (2011) How does mindfulness meditation work? Proposing mechanisms of action from a conceptual and neural perspective, *Perspectives in Psychological Science*, **6**, pp. 537–559.

Horovitz, S.G., Braun, A.R., Carr, W.S., Picchioni, D., Balkin, T.J., Fukunaga, M., *et al.* (2009) Decoupling of the brain's default mode network during deep sleep, *Proceedings of the National Academy of Sciences*, **106**, pp. 11376–11381.

Irving, Z.C. (2015) Mind-wandering is unguided attention: Accounting for the 'purposeful' wanderer, *Philosophical Studies*, pp. 1–25, [Online], http://link.springer.com/article/10.1007%2Fs11098-015-0506-1.

Kane, M.J., Brown, L.H., McVay, J.C., Silvia, P.J., Myin-Germeys, I. & Kwapil, T.R. (2007) For whom the mind wanders, and when: An experience-sampling study of working memory and executive control in daily life, *Psychological Science*, **18**, pp. 614–621.

Killingsworth, M.A. & Gilbert, D.T. (2010) A wandering mind is an unhappy mind, *Science*, **330**, p. 932.

Klinger, E. (2013) Goal commitments and the content of thoughts and dreams: Basic principles, *Frontiers in Psychology*, **4**, p. 415.

Kühn, S., Haggard, P. & Brass, M. (2009) Intentional inhibition: How the 'veto-area' exerts control, *Human Brain Mapping*, **30**, pp. 2834–2843.

Limanowski, J. & Blankenburg, F. (2013) Minimal self-models and the free energy principle, *Frontiers in Human Neuroscience*, **7**, p. 547.

Lu, H., Zou, Q., Gu, H., Raichle, M.E., Stein, E.A. & Yang, Y. (2012) Rat brains also have a default mode network, *Proceedings of the National Academy of Sciences*, **109**, pp. 3979–3984.

Mantini, D. & Vanduffel, W. (2012) Emerging roles of the brain's default network, *Neuroscientist*, **19**, pp. 76–87.

Mason, M.F., Norton, M.I., Van Horn, J.D., Wegner, D.M., Grafton, S.T., *et al.* (2007) Wandering minds: The default network and stimulus-independent thought, *Science*, **315**, pp. 393–395.

McCauley, R.N. & Bechtel, W. (2001) Explanatory pluralism and heuristic identity theory, *Theory & Psychology*, **11**, pp. 736–760.

McVay, J.C. & Kane, M.J. (2009) Conducting the train of thought: Working memory capacity, goal neglect, and mind wandering in an executive-control task, *Journal of Experimental Psychology: Learning, Memory & Cognition*, **35**, p. 196.

McVay, J.C. & Kane, M.J. (2010) Does mind wandering reflect executive function or executive failure? Comment on Smallwood and Schooler (2006) and Watkins (2008), *Psychological Bulletin*, **136**, pp. 188–197.

McVay, J.C. & Kane, M.J. (2013) Dispatching the wandering mind? Toward a laboratory method for cuing 'spontaneous' off-task thought, *Frontiers in Psychology*, **4**, p. 570.

Metzinger, T. (ed.) (1995) *Conscious Experience*, Exeter: Imprint Academic.

Metzinger, T. (2003a) *Being No One: The Self-Model Theory of Subjectivity*, Cambridge, MA: MIT Press.

Metzinger, T. (2003b) Phenomenal transparency and cognitive self-reference, *Phenomenology and the Cognitive Sciences*, **2**, pp. 353–393.

Metzinger, T. (2006) Précis: Being no one, *Psyche (Stuttg)*, **11**, pp. 1–35.

Metzinger, T. (2007) Self models, *Scholarpedia*, **2**, p. 4174.

Metzinger, T. (2008) Empirical perspectives from the self-model theory of subjectivity: A brief summary with examples, *Progress in Brain Research*, **168**, pp. 215–278.

Metzinger, T. (2013a) The myth of cognitive agency: Subpersonal thinking as a cyclically recurring loss of mental autonomy, *Frontiers in Psychology*, **4** (931), [Online], http://journal.frontiersin.org/article/10.3389/fpsyg.2013.00931/abstract

Metzinger, T. (2013b) Why are dreams interesting for philosophers? The example of minimal phenomenal selfhood, plus an agenda for future research, *Frontiers in Psychology*, **4** (746), [Online], http://journal.frontiersin.org/article/10.3389/fpsyg.2013.00746/abstract.

Metzinger, T. (2014) First-order embodiment, second-order embodiment, third-order embodiment, in Shapiro, L. (ed.) *The Routledge Handbook of Embodied Cognition,* London: Routledge.

Metzinger, T. & Windt, J.M. (2014) Die phänomenale Signatur des Wissens: Experimentelle Philosophie des Geistes mit oder ohne Intuitionen?, in Grundmann, T., Horvath, J. & Kipper, J. (eds.) *Die Experimentelle Philosophie in der Diskussion*, Berlin: Suhrkamp.

Metzinger, T. & Windt, J.M. (2015) What does it mean to have an open mind?, in Metzinger, T. & Windt, J.M. (eds.) *OpenMIND,* Frankfurt am Main: MIND Group, [Online], http://open-mind.net/papers/general-introduction-what-does-it-mean-to-have-an-open-mind/paperPDF.

Mooneyham, B.W. & Schooler, J.W. (2013) The costs and benefits of mind-wandering: A review, *Canadian Journal of Experimental Psychology*, **67**, pp. 11–18.

Mrazek, M.D., Smallwood, J. & Schooler, J.W. (2012) Mindfulness and mind-wandering: Finding convergence through opposing constructs, *Emotion*, **12**, p. 442.

Nielsen, T.A. (2000) A review of mentation in REM and NREM sleep: 'Covert' REM sleep as a possible reconciliation of two opposing models, *Behavioral & Brain Sciences*, **23**, pp. 851–866.

Noreika, V., Valli, K., Lahtela, H. & Revonsuo, A. (2009) Early-night serial awakenings as a new paradigm for studies on NREM dreaming, *International Journal of Psychophysiology*, **74**, pp. 14–18.

Noreika, V., Windt, J.M., Lenggenhager, B. & Karim, A.A. (2010) New perspectives for the study of lucid dreaming: From brain stimulation to philosophical theories of self-consciousness, *International Journal of Dream Research*, **3**, pp. 36–45.

Pliushch, I. & Metzinger, T. (2015) Self-deception and the dolphin model of cognition, in Gennaro, R.J. (ed.) *Disturbed Consciousness: New Essays on Psychopathology and Theories of Consciousness*, Cambridge, MA: MIT Press.

Raichle, M.E., MacLeod, A.M., Snyder, A.Z., Powers, W.J., Gusnard, D.A. & Shulman, G.L. (2001) Inaugural article: A default mode of brain function, *Proceedings of the National Academy of Sciences*, **98**, pp. 676–682.

Redshaw, J. & Suddendorf, T. (2013) Foresight beyond the very next event: Four-year-olds can link past and deferred future episodes, *Frontiers in Psychology*, **4**, p. 404.

Samann, P.G., Wehrle, R., Hoehn, D., Spoormaker, V.I., Peters, H., Tully, C., *et al.* (2011) Development of the brain's default mode network from wakefulness to slow wave sleep, *Cerebral Cortex*, **21**, pp. 2082–2093.

Schmidt, R.E. & van der Linden, M. (2009) The aftermath of rash action: Sleep-interfering counterfactual thoughts and emotions, *Emotion*, **9**, pp. 549–553.

Schmidt, R.E., Harvey, A.G. & van der Linden, M. (2011) Cognitive and affective control in insomnia, *Frontiers in Psychology*, **2**, p. 349.

Schooler, J.W., Smallwood, J., Christoff, K., Handy, T.C., Reichle, E.D. & Sayette, M.A. (2011) Meta-awareness, perceptual decoupling and the wandering mind, *Trends in Cognitive Sciences*, **15**, pp. 319–326.

Schupak, C. & Rosenthal, J. (2009) Excessive daydreaming: A case history and discussion of mind wandering and high fantasy proneness, *Consciousness & Cognition*, **18**, pp. 290–292.

Seth, A.K. (2010) Measuring autonomy and emergence via granger causality, *Artificial Life*, **16**, pp. 179–196.

Siclari, F., La Rocque, J.J., Postle, B.R. & Tononi, G. (2013) Assessing sleep consciousness within subjects using a serial awakening paradigm, *Frontiers in Psychology*, **4**, p. 542.

Slagter, H.A., Davidson, R.J. & Lutz, A. (2011) Mental training as a tool in the neuroscientific study of brain and cognitive plasticity, *Frontiers in Human Neuroscience*, **5**, p. 17.

Smallwood, J. (2013) Distinguishing how from why the mind wanders: A process-occurrence framework for self-generated mental activity, *Psychological Bulletin*, **139**, p. 519.

Smallwood, J., McSpadden, M. & Schooler, J.W. (2007) The lights are on but no one's home: Meta-awareness and the decoupling of attention when the mind wanders, *Psychonomic Bulletin & Review*, **14**, pp. 527–533.

Smallwood, J., McSpadden, M. & Schooler, J.W. (2008) When attention matters: The curious incident of the wandering mind, *Memory and Cognition*, **36** (6), pp. 1144–1150.

Smallwood, J., Brown, K., Baird, B. & Schooler, J.W. (2012) Cooperation between the default mode network and the frontal-parietal network in the production of an internal train of thought, *Brain Research*, **1428**, pp. 60–70.

Smallwood, J. & Schooler, J.W. (2015) The science of mind wandering: Empirically navigating the stream of consciousness, *Annual Review of Psychology*, **66**, pp. 487–518.

Spreng, R.N., Mar, R.A. & Kim, A.S.N. (2009) The common neural basis of auto-biographical memory, prospection, navigation, theory of mind, and the default mode: A quantitative meta-analysis, *Journal of Cognitive Neuroscience*, **21**, pp. 489–510.

Stawarczyk, D., Majerus, S., Maquet, P., D'Argembeau, A. & Gilbert, S. (2011) Neural correlates of ongoing conscious experience: Both task-unrelatedness and stimulus-independence are related to default network activity, *PLoSONE*, **6**, e16997.

Vanhaudenhuyse, A., Noirhomme, Q., Tshibanda, L.J.-F., Bruno, M.-A., Boveroux, P., Schnakers, C., *et al.* (2010) Default network connectivity reflects the level of consciousness in non-communicative brain-damaged patients, *Brain*, **133**, pp. 161–171.

Voss, U., Holzmann, R., Tuin, I. & Hobson, J. (2009) Lucid dreaming: A state of consciousness with features of both waking and non-lucid dreaming, *Sleep*, **32**, p. 1191.

Voss, U., Schermelleh-Engel, K., Windt, J., Frenzel, C. & Hobson, A. (2013) Measuring consciousness in dreams: The lucidity and consciousness in dreams scale, *Consciousness & Cognition*, **22**, pp. 8–21.

Voss, U. & Hobson, A. (2015) What is the state-of-the-art on lucid dreaming?, in Metzinger, T. & Windt, J.M. (eds.) *OpenMIND,* Frankfurt am Main: MIND Group, [Online], http://open-mind.net/papers/what-is-the-state-of-the-art-on-lucid-dreaming-recent-advances-and-questions-for-future-research/at_download/paperPDF.

Wamsley, E.J. (2013) Dreaming as an extension of waking conscious experience and a tractable problem for cognitive neuroscience, *Frontiers in Psychology*, **4**, p. 637.

Ward, A.F. & Wegner, D.M. (2013) Mind-blanking: When the mind goes away, *Frontiers in Psychology*, **4**, p. 650.

Wegner, D.M. (2002) *The Illusion of Conscious Will*, Cambridge, MA: MIT Press.

Weissman, D.H., Roberts, K.C., Visscher, K.M. & Woldorff, M.G. (2006) The neural bases of momentary lapses in attention, *Nature Neuroscience*, **9**, pp. 971–978.

Windt, J.M. (2014) *Dreaming: A Conceptual Framework for Philosophy of Mind and Empirical Research*, Cambridge, MA: MIT Press.

Windt, J.M. (2015) *Dreaming: A Conceptual Framework for Philosophy of Mind and Empirical Research*, Cambridge, MA: MIT Press.

Windt, J.M. & Metzinger, T. (2007) The philosophy of dreaming and self-consciousness: What happens to the experiential subject during the dream state?, in *Praeger Perspectives: The New Science of Dreaming*, Vol. 3., *Cultural and Theoretical Perspectives*, pp. 193–247, Westport, CT: Praeger Publishers/Greenwood Publishing Group.